THE PROBLEM WITH PLEASURE

THE PROBLEM
WITH PLEASURE

MODERNISM AND ITS DISCONTENTS

Laura Frost

Columbia University Press   New York

Columbia University Press
Publishers Since 1893
New York   Chichester, West Sussex
cup.columbia.edu

Versions of chapters 3, 4, and 6 were published as:
"The Romance of Cliché: E. M. Hull, D. H. Lawrence, and Interwar Erotic
Fiction" in *Bad Modernisms*, ed. Douglas Mao and Rebecca Walkowitz
(Durham: Duke University Press, 2006), 94–118.
"Huxley's Feelies: The Cinema of Sensation in *Brave New World*,"
Twentieth-Century Literature 52, no. 4 (Winter 2006): 443–473.
"Blondes Have More Fun: Anita Loos and the Language of Silent
Cinema," *Modernism/modernity* 17, no. 2 (April 2010): 291–311.

Library of Congress Cataloging-in-Publication Data
Frost, Laura Catherine, 1967–
The problem with pleasure : modernism and its discontents /
Laura Frost.
   p.   cm.
Includes bibliographical references and index.
ISBN 978-0-231-15272-3 (cloth : acid-free paper) —
ISBN 978-0-231-52646-3 (electronic)
1. Modernism (Literature) 2. Pleasure in literature. I. Title.

PN56.M54F76   2013
809'.9112—dc23   2012036521

c 10 9 8 7 6 5 4 3 2 1

Cover design by Noah Arlow. Cover art: © The Museum of Modern Art/
Licensed by SCALA / Art Resource, NY

Contents

Illustrations

Acknowledgments

This project began at Yale and was funded by a Senior Faculty Fellowship, a Morse Fellowship in the Humanities, and a series of A. Whitney Griswold Faculty Research Grants from the Whitney Humanities Center. A semester teaching in London was felicitous in many ways, not the least of which was a marvelous Bloomsbury book collection. I am grateful to my colleagues at Yale—Michael Thurston, Elizabeth Dillon, Michael Trask, Nigel Alderman, Pericles Lewis, Tanya Agathocleous, Amy Hungerford, Sandy Welsh, Ruth Yeazell—and my students there. Rebecca Walkowitz and Doug Mao's invitation to join their band of bad modernists was an early impetus for this project, and I thank them for their editorial input, which helped put me on the road to pleasure. John Paul Riquelme generously invited me to present parts of the book in their early stages, and those events (at the Modernist Studies Association, Modern Language Association, and Harvard Humanities Center Modernism Seminar) were also instrumental in defining the project. I am grateful to Lawrence Rainey for bringing my Anita Loos article to *Modernism/modernity*; Bryan Radley for his editorial skills; Gregory Robison for our exchange about cinema history; and Cari Beauchamp for sharing her knowledge of Anita Loos with me. My New School colleagues Dominic Pettman, Laura Liu, Carolyn Berman, Paul Kottman, Alex Chasin, Inessa Medhibovskaya, Oz Frankel, Michael Schober, Elaine Savory, and Jim Miller got me through the home stretch. Others read and/or inspired me along the way: Nico Israel, Sarah Cole, Clover Bachman, Yvonne McDevitt, Miranda Sherwin, Karen Gehres, Ron Rosenbaum, Chris Wiggins, Aya Horikoshi, Randi Saloman, Nancy Miller, David Damrosch, D. A. Miller, and Carol Siegel. Teri Reynolds is the kind of friend who will wake up in the middle of a jet-lagged nap to edit your paper on Gertrude Stein; she stepped in at other crucial moments. I am especially indebted to my anonymous readers at Columbia University Press, and to Philip Leventhal for his patience and intelligence in helping me shape the book. The best part of this process was writing for the members of my Modernist Ladies Auxiliary writing group, Celia Marshik and Allison Pease, whose brilliant readings are second only to their bibulous lunch camaraderie. Victoria Rosner is my constant reader and advisor; I thank her for her friendship, wit, and genius for figuring out what needs to be said. My parents' unflagging enthusiasm and interest make academic work seem worthwhile. Finally, this book is for Chris, whose love, support, and IT triage have helped me rediscover the delights of creation and the allure of the left brain; and for Max, our in-house hedonist, whose untroubled relationship to pleasure constantly reminds me, in the words of Dr. Seuss, that:

These things are fun
And fun is good.

THE PROBLEM WITH PLEASURE

INTRODUCTION
The Repudiation of Pleasure

"Pleasure is not always fun. . . ."
—Lauren Berlant[1]

In Jean Rhys's 1939 novel *Good Morning, Midnight*, the protagonist, who calls herself Sasha, is picked up by a male stranger on the Boulevard Arago during an evening walk. They go to a café and drink Pernod: one, two. . . . "I feel like a goddess," she thinks. "I want more of this feeling—fire and wings." The man puts his hand on her knee and invites her back to his flat. Sasha doesn't particularly like him, but she remarks, "Well, why not?" When they walk out onto the street, she stumbles. "What's the matter?" he asks. "Have you been dancing too much? . . . All you young women . . . dance too much. Mad for pleasure, all the young people. . . . Ah, what will happen to this after-war generation? I ask myself. What will happen? Mad for pleasure."[2]

This is a comically flawed conclusion, as the man mistakes Sasha for a good-time girl, a shingled flapper out for thrills. Although Sasha is, in fact, eager to get drunk, she is poor, alone, and depressed, a broken marriage and a child's death in her past. She sleeps most of the time and contemplates chloroforming herself, were it not for the fact that her hotel board has been paid for the month. She lurches in the street not because she is giddy from dancing, but because she is hungry and drinks on an empty stomach. Sasha goes along with the stranger even though she describes the encounter as "unhoped-for" and "quite unwanted" (397). In the novel's final act, when she leaves her hotel-room door propped open to invite a menacing neighbor into her bed, her pleasure is dubious by any conventional definition.

Rhys's transnational flâneuse would seem to epitomize modern feminine cosmopolitanism, as a creature who orbits contemporary amusements (clubs and restaurants, the cinema, popular music, cocktails, and freely chosen sexual companionship), yet she is plagued by anxiety and alienation. Sasha's decisions are not calculated to produce what most would recognize as bliss or joy. Rhys's narrative enacts Sasha's erratic psychology through its fragmented form, shifting abruptly from one time frame and one scene to another, and dispensing with causality. Communication is cryptic; people are ciphers. On a local level, some individual scenes are poetic, playful, or witty, but the overall impression is one of disorientation and dislocation. Like Sasha, Rhys's reader lurches from one episode to the next, a succession of flights and drops, delight and mostly dysphoria.

Sasha's companion's conception of "this after-war generation" as "mad for pleasure" echoes stereotypes of the interwar period: Daisy Buchanan jazz babies drinking cocktails and dancing in sleek art deco dresses, swooning in the cinema or listening to the latest thing on the gramophone. Rhys subsumes these experiences into the landscape of malaise and depression through which her protagonist drifts. In other modernist texts from the period—an era preoccupied by the miseries of the past war and the impending rise of fascism as well as the exhilaration and anxiety of shifting gender roles and new sensory cultures—embodied, direct, and easy pleasures have a dark side. Figured as a siren call, alluring and dangerous, they are both a compulsion and a disorder of the age. What would usually register as pleasure often becomes empty, dangerous, or even anhedonic. "Well now that's done: and I'm glad it's over," T. S. Eliot's typist in *The Waste Land* remarks, following a mechanical lovemaking session.[3] As with Rhys's novel, the form of Eliot's poem echoes its representations of compromised pleasure, confronting its reader with language that is as demanding as it is captivating. Between the disjointed imagery, the foreign languages, and recondite, dense allusions, by the time the (at least first-time) reader reaches the poem's final "Shantih shantih shantih" (69), she may breathe a sigh of relief too: "Well now that's done."

Many other modern and most high modernist texts complicate or defy classical conceptions of literature as an experience of pleasure (Aristotle[4]) or delight (Horace[5]) that continue into contemporary criticism. Posing the query, "What do stories do?" Jonathan Culler specifies that "First, they give pleasure." Harold Bloom, who bemoans that "reading is scarcely taught as a pleasure, in any of the deeper senses of the aesthetics of pleasure," proposes that literature's purpose is rehabilitative and redemptive: it is "healing" and "alleviates loneliness."[6] To the contrary, modernists offer a challenging and even hostile reading experience that calls into question the most axiomatic premises of what literature and pleasure can do.

The man in *Good Morning, Midnight* misunderstands Sasha, but his notion of a generation "mad for pleasure" reflects two truths about the interwar period: that there was widespread suspicion of particular categories of pleasure, and that the broader idea of pleasure itself was undergoing a radical reconceptualization, and nowhere more than in the literary culture of the time. This book will argue that the fundamental goal of modernism is the redefinition of pleasure: specifically, exposing easily achieved and primarily somatic pleasures as facile, hollow, and false, and cultivating those that require more ambitious analytical work. Essential paradigms of modernism, such as the high/low or elite/popular culture divide and the attention to formal difficulty, I claim, revolve around pleasure. That is, the so-called "great divide"[7] is fundamentally a way of managing different kinds of pleasure, and modernism's signature formal rhetorics, including irony, fragmentation, indirection, and allusiveness, are a parallel means of promoting a particularly knotty, arduous reading effect. The discrepancies between the modernist theory and practice of pleasure signal how denigrated pleasures are never actually banished, but are rather presented in a reformulated guise. Focusing on the tension in modernist literature between the artistic commitment to discipline—of ideas, form, and cultural activity—and the voluptuous appeal of embodied, accessible culture, the following chapters will show that modernists disavow but nevertheless engage with the pleasures they otherwise reject and, at the same time, invent textual effects that include daunting, onerous, and demanding reading practices.

In a 1963 essay called "The Fate of Pleasure," Lionel Trilling contends that "at some point in modern history, the principle of pleasure came to be regarded with . . . ambivalence."[8] Trilling points to Romanticism as a contrast, exemplified by Keats's writing ("O for a Life of Sensations rather than of Thoughts") as well as Wordsworth's praise in his preface to *Lyrical Ballads* for "the naked and native dignity of man" that is found in "the grand elementary principle of pleasure" (Trilling, 428). Trilling argues that early twentieth-century writers came to regard sensuous, simple, mainstream pleasures as a false consolation, a "specious good" (445). Conventional bliss, Trilling maintains, did not interest a generation of artists committed to exploring the "dark places of psychology," as Virginia Woolf put it.[9] Trilling describes modernists as a group of writers who "imposed upon themselves difficult and painful tasks, they committed themselves to strange, 'unnatural' modes of life, they sought out distressing emotions, in order to know psychic energies which are not to be summoned up in felicity."[10] This, along with the desire to destroy "the habits, manners, and 'values' of the bourgeois world" (442), resulted in a full-blown "repudiation" of pleasure (439). While acknowledging that the impulse to look beyond the pleasure principle is not exclusive to the twentieth century—for example, Keats explored a "dialectic of pleasure," a "divided state of feeling" by which "the desire for pleasure denies itself" (433–434)—Trilling asserts that this impulse to free "the self from its thralldom to pleasure" (445) reached an unprecedented peak in modernism.

Trilling was a great promoter of modern literature as an art of disruption, rebellion, opposition, and crisis. Like any myth, this is in part a distortion. Recent scholarship informed by cultural studies tells another story about pleasure. Instead of Trilling's brooding, ponderous modernism, we now have a more effervescent one that writes for *Vogue*, courts celebrity, and adores Chaplin films. Through this lens, even high modernism can look downright user-friendly. However, at the same time that scholars produce a more vernacular, culturally savvy, and accessible field, modernism's own overt rhetoric about its relationship to pleasure upholds the great divide. Neither Trilling's "repudiation" nor cultural studies' enthusiasm exactly captures modernism's central conflict about pleasure.

While Trilling is right that pleasure is a major preoccupation of modern literature, it is not precisely "bourgeois" pleasure that modern writers purport to reject; nor is the defense against pleasure as straightforward as "repudiation." To choose two memorable episodes from canonical high modernism, we might think of Leopold Bloom's breakfast of organ meats at 7 Eccles Street or Clarissa Dalloway's rumination on her feelings for women that culminates in "some pressure of rapture, which split its thin skin and gushed and poured with an extraordinary alleviation over the cracks and sores!" Notably, these visceral, powerful moments are closely related to negativity and angst, including Bloom's more representative moods of compulsive avoidance and guilt and Clarissa's depressing realization that passion is a thing of the past.[11] Woolf's famous remark, inscribed on coffee cups and t-shirts in our own century, "One cannot think well, love well, sleep well, if one has not dined well," is not a rallying cry for the sybaritic life, but rather appears in the context of a discussion of women's educational deprivation.[12] Likewise, the magnificent boeuf en daube scene in *To the Lighthouse* cannot be read apart from the conflict and violence elsewhere in the novel, which Mrs. Ramsay's meal only temporarily and partly assuages.[13] In modernism, sensual pleasure appears in a climate of tension and fragmentation, only very provisionally transcending rifts and anxieties.

Literary pleasure exists in two related registers: the thematic and the linguistic. As with Rhys's and Eliot's texts, the delectation of passages such as the one detailing Bloom's "nutty gizzards" is generated not only by the objects represented but also by the linguistic play through which they are rendered. The "grilled mutton kidneys which gave to his palate a fine tang of faintly scented urine"[14] are hardly epicurean delicacies, although Bloom clearly relishes them. Rather, it is Bloom's earthy, carnal appetite for "the inner organs of beasts and fowls" and the irony of his delicately wrought tastes ("fine tang," "faintly scented") alongside the clinical "urine" that amuse and prepare us for the still more unorthodox appetites to come. Woolf's luminous prose requires the reader to identify and ponder the collapse of temporality and the associative leaps of consciousness that happen in Clarissa's moment of illumination. The words themselves, "swollen with some astonishing significance," effect an ecstatic swoon in the text. The bliss of modernism emerges from highly self-conscious writing that demands a heightened attention to form and the construction of pleasure itself.

Despite its interest in polyphony and suggestion, fragmentation and open-endedness, modernism is highly pedantic insofar as it dictates to readers what kind of enjoyment is permissible. Its assertion of the value of deliberate, intricate, cognitive effort often comes at the expense of more immediate, sensual enjoyment. "Modernism," Richard Poirier writes, "happened when reading got to be grim."[15] It is worth noting that modernism was at the center of the post–World War One institutionalization of English literature as an academic discipline and a shift away from the study of literature as philology to a field of criticism and interpretation. No longer assumed to be a form of entertainment available to anyone who could read, literature now *required* professors. It took modernism to constitute literature as a field of inquiry that was, as Terry Eagleton puts it, "unpleasant enough to qualify as a proper academic pursuit."[16] Modernist texts do not appear on summer reading lists: for all its attractions, modernism is no picnic. Its pathways to readerly bliss often require secondary sources and footnotes as dense as the original text. Yet the modernist doxa of difficulty gives rise to new kinds of pleasure. Along with offering thrilling and powerful innovation, modernist writers ask their readers not just to tolerate but also to embrace discomfort, confusion, and hard cognitive labor. Modernism, in short, instructs its reader in the art of unpleasure.

◈ ◈ ◈

Let me be clear: unpleasure is not the opposite of pleasure, but rather its modification. The concept of unpleasure breaks with the conventional separation of human experience into two tendencies, as expressed in Bentham's ominous opening of *The Principles of Morals and Legislation*: "Nature has placed mankind under the governance of two sovereign masters, *pain* and *pleasure*. It is for them alone to point out what we ought to do, as well as to determine what we shall do. . . . They govern us in all we do, in all we say, in all we think: every effort we can make to throw off our subjugation, will serve but to demonstrate and confirm it."[17] Unpleasure denaturalizes this distinction between two rival governing bodies and introduces another, less regal category of motivation that operates between them. Unpleasure, from "Unlust" in *Beyond the Pleasure Principle*, a text written in the shadow of World War One, is characterized by gratification attained through tension, obstacles, delay, convolution, and pain, as opposed to accessible, direct satisfaction. Unpleasure can be grim, but it can also be ironic and funny and offer engagements and intensities on par with pleasure. I will elaborate on the theory of unpleasure later and propose that it offers a dialectical approach to the opposition of pain and pleasure that describes modernist sensibilities. First, though, a note about the parameters of pleasure itself is in order.

The discourse of pleasure is complicated by two long-standing ontological problems. On the one hand, pleasure is exasperatingly unbound; on the other, it remains subject to millennia-old postulates about its nature. Pleasure in general is such an expansive concept that it is useful to begin by estranging ourselves from what we think we know about it. Both second nature and so familiar as to be beneath or beyond definition, pleasure is, as the neurobiologists would have it (in research that postdated modernism), whatever tickles our limbic system or sets our dopamine surging.[18] It's what makes us feel good. We know, to take a page from Potter Stewart, what it is when we see or feel or experience it—we laugh or swoon, or are energized, excited, or riveted. It's bliss. Ecstasy. Enjoyment. Delight. These near-synonyms all have specialized connotations, but pleasure is semantically unconstrained and apparently ahistorical, although close attention to the way the word is deployed will reveal that one era's pleasure is not the same as another's. Geoffrey Hartman contends that "The word *pleasure* is problematic. . . . First, for its onomatopoeic pallor, then for its inability to carry with it the nimbus of its historical associations. . . . Though literary elaboration has augmented the vocabulary of feeling and affect, pleasure as a critical term remains descriptively poor."[19] I find the word itself more evocative than Hartman does: I hear a plosive that relaxes into a sinuous buzz followed by a purr. However, he is right that "pleasure" lacks the connotative richness of words such as *jouissance* (downgraded to "bliss" in Richard Howard's translation of Roland Barthes' *Pleasure of the Text*); by contrast, the terms that modernists use to dismiss somatic, accessible pleasures are sneeringly effective: the trivializing "fun" or "amusement" and the banalizing "recreation."

Even as the word is overwhelmingly diffuse, the practice of pleasure has always been kept in tight ethical check. For most ancient Greek philosophers, *hedone* (pleasure) is only one unruly factor in *eudaimonia* (happiness). Pleasure is integrally tied to bodily, sensual experience, while happiness is more abstract and metaphysical, correlated with truth, contemplation, and wisdom. A spectrum with asceticism and gluttony at its extremes, pleasure can easily become disruptive, antisocial, or excessive. Pleasure can get out of hand; happiness, never. The relatively recent science of pleasure supports this axiom. In the 1950s, James Olds and Peter Milner embedded electrodes in the brains of rats. When the animals pressed designated levers, the electrodes would deliver local currents. Given the opportunity, the rats with electrodes in pleasure-stimulating areas would press the levers repeatedly, neglecting food, water, and their young.[20] Subsequent studies in fields such as affective neuroscience have demonstrated the biological basis of hedonic compulsions and addictions in humans. Many of us are, it seems, only a step away from falling into the vortex of pleasure.

Many early philosophers imagined well-being as a physiological model with two states, pain and pleasure, that need to be balanced in order to achieve *ataraxia* (tranquility). Only extreme hedonists such as Aristippus of Cyrene (435–356 B.C.E.) declared that pleasure, including immediate and bodily sensation, was the highest good.[21] Others, such as Epicurus, were more conservative about indulgence and defined pleasure as *aponia* (absence of pain) and a lowering of tension. By this logic, pleasure is not intrinsically desirable, but is rather a relief from negative states: a negation of a negation. It is in this spirit that Plato's *Philebus*, a dialogue about whether pleasure or reason is the highest good, begins with Socrates's premise that "the majority of pleasures are bad, though some are good,"[22] and proposes a calibration of pleasure according to quality and quantity. Socrates imagines a sort of doorman who chooses to admit pleasures or turn them away: "'We know about true pleasures,' we'll say, 'but do you also need to share your house with pleasures which are very great and intense?' 'Of course not,' they would probably say. 'There's no end to the trouble they make for us: with their frenzied irrationality they disturb the souls we inhabit'" (77). Cogitation, you're in; lust and gluttony, move along. The aim of pleasure, according to this view, is to eliminate tension and to restore harmony.

Plato also introduced an influential distinction between "true" and "false" pleasures (39), aligning mental pursuits with the former and the pleasures of the body with the latter. A life of physical stimulation without reason, intellect, memory, knowledge, and judgment, Sophocles remarks, is "not the life of a human being, but of a jellyfish or some sea creature which is merely a body endowed with life, a companion of oysters" (16). In contrast to these blissed-out blobs at the bottom of the sea, the highest form of gratification belongs to the philosopher, with his head in the clouds.[23] This basic formulation has endured. Bentham's hedonic calculus was scandalous—"Pig Philosophy," as Thomas Carlyle put it, giving a mammalian backbone to the oyster metaphor[24]—because it jettisoned qualitative distinctions: "Prejudice apart, the game of push-pin is of equal value with the arts and sciences of music and poetry. If the game of push-pin furnish more pleasure, it is more valuable than either. Everybody can play at push-pin: poetry and music are relished only by a few."[25] John Stuart Mill refined Bentham's formulation by reasserting a hierarchy of "higher" and "lower" pleasures that was in keeping with Plato's hypothesis. "It is better to be a human being dissatisfied than a pig satisfied," Mill wrote, and "better to be Socrates dissatisfied than a fool satisfied."[26] This hierarchization of pleasure reaches its theoretical zenith in Kantian aesthetics, where rational, universal taste and appreciation are distinguished from embodied, instinctual, voluptuous stimulation.[27] Bifurcating experience into a pure (abstract, disinterested) and an impure (sensual, engaged) form exacerbates the semantic problems with pleasure. Adorno points out that "For Kant, aesthetics becomes paradoxically a castrated hedonism, desire without desire."[28] Bourdieu too describes Kant's "pure pleasure" as "ascetic, empty pleasure which implies the renunciation of pleasure, pleasure purified of pleasure."[29] As paradoxical as the formulation is, it nevertheless became a fundamental principle in articulating a refined aesthetic sensibility, and it underpins modernism's dismissal of accessible pleasure as facile and trite, and its valorization of that which requires effort and training.

Modernist era philosophy is characteristically contrasted to the crude instrumentalism of utilitarianism, yet the separation of pursuits of the rational mind from sensual, bodily experience proved to be lasting, as philosophers such as G. E. Moore emphasized the cerebral processes or "states of mind" involved in pleasure.[30] Modern writers reject the hedonic calculus of utilitarianism and seem to appeal deliberately not to the greatest possible number, but to the least; however, when considering contemporary (vernacular, mass, sensorial) pleasure, modernists substitute their own kind of utilitarian calculus, inverting Bentham's hierarchy by putting poetry at the top and pushpin at the bottom. Meaningful pleasure is intellectually or aesthetically useful. So Moore, following Plato's argument in the *Philebus*, asserts that "pleasure would be comparatively valueless without . . . consciousness" (92) and that "a pleasurable Contemplation of Beauty has certainly an immeasurably greater value than mere Consciousness of Pleasure" (96). Moore specifies that "pleasure is *not* the only end, that some consciousness at least must be included with it as a veritable part of the end" (92). Moving valorized pleasure still further from the somatic to the cerebral, Roger Fry writes, in *Vision and Design*, that "the specifically aesthetic" experience involves an apprehension that "corresponds in science to the purely logical process," proposing that "Perhaps the highest pleasure in art is identical with the highest pleasure in scientific theory."[31] (Virginia Woolf records Bertrand Russell proclaiming, "I get the keenest aesthetic pleasure from reading well written mathematics."[32]) Despite its devotion to aesthetics and beauty and its interest in interior psychological states, most modernism remains largely tethered to aesthetic instrumentalism when it comes to pleasure.

Modernism steers a curious path between Victorian attitudes toward pleasure and those of decadence and aestheticism. Its energies are more in line with the decadent idea of artistic autonomy than they are with the Victorian insistence that art is integrally related to morality; however, modernists consistently frame pleasure as an ethical and aesthetic problem. And while modernism draws from the decadent understanding of the artist's rarified relationship to pleasure ("Harlots and / Hunted have pleasures of their own to give, / The vulgar herd can never understand," Baudelaire writes in his epigraph to *Les Fleurs du Mal*[33]), decadence, with its swooning sadomasochism, does not typically include the overtly antipleasure rhetoric in which modernism is so invested. What marks the modernist period in the genealogy of pleasure is that unpleasure and difficult pleasure are elevated as aesthetic practices that require extraordinary kinds of reading practices and often entail a hostile relationship to the reader, and that those modes are predicated on a struggle with other—lesser—kinds of pleasure.

Explicated through these categories of value over time, pleasure itself has been strikingly elusive even as it has been a principal term in modern critical discourse. Lord Henry Wotton's quip, in *The Picture of Dorian Gray*, that "Pleasure is the only thing worth having a theory about," sets the tone for a century and a half of exposition about pleasure.[34] Just as his "New Hedonism," at least in the way it is represented in the text, is less about sensual indulgence than about verbal irony, paradox, and coy wordplay, literary critical discourse is dependent upon but largely elides pleasure. In Barthes's *Pleasure of the Text*, the primary subject is teasingly vague, and deliberately so. *Jouissance*, Barthes claims, cannot be put into words; "no 'thesis' on the pleasure of the text is possible."[35] Pleasure is thereby relegated to the category of things that are beyond articulation and "can never be fixed directly by the naked eye—let alone pursued as an end, or conceptualized—but only experienced laterally, or after the fact, as something like the by-product of something else," as Frederic Jameson has observed.[36] This is borne out by twentieth-century cultural critics who have applied themselves to the problem of pleasure as an occasion to discuss something else—for example, politics, censorship, or aesthetics—while never quite registering pleasure's palpable effects or rendering it as a concrete, immediate, or phenomenological experience. Despite its powerfully specific, local, and stimulating effects, pleasure remains mainly abstract and offstage, a means of getting to another topic rather than something worth pondering for its own intrinsic value.

"We are always being told about Desire, never about Pleasure," Barthes laments.[37] The usually psychoanalytically inflected "desire," defined by lack and frustration, is much more often the object of analysis than aim-achieving pleasure.[38] Desire is compelling, perhaps, because it is, by definition, always seeking, always active, always still unfolding, and hence conducive to analysis. Pleasure, by contrast, is the achieved end point, the need satisfied, the desire slaked. In Slavoj Žižek's Lacanian terms, for example, the pleasure principle represents limitations, whereas *jouissance*, or enjoyment, transgresses those limitations.[39] Similarly, reflecting on a dialogue with Michel Foucault, Gilles Deleuze complains, "I can barely stand the word pleasure." Casting pleasure on the side of dull "strata and organization," a stabilizing "re-territorialisation" in contrast to desire's chaotically sexy "zones of intensity," Deleuze maintains, "I cannot give any positive value to pleasure, because pleasure seems to interrupt the immanent process of desire."[40] Pleasure is, by this assessment, desire's killjoy. Desire is a work in progress, while pleasure is a narrative punctuation that is also, apparently, the end of theoretical and critical speculation. This is why, for many critics, middle- and lowbrow texts—texts of pandering pleasure (Barthes's "readerly" text) rather than inscrutable bliss (the "writerly" text)—do not seem to require analysis. Certainly, pleasure has a temporary character, followed by a renewal and repetition. Unlike desire, which can be endlessly attenuated, pleasure is periodic. But in the same way that an orgasm-centered theory of sexuality does not account for vast registers of eroticism, the idea of pleasure as a performance that has ended or a dam that has burst imposes false borders on the experience.

There is something unseemly about pleasure, something too direct, selfish, nonrelational. Hedonism is distinctly out of step with the current theoretical climate of other-oriented, ethical, relational philosophy and cultural criticism. While desire is constantly turned outward, pleasure is, in its most basic sense, brazenly self-centered. We might think of Lacan's response to Bernini's sculpture of St. Teresa's ecstasy. Lacan is sure that "she's coming [*qu'elle jouit*], there is no doubt about it," yet he famously claims that "the woman knows nothing of this *jouissance*" even while she experiences it, and that despite his "begging" female analysts to disclose the secrets of such pleasure, he got, "well, not a word!"[41] Where desire is essentially communicative, discursive, other-seeking, and expansive, pleasure is, on a physical, neural level, a fundamentally insular experience (although it can be shared with others in a mediated fashion). It's no coincidence that the mystery of pleasure, for Lacan, is symbolized by a woman. Embodied, immediate pleasure has long been aligned with femininity. As we will see, women's increasing ability to articulate and participate in the discourse of pleasure in the twentieth century is a key development of modernity. In the chapters that follow, I hope to demonstrate that pleasure is every bit as structurally, narratively, and historically complex as desire. The concept of unpleasure amplifies the intricacy of pleasure, as modernists knew well.

MODERNISM'S TIRED TOPOI

Screeds against the "culture industry" in which pleasure is cast as "mass deception" have become familiar parts of modernism. "One of the most tired topoi of the modernist aesthetic and of bourgeois culture at large," Andreas Huyssen remarks, is that "there are the lower pleasures for the rabble, i.e., mass culture, and then there is the *nouvelle cuisine* of the pleasure of the text, of *jouissance*."[42] This tired but tenacious bias is routinely interpreted as a function of the dichotomy between high and low that has, as Robert Scholes notes, "been the founding binary opposition for all Modernist critical terminology."[43] Although it is useful for schematizing modernism's overt rhetoric about its priorities, this conceptual scaffolding has limitations: the dichotomies inevitably break down, and the scaffolding masks what motivates the dichotomies. As some of the richest work in modernist studies of the past twenty years or so has demonstrated, modernism constantly participates in the vernacular culture (to adopt Miriam Hansen's nuanced alternative to "popular"[44]) that it purports to reject. The relationship between modernism and mass or popular culture is more complex than simple opposition, entailing local histories that elude the dichotomy of the great divide.[45]

So far, so good. However, the same deconstructive analysis has not been applied to pleasure as it structures the terms of the debate. What is fundamentally at stake in the tension between modern literature and vernacular modernism is not just class, aesthetics, or institutions of culture, but even more centrally, judgments about different types of pleasure. That is, distinctions about pleasure are not the by-product of but rather *motivate* classic articulations of modernist cultural hierarchy. For Q. D. Leavis, for example, the distinction between modern and popular culture is a function of the quality of pleasure each produces. She praises Puritan reading habits and the "extremely subtle kind of pleasure" of the eighteenth century "public prepared to take some trouble for its pleasures," as opposed to the "immediate," "cheap and easy pleasures offered by the cinema, the circulating library, the magazine, the newspaper, the dance-hall, and the loud-speaker."[46] All of these amusements have had the effect of diminishing readers' capacity for tackling challenging texts and appreciating subtle pleasures.

> We have no practice in making the effort necessary to master a work that presents some surface difficulty or offers no immediate repayment; we have not trained ourselves to persevere at works of the extent of *Clarissa* and the seriousness of Johnson's essays, and all our habits incline us towards preferring the immediate to the cumulative pleasure. (226)

The premise that reading enjoyment requires training beyond literacy itself, and that enjoyment should require serious exertion as well as a tolerance for delayed gratification, is key to Leavis's argument about cultural value. She notes that "Post-war books are apt to be praised by reviewers and advertised as 'readable'" (227), as if that is an indictment in itself. If a text is too "readable" it is classified with the easy, accessible, trite pleasures of movies and newspapers. Hence the frequency with which many cornerstones of modernist literature are pronounced "unreadable." What distinguishes modernist productions from amusement is the *effort* entailed. Quality pleasure is challenging, flexible, and innovative; inferior versions are ossified and boring, their obvious popular attraction notwithstanding. "Pleasure hardens into boredom," Horkheimer and Adorno remark, "because, if it is to remain pleasure, it must not demand any effort."[47]

Modern fiction writers explicitly address these questions of pleasure's variable disposition. The following examples display the predictable hierarchies of the great divide, but they also invoke the definition of pleasure and its effects as an essential problem to be solved. This sequence of authors—Lawrence, Eliot, Huxley, and Orwell—indicates the way I am using the term "modernism" here. Not long ago, "modernism" typically only included those authors who practiced radical formal innovation (Pound, Eliot, Joyce, Stein, Faulkner, Woolf, and the like): that is, "high modernists." However, in recent years, scholars have been expanding the field of inquiry designated as modernism or modernist to include writers from the period who do not experiment extensively with form but who participate in the same ideological discussions. If we prioritize the historical contours of modernism, rather than fetishizing form, as modernists themselves did, the field looks very different. The preoccupation with pleasure is one of the hallmarks of modernity and a means of uniting those authors who are often excluded from canonical modernism but are important figures of the period. Writers such as Lawrence and Huxley, for example, do not engage in the radical aesthetic innovations of high modernism, but they do share many of the signature cultural concerns of the period, and they notably seek to recalibrate their readers' ideas about pleasure in ways that have surprising affinities with authors such as Joyce and Stein. I present the interwar debate about pleasure and the rise of unpleasure, then, as a new way of defining literary modernism more capaciously.

Near the conclusion of *Lady Chatterley's Lover*, a novel that seems consecrated to bodily, immediate delights and that details its protagonists' every orgasmic stroke, Constance Chatterley travels to Europe, away from her gamekeeper lover, Mellors. She observes tourists in Italy indulging in "Far too much enjoyment! . . . It was pleasant in a way. It was *almost* enjoyment. But anyhow, with all the cocktails, all the lying in warmish water and sun-bathing on hot sand in hot sun, jazzing with your stomach against some fellow in the warm nights, cooling off with ices, it was a complete narcotic. And that was what they all wanted, a drug. . . . To be drugged! Enjoying! Enjoyment!"; "Oh, the joy-hogs! Oh 'enjoying oneself'! Another modern form of sickness."[48] In this moment, the protagonist's voice is notably overshadowed by the author's own near-hysterical expression (recognizable from essays such as "Pornography and Obscenity"). Lest cocktails, sunbathing, and frottage sound too pleasant, Lawrence insists, they are bad! sick! a drug! Lawrence's authorial presence regularly intrudes on his fictional world when he writes about pleasure, whether he is arguing about the correct form of leisure activity or the correct kind of orgasm for women. His quotation marks ("Oh 'enjoying oneself'") appeal to the reader's sense of semantic distinction and imply that these enjoyments are delusions or a kind of false consciousness.

Some, but not all of these activities are related to mass culture. What bothers Lawrence about cocktails, sunbathing, sexual promiscuity, and jazz, when he believes so passionately in sensual life itself, is that these body-centered activities are effortless, narcotizing, and collective, and decrease awareness. Unlike the forms of eroticism that Lawrence exalts as a means of personal and social enlightenment, a transcending of "sex in the head" that is, paradoxically, very much related to the linguistic expression of consciousness, these modern enjoyments lack any purpose except pleasure. The most threatening pleasures are tautological, with no "added value." They "mean," as Aldous Huxley writes of the "feelies" in *Brave New World*, only "themselves; they mean a lot of agreeable sensations to the audience."[49] Art for art's sake is a worthy endeavor, but not pleasure for pleasure's sake. T. S. Eliot makes a similar point in his 1934 essay on "Religion and Literature," where he investigates the attraction of popular literature.

I incline to come to the alarming conclusion that it is just the literature that we read for "amusement," or "purely for pleasure" that may have the greatest, and least suspected influence upon us. It is the literature which we read with the least effort that can have the easiest and most insidious influence upon us. Hence it is that the influence of popular novelists, and of popular plays of contemporary life, requires to be scrutinized most closely. And it is chiefly *contemporary* literature that the majority of people ever read in this attitude of "purely for pleasure," of pure passivity.[50]

According to this view, popular contemporary literature surreptitiously bypasses consciousness and obviates effort. The same argument, as we will see, was made about cinema, which was thought to lower people's defenses, lulling them into a relaxed or hypnotized condition. Again, ironic quotation marks around the operative terms "amusement" and "pleasure" suggest that Eliot, like Lawrence, views the sociological problem of pleasure as importantly related to language. Modern writers confront pleasure from within language itself, by advocating closer textual scrutiny and pressing the word to signify not one but several different ranks of phenomena. ("Life is a well of joy," Nietzsche wrote, "but where the rabble drinks too, all wells are poisoned. . . . They have poisoned the holy water with their lustfulness; and when they called their dirty dreams 'pleasure,' they poisoned the language too."[51]) Such self-consciousness and linguistic defamiliarization are standard modernist strategies. This is not just irony, but an attempt to subject the sensation of pleasure to the same concerns modernists voice about aesthetic experience.

Although they would have been loath to admit it, modern writers, in these arguments for the necessity of putting more effort into amusement, overlapped significantly with contemporary "leisure theorists": philosophers and social scientists who emphasized the importance of pursuing cultivated pleasures as a bulwark against cultural degeneration. The popular (and anti-Bloomsbury) philosopher C. E. M. Joad, whose misogynist writings Woolf cites extensively in *Three Guineas*, argues in his 1928 tract *Diogenes or the Future of Leisure* against easy, popular pleasures in favor of activities and tastes that "must be worked for; they must be pursued with effort and through boredom." Labor and difficulty, Joad claims, are exactly what the modern situation requires. Our cultural development depends on our willingness to shun simple, easy pleasures, forsaking "festering on the beach at Margate" (23) for reading "good novels" (25) and other challenging pastimes. If, Joad maintains, we "force ourselves to

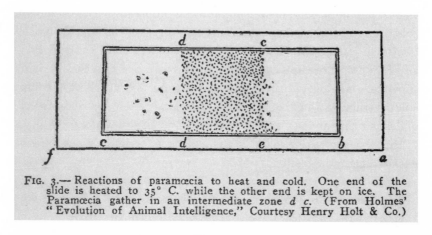

FIG. 3.— Reactions of paramœcia to heat and cold. One end of the slide is heated to 35° C. while the other end is kept on ice. The Paramœcia gather in an intermediate zone *d c.* (From Holmes' "Evolution of Animal Intelligence," Courtesy Henry Holt & Co.)

Figure 0.1
"Reactions of paramoecia to heat and cold" from
Henry Thomas Moore, *Pain and Pleasure,* 1917.

undergo a severe training," we will "enjoy the happiness which comes to all who struggle."[52]

Henry Thomas Moore's treatise on *Pain and Pleasure* (1917) makes a similar point by invoking experiments on single-celled animals: for example, paramecia put in a trough with progressively freezing to very hot water were found to gravitate toward the pleasant, tepid temperatures in the middle. Humans must distinguish themselves from such lowly creatures, Moore argues, by striving to develop more complex and demanding inclinations. Moving from the petri dish to the concert hall, Moore contends that the most worthy pleasure must be cultivated and "results from conflict."

The music that we most enjoy to-day would have been laughed out of court as unspeakably disagreeable two hundred years ago.

More and more dissonant intervals have challenged the ears of each successive generation, and while each new innovation has created confusion and unpleasantness, it has been gradually mastered by the music-going public, which now demands that music be complex and even harsh in order to be enjoyable.[53]

Confusion, unpleasantness, complexity, and harshness are positive values. Aesthetic enjoyment is figured as a punishing series of hot and cold plunge pools (as opposed to the paramecia's bath or Lawrence's "warmish water") that stun the mind awake. This is art as shock therapy. Moore is more optimistic than Eliot, Lawrence, and Huxley in his conviction that people can be and are being trained to value more difficult pursuits. Among modernist literary critics, there is a shared sense of despair that amusement is winning the war on pleasure.

Huxley's 1923 essay called "Pleasures" is a particularly despondent dispatch from the front:

Of all the various poisons which modern civilization, by a process of auto-intoxication, brews quietly up within its own bowels, few, it seems to me, are more deadly (while none appears more harmless) than that curious and appalling thing that is technically known as "pleasure." "Pleasure" (I place the word between inverted commas to show that I mean, not real pleasure, but the organized activities officially known by the same name) "pleasure"—what nightmare visions the word evokes! . . . The horrors of modern "pleasure" arise from the fact that every kind of organized distraction tends to become progressively more and more imbecile. . . . In place of the old pleasures demanding intelligence and personal initiative, we have vast organizations that provide us with ready-made distractions—distractions which demand from pleasure-seekers no personal participation and no intellectual effort of any sort. To the interminable democracies of the world a million cinemas bring the same balderdash. . . . Countless audiences soak passively in the tepid bath of nonsense. No mental effort is demanded of them, no participation; they need only sit and keep their eyes open.[54]

Huxley starkly juxtaposes "old" pleasure—"real pleasure" that is individualized and intellectually demanding—with "ready-made," collective, and immediate distractions (described, once again, through the metaphor of the warm bath). Mindfulness and individualism are the supreme virtues that separate humans from beasts. For Huxley, there is something especially disturbing about the creation of pleasures that materialize as effortlessly as waste brewed in modern civilization's bowels. (It is not just their novelty that bothers Huxley; he is more approving of the engineered phenomenon of speed, which he claims in a 1931 essay "provides the one genuinely modern pleasure."[55] Unlike more complex forms of culture that require explanation and *effort*, the production of these new pleasures is just as automatic as their consumption. Old pleasures, by contrast, are hard to achieve and require education to create and properly digest.

In metaphors from the barnyard to the pharmacy, from Q. D. Leavis's descriptions of the consumption of vernacular culture as masturbation or a drug habit[56] to the Frankfurt School critique of "distraction factories,"[57] passive and corporeal pleasures—often associated with femininity and with the new sensorium—are posited as inferior to the deliberately chosen, cerebral, and *difficult* pleasures of modernism. All of the aforementioned attacks on pleasure are predicated on challenging the dominant idea of the word itself. (Orwell's 1946 essay "Pleasure Spots" sounds the same notes: "Much of what goes by the name of pleasure is simply an effort to destroy consciousness. . . . The tendency of many modern inventions—in particular the film, the radio and the aeroplane—is to weaken [man's] consciousness, dull his curiosity, and, in general, drive him nearer to the animals."[58]) Signposts around pleasure set off the writer's sensibilities from common usage, a recurrent rhetorical maneuver that is further evidence that modern writers thought of pleasure not merely as a matter of what people did with their spare time, but as a potential threat to language itself that needed to be fought, in kind, through language. Hence, modern writers managed their readers' response to pleasure and actively inscribed their own alternatives into the grain of their writing.

DIFFICULTY AND UNPLEASURE

"We do not take pleasure seriously enough," Robert Scholes remarks, "and Modernism, with its emphasis on the connection between greatness and difficulty, is to some extent responsible for this" (xiii).

Significantly, we have elaborate analyses of the anatomy of difficulty—for example, William Empson's *Seven Types of Ambiguity* or George Steiner's "On Difficulty"[59]—but no equivalent for pleasure. In tandem with disparaging embodied, accessible pleasure, modernists revise the conventional relationship between the artist and the audience from entertainment to intellectual challenge. The hallmarks of modernism—including fragmentation, disjunction, and irony—are strategies that demand interpretive work from the reader as well as a certain kind of tolerance and submission.[60] Trilling observes that

> Our typical experience of a work which will eventually have authority with us is to begin our relation to it at a conscious disadvantage, and to wrestle with it until it consents to bless us. We express our high esteem for such a work by supposing that it judges us. . . . In short, our contemporary aesthetic culture does not set great store by the principle of pleasure in its simple and primitive meaning and it may even be said to maintain an antagonism to the principle of pleasure. (438)

The reader genuflects before an arrogant, hostile text. Here Trilling presupposes a combative or masochistic model of readership, an engagement with an arrogant opponent that will eventually be enriching. This is very different from collaboration or seduction, more conventional conceptual models of readership. Indeed, modernism has a confrontational edge: Eliot's insistence that "poets in our civilization, as it exists at present, must be difficult,"[61] for example, or Dorothy Richardson's quip that "Plot, nowadays, save the cosmic plot, is inexcusable. Lollipops for children."[62] Joyce's only half-joking claim that "the demand that I make of my reader is that he should devote his whole life to reading my works" is confirmed by his prose, which seems to have been written for an "ideal reader suffering from an ideal insomnia."[63] Difficulty becomes an inherent value and is a deliberate aesthetic ambition set against too pleasing, harmonious reading effects. Conventional pleasure is dismissed precisely because it is too easy and seems to pander to the dumb happiness of beasts.

Rather than become more conventionally captivating, modernists invented new modes of engagement. Against the saccharine, predictable, easy amusement of popular novels, newspapers, and cinema, they offered cognitive tension, irony, and analytical rigor. Leonard Diepeveen has made a convincing case that when disparaged for "block[ing] reading pleasure, creating anxiety and irritation instead," modernists claimed that the struggle with difficult texts had its own intrinsic rewards: the satisfaction of solving a puzzle or recognizing arcane references, sorting out the voices of *The Waves*, or decoding Pound's *Cantos*.[64] Those of us who have to coax recalcitrant undergraduates into reading *Ulysses* will recognize this argument: really, it's FUN.

An important motivation for modern art's aesthetic difficulty was competition with the undeniable charms of vernacular culture. In Orwell's 1936 novel *Keep the Aspidistra Flying*, which wittily stages the cultural battle of the brows in a bookshop scene, the self-defeating would-be poet Gordon Comstock is undone by his attempt to compose a massive work in rhyme royal, an Eliotic pastiche caustically called "London Pleasures."[65] Gordon sneers at the common urban pleasures around him even as he acknowledges their allure:

> The pubs were open, oozing sour whiffs of beer. People were trickling by ones and twos into the picture-houses. Gordon halted outside a great garish picture-house, under the weary eye of the commissionaire, to examine the photographs. Greta Garbo in *The Painted Veil*. He yearned to go inside, not for Greta's sake, but just for the warmth and the softness of the velvet seat. He hated the pictures, of course, seldom went there even when he could afford it. Why encourage the art that is destined to replace literature? But still, there is a kind of soggy attraction about it. To sit on the padded seat in the warm smoke-scented darkness, letting the flickering drivel on the screen gradually overwhelm you—feeling the waves of its silliness lap you round till you seem to drown, intoxicated, in a viscous sea—after all, it's the kind of drug we need. (71–72)

Here we see, in characteristic Orwellian clarity, anxiety about cinema's appeal (such bad food and such small portions!), felt all the more now that cinema was superseding or cannibalizing literature. Unlike Graham Greene's sociopathic Pinkie in *Brighton Rock*, who has an extreme antipathy to somatic enjoyment—dancing, alcohol, and sex fill him with "the nausea of other people's pleasures"[66]—Gordon senses but tries to resist the cinema's "soggy attraction." Gordon is a comical failure whose negativity and pretentious rebellion keep him from enjoying anything. Orwell understood the power of "good bad books"[67]; nevertheless, like Huxley, Eliot, and others, he articulates the common concerns about vernacular culture here and in 1984, where he imagines a dystopia that secures its drone-citizens' compliance through "pornosec" and fiction produced by "novel writing machines." The new landscape of vernacular pleasure is both stimulating and threatening to modern writers, as evidenced by the defensive mode that often underlies their seeming autonomy and innovation.

Diepeveen contends that

> high moderns moved too briskly away from mainstream notions of pleasure. Looking askance at forms of pleasure that didn't have its vigorous ethic attached to it, difficult modernism presented the hard and serious work required for reading *Ulysses* as the only worthwhile pleasure. Thus, even though difficult modernism shed light on an important aspect of art when they described difficulty's anxiety, and why that anxiety might be important, it was less adept at imagining the validity of other forms of pleasure. . . . When they asserted their vigorous morality, difficulty's apologists also couldn't deal with the pleasure of physical abandonment and sensual indulgence. (173)

This kind of pleasure, Diepeveen argues, is modernism's "blind spot." Certainly, modernism privileges serious cultural work, but its resistance to vernacular and sensual pleasures suggests that it is anything but blind to them—rather, it never takes its eyes off them. The writers collected here often draw on simple, immediate pleasures, but present them through devices of refinement, indirection, irony, and distance that mitigate against a reader enjoying them too easily or too much. Modernism's contribution to the genealogy of pleasure is the declared substitution of one set of pleasures (refined, acquired, and cognitive) for another (embodied, accessible), in which the disavowal of the latter is promoted as an aesthetic principle. The construction of pleasure hierarchies, the resistance to certain stimulation, and the obstacles to reading pleasure, culminate in their own kind of contorted satisfaction.[68] (This did not only happen in literary modernism: there was a concomitant problematicizing of pleasure in fine art as abstract, non-mimetic modernist and avant-garde works challenged traditional conceptions of art and the experience of viewing it. Clement Greenberg, for example, in his influential 1939 essay "Avant-Garde and Kitsch," contrasts the ersatz culture of kitsch, "vicarious experience and faked sensations," to "what is necessarily difficult in genuine art."[69]) This premise has been one of modernism's enduring cultural legacies: the philosopher Susanne Langer argued that "Now that everyone can read, go to museums, listen to great music, at least on the radio, the judgment of the masses about these things has become a reality and through this it has become clear that great art is not a direct sensuous pleasure. Otherwise, like cookies or cocktails, it would flatter uneducated taste as much as cultured taste." Modernism is the first moment when "great art" so consistently asserted formal experimentation and allusiveness—pleasure and unpleasure that had to be learned—and withheld from its audience cookies and cocktails.[70]

What, then, should we call this aesthetic response that must be earned or learned, and that distinguishes itself from facile amusement? Commenting on the reading experience of *The Waste Land*, Frank Kermode detects a "pleasure that is accompanied by loss and even dismay—something quite different from the ordinary pleasures of reading . . . an experience hardly to be called pleasure, a moment of ecstatic dismay."[71] Ecstatic dismay is a suggestive description, but not wide enough to cover the range of dysphoric effects in modernism. Earlier writers had anecdotally described the paradoxical attraction of unpleasant experiences (itching for Plato, ecstatic martyrdom for the early saints, spanking for Rousseau, the sublime for Kant), and late nineteenth-century sexologists such as Krafft-Ebing and Havelock Ellis catalogued masochistic and sadistic practices in the realm of human sexuality that blurred the distinction between pleasure and pain. But it was Freud who moved the discussion to more general principles of psychology, offering in *Beyond the Pleasure Principle* (1920) a metapsychological theory of "Unlust," translated as unpleasure, which unmoors the premise that people seek pleasure and avoid pain. Unpleasure (as distinct from "Schmerz," or "pain," which Freud uses to designate more uniform negative experiences[72]) is not an abdication of pleasure entirely, nor is it the same as anhedonia. "Lust" is embedded in "Unlust," and this is key to grasping the relationship between the two drives. Recasting the classical model of pleasure as a lessening of tension—"unpleasure corresponds to an *increase* in the quantity of excitation and pleasure to a *diminution*"[73]—Freud describes enactments of "unpleasurable tension" such as the repetition compulsion that circuitously produce pleasure. Here, as a dialectical resolution of apparently oppositional forces, unpleasure is useful for describing the modernist approach to pleasure. That Freud elaborated the concept of unpleasure in the context of interwar culture strengthens its aptness for literary modernism and demonstrates further how views about pleasure are subject to historical fluctuations.

The force of *Beyond the Pleasure Principle* is its suggestion that people commonly seek out convoluted and distressing experiences, and that what seems like pain or unbearable conflict can produce pleasure. Leo Bersani has drawn out the implications of Freud's argument about "the pleasureable unpleasurable tension of sexual excitement" to suggest that "The *mystery* of sexuality is that we seek not only to get rid of this shattering tension but also to repeat, even to increase it. . . . Sexuality—at least in the mode in which it is constituted—could be thought of as a tautology for masochism."[74] Far from a perverse experience, unpleasure can be part of commonplace experience, and not just in the sexual realm. The reality principle itself, Freud maintains, requires "the temporary toleration of unpleasure as a step on the long indirect road to pleasure" (*Beyond the Pleasure Principle,* 7). Sublimation itself is a form of unpleasure.

Freud's idea that we must renounce what we actually want (presented, for example, in *Civilization and Its Discontents*) is useful for complicating what Trilling deems modernism's "repudiation" of pleasure. The fort/da game of *Beyond the Pleasure Principle,* which Freud calls "the child's great cultural achievement—the instinctual renunciation (that is, the renunciation of instinctual satisfaction)" (14), a ruse of postponement and simulated control that masters emotional attachment to the mother, is suggestive of modernism's distrust of instinctive, comforting, *bodily* pleasure and its validation of difficulty. What may look like a suppression of sensual, embodied, immediate, and easy pleasure in the service of cognitive effort is a means of assuaging an attraction to those disavowed pleasures. Modernism redefines pleasure not just to include but to require tension, difficulty, and obstacles. Unpleasure, to adapt Bersani, may be a tautology for modernism.

"Unpleasure" is a big umbrella. How is it different from, say, the sublime's pleasurable terror? While the sublime taps into deep instinctive impulses (the natural sublime is involuntary, although it can then be consciously constructed in literature), the modern repudiation of pleasure must be cultivated and learned. With authors like Joyce, Rhys, and Patrick Hamilton, terms such as "masochism," "abjection," or "*jouissance*" are plausible explanations for some of the experiences they describe. However, these are only subsets of a broader category. I will use "unpleasure," then, as it reflects the self-conscious and explicit interwar discourse about pleasure. More than any other term, "unpleasure" is able to encompass both the complex, dialectical representations of pleasure and the readerly affects modernism puts into play.

READING FOR (UN)PLEASURE

Laura Mulvey famously declared, in "Visual Pleasure and Narrative Cinema," "It is said that analysing pleasure, or beauty, destroys it. That is the intention of this article."[75] The intention of this book is the opposite. It is, rather, to analyze, magnify, and participate in the varieties of delight and unpleasure that texts display. How should we go about grasping pleasure? How can we catch it in the act? First, we have to move past the idea that pleasure must be veiled or obscure: an affect that dare not speak its name. While it is true that analyzing pleasure, like analyzing jokes, runs the risk of ruining the fun (hence, *Beyond the Pleasure Principle* is really no more pleasurable than *Jokes and Their Relation to the Unconscious* is funny), it is a risk worth taking. The linguistic barriers to sense impression mean that pleasure is always and necessarily mediated in literature. Recent studies such as Sianne Ngai's *Ugly Feelings* and Lauren Berlant's *The Female Complaint* have provided useful models for reading the aesthetic, political, and social implications of affect, and I will follow their lead in conceptualizing pleasure as a bodily, individual experience that is simultaneously located in a social field as well as, most importantly, a textual one.[76] The challenge of analyzing pleasure rendered in language lies in teasing out its texture and effects: its ticklish play on the page, its moments of affectual intensity, the "fire and wings" in *Good Morning, Midnight*, for example, or in Katherine Mansfield's short story "Bliss" (1920), the protagonist's sensation that she'd "suddenly swallowed a piece of that late afternoon sun and it burned in [her] bosom, sending out a little shower of sparks into every particle, into every finger and toe."[77] Such moments solicit the reader's feelings and body through both the objects or states represented and the language itself. A text of bliss, Barthes writes, must "cruise" its reader (4); "whenever I attempt to 'analyze' a text which has given me pleasure . . . it is my body of bliss I encounter" (62). The text does not have to be a sensation novel; this happens when we admire a felicitous phrase, laugh, are aroused, or find ourselves drawn in through textual challenges, mysteries, or riddles. Of course, a text can appeal to different readers in different ways, so the focus here is primarily on the rhetorical management of pleasure for what Wolfgang Iser has called an "implied reader."[78] We do not read modernist works now in exactly the same way readers did in the 1920s and '30s. Retrieving that experience is impossible, but the author's linguistic cues give a strong sense of what kind of response was expected and desired. Barthes insists that pleasure is never so obvious as to be literal—"the text of bliss is never the text that recounts the kind of bliss afforded literally by an ejaculation. The pleasure of representation is not attached to its object"—but rather is linguistic and "occurs in the volume of the languages" (55, 13). This conforms to modernism's own story about itself (nothing so low as *representational* pleasure: but can one cruise without a body?), but it is not the whole story. Modernism simulates or curtails pleasure—thematically and linguistically—in order to achieve a particular effect. So Mansfield's story, for example, is both a catalogue of sensations and a text of aporias, ellipses, and indirection that reflects the incoherence of her protagonist's feelings and demands an analytical and mediated kind of engagement. Reading for modernist pleasure, then, requires an attention to how a text represents, produces, and thwarts bliss at once.

For all its elusiveness, modernism is profoundly pedagogical. It continually teaches readers how to approach its texts. Modernist fictions are full of implied or explicit injunctions—notice this, admire this, reject this, puzzle over this—and scenes that model correct and incorrect readerly affect. So Joyce, for example, exhibits and creates models of different kinds of pleasure—readerly, aesthetic, and sensuous—in *Ulysses*. Lawrence, through overt polemic and textual guidance, aims to shape his audience's experience of reading and of sexuality together. Stein trains her reader to tolerate repetition and indeterminacy. Huxley expounds on the idea that people's pleasures can be upgraded through pedagogy and other modes of cultural conditioning.

That said, in modernism, pleasure is often the place where the text contradicts itself. Pleasure may exert itself through ideology-defying magnetisms and irrational attractions. It is important to note an author's avowed stance but also to pay close attention to how pleasure plays out in the text. Barthes writes, "The pleasure of the text is that moment when my body pursues its own ideas—for my body does not have the same ideas I do" (17). Although modernists attempt to tightly control their effects, scorned delights appear everywhere in disguised or disavowed forms. So, for example, the language that Lawrence uses when he writes about eroticism makes use of the same clichés and stereotypes that he condemns in popular genre fiction; and when Huxley depicts *Brave New World*'s pneumatic woman Lenina Crowne, he appeals to the same prurience that he abhors in popular culture. Modernists often use, in the guise of irony, the same formulas of vernacular culture that they otherwise reject as corrosive precisely for the attractions they offer. Pleasure is often where the text goes beyond or gets away from itself.

It is not my goal here to account for all kinds of subjects responding to all kinds of pleasure, but rather to suggest, through a series of heuristic readings, how centrally modern literature is concerned with the reconceptualization of pleasure. In the following chapters, I will analyze stimulants as diverse as perfume, bearskin rugs, Rudolph Valentino, and linguistic puzzles, and experiences ranging from wordplay to foreplay to tickling to drunkenness. Widening the field to include both somatic and cognitive pleasure and to show the imbrication of the two is a strategic choice that I hope will reflect unexpected connections, combinations, transfer points, and associations between and among different types of pleasure.

I aim to capture a panorama of pleasures while emphasizing those about which modernists were most overtly concerned. It was an era shadowed by the Great War and the impending signs of another; it was also a time of gender upheaval and novel forms of mass culture: the disembodied sounds of the radio, the gramophone, and interwar cinema's momentous transition from silence to sound. The "mass production of the senses," Miriam Hansen writes, offered "new modes of organizing vision and sensory perception, a new relationship with 'things,' different forms of mimetic experience and expression, of affectivity, temporality, and reflexivity, a changing fabric of everyday life, sociability, and leisure" (60). This mass production initiated modes of pleasure and means of stimulation that troubled as well as excited modernists. This is not merely about the invention of new technologies or a shift in perception or cognition: it is about shifts in the value of particular pleasures and the understanding of how modernity is experienced through the body and the brain, and also how those shifts impact aesthetics. If, as Walter Benjamin remarked, "technology has subjected the human sensorium to a complex kind of training,"[79] literary modernists counter this with their own kind of training in reading that ratifies certain pleasures as legitimate and casts doubt on others. There is a thread running through these chapters about emergent technology facilitating this effortlessness, in which machines do not so much alienate (like the gears and gadgetry of Chaplin's *Modern Times*, for example) as they generate easy, debased, bodily pleasure. Modernist prose is the opposite of technological efficiency. It means to discomfit its readers, to make them focus, think, and grapple with language. It is conspicuously labor intensive.

There are two strong currents running through the dominant representation of pleasure in modernism. Literary modernity corresponded to the emergence of women as politically empowered subjects and also to the establishment of cinema, newly imbued with sound, as a massively popular pastime. Female voices and the cinema, both figured as intensely somatic and largely noncerebral, are often the foil for modernist unpleasure. The twentieth-century equivalents of Bentham's pushpins were popular women's novels and films. In the late 1920s and early '30s, modernists continually focused on the nexus of popular fiction—which Lawrence personifies and pointedly feminizes as "that smirking, rather plausible hussy, the popular novel"[80]—and cinema as a site of controversial pleasure.

My focus here has been necessarily selective, and this project largely addresses British modernists as well as some American writers. All of them, however, were strongly influenced by other national literatures, and most spent substantial amounts of time living outside of their native countries.[81] Their work therefore offers a more cosmopolitan vision of pleasure than their national origins might suggest. Mapping complex linguistic traditions and nationalities onto a concept like pleasure is a complicated matter. Pleasure is typically experienced as an individual, local, and intimate event, but affiliations of race, class, gender, and nationality all exert an influence over how and where particular pleasures flourish. The dominant discourse of bliss has been largely Western, white, male, privileged, and heterosexual. Female Harlem Renaissance writers such as Nella Larsen or Zora Neale Hurston, for example, had a different set of political pressures around their representation of pleasure than did white, male, British writers such as Huxley, Lawrence, or Patrick Hamilton.[82] This study never loses sight of that fundamental difference, but I also argue that Huxley's treatment of the black male body, Lawrence's orientalist sheiks, and Hamilton's prostitutes, among other examples, illustrate how stereotypes of race, gender, and nation shape pleasure.

Most criticism on the modernist sensorium focuses on visual or auditory pleasure. I begin with the less considered realm of olfaction. Chapter 1, "James Joyce and the Scent of Modernity," examines one of modernism's great hedonists who is also one of the great artists of unpleasure. Numerous odors, fragrant and foul, waft through *Ulysses*, charged with erotic and mnemonic symbolism. For Joyce, odor is significant because it hovers on the threshold between body and mind, confounding the bifurcation of these qualities in contemporary theories of pleasure. Odor in general has a formal dimension: its dispersal is analogous to the mechanisms of the mind that produce involuntary memory and stream of consciousness. Perfume would seem to embody the simple, somatic pleasures against which high modernism often sets itself, but Joyce is also interested in the cultural connotations of perfume, and especially the synthetic creations of modern perfumery, which strikingly dovetail with the history of aesthetic modernism. Modern perfume's most compelling qualities, for Joyce, are its contradictions: its combination of artificial and natural scents, its abstract and mimetic characteristics, and its blend of the putrid and pleasing. Perfume is a metaphor for Joyce's response to pleasure in general. His "perfumance" in *Ulysses*,[83] which includes inventing his own fragrance, "Sweets of Sin," poses counterintuitive acts of olfactory pleasure as a model of eroticism and readership that seeks to expand his audience's repertoire of sensation in idiosyncratic ways.

Chapter 2, "Stein's Tickle," takes up one of the outstanding questions in Stein criticism: how and whether she gives pleasure. There has been a strong turn in recent Stein criticism toward interpreting her as a purveyor of sensuous pleasure that is secured by her hermeticism and indeterminacy. That is, the same formal features in her work that are deemed irritating or confusing have increasingly been read as the source of her appeal. Looking at Stein's experimental writing from 1914 to her lectures of the mid-1930s, I will suggest a new model for approaching her work: tickling. Both infantile and erotic, delight-inducing and irritating, physically reflexive and intersubjective, tickling is an enduring social and scientific mystery whose patterns, I will argue, illuminate Stein's methods and her reading effects. The gesture of tickling describes both the delights and difficulties of Stein's texts and also accounts for the wide discrepancies in readers' responses to her writing.

Chapter 3, "Orgasmic Discipline: D. H. Lawrence, E. M. Hull, and Interwar Erotic Fiction," considers the relationship between innovation and repetition in the structure of pleasure, and Lawrence's effort to direct readerly pleasure around those poles. For most modernists, vernacular culture has its own language: cliché, stereotype, and banal formula, all of which would seem to work against the modernist maxim to "make it New." Lawrence's representation of sexuality is understood to be among the most original of the modernist period. However, just as British genre novels and popular films exerted an important influence on many modernist representations of sexual pleasure, Lawrence criticized but also borrowed from the formulaic language of popular romance by turning it toward antierotic purposes. I will examine Lawrence's charged reaction, in his essays and in fiction, to E. M. Hull, whose 1919 novel *The Sheik* was the supreme interwar desert romance novel. Lawrence's appropriation and manipulation of Hull's work demonstrates how circuits of pleasure favor both novelty (the shock of the new) and familiarity (the sure thing). Lawrence's effort to actively reform pleasure is most evident in his strategies of orgasmic discipline, through which he demands that his characters, along with his readers, embrace arduous ecstasy.

Chapter 4, "Huxley's Feelies: Engineered Pleasure in *Brave New World*," considers Huxley's most famous novel as an intricate balance of pleasure and unpleasure. Huxley highlights the management of vernacular pleasure in *Brave New World* as a means of bolstering other techniques of social and political conditioning. In so doing, he addresses one of the central assumptions of modernism: that pleasure can be manipulated and upgraded through training. Huxley is interested in the ways pleasure is malleable and the uses to which it can be put, and he casts the cinema as a key manifestation of engineered pleasure. His response to early cinema—and especially the transition to sound—recognizes its stimulation of the body as well as the mind and imagines film's potential to be either an instrument of sociopolitical reform or a medium of cultural degeneracy. This chapter traces the dense composite of references around the "feelies" in *Brave New World*, from a popular women's romance novel to Shakespeare to race cinema and nature documentaries. Just as Lawrence's work registers the attraction of the material he claims to reject, the engineered pleasures in *Brave New World*, including the feelies, exert a frivolous, sleazy magnetism that often contradicts the novel's argument against careless hedonism. The totalitarian culture that is meant to be repellent is secured by a wide variety of vernacular pleasures that are, from a readerly perspective, paradoxically engaging. This irony is extended in Huxley's subsequent adaptation of *Brave New World* to the form that is perhaps least likely: a musical comedy.

If some modernists foreground cognitive and aesthetic difficulty in their work, others replace conventional, sensory, popular, and stereotypical enjoyment with forms of somatic and aesthetic unpleasure that are contorted, violent, or masochistic. Chapter 5, "The Impasse of Pleasure: Patrick Hamilton and Jean Rhys," pairs two late-modernist authors who are rarely thought of as pleasure seekers but rather as chroniclers of urban misery. Like other writers of the period, Hamilton and Rhys are highly attuned to vernacular culture as the main force of conventional, bodily pleasure. However, in fictions in which the losses of the Great War and the menacing rise of fascism are felt, these authors extend the critique of pleasure in a new direction as vernacular culture becomes the primary realm for their protagonists to achieve negative distinction. Effacing the conceptual boundaries between pleasure and pain, Hamilton and Rhys deploy several common vehicles—including alcohol, cinema, and prostitution—to redefine the texture and terms of the pleasure principle and to show the allure of intense experience that is obliterating, repetitive, and self-destructive. Through representations of visceral distress, dark humor, and characters of determined dissolution, Rhys and Hamilton both frustrate reading for pleasure and beckon their audience to read for unpleasure.

Chapter 6, "Blondes Have More Fun: Anita Loos and the Language of Silent Cinema," turns to an author for whom the modernist debate about pleasure is a source of amusement, creativity, and aesthetic play rather than a vexing problem and who, in this respect, anticipates the movement beyond modernism, postmodernism. Loos's 1925 best-selling novel *Gentlemen Prefer Blondes* was simultaneously lambasted by Q. D. Leavis and Wyndham Lewis and praised by pleasure critics such as Huxley and Mencken. *Blondes*'s appeal to modernist audiences turns on the way Loos develops a linguistically witty and self-conscious reading pleasure within one of the most reviled of the interwar genres: popular women's writing and film. Loos honed her linguistic strategies in the early silent cinema writing screenplays and subtitles, which until that point had been largely dismissed as superfluous and artless: a means of making an undemanding art form even more effortless. At a transitional moment when literary institutions were changing and the cinema was being born, Loos cross-pollinated the novel with the cinema to invent new forms of vernacular pleasure and slyly demonstrated how acts of cultural classification (and their undoing) are themselves pleasurable. Along the way, she sends up the pretentions of modernist pedagogy, asserting the possibility of witty innovation without the vexation of unpleasure. For these reasons, I position Loos as a transitional figure out of the thicket of modernism into postmodernism.

The book concludes with a coda, "Modernism's Afterlife in the Age of Prosthetic Pleasure." Although summing up six decades of pleasure after modernism is impossible, by way of a necessarily impressionistic conclusion, I will look at David Foster Wallace's novel *Infinite Jest* (1996), as it demonstrates how, despite postmodernism's divergence from many of modernism's premises, the conception of pleasure as a problem remains strong into our century.

My goal is to place pleasure at the center of the twentieth century and to cast the history of literary modernism in a way it has not been seen before: as a tumultuous and revealing chapter in the history of bliss. Although this book investigates the counterintuitive condemnation of experiences of delight and enjoyment as a discursive issue in modernism, my fundamental premise is hedonistic. No matter how circuitous the paths may be, there is, in every aesthetic act, a basic impulse toward an engaged incitement, but we need to expand and even revise our concept of pleasure in order to perceive that effect throughout modernism. What looks like a story about limiting pleasure, then, is also a story about its proliferation.

1

JAMES JOYCE AND THE SCENT OF MODERNITY

Is it perfume from a dress
That makes me so digress?
—T. S. Eliot, "The Love Song of J. Alfred Prufrock"[1]

That is horse piss and rotted straw, he thought.
It is a good odour to breathe. It will calm my heart.
—James Joyce, *A Portrait of the Artist as a Young Man*[2]

The interwar debate about pleasure clusters most intensely around cinema and popular literature. However, I will begin with a sensual experience that has received far less attention: smell, and specifically perfume, viewed as a vehicle of pleasure that is as interpretable as any text. Recent scholarship on the modernist sensorium focuses almost exclusively on vision and hearing, and few literary critics have attended to the olfactory sense. Historically, smell has been construed as vision's other: the archaic to the modern, the spontaneous to the cultivated, the irrational to the logical. Accordingly, the pleasures of scent have been dismissed as frivolous and nonaesthetic. Just so, while the impact of cultural innovations in cinema, music, and the fine arts on modern literature has been carefully documented, the remarkable conceptual and material innovations in perfumery during the modern period have gone largely unnoticed. (An exception is Chanel No. 5, which is usually highlighted more for its bottle shape, typography, and abstract name or for its maker's biography than for the substance itself.[3]) The history of perfume from the 1880s to the early years of the twentieth century strikingly dovetails with the history of literary modernism.

Perfume would seem to be an extreme embodiment of the somatic, commodified pleasures that modernists decry. Aside from the aesthetic choice of which perfume to wear, scent is a largely passive pleasure that plays on the senses. However, as Jennifer Wicke reminds us, commodities and the activity of their consumption offer an important window into the experience of modernity.[4] A peculiar kind of pleasure, perfume is mostly mass-produced but also intimate and individual, thought to disclose the essence of the wearer and publicly advertise his or her taste, passion, and predilections. Ephemeral (it evaporates and fades from the skin; when specific brands or formulas are discontinued, they may disappear forever), perfume can evoke deep-seated, unconscious responses and memories. A product that becomes part of the body itself by seeping into the skin, perfume elicits equally somatic reactions from those who smell it.

This chapter will first give a brief history of perfume's synthetic revolution and demonstrate how modern writers, including T. S. Eliot, Virginia Woolf, Aldous Huxley, and George Orwell, registered the impact of these material changes in their work. Subsequently, I will examine how James Joyce deploys scent, and particularly perfume, as a means of expanding the conventional boundaries of what is "scentually" appealing to include the repulsive and the repellent in a pungent dialectic of pleasure and unpleasure. Joyce notably engages with sensual and popular pleasures at the same time that he upholds the vaunted modernist value of difficulty. He is far less defensive about vernacular culture than many other modernists. Indeed, he revels in the absurd, cliché, and shameless side of mass culture and literary genres such as pornography and romance: hence, his work immediately complicates the stark polarities of the great divide. However, Joyce's work—and *Ulysses* in particular—demonstrates how modernism incorporates easy, somatic pleasures but renders them through contorted kinds of unpleasure and challenging reading effects. Although contemporary criticism gives the impression that Joycean texts are most attuned to auditory pleasures and early visual technologies, Joyce also constantly registers the appeal—and repulsion—of olfactory sensation, and these moments are fundamental to his hedonistic universe.[5]

Joyce had a keen understanding of what Barthes called the "texture of perfume."[6] The representation of perfume in *Ulysses* indicates that Joyce thought of it as a commodity as well as a sensuous experience, a material substance, and an aesthetic creation. For example, in a December 17, 1931, letter to Harriet Shaw Weaver, Joyce remarks that an unauthorized edition of *Ulysses* is "a *contrefaçon* [forgery] of a French printer's output just as a falsified French perfume would be."[7] Joyce understood that perfume formulas, like literary texts, had a kind of aesthetic autonomy, particularly in the early years of the twentieth century, when perfumery had reached new heights of invention. Joyce's textual scents are never single-note; rather, they are constructed through layers of memory, bodily response, attraction, and resistance. Perfume is a pleasure with unexpected depths. It is, to borrow a felicitous metaphor from Wicke, one way "fashion intelligence is sprayed all over *Ulysses*."[8] Odor in general, and modern perfume in particular, is a means through which Joyce models a complex eroticism and an equally intricate reading experience.

"STRANGER FLOWERS, PLEASURES NOT YET DISCOVERED"

When Stephen Dedalus walks on the beach in the "Proteus" episode of *Ulysses*, he tests Aristotle's theories of perception by experimenting with his vision and hearing. Western philosophy has always ranked vision at the top of the sense hierarchy, along with hearing, above smell, taste, and touch.[9] The eyes and ears were thought to put more distance between the perceiver and the source of stimulation than the lowly nose, skin, or mouth: the farther the object of perception from the body, the more opportunity for reason to exert its influence. Most early philosophers argued that the most valuable forms of sensual pleasure are rational and ethical. Smell, by contrast, was thought to be somatically reflexive and so not subject to the higher mechanisms of the mind. Smell was also pronounced aesthetically deficient. Vision and hearing had corresponding arts (the fine arts and music), but perfumery was, and still is, not thought to constitute a disciplined or principled artistic activity.[10]

The Enlightenment inquiry into the nature of the senses demoted olfactory experience even further. Étienne Bonnot de Condillac's *Treatise on the Sensations* maintains that smell "is the one [sense] that seems to contribute the least to the operations of the human mind."[11] Kant asks, "Which organic sense is the most ungrateful and also seems to be the most dispensable? The sense of *smell*. It does not pay to cultivate it or refine it at all in order to enjoy; for there are more disgusting objects than pleasant ones (especially in crowded places), and even when we come across something fragrant, the pleasure coming from the sense of smell is always fleeting and transient."[12] For Kant, smells—ephemeral and mostly foul—are associated with the masses and the irrational body. Olfaction was not thought to be connected to aesthetics, and the pleasure it did produce was deemed too ephemeral to merit contemplation.

Most mid-to-late nineteenth- and early twentieth-century social scientists continued to regard olfaction as a crude and primitive sense. Both Darwin and Freud assert that smell is a faculty more useful to animals than humans, and that vision, rather than scent, guides civilized culture.[13] Freud speculates that vision gained dominance over smell when humans began to walk upright and their noses were no longer on the same level as their genitals.[14] In *Three Essays on the Theory of Sexuality*, he remarks that "coprophilic pleasure in smelling . . . has disappeared owing to repression," at least among those who are properly socialized.[15] Sexologists such as Krafft-Ebing and Havelock Ellis, whose *Studies in the Psychology of Sex* devotes a substantial section to the sense of smell, recognized the role of odors in mental life and, like Freud, linked unconventional olfactory pleasure to deviance.[16]

Ellis remarks that "odors do not, as vision does, give you information that is very largely intellectual; they make an appeal that is mainly of an intimate, emotional, imaginative character."[17] This is partly right. The olfactory sense is reflexive, involuntary, and somatic; however, it also involves the capacities of the mind insofar as it is highly associative and mnemonic. "No sense," Ellis asserts, "has so strong a power of suggestion, the power of calling up ancient memories with a wider and deeper emotional reverberation" than smell.[18] Smell is both an immediate, somatic response and a trigger to emotional retrospection; it is a sensual impression in the present as well as a door to the past. Olfaction is closely related to memory and cognition; however, contemporary scientists agree that most humans find it difficult to describe specific odors in words (although they are more successful at matching smells with their sources). "In evolutionary terms," Piet Vroon writes, "the sense of smell is an old one, with relatively few direct connections with the youngest part of the brain—namely, the left neocortex, a system which houses, for example, 'language centers.'"[19] Significantly, smell is understood as beyond or outside language, similarly to the way that pleasure has often been theorized.

At various points in history, perfume has been a tool for hygiene, a means of fumigation, a spiritual substance, or a sensual accessory. Homer associated perfume with divinity, and ancient Greeks also thought of it as a luxury.[20] In the Middle Ages, scent was a prophylactic against the fumes of the plague and poor sanitation, making the smell of dirty bodies bearable. The early Church frowned upon perfume, as it did other sensual indulgences. However, in the fourth century, it adopted the use of scent in ritual.[21] Incense signifies purification, a religious offering that converts the aromatics of pagan practices into a spiritual show of holiness. A fundamental change occurred at the end of the nineteenth century. Like so many innovations, it happened in the 1880s in France. Chemists and perfumers developed synthetic, artificial scents to supplement the costly and often rare natural fragrances that had been the palette of perfumery. Like the synthetic pigments that expanded the array of colors available to late nineteenth-century painters and hence the course of art, the perfume innovations made possible, writes Richard Stamelman, an unprecedented "scale of perfume notes and accords, an 'immense register of scents,' completely unknown" to earlier perfumers.[22] In the years that followed, there was a radical reconceptualization of what a perfume could be. Many perfumers developed abstract rather than mimetic compositions. Scents such as Coty's Chypre and Chanel No. 5 were nonreferential. Rather than striving to imitate a perfect rose or a convincing violet, they presented a heady blend of abstract and unnatural odors that Luca Turin, biophysicist and perfume critic, likens to "jumping from Delacroix's neoclassic people with arms that looked like, well, human arms into a nonhuman, natureless Kandinsky world of triangles, dots, and machine-tooled blobs."[23] L'Heure Bleue, Guerlain's sweetly melancholic creation of 1912—and also, supposedly, Jean Rhys's favorite perfume—was said to have been inspired by the "fleeting sensation" captured by impressionist painters.[24] Just as impressionism changed the lens through which painters represented the world, from the colors they employed and the quality of their brushstrokes to their understanding of vision and cognition, and just as abstraction changed the premises of mimesis itself, the new perfumery altered the kinds of fragrances people could smell as well as their ideas about what perfume could be.[25]

Other changes were afoot. Particularly during the Renaissance and up until the eighteenth century, strong, "animalic" scents (as bestial odors are known by perfumers) had been popular. The most common were musk, a substance that comes from a musk deer's scent gland; ambergris, which is extracted from the excrement or vomit of sperm whales; and civet, from the anal gland of a civet cat. To be sure, these ingredients were and continue to be used in very sparing amounts in perfume, but they nevertheless added a hint of dissonance to the dominant notes.[26] The nineteenth-century hygiene movement with its "growing deodorization of society" meant that perfumes were no longer used as health remedies but were classified as cosmetics, and advertised and sold as luxury products.[27] The scent of cleanliness—or no odor at all—had become the new standard, and scents that had once been hugely popular fell out of favor. In the Victorian era, animalic scents were superseded by more delicate and less bodily fragrances, including violet, lavender, and rose, as the cult of female purity took hold. Floral and herbal perfumes were the scents of choice for the Angel in the House, while "The thick vapors of impregnated flesh, heavy scents, and musky powders were for the courtesan's boudoir or even the brothel salon."[28] But French perfumers, armed with the new synthetics, extended their formulas to include animalics. The first perfume with man-made ingredients was Houbigant's Fougère Royale (Royal Fern, 1882), featuring a synthetic reproduction of coumarin, which simulates the smell of freshly mown hay and other, more corporeal odors. Luca Turin describes the now defunct scent, which can only be smelled in the archives of the International Perfume Museum in Grasse:

Fougère Royale starts the way some Bruckner symphonies do, with a muted pianissimo of strings, giving an impression of tremendous ease and quiet power. It does smell of coumarin, to be sure, but it is also fresh, clean, austere, almost bitter. This is the reference smell of scrubbed bathrooms, suggestive of black and white tiles, clean, slightly damp towels, a freshly shaven daddy. But wait! There's a funny thing in there, something not altogether pleasant. It's a touch of natural civet, stuff that comes from the rear end of an Asian cat and smells like it does. . . . Small wonder Fougère Royale was such a success. At a distance, he who wears it is everyone's favourite son-in-law; up close, a bit of an animal.[29]

Turin's description vividly conveys the subtle blending of clean and "dirty" odors that destabilizes the strong cultural imperative to separate such entities, as detailed by Mary Douglas.[30] This blend of artificial and natural, fragrant and foul smells produced a combination of referents and textures that was more challenging to the nose—and the brain—than a conventional floral perfume. The most innovative fragrances of this and the modern era, including Jicky, Shalimar, and Chanel No. 5, feature civet. If perfume is connected to memory, then the reminiscences triggered by the new synthetics included the primal, the infantile, the bestial, and the excremental.

Fin-de-siècle decadent writers were the bards of the new scents. Glorifying modern perfume was a way to flout bourgeois conventions, but it also reflected a fascination with aesthetic innovation in perfumery. In poems such as "The Double Room," "Lethe," "The Cat," and "Exotic Perfume," Baudelaire praises odors that arouse melancholy and macabre eroticism; perfume reflects the interior landscape of the moody modern subject.[31] The *ur*-scene of synthetic poesis is chapter 10 of Huysmans's *À Rebours* (1884), in which Des Esseintes sets out "to master the grammar and understand the syntax of odors." He strives to create "New perfumes . . . stranger flowers . . . pleasures not yet discovered,"[32] asserting that smell "could give one delights equal to those of hearing and sight; each sense being susceptible, if naturally keen and if properly cultivated, to new impressions, which it could intensify, coordinate and compose into that unity which constitutes a creative work" (168–169). His experiments, then, challenge both the traditional classification of olfaction as inferior to hearing and sight and the idea that perfumery is not an art. Moreover, they defy the conception of odor as extralinguistic, as Des Esseintes deploys "effects analogous to those of the poets" (176), using metaphors and layering odors like lines of a stanza: a prosody of perfume. His fragrance referents are distinctively modern and industrial. He produces, for example, the smell of factories "whose tall chimneys flared like bowls of punch . . . chemical products . . . sweet effluvia amid this putrescence" (177). In another creation, he conjures "a singular odor, at once repugnant and exquisite" that "partook of the delicious fragrance of jonquil and of the stench of gutta percha and coal oil" (177–178).[33] Des Esseintes's scents are narratives of dissonance and perversity, referencing experiences such as those with his "unbalanced" former mistress who could have been a Krafft-Ebing case study: she "loved to steep the nipples of her breasts in perfumes, but [she] never really experienced a delicious and overpowering ecstasy save when her head was scraped with a comb or when she could inhale, amid caresses, the odor of perspiration, or the plaster of unfinished houses on rainy days, or of dust splashed by huge drops of rain during summer storms" (180–181). Des Esseintes's experiments in olfaction, like his lover's libido, map circuitous routes to ecstasy through byways of negation and revulsion. Joyce was markedly influenced by Huysmans's aestheticized approach to the senses and his linguistic-aromatic odorscapes.

Such paeans to synthetic scents were not the order of the day. More typical was Augustin Galopin's study *Le Parfum de la femme* (1886), which warns against the effect of artificial perfumes: "Men who frequent the society of women" who are heavily perfumed, the author cautions, "often have their own sense of odor perverted," as the "strange and dangerous perfumes that temporarily heighten the senses" confound the distinction between illusion and reality. Galopin laments men who have been "ruined" by women "saturated with artificial perfumes."[34] The new perfumes were disparaged by many as unclean and immoral. In an era of (relatively) advanced hygiene, the ideal was deodorization: the less odor, the better. Heavy perfume had to be hiding something, whether it was a dirty body or moral licentiousness.

While there was an animalic upswing in French perfumes from the turn of the century to the early years of the twentieth century, UK consumers continued to prefer light floral and herbal scents. British perfume preferences were different from the French—the central scents of Yardley, a classic British perfumer, for example, are English Lavender, Lily of the Valley, and English Rose. A 1902 notice for a British perfumer underscores the distinctive character of its scents: "Bayley's new perfumes for this season are, if one may say so, the very essence of patriotism. They are really British perfumes, made here in England from British flowers, and are in all respects most excellent, as everything British should be."[35] Flowers: not factories or feral cats. In contrast to the Continental (particularly French) literary decadents and aesthetes who were infatuated by artificial and conceptual perfumes, many British and American modernists were suspicious of these contrived scents.

In *Brave New World*, synthetic perfume is one among numerous engineered sensual pleasures that pacify the masses. It is a feature of public space: restrooms, hotels, and even hospitals are fitted with scent dispensers offering a medley of synthetic odors. When John the Savage and Lenina, the epitome of an artificial woman, attend the feelies, the show is accompanied by a "synchronized scent-organ" whose "Herbal Capriccio" includes "a whiff of kidney pudding, the faintest suspicion of pig's dung," parodying both Huysmans's scene of synaesthesia and what Huxley sees as modern perfumery's infatuation with farfetched innovation and aesthetic excess in its exotic fecal odors.[36] (Lawrence similarly lampoons modernist olfaction in "Surgery for the Novel—Or a Bomb," where he characterizes the "serious" novel of Joyce, Richardson, and Proust as obsessed with the minutiae of idiosyncratic scent impressions: "Is my aura a blend of frankincense and orange pekoe and boot-blacking, or is it myrrh and bacon-fat and Shetland tweed?")[37]

For T. S. Eliot, modern scent signals decay and spiritual corrosion, and perfume is a particularly toxic sign of depraved femininity. At the beginning of "A Game of Chess" in *The Waste Land*, for example, Eliot alludes to Shakespeare's *Antony and Cleopatra*, in which the queen's barge sports sails "so perfumed that / The winds were love-sick with them" (II, ii, 217). Eliot's glittering woman is exotic, orientalized, and foreign. She sits surrounded by "vials of ivory and coloured glass," both natural and artificial, in which, "Unstoppered,"

> lurked strange synthetic perfumes,
> Unguent, powdered, or liquid—troubled, confused
> And drowned the sense in odours. . . .[38]

The scents are the product of some malicious alchemy: "strange synthetic" substances that do not inspire love and devotion but rather befuddlement and engulfment, amplifying the theme of drowning that runs throughout the poem. The prostitute in Eliot's "Rhapsody on a Windy Night" "twists a paper rose, / That smells of dust and eau de Cologne, / She is alone / With all the old nocturnal smells / That cross and cross across her brain." These odors summon a "reminiscence" of still more smells, including "sunless dry geraniums" and "female smells in shuttered rooms."[39] The second half of "Whispers of Immortality" introduces the very modern, eyeliner-wearing Grishkin, with her "promise of pneumatic bliss." She is compared to a "sleek Brazilian jaguar," but even that cat "Does not in its aboreal gloom / Distil so rank a feline smell / As Grishkin in a drawing room."[40] For Eliot, heavy perfume is a sign of female sexual aggression that crosses over into animalistic behavior. Colleen Lamos notes his frequent invocations of "feminine effluvia" and "noxious fumes" to "suggest the pestilential atmosphere of . . . female spaces, an odor that attracts and distracts."[41] Lamos points out the resemblance between Grishkin and Fresca, another odiferous cat woman who appears in outtakes from *The Waste Land*. A "can-can salonnière" who awakens "from dreams of love and pleasant rapes," Fresca radiates "Odours, confected by the cunning French" that "Disguise the good old hearty female stench." Pound suggested that "cunning" should be changed to "artful," a snide comment on the pretentions of the new perfumer).[42] Eliot's palpable disgust at these funky-smelling women betrays his anxiety about sexually powerful female bodies. While he represents Victorian perfumes such as hyacinth and lilac favorably, his rapacious and slatternly women wear animalic, artificial—and significantly, *French*—perfumes.

Virginia Woolf's acerbic comment about Katherine Mansfield in her 1917 diary is a further illustration of the modernist bias against the new perfume. She remarks that she and Leonard "could both wish that ones first impression of K.M. was not that she stinks like a—well civet cat that had taken to street walking. In truth, I'm a little shocked by her commonness at first sight; lines so hard & cheap."[43] "Cheap" is a word that comes up with some regularity among modernists disparaging perfume. Although the decadents saw synthetic perfumes as a rarified and sophisticated pleasure, in the British context, they indicate popular tastes, coarse female sexuality, and specifically prostitution.[44] Even after Mansfield and Woolf had struck up a close friendship and after Mansfield's death, Woolf wrote, "I mean she could permeate one with her quality; and if one felt this cheap scent in it, it reeked in ones nostrils."[45] (Mansfield's biographer, Antony Alpers, came to her defense, explaining that Mansfield wore fashionable French perfume.[46] Indeed, her stories suggest that she was inspired by Continental decadents' aromatic combinations; for instance, she describes the smell "of soap and burnt paper and wallflower brilliantine," "tar and ropes and slime and salt," and "paint and burnt chop-bones and indiarubber."[47])

Joyce's olfactory instincts are quite different from Eliot's or Woolf's. He capitalizes on the tensions of modern perfume: its artificiality and naturalness, its somatic and emotional qualities, its discordant compositions, and its evocation of exotic erotic pleasure. Extending the decadent exploitation of perfume as a palette of aesthetic possibilities, Joyce uses odor to explore the structure of pleasure itself.

"PERFUME OF EMBRACES ALL HIM ASSAILED"

The opening pages of *Portrait of the Artist as a Young Man* famously rouse the five senses. Stephen Dedalus is highly attuned to smell, from the "queer" odor of the oilsheet on his bed to the "nicer" aroma of his mother.[48] His Irish Catholic inculcation, redolent of cool, dark churches and sweet, dusty incense, creates powerful olfactory associations among sex, smell, and sin. The herbs burning in the thurible counter the stench of sin, as Father Arnall emphasizes in his terrifying Hell Sermon of chapter 3:

> The horror of this strait and dark prison is increased by its awful stench. All the filth of the world, all the offal and scum of the world, we are told, shall run there as to a vast reeking sewer when the terrible conflagration of the last day has purged the world. The brimstone too which burns there in such prodigious quantity fills all hell with its intolerable stench; and the bodies of the damned themselves exhale such a pestilential odour that as saint Bonaventure says, one of them alone would suffice to infect the whole world. (120)

Borrowing from Dante's descriptions in *Inferno*, with its abysses of "outrageous stench"[49] and sinners mired in shit (contrasted to the ambrosial smells of *Paradiso*), Arnall likens the reek of hell to those in the boys' own environment: offal, scum, sewers, fungus, and various smells emanating from bodies. Human bodies, for a Catholic adolescent, are a miasma of spiritual contagion and damnation. Hell is right here on earth, in our bodies, if we are not careful. Stephen absorbs this lesson and uses it to torture himself. Stench features prominently in his "putrid" nightmare of the "hell reserved for his sins" (138), in which goatish men move in circles while "An evil smell,

faint and foul as the light, curled upwards sluggishly out of the can-
isters and from the stale crusted dung" (137). Stephen is overcome by
"the reeking odour pouring down his throat, clogging and revolting
his entrails" and he gasps for "Air! The air of heaven!" (138). Similarly, after his dramatic confession in chapter 3, Stephen "knelt to
say his penance, praying in a corner of the dark nave: and his prayers
ascended to heaven from his purified heart like perfume streaming
upwards from a heart of white rose" (145). He selects the right perfume for the occasion: the white rose is Mary's symbol, representing purity. Dante pictures the Empyrean heaven as a huge white rose
inhabited by the blessed.

The bifurcation of smells into the pure, celestial odors of Catholic
grace and the stink of earthy and bodily sin complements the many
other Catholic dichotomies (saved/damned, virgin/whore, etc.) that
shape Stephen's consciousness. However, his sense of smell leads
him to confound these divisions. "The names of articles of dress worn
by women or of certain soft and delicate stuffs used in their making
brought always to his mind a delicate and sinful perfume" (155). The
religious rituals that have impressed upon him that smell can be holy
(incense) or sinful (the stench of hell) become attached to signifiers
that allude to the mysterious female body. This chiastic sentence indicates Stephen's confusion about whether women are soft and delicate
or delicate and sinful, like perfume. His linguistic sensitivity and his
synaesthetic sensibility that associates words with smells are tendencies Joyce develops further in *Ulysses* to connect smells with linguistic
creativity and forbidden pleasures.

Stephen's body itself, and his nose in particular, resists the demoni-
zation of odor that the Church tries to impress upon him. When
he sets out to mortify his senses as a means of bringing his unruly
body into line, he finds ways to discipline his senses of vision, touch,
taste, and hearing, but he has difficulty restraining his sense of smell.
Although the scent of white rose leads "upwards" to the heavens, he
looks downward, towards the earth, to focus on odor.

> To mortify his smell was more difficult as he found in himself
> no instinctive repugnance to bad odours, whether they were the
> odours of the outdoor world such as those of dung or tar or the
> odours of his own person among which he had made many curious

comparisons and experiments. He found in the end that the only odour against which his sense of smell revolted was a certain stale fishy stink like that of longstanding urine; and whenever it was possible he subjected himself to this unpleasant odour. (151)

There is something quite wonderful about Stephen's discovery: he has found a part of himself that has eluded his Catholic indoctrination. The allusion to his "many curious comparisons and experiments" with "the odours of his own person" suggests a stealth or Faustian exploration. His olfactory revolt proves an advantage to a boy looking to fly by the nets of Catholic conscience. When, agitated after a school drama, Stephen flees from his family and schoolmates to a filthy alley.

He saw the word *Lotts* on the wall of the lane and breathed slowly the rank heavy air.

That is horse piss and rotted straw, he thought. It is a good odour to breathe. It will calm my heart. (86)

Stephen is viscerally soothed by rank odors; they pacify him by reflecting his fallen nature: a sensual creature, driven by bodily and blasphemous desire. He savors foul smells because they align the external world ("the outdoor world") with his interior sense of self as well as his body. When Stephen realizes that he does not have a vocation, "The faint sour stink of rotted cabbages came towards him from the kitchengardens on the rising ground above the river. He smiled to think that it was this disorder, the misrule and confusion of his father's house and the stagnation of vegetable life, which was to win the day in his soul" (162). Relinquishing the idealism of cleanliness and purity represented by the white rose scent, he gravitates toward putrid, grimy, earthy odors.

Stephen's tolerance for, and even attraction to, noxious smells—urine, excrement, and rotting matter—is surpassed by Leopold Bloom's in *Ulysses*. While Bloom does not have as much to prove to the world as Stephen does, olfaction is a means through which he can explore his transgressive desires. Bloom's first appearance in the novel signals how he relishes unconventional odors: "Most of all he liked grilled mutton kidneys which gave to his palate a fine tang of faintly scented urine."[50] In the WC, he is "seated calm above his own rising smell" ("calm" is the word that Stephen uses to describe the effect that horse piss and rotten straw have on him) (4:512). Much later in the day, in "Ithaca," Bloom picks his toe and "raised the part lacerated to his nostrils and inhaled the odour of the quick, then, with satisfaction, threw away the lacerated ungual fragment" (17:1489). Reviewing *Ulysses* in *The New York Times*, Joseph Collins aptly described the novel as having a "mephitic atmosphere."[51]

That said, natural, fresh odors and sweet perfumes are equally important to the novel's environment, including the "creamfruit smell" (3:369) that symbolizes Molly ("heavy, sweet, wild perfume. Always the same, year after year" [4:208–209]) and in her scented lotion of "sweet almond oil and tincture of benzoin" and "orangeflower water" (5:490-491), as Bloom recites the "recipe" to the chemist. "Know her smell in a thousand," he thinks. "Reminds me of strawberries and cream" (13:1024–1025). In "Sirens," Bloom recalls the "First night when first I saw her at Mat Dillon's in Terenure. . . . *Waiting* she sang. I turned her music. Full voice of perfume of what perfume does your lilactrees. Bosom I saw, both full, throat warbling" (11:725–732). Molly's lilac-perfumed voice is a synaesthetic aphrodisiac to Bloom, and throughout the novel, she is connected to fragrance. Even Martha Clifford, who seems otherwise befuddled, knows enough to inquire about Molly's bouquet: "P.S. Do tell me what kind of perfume does your wife use. I want to know" (5:258).

For Joyce, odor is significant because it so hauntingly hovers on the threshold between body and mind, confounding the bifurcation that has always been central to the cultural hierarchy of pleasure. His understanding of smell is predicated on the idea that it is a primitive, irrational sense that expresses base instincts and has strongly associative, mnemonic properties.[52] Odor is one of the key means of accessing memory in *Ulysses*. Bloom vividly recalls odors he smelled ten years earlier. Whereas in the case of Proust's madeleine, a sensuous experience in the present triggers the journey to the past, for Joyce, even the mere contemplation of odors from the distant past can prompt a profound reverie. Scent is one of the great unifiers of Molly and Bloom— at least in their memories. Although they are sexually estranged, perfume bridges the gap between them. In "Lestrygonians," Bloom reprises a moment on Howth with Molly: "A warm human plumpness settled down on his brain. His brain yielded. Perfume of embraces all him assailed. With hungered flesh obscurely, he mutely craved to adore" (8:637–639); "Perfumed bodies, warm, full. All kissed, yielded: in deep summer fields, tangled pressed grass" (8:642–643). Both Molly and Bloom have a heightened sensual recollection of that scene. In her famous last utterance, Molly recalls, "he could feel my breasts all perfume yes and his heart was going like mad and yes I said yes I will Yes" (18:1607–1609). Yet perfume also represents the couple's respective acts of adultery. While Bloom imagines Molly's scent as "always the same, year after year," throughout *Ulysses*, perfume marks the modulations of her, and his, fidelity. Memories of his courtship with Molly ("Full voice of perfume of what perfume does your lilactrees" [11:730]) also prompt thoughts about the perfume she was wearing the night she met Blazes Boylan. In "Sirens," perfume is the direct link to Bloom's vivid fantasy of Blazes arriving at their home: "Perfumed for him. What perfume does your wife? I want to know. Jing. Stop. Knock. Last look at mirror always before she answers the door" (11:687–689). Bloom knows that Molly has perfumed herself for Blazes just as she had once done for him. Martha's postscript is woven into this thought, but she encloses a nearly odorless flower in her letter to Bloom ("He tore the flower gravely from its pinhold smelt its almost no smell and placed it in his heart pocket" [5.260–261]). She and Bloom have no past--and no embodied present—together, and this is part of Martha's appeal to him as an alternative to the passionate, perfumed woman he loves, redolent as much of the past as the present.

Joyce was interested in the cultural meanings of scent. He knew sexology texts that linked olfaction to eroticism,[53] and he owned Galopin's *Le Parfum de la femme*, which argues that women's odors are determined by characteristics such as hair color and race: a sort of phrenological approach to scent. At points, Joyce imagines perfume as disclosing the wearer's character traits, and also as a sort of Victorian language of flowers, signaling the wearer's desires.[54] But he is also interested in its material, phenomenological, and structural dimensions. When Bloom smells Gerty's scent in "Nausicaa," he meditates on the physics of perfume. He interprets its transmission as an insinuating influence of dispersal, delay, and involuntary response that is analogous to memory.

Wait. Hm. Hm. Yes. That's her perfume. Why she waved her hand. I leave you this to think of me when I'm far away on the pillow. . . . Why did I smell it only now? Took its time in coming like herself, slow but sure. Suppose it's ever so many millions of tiny grains blown across. Yes, it is. Because those spice islands, Cinghalese this morning, smell them leagues off. Tell you what it is. It's like a fine veil or web they have all over the skin, fine like what do you call it gossamer, and they're always spinning it out of them, fine as anything, like rainbow colours without knowing it. Clings to everything she takes off. (13.1007–1023)

Bloom attributes the diffusion of scent to physiognomy, speculating that, using traditionally feminine metaphors, "It's like a fine veil or web" on a woman's skin, "and they're always spinning it out of them, fine as anything, rainbow colours without knowing it." He imagines women as both passive and active atomizers. Scent is an involuntary secretion issuing from the body, but it is also a deliberate enticement women choose to send out into the world. Perfume here is simultaneously an immediate, somatic experience (likened, punningly, to orgasm: "took its time in coming like herself") and also a conjuring of memory ("I leave you this to think of me when I'm far away").

Like Huysmans, Joyce imagines odor in terms of linguistic structure and syntax. The dispersal of scent also resembles the production of stream of consciousness, a spontaneous spinning of words that bypasses censorship ("always spinning it out of them . . . without knowing it"). Joyce's characters' thoughts are generated like a sort of time-delayed perfume, with words and refrains scattered across the text, repeated later, inevitably, "slow but sure." Joyce's prose, even outside of stream of consciousness, operates similarly, through suggestion and slow disclosure. But unlike perfume, which automatically registers in the nose and the brain, Joyce's language requires an alert tracking of those "tiny grains." Ideas and images that may not make sense in the moment will eventually, with dedicated reading, become clear, strengthening and shifting as they develop just as a perfume changes over time. ("Wandering Rocks" is an intensified version of this principle that operates throughout the novel.) In "Nausicaa," Joyce uses the metaphor of perfume's dispersal not just to establish a material history of perfume and the tension between Victorian and Catholic odors and more modern, carnal scents, but also to assert the erotic appeal of difficult and contorted pleasure.

"NAUSICAA": THE PERFUME OF PERVERSITY

While olfactory pleasure influences every episode of *Ulysses*, the jocoserious Gilbert and Linati schemas for *Ulysses* steer us toward understanding "Nausicaa" as the "eye and nose" episode of the novel. The first half of the episode emphasizes visual effects, as the couple on the beach gaze at each other, and the second half calls attention to olfactory experiences, pivoting in the switch from Gerty's narrative to Bloom's stream of consciousness. John Bishop discusses the shift in his essay "A Metaphysics of Coitus in 'Nausicaa'": "as the dominant colors in the first half of the episode—mystical 'rose' . . . and shrinking 'violet' . . . evaporate into invisible fragrances . . . Bloom's nose gains ascendancy over the idealizing eye."[55] Rose and violet, which are odors as well as colors, were dominant scents in the Victorian and Edwardian period, before the synthetic revolution caught up to Ireland. The episode enacts, through its two parts, the differences between the Roman Catholic approach to odor, perfume, and bodily pleasure, which favors the visual, the rational, and the hygienic, and a pagan (Homeric) or secular stance that engages with olfactory and haptic senses and the messy realities of the body. Joyce demonstrates these differences by aligning different kinds of odors and perfumes as well as different reading effects with each part of the chapter.

As Gerty is introduced early in the episode, she is the picture of fashionable, if fastidious womanhood:

> A neat blouse of electric blue selftinted by dolly dyes (because it was expected in the *Lady's Pictorial* that electric blue would be worn) with a smart vee opening down to the division and kerchief pocket (in which she always kept a piece of cottonwool scented with her favourite perfume because the handkerchief spoiled the sit) and a navy threequarter skirt cut to the stride showed off her slim graceful figure to perfection. (13:150–155)

Gerty thinks in fussy language that reflects her preoccupation with appearance and tidiness. She applies perfume the economical way, on a handkerchief or cotton ball, rather than directly to the skin. The way she stores her scent is similarly sanitized: in "the drawer of her toilettable which, though it did not err on the side of luxury, was scrupulously neat and clean" (13:637–638); it contains "her girlish treasures trove, the tortoiseshell combs, her child of Mary badge, the whiterose scent, the eyebrowleine, her alabaster pouncetbox" (13:638–640). Gerty's scent, like Stephen's in his spiritually devout phase, is the virginal white rose. Her perfume, then, reflects her commitment to hygiene and Catholic purity. While indulging in the pleasures of consumption—perfume is a fashion statement, like the "eyebrowleine" and the other products that Gerty collects to effect her "winsome womanhood" and attract a "dreamhusband"—Gerty does "not err on the side of luxury": the white rose is not a rarified or opulent scent.

Joyce's choreography of odors in this episode seems influenced by Galopin. In *Le Parfum de la femme*, Galopin ponders the smells of various classes of people, including masturbators (who smell like "rancid butter"), virgins, homosexuals, and religious women—"l'odeur de Sainteté" (199). Gerty's scent is named but not described in the first half of the episode, in which she is rendered odorless, like the other deodorized woman in *Ulysses*, Martha Clifford, Bloom's other quasi-adulterous partner. Bloom does not smell Gerty's perfume until the second half of the episode, when she waves the "wadding" at him as she leaves the beach. The dominant odor of the first part of the episode is the incense that issues from the temperance meeting:

> Through the open window of the church the fragrant incense was wafted and with it the fragrant names of her who was conceived without stain of original sin, spiritual vessel, pray for us, honourable vessel, pray for us, vessel of singular devotion, pray for us, mystical rose. (13:371–374)

> She gazed out towards the distant sea. It was like the paintings that man used to do on the pavement with all the coloured chalks and such a pity too leaving them there to be all blotted out, the evening and the clouds coming out and the Bailey light on Howth and to hear the music like that and the perfume of those incense they burned in the church like a kind of waft. And while she gazed her heart went pitapat.... (13:406–411)

Incense becomes Gerty's perfume; she displays herself to Bloom as a parodic offering to the "mystical rose" (she imagines Bloom "literally worshipping at her shrine" [13:564]). The odors on Sandymount Strand present an ironic history of Catholicism's co-optation of pagan perfumery. Just as the action on the beach is converted through Gerty's sentimental discourse into a humorously deluded romantic encounter, incense is the smokescreen for the more earthly activities that unfold between Bloom and Gerty: it becomes the perfume of perversity.[56]

The two parts of "Nausicaa" are marked by the contrast between the romanticized, fantasy-driven vision that leads up to orgasm and Bloom's "profoundly anti-idealizing nose" and his postorgasmic thoughts (Bishop, 199). The shift in narrative voice from Gerty to Bloom also signals a change in the kinds of smells that are represented. While Gerty's thoughts are bound by propriety and fashion— with some jarring slips when she mentions matters such as "those iron jelloids" and "those discharges she used to get" (13:84–86)—Bloom's musings are freewheeling, bawdy, and base.

After Gerty walks away, Bloom ponders a number of unusual odors, both present and imagined, in the second part of the episode, including "mansmell" (13:1036), the fragrance of priests ("Women buzz round . . . like flies round treacle . . . The tree of forbidden priest" [13:1037–38]), armpits, and bad breath. This is typical of his curious nature: he sniffs his own waistcoat for a whiff of his ejaculate ("celery sauce" [13:1040]), but finds it masked by the almond-lemon smell of the soap. Gerty's retreat triggers a joke about a foul smell. "Watch! Watch! See! Looked round. She smelt an onion. Darling, I saw your. I saw all" [13:935]. Don Gifford explains that this reference is

From a joke about the man who determined to keep himself free from any entanglement with women. In order to fulfill his determination, he ate a raw onion whenever contact with women was imminent. His scheme and his self-discipline collapsed when he met a woman who found his oniony breath extraordinarily attractive.[57]

This recollection of a quip about bad breath that is strangely compelling[58] sets Bloom's thoughts toward a series of imagined odors, including diapers (13:957–958), a "husband rolling in drunk, stink of pub off him like a polecat" (13:964), "the dark, whiff of stale boose" (13:965), violets, and turpentine (13:1002), a jumble of associations that create a bouquet as strange and various as Des Esseintes's. This is the olfactory overture to Gerty's scent, which finally drifts across the beach and reaches Bloom's nose. "What is it? Heliotrope? No. Hyacinth? Hm. Roses, I think. She'd like scent of that kind. Sweet and cheap: soon sour" (13:1008–1010). The same rose scent that is exalted for its purity and sacramental nature in the first half of the episode is now pronounced "cheap." As for Woolf and Eliot, in Joyce's vocabulary, that word is closely associated with prostitution. Molly scorns the "cheap" perfume of her youth; she also associates cheapness with sexual promiscuity (18:864).[59] The irony here is that Gerty acts like an "amateur" in "Nausicaa": she is "cheaper" than a prostitute.[60] That said, even as Joyce draws on the familiar modernist connotations of cheapness, when Bloom's erotic imagination is really unloosed, particularly in "Circe," "cheap" perfume is strongly attractive.

In the first half of "Nausicaa," the rose is "poetical" and religious, but in Bloom's mind it is connected to menstruation through the euphemism "roses," and leads him to ponder a particularly foul smell: "Some women, instance, warn you off when they have their period. Come near. Then get a hogo you could hang your hat on. Like what? Potted herrings gone stale or. Boof! Please keep off the grass" (13:1031–1033). The stench resembles the "certain stale fishy stink like that of long-standing urine" that repels Stephen in *Portrait*. There is, in these musings on *odor di femina*, a misogynist streak of repulsion at the female body, as with Eliot.[61] Unlike Eliot's Grishkin, however, or his other reeking cat women, Joyce's off-odors become aphrodisiacs.[62]

Adopting the structural grammar of perfume, the first half of "Nausicaa" reveals "top notes" of incense and white rose, while the "base notes" in the second half are darker, earthier, and smellier. Gerty's scent leads away from the body, toward religious sublimation, hygiene, and heaven; Bloom's preferred odors lead to secular, corporeal experience. He speculates about the source of scent.

> Wonder where it is really. There or the armpits or under the neck. Because you get it out of all holes and corners. Hyacinth perfume made of oil of ether or something. Muskrat. Bag under their tails.

One grain pour off odour for years. Dogs at each other behind. Good evening. Evening. How do you sniff? Hm. Hm. Very well, thank you. Animals go by that. Yes now, look at it that way. We're the same. (13:1025–1031)

Muskrat turns Bloom's mind to the bodily folds and orifices that most Victorian scents sought to conceal. He goes right to the source—"bag under their tails"—and imagines humans as driven by the same kind of primitive desires as animals. Artificial musk was part of the synthetic revolution, but Bloom is drawn to the idea of musk precisely because of its origins in base parts of the body.[63]

Odor appeals to Joyce for the same reasons it is often devalued: its emotional, irrational, archaic dimensions. Ellis explains that the "anatomical seat" of smells "is the most ancient part of the brain. They lie in a remote and almost disused storehouse of our minds and show the fascination or the repulsiveness of all vague and remote things" (vol. 1, part 3, 54–55). Joyce was interested in depicting the primal allure of desublimated desire, as he told Arthur Power, and the "motives, the secret currents of life which govern everything . . . the hidden world, those undercurrents which flow beneath the apparently firm surface. . . . We believe that it is in the abnormal that we approach closer to reality."[64] For Joyce, the "abnormal" is best accessed through the unconscious, as it makes itself known through fantasies and uncensored associations, including memory, rather than the willed, rational, "daylight" world of the "active mind." Involuntary olfactory impulses are not subject to civilizing sublimation, so they open pathways to such "undercurrents." Joyce could not have known it, but recent neuroscience research suggests that unpleasant smells may have more impact on memory than pleasant ones.[65] Foul odors may, in fact, be a secret path to the unconscious.

PEAU D'ESPAGNE

In her recollections of Joyce, Djuna Barnes said he "loved pointless jokes . . . carried the calendar of saints wherever he went, even into the red light district [and] likes the perfume known as opoponax."[66] If this is true, then Joyce shared this preference with his earthy heroine. In "Nausicaa," Bloom recalls the perfume Molly wore when she met his rival, Blazes:

Molly likes opoponax. Suits her, with a little jessamine mixed. Her high notes and her low notes. At the dance night she met him, dance of the hours. Heat brought it out. She was wearing her black and it had the perfume of the time before. . . . Clings to everything she takes off. (13:1010–1022)

When Bloom returns to the marital bedroom after a day of wandering, he surveys Molly's scattered lingerie, including "a pair of outsize ladies' drawers of India mull, cut on generous lines, redolent of opoponax, jessamine and Muratti's Turkish cigarettes" (17:2092). The Turkish cigarettes reinforce Bloom's orientalist dreams about Molly. Jessamine, or jasmine, has such a pungent scent that it is often recommended for planting near outhouses: the sort of incongruity that would have amused Joyce.[67] Molly's primary scent, opoponax, is etymologically related to a Greek word meaning "all-healing juice,"[68] which is appropriate for the woman who holds out this curative promise to Bloom. Opoponax is a sumptuous scent. Huysmans once referred to "the libertine virtues of that glorious perfume."[69] Iwan Bloch writes that "If [a woman] is silent and reserved, a few drops of ancient oil charged with extract of violet will suffice her; if fiery, she will love the haughty zinnia . . . the violently voluptuous will have as favorites, stephanotis [otherwise known as jasmine], chypre, and the opulent opoponax" (*Odoratus Sexualis*, 219). Tracing the variable nature of this scent, Judith Harrington points out that there is more than one material basis for it: "Opoponax for healing and opoponax for perfume were not always from the same sources." All of Harrington's sources note the pleasant *and* off-putting nature of opoponax. The *OED* describes it as "a fetid gum-resin. . . . In perfumery, it has a slightly pleasant and quite distinctive odour."[70] George William Septimus Piesse's *Art of Perfumery* describes it as "a very remarkably strong and aromatic odour, much abused by some as being nauseous, and praised by others for its fragrance."[71]

Bloom both dreads and enjoys thinking about Molly as a "violently voluptuous" woman. In his mind, the smell of opoponax links his own passion for her—"Know her smell in a thousand" (13:1024)—to her first meeting with his rival. Like many of Bloom's erotic thoughts, opoponax combines sweet notes (indicating sentimentality and faithfulness) with rancid ones (signaling discord and adultery). Here is the crux of Bloom's erotic temperament and the basic syntax of his pleasure: his nostalgic longing for romance ("Love's Old Sweet Song") is constantly juxtaposed with a desire for painful experiences. This complexity of smell, nauseating and pleasant, like the way ingredients such as civet can be pleasing in the right amount but atrocious in excess, reflects Joyce's eroticization of paradox.

The perfume Bloom tells Martha that Molly uses, Peau d'Espagne, is a similarly complex fragrance, straddling the line between delicious and noxious. It features leather, musk, and civet in its composition. Its name, "Spanish Skin," is fitting for Molly's Gibraltar heritage, and for Bloom's erotic fantasies about his wife's "animalic" tendencies. Ellis writes at length on this scent in *Studies in the Psychology of Sex*:

> Peau d'Espagne may be mentioned as a highly complex and lux-
> urious perfume, often the favorite scent of sensuous persons,
> which really owes a large part of its potency to the presence of the
> crude animal sexual odors of musk and civet. It consists of wash-
> leather steeped in ottos of neroli, rose, santal, lavender, verbena,
> bergamot, cloves, and cinnamon, subsequently smeared with
> civet and musk. It is said by some, probably with a certain degree
> of truth, that Peau d'Espagne is of all perfumes that which most
> nearly approaches the odor of a woman's skin. Whether it also
> suggests the odor of leather is not so clear. (vol. 1, part 3, 99–100)

Unlike perfumes that mask human odors, Peau d'Espagne emphasizes carnal, mammalian scents: musk smeared on leather, the animal in the human. Contemporary perfumer Santa Maria Novella produces a Peau d'Espagne that lives up to the description. Two sprays of the perfume on a paper tester strip fill a room for an entire day with a sweet leather fragrance with a slightly rotten undertone. If this is the scent of a woman's skin, she has been astride a horse all day in the hot sun. It is the reek of Bella Cohen. Marketed now for men as a "very masculine" scent, Peau d'Espagne also captures the bisexual qualities of Joyce's huntswoman. Peau d'Espagne was anomalously popular in the UK even when floral perfumes were at their peak of popularity. An advertisement for wholesale perfumers H. Labern & Son in 1893 boasts that they offer the "'best' genuine perfumes in all the charming, fashionable odours, including Violette de Parma, Wildflower, Violet de Nice, Chypre, Lily of the Valley, Peau d'Espagne, White Rose, etc."[72] Peau d'Espagne is the odd scent out in this sequence, a blast of beast in a forest of florals.

Peau d'Espagne exemplifies the intricacy of scent in *Ulysses*. Its sweet and bracing blend of odors invokes pleasant and painful memory, romantic and brutish fantasies, as well as deception and honesty. In fact, Peau d'Espagne is pure memory and fantasy in *Ulysses*: it never actually appears in the novel's present. Rather, it is Bloom's fabrication for Martha, as he tries to coax out the "dormant tigress" in her. Molly herself dismisses Peau d'Espagne as "cheap": "there was no decent perfume to be got in that Gibraltar only that cheap peau dEspagne that faded and left a stink on you more than anything else" (18:864–865). Molly shares some of Bloom's olfactory kinks,[73] but she does not share his love of "stink."

The second half of "Nausicaa" does not merely undermine a sentimental and romanticized narrative.[74] It introduces a Rabelaisian counternarrative in which foul odors have a dialectical relationship to fragrant ones. This is true of pleasure in general for Joyce: it is never far from—and is heightened by—unpleasure. For example, in "Circe," Bloom shares a fond memory of his school days: "I was in my teens, a growing boy. A little then sufficed, a jolting car, the mingling odours of the ladies' cloakroom and lavatory, the throng penned tight on the old Royal stairs (for they love crushes, instincts of the herd, and the dark sexsmelling theatre unbridles vice). . . . Halcyon days" (15:3318–3324). It is notable that the odors themselves are not transformed into ambrosia; their foulness renders them arousing to Bloom. From his excitement in "Circe" at inhaling "Rut. Onions. Stale. Sulphur. Grease" (15:3477) to being commanded by Bella/The Hoof to "Smell my hot goathide" (15:2820) and to "souse and bat our smelling underclothes also when we ladies are unwell, and swab out our latrines" (15:3065–3066), Bloom is stimulated by the animalic and lavatorial smells that transgress the deodorizing modern impulse. When Judge John M. Woolsey argues that "Whilst in many places the effect of *Ulysses* on the reader undoubtedly is somewhat emetic, nowhere does it tend to be an aphrodisiac," he misses the point that the emetic *is* an aphrodisiac—at least to Bloom, if not to the reader.[75]

In the clinical literature of Joyce's time, a predilection for bad odors was considered a sign of deviance and mental unbalance. Both

Krafft-Ebing and Havelock Ellis associate a fetishistic attachment to foul odors, and particularly what Freud called "coprophilic pleasure," with masochism. Krafft-Ebing defines masochism as a disorder in which "Impressions obtained through the senses of smell and taste, which in the normal man produce only feelings of nausea and disgust, are made the basis of the most vivid emotions of lust, producing in the perverse subject mighty impulses to orgasm and even ejaculation."[76] The description corresponds to the many moments in *Ulysses* that reflect what H. G. Wells calls Joyce's "cloacal obsession"[77] and also brings to mind the infamous series of so-called "dirty letters" that Joyce wrote to Nora Barnacle when they were separated. Joyce rhapsodizes about "the perfume" of Nora's "drawers" as well as the "warm odour of [her] cunt and the heavy smell of [her] behind" (*Selected Letters*, 184). Praising her body in the language of *The Dead*, "musical and strange and perfumed" (163), Joyce exalts the smell of her farts as if they are the winds to Cleopatra's barge: they "com[e] blowing . . . like a wind of spices" (181). Joyce even gives Nora a sort of "recipe" for scent: "My sweet naughty little fuckbird, Here is another note to buy pretty drawers or stockings or garters. Buy whorish drawers, love, and be sure you sprinkle the legs of them with some nice scent and also discolour them just a little behind" (185). Were it not for the writer's earnestness, the proposed combination of "nice scent" and excrement would seem like a parody of modern perfume, with its whisper of civet blended with "nice" notes.

For Joyce, pleasure is heightened by and even constituted through obstacles and tension. This applies as much to perfume, in which base notes enhance sweeter top notes, as it does to eroticism and to Joyce's reading effects in *Ulysses*, where attention to form and linguistic pyrotechnics actively work against the kind of direct somatic pleasure of his letters to Nora. We see this particularly clearly in one of the novel's most striking depictions of readerly pleasure that also features a dizzyingly complex smell.

SWEETS OF SIN

The structural midpoint of *Ulysses*, as Hugh Kenner and others have noted, is the episode called "Wandering Rocks." The middle section shows Bloom at a bookseller, ostensibly looking for reading material for Molly. Having rejected *Fair Tyrants* by James Lovebirch ("she wouldn't like that much. Got her it once" [10:605]), he is drawn to a volume called *Sweets of Sin,* which he claims seems to be "more in her line." He reads from "where his finger opened" (10:607):

> —*All the dollarbills her husband gave her were spent in the stores on wondrous gowns and costliest frillies. For him! For Raoul!* . . .
>
> *Her mouth glued on his in a luscious voluptuous kiss while his hands felt for the opulent curves inside her deshabille.* . . .
>
> *You are late, he spoke hoarsely, eying her with a suspicious glare. The beautiful woman threw off her sabletrimmed wrap, displaying her queenly shoulders and heaving embonpoint. An imperceptible smile played round her perfect lips as she turned to him calmly.* (10:608–617)

Captivated by the selection, Bloom takes up this "book of inferior literary style" (17:733), and its phrases appear throughout *Ulysses* as one of several "coincidences" that perfectly mirror Bloom's own situation: here is a cuckold buying a book about a cuckold for his wife. It is also important as it signals a moment of reflection in which the distance between the reader of *Ulysses* and Joyce's character is temporarily collapsed while they share a common text of pleasure.

Critics generally agree that among the many humorous, sentimental, naughty, and absurd intertexts (popular songs, postcards, advertisements, magazines, pulp novels, etc.) that Joyce embeds in *Ulysses, Sweets of Sin* plays an important role.[78] For one thing, Bloom carries the book around with him for the rest of the day, along with the heirloom potato and his soap, both of which have symbolic weight. For another, it is supposedly a book to please Molly, although it clearly appeals to his own sensibilities. The ridiculous phrases that enrapture Bloom are cast "like a fine veil or web" across the subsequent hours of the day as he thinks through his relationship to his wife and his rival. *Sweets of Sin* is all the more intriguing because the real-world referent text, if there is one, remains elusive. Gifford suggests that *Sweets* may be "Joyce's own coinage" (272); others have concluded that it simply has not been located yet. The major obstacle to the identification of *Sweets* is uncertainty about its genre. The pretentious "embonpoint" and "deshabille" might appear in a women's romance novel, and the "sabletrimmed wrap" and "queenly shoulders" are plausibly erotic in the Sacher-Masochian sense. However, a woman is unlikely to "glue" a kiss on a man in a romance or "a volume of peccaminous porno-graphical tendency," as *Sweets of Sin* is described in "Ithaca" (17:2259). In Bloom's own memories, in "Calypso," however, "Lips kissed, kissing kissed. Full gluey woman's lips" (4:450). "Costliest frillies" also rings false, or rather, Bloomian. Both these phrases seem directly from the mind of Bloom, suggesting an intimacy between him as reader and the mysterious author of *Sweets of Sin* ("a gentleman of fashion"), but just the opposite between the reader of *Ulysses* and Joyce. That is, the incongruous phrases in *Sweets of Sin* draw attention to strange word choice and tone and generic oddity, and necessarily interrupt the kind of immersive reading effects that pornography or romance elicits. This manipulation of readerly response grows stronger as the episode moves on.

One gets further in the hunt for the "original" *Sweets of Sin* by looking not at racy fiction but at a (somewhat) less steamy source: the Bible. The phrase "sweets of sin" appears throughout early Chris-tian texts to signify worldly temptation, such as adultery. One ver-sion of Psalm 141, "A Prayer for the Preservation from Evil," which begins with an invocation of incense, warns that "Sinners pretend to find dainties in sin; stolen waters are sweet, forbidden fruit is pleas-ant to the eye: but they that consider how soon the dainties of sin will turn into wormwood and gall, how certainly it will, at last, bite like a serpent. . . . Good men will pray against even the sweets of sin."[79] Alison Shell asserts that the phrase "sweets of sin" appears so often in fifteenth- and sixteenth-century Catholic texts as to constitute a "sweets-of-sin topos," throughout which "Perfumes as well as tastes convey the synesthaesia of Catholic sin."[80] Just as for Stephen Dedalus the "delicate" and "sinful" are linked in his erotic imagination, "sweets of sin" slyly combines the threat of damnation with its lusciousness.[81] Given how Catholicism shapes Joyce's most fundamental understand-ing of sensual pleasure, it is appropriate that *Sweets of Sin* should be underwritten by a theological text that warns against the provocation represented by Raoul and his lover. The play of the novel's title, with its titillating co-optation of a biblical phrase, becomes, for Joyce, a ref-erence to didactic texts and their management of readerly pleasure.

Before Bloom opens *Sweets of Sin*, he encounters the insalubrious bookseller, who speaks in a demotic voice: "Them are two good ones"

(*Fair Tyrants* and *Sweets of Sin*). Like Molly's voice, "full of perfume," the bookseller's voice is scented: "Onions of his breath came across the counter out of his ruined mouth" (10:596–597). This unkempt, odiferous man (who coughs and "puked phlegm on the floor" [10:633–645]) sets the stage for Bloom's unusual (to put it mildly) response to the snippets from *Sweets of Sin:*

> Warmth showered gently over him, cowing his flesh. Flesh yielded amply amid rumpled clothes: whites of eyes swooning up. His nostrils arched themselves for prey. Melting breast ointments (*For him! For Raoul!*). Armpits' oniony sweat. Fishgluey slime (*her heaving embonpoint!*). Feel! Press! Chrished! Sulphur dung of lions! (10:619–623)

Bloom's reading, or rather, his interpretation of *Sweets of Sin* combines the haptic and the olfactory senses in a flurry of synaesthetic associations that are possibly fragrant (melting breast ointments?) but mostly foul. If *Sweets of Sin* were a perfume—the name would certainly be appropriate, as Lanvin launched Mon Pêche (My Sin) in 1924—its top notes would be fur, cash, and lacy underwear, giving way to rank, excremental undertones. The smells are bizarre, counterintuitive, and nonmimetic. The fecal theme, as we have seen, has its place in the world of perfume, but the smells of sulphur, onions, and fish virtually never appear. Fishy smells are singled out as repulsive to both Stephen and Bloom; an eccentric affection for onion breath is a joke in "Nausicaa." Sulphur, or brimstone, as Father Arnall emphasizes, is the dominant odor of hell.

Yet this is a scene of arousal, as Joyce conveys through Bloom's physical response to erotic content: eyes rolling, swooning, and flesh yielding. Joyce's readers are prevented from participating in this when they are brought up short by the highly idiosyncratic images that ensue. "Fishgluey slime" and "sulphur dung of lions" hardly follow from the banally salacious text of *Sweets*. If we think back on what we know about Bloom's gravitation toward unpleasure and the images that made an impression on him earlier in the day (the lions, for example, from *Ruby: Pride of the Ring*, another book he reads in a highly imaginative way), they begin to make a kind of absurd sense. Still, that required step of interpretation puts the reader in an analytical rather than a concupiscent mode of engagement with the text.

Some of the most perplexing scents Bloom imagines in response to *Sweets of Sin* reprise those from a passage of *Giacomo Joyce* (1907) that describes the audience at an opera:

> A symphony of smells fuses the mass of huddled human forms; sour reek of armpits, nozzled oranges, melting breast ointments, mastick water, the breath of suppers of sulphurous garlic, foul phosphorescent farts, opoponax, the frank sweat of marriage-able and married womankind, the soapy stink of men.[82]

In this Huysmans-inspired composition, smells become the notes of a "symphony" that includes many odors from *Sweets of Sin*—armpits, sweat, "melting breast ointments," "sulphurous garlic" breath—and places the almightly opoponax right in the middle of it all, balanced between disgust and desire. Joining words that would seem to contra-dict one another, such as "soapy" and "stink," with cryptic images such as "nozzled oranges," "phosphorescent farts" and the sweat of women differentiated by their marital status, the strange odors Joyce forges in his lexical laboratory are aimed less at evoking the senses than at displaying the author's linguistic virtuosity and playful imagination. *Sweets of Sin* is a more concentrated passage, but it similarly distances Joyce's reader from the olfactory images and calls attention to the author's manipulation of language.

Joyce does not invite the reader to enjoy *Sweets of Sin* in the direct and somatic way that such texts, like the explicitly masturbatory "dirty" letters, are typically consumed. Rather, the passage's incongru-ities and ironies ask us to read with a strong sense of critical distance: we might laugh, but it is an arch, knowing kind of laugh. This effect is repeated throughout *Ulysses* in other scenes of pleasure: the orgasm on the beach in "Nausicaa," for example, or Molly Bloom's raunchy monologue. In both cases, the racy passages are rendered through ostentatiously parodic or inventive prose that has the effect of focus-ing the reader on the construction of language itself rather than per-mitting a direct, sensuous reaction to the text. As Allison Pease puts it, "potential pornographic pleasure [in Joyce] is always disrupted, held at bay by an intervening discourse"—namely, Joyce's "modernist form [which] necessarily violates the pornographic forms within, recoding such works for the high-brow reader." Ultimately, Pease argues, "the sensuous content of *Ulysses*'s narrative is rendered impotent by form."[83] Joyce invokes but contains sensuous pleasures: like Stephen mortifying his senses, he contorts and pushes them beyond their limits through language.

Joyce's sensuous material is not exactly impotent, but it is crucially qualified by linguistic convolution that is an acquired taste gained by reading the text. Through Bloom's response to *Sweets of Sin* and many similar passages in *Ulysses*, Joyce models the approach to pleasure that he wants the reader to adopt. It is a very different kind of pleasure from reading pornography or a romance novel, just as inhaling Peau d'Espagne is very different from sniffing Yardley's English Rose. In a letter to Ezra Pound on September 7, 1915, Joyce vents about the state of contemporary theatre. "The prudery of my country (i.e. all of it that isn't lured by vulgarity.) The sheer numbers to which a play must appeal before it is any use to a manager. Bed room scenes where the audience can be tittivated, eroticised . . . excited and NOT expected to think."[84] *Ulysses* offers the thematic titillation of bedroom scenes, but the novel's allusive and ironic layers demand active, analytical reading practices. Joyce mediates somatic pleasures by rendering them aestheticized, self-reflexive, and textually difficult, but puts forward that mindful, complex process of reading as its own reward and as superior to other kinds of reading. Hence the irony of the censorship of modernist works such as *Ulysses*. If we are reading the correct way—the way that Joyce instructs us—we are never in the realm of unadulterated sensuous pleasure, but rather always aware of the work's textuality and the author's deliberate effects. The ideal reader—the well-trained reader--is constantly aware of the construction of the reading experience alongside Joyce's appeal and obstacles to pleasure. Once we have followed Joyce's "perfumance," it is doubtful that we will regard olfaction or scents as neutral, simple commodities; just so, once we have learned to read *Ulysses*, our horizon of what constitutes readerly pleasure has been irrevocably altered.

2

STEIN'S TICKLE

"Please be the beef, please beef, pleasure is not wailing. Please beef,
please be carved clear, please be a case of consideration."
—*Tender Buttons*[1]

"Tickle tickle tickle you for education."
—"Sacred Emily," *Geography and Plays*[2]

Gertrude Stein's early mentor William James prefaces his *Principles
of Psychology* (1890) with an apology: "the work has grown to a length
which no one can regret more than the writer himself. The man must
indeed be sanguine who, in this crowded age, can hope to have many
readers for fourteen hundred continuous pages from his pen."[3] Stein
did not share James's hesitation about making such demands on her
readers, and not just in terms of length. As she explained, in one of her
1934–35 lectures in America, of her "enormously long" *Making of Americans*, "I went on and on and then one day after I had written a thousand pages, this was in 1908 I just did not go on any more. I did however immediately begin again," with the intention of writing an "even
longer . . . even more complicated" book.[4] Stein's announced ambition
to "describe not only every possible kind of a human being, but every
possible kind" of group of human beings stemmed, she claims, from
working with James, from whom she learned that "science is contin-
uously busy with the complete description of something, with ultimately the complete description of everything." If science could have
such monumental goals, then "what else is there to do" (*Selected Writings,* 255) but pursue the same encyclopedic objective in her writing,

which Stein describes, in her essay "Composition as Explanation," as "using everything" (*Selected Writings*, 518).

James, however, pointedly admits the areas he neglects in *The Principles of Psychology*: in particular, he states his regret for "the exclusion of the important subjects of pleasure and pain" in human experience. But James does emphatically reject the still dominant understanding of pleasure and pain as exclusively oppositional impulses, criticizing other writers (such as Herbert Spencer and Leslie Stephen) who took this approach. In *Varieties of Religious Experience*, James suggests that *all* pleasure has a hybrid quality that frustrates the bifurcated pleasure/pain model:

> Unsuspectedly from the bottom of every fountain of pleasure, as the old poet said, something bitter rises up: a touch of nausea, a falling dead of the delight, a whiff of melancholy, things that sound a knell, for fugitive as they may be, they bring a feeling of coming from a deeper region and often have an appalling convincingness. The buzz of life ceases at their touch as a piano-string stops sounding when the damper falls upon it.
>
> Of course the music can commence again;—and again and again,—at intervals. But with this the healthy-minded consciousness is left with an irremediable sense of precariousness. It is a bell with a crack; it draws its breath on sufferance and by an accident.[5]

By this account, pleasure is inherently volatile and vacillating, and contains dissonance as well as its own undoing. In a review of Grant Allen's *Physiological Aesthetics* (1877), James contends that no theory of pleasure is complete without accounting for phenomena in which pleasure and displeasure intermingle, such as "tickling, . . . the comical, . . . the bliss of incipient anaesthesia, . . . various intoxicants; . . . the pleasures of a slow crescendo simply as such."[6]

James's description of pleasure as constitutionally variable, intermittent, and repetitive ("commence again;—and again and again—at intervals") is apt for Stein's work. The nature of Steinian pleasure—how and whether she gives delight—remains an outstanding question. Even Stein's greatest admirers concede that much of her work is insurmountably obscure or unduly demanding—and the length is the least of the obstacles. "Stein remains more confusing and irritating than other modernists"[7]; "Reading Gertrude Stein at length is not unlike making one's way through an interminable and badly printed game book"[8]; "exhilarating, but the treatment is so drastic that it kills the patient."[9] Stein presents not what George Steiner calls "contingent difficulty," requiring specialized knowledge or research, but rather a more sweeping "ontological" or "tactical" difficulty.[10] As Ulla E. Dydo points out, "We have learned to read Joyce, Pound, Olson, and others with the help of scholarly tools. But Stein, older than they, remains difficult because she is primitive and naïf. Her simple vocabulary requires little learning. Her refusal of the conventions of English defamiliarizes her writing and angers readers. She demands total concentration on the naked text before eye and ear. The rewards are as great as the effort is difficult" (*The Language That Rises*, 63).

Stein's relationship to literary high modernism is unsettled. She is both of it and apart. In her own time, she was represented as both approachable to general audiences and "unreadable."[11] In recent years, Stein has become queerer still: not because of the critical attention to coded and not so coded lesbian sexuality in her work—which at this point seems so well established that it is the *least* queer thing about Stein—but because there has been a distinct turn toward interpreting Stein as a purveyor of sensuous pleasure that is *secured* by its hermeticism and indeterminacy. That is, the same formal features that were once deemed off-putting have increasingly been read as the source of delight and even accessibility.[12] Ann Douglas, for example, positions Stein as an opponent of modernist cultural snobbery, contending that Stein "loved the effortlessness and abundance created by the new technology of consumer-oriented mass production and saw her own art as its ally and analogue." Contrasting Stein to Freud, who "reified productivity and hard, unrelenting work" (evidence of which is that he "never, so far as we know, went to a movie"), Douglas argues that "While Freud espoused 'the reality principle,' [Stein] explored 'the pleasure principle.'"[13] In a similar vein, Leisl Olson writes that Stein's "incomprehensibility . . . actually had the effect of promoting simple sensory pleasure," and that "the primary aim of a literary text," for Stein, was "immediate, effortless pleasure."[14] (Wayne Koestenbaum takes this line of appraisal further, declaring that "Gertrude Stein is the most pornographic writer I know."[15]) These interpretations square with *Time*'s 1933 cover story about Stein, in which she was described as "very democratic" and "always accessible to strangers," but they are out of synch with the *New York Times* headline on the occasion of her American lecture tour, "Miss Stein Speaks to Bewildered 500," and a large percentage of popular and academic criticism.[16]

Immediacy and effortlessness may describe texts such as *Three Lives* or *The Autobiography of Alice B. Toklas*, but their applicability to Stein's more formally innovative pieces published between 1914 and the mid-1930s is a harder case to make. As Edmund Wilson remarks of Stein's work, "If other persons say they do respond, and derive from doing so pleasure or profit, we must take them at their word."[17] The welcoming, sensual Stein needs to be reconciled with the hermetic, opaque, and tedious Stein. The author herself was alert to this mixed reception. Although she claims, in *The Making of Americans*, that she writes for herself and strangers, she knows that "There are some who like it" but "there are many who never can really like it (*Selected Writings*, 262). Of course, readers always have the latitude of their own bliss. However, there is massive disagreement about the most basic nature of Stein's reading effects. Cyril Connolly's comment in *Enemies of Promise* (1938) that "Any estimate of Miss Stein must largely depend on the pleasure derivable from her creations" remains relevant, as that issue is still contentious.[18]

Various models have been suggested to describe Steinian pleasure, including *écriture feminine*, preoedipal orality, and anality.[19] I want to suggest a new model for approaching Stein's work that takes into account both the appeal and the difficulties of her texts: tickling. I do not mean just the general metaphorical sense of the word—tickling as amusement or interest—but tickling in its physical incarnation, to which, structurally and experientially, Stein's method and her literary effects are analogous. Tickling has long been understood as a form of childish physical play and a preverbal mode of communication between infants and adults.[20] Stein's estranged approach to words and language and her love of repetition are regularly characterized as regressive and infantile, from Wyndham Lewis's excoriating critique to Koestenbaum's salute to Stein as the "Baby Queen."[21] Significantly, even beyond childhood, tickling fuses pleasure with irritation, intimacy, and estrangement in a way that resembles Stein's textuality. Tickling is somatic and extraverbal, but it entails an unusual kind of coordination between reflex and social context and between self and other. James cites tickling as a primary example of states that mix pleasure and pain; at one point in *Tender Buttons*, Stein remarks, "What is the use of a violent kind of delightfulness if there is no pleasure in not getting tired of it" (462). This is a marvelously acute description of tickling as well as, I will argue, the ways Stein taxes and teases her reader. Tickling, whose mysterious idiosyncrasies have intrigued theorists from Plato to James to Adam Phillips, strikingly characterizes Stein's infantile and erotic impulses, her abstraction and sensuality, and the sliding scale of pleasure to irritation that her work arouses.

◙ ◙ ◙

Stein had many of her major aesthetic breakthroughs before World War I (notably, in *Three Lives*, *The Making of Americans*, her word portraits, and *Tender Buttons*) and spent much of her career afterward refining them. Before *The Autobiography of Alice B. Toklas*, *Tender Buttons* was one of Stein's most widely known experimental works and it remains a cornerstone of contemporary Stein criticism. It was also the main inspiration of contemporary Stein parodies. The length of *Tender Buttons* renders it more accessible than *Making of Americans*, but it is more compressed and elusive. Superficially grounded in the noun but set adrift by other linguistic elements, the still-life quality of *Tender Buttons* is ruptured by Stein's wayward syntax and grammar. In the first two sections, objects and food are set forth and named and then immediately recede in a stream of apparently random, or at least highly idiosyncratic, associations.[22] Images are not sustained, except as they are implied by the section titles. Stein mocks descriptive and metaphorical language: "What is the sash like. The sash is not like anything mustard it is not like a same thing that has stripes, it is not even more hurt than that, it has a little top"; "Change a single stream of denting and change it hurriedly, what does it express, it expresses nausea. Like a very strange likeness and pink, like that and not more like that than the same resemblance and not more like that than no middle space in cutting." Seeming similes promise definition but then become occluded by negation and non sequiturs. There are cohesive, focused moments throughout *Tender Buttons*, but far more moments of surreal disjunction. The section called "Suppose an Eyes," for example, offers a succession of sensuous word combinations that draw attention to the surface of words and the dance of syllables on the page.

> Go red go red, laugh white.
> Suppose a collapse in rubbed purr, in rubbed purr get.
> Little sales ladies little sales ladies little saddles of mutton.
> Little sales of leather and such beautiful beautiful, beautiful
>   beautiful. (*Selected Writings*, 475)

The witty transformation of "little sales ladies" into "little saddles of mutton" is initially effected through sound. "Sales" becomes "saddles," which is associated with mutton, a cut of aged sheep that evokes the catty phrase, "mutton dressed as lamb." The quick, tripping quip is softened on both sides by the slower, more sonorous "rubbed purr" and the petting strokes of "beautiful, beautiful beautiful." As this passage demonstrates, and feminist criticism of the 1970s celebrated, Stein's work often evokes tactile sensation, both thematically and through sonic oral play. The "rubbed purr" fondles not just language but also the reader's lips, mouth, and skin as the line is read. However, such sensations are rarely extended; they are aroused suddenly, seemingly out of the blue, and they dissipate just as quickly.

In a different tonal range, but equally abruptly, a notable paragraph of "Roastbeef" charms through a pulsing tempo and captivating imagery evoking Lewis Carroll.

> Lovely snipe and tender turn, excellent vapor and slender butter,
> all the splinter and the trunk, all the poisonous darkening drunk,
> all the joy in weak success, all the joyful tenderness, all the section and the tea, all the stouter symmetry. (479)

The passage is playful, erotic, and elusive at once ("Roastbeef" picks up on the earlier theme of eros and age: "Why should ancient lambs be goats and young colts and never beef, why should they, they should because there is so much difference in age" [480]). Stein preserves the syntax of traditional sentence structure so that even the nonsensical words make a certain kind of sense. The beat of the syllables is cumulative, binding the dissonant words ("poisonous," "splinter," "weak success") together with the more "tender" and "joyful" ones to achieve a lyrical effect. A similarly compelling moment appears in "Lifting Belly" (written 1915 to 1917) when Stein breaks into an anomalous nursery rhyme-like voice:

Here is a bun for my bunny.
Every little bun is of honey.
On the little bun is my oney.
My little bun is so funny.[23]

Although this is baby prattle (or pillow talk), the voice is clear and inviting. These and similar passages inexplicably appear among pages of fractured language that moves—or lurches—to entirely different rhythms. Just when the reader latches on to a rhythm, an image, or an evocative combination of words, Stein switches gaits.

The other, and far more typical, extreme is when Stein falls into repetition or lengthy, convoluted passages that barrage the reader with words and sounds that seem to gain no—or only fleeting—traction in terms of meaning or pattern. "Lifting Belly," for example, which has become a primary example of the accessible, sensual Stein, has many strikingly approachable passages but is also monotonous and meandering.[24] After the short preamble, from part II onward, almost all the lines are very short, with a staccato rhythm, and end-stopped. The lack of enjambment means that every line, unless it repeats an element from the line before, introduces a new idea. For example,

Angry we are not angry.
Pleasing.
Lifting belly raining.
I am good looking.
A magazine of lifting belly. Excitement sisters. (18)

Most of these lines are self-contained, possibly relating to their predecessor and successor, but not in an obvious way. The reader might want to linger on the image of "lifting belly raining" or hear more about those intriguing "excitement sisters," but that desire is frustrated as Stein moves on. The dynamic brings to mind Virginia Woolf's comment, in "Mr. Bennett and Mrs. Brown," on the sensation of reading Eliot's poetry:

I think that Mr. Eliot has written some of the loveliest single lines in modern poetry. But how intolerant he is of the old usages and politenesses of society—respect for the weak, consideration for the dull! As I sun myself upon the intense and ravishing beauty of one of his lines, and reflect that I must make a dizzy and dangerous leap to the next, and so on from line to line, like an acrobat flying precariously from bar to bar, I cry out, I confess, for the old decorums, and envy the indolence of my ancestors who, instead of spinning madly through mid-air, dreamt quietly in the shade with a book.[25]

In fact, Eliot gives his reader much more of a bridge between lines than Stein does; if his references are more obscure, the stepping-stones between images and words are much firmer. In "Lifting Belly," the mixing of occasionally rhymed, emotionally evocative lines— "Lifting belly is so dear. / Lifting belly is here" (19)—and nonrhymed, more analytical lines—"Lifting belly is a rare instance. I am fond of it. I am attached to the accentuation" (18)—has the effect of constantly unsettling tempo, tone, and mood. Lines such as "Lifting belly was very fatiguing" and "Hurry up. / Hurry up with it" (15) could be commenting on sexual performance or on the prolix nature of the poem itself. "Pussy how pretty you are. / That goes very quickly unless you have been there too long" (17); "I can go on with lifting belly forever. And you do" (39). And she does.

Throughout her work, Stein's continuous present functions as a kind of parataxis that refuses the reader a temporal or spatial orientation, a linear sense of tense or a hierarchical sense of foreground and background, and also denies "resting places," as Richard Bridgman observes (60). Her unconventional punctuation similarly thwarts traditional linguistic signals that help the reader organize meaning around space and time. Sianne Ngai writes of the sludgelike, dense, boring, exhausting quality of Stein's writing—the sheer *demand*— that is particularly evident in *The Making of Americans* but is also featured in less volume in the shorter works.[26] That Wyndham Lewis makes a similar argument about *Three Lives*, but to a dismissive end, demonstrates the range of responses the same textual dynamic can solicit from different readers. What is most important about Stein's insistence, her "sludge," is that it is leavened—always unpredictably, seemingly haphazardly—by local moments of sprightly wordplay, brief felicity, and seeming coherence amongst the torrent. The vacillation between these effects is important: it taxes readers, challenging them to observe other features (sound, lexical structure, and shape) in place of significance and to endure estrangement and repetition in hopes of something delightful or graspable on the horizon. In most of Stein's work, the ratio between the cryptic and repetitive passages and the moments that "bind" the reader to the text is strikingly unbalanced.

Steinian pleasure is irregular, sporadic, and spasmodic: too short or too long; too much or not enough. Even repetition is paradoxically erratic as sentences fold back on themselves, but rarely predictably. This sense of randomness and the switching to new tonal frequencies and rhythms every couple of lines or even within the same line, which demands the reader's constant adjustment, are countered by Stein's purposeful, expository—but not descriptive—tone. Throughout *Tender Buttons*, the voice is firm, precise, composed. The piece's triptych organization around the headings "OBJECTS," "FOOD," and "ROOMS" implies a solid architectural structure, but the plan is undermined by, among other things, the free play of misclassified items. "A time to eat," for example, appears under "OBJECTS," and "END OF SUMMER" is included under "FOOD," as well as phrases such as "A puzzle, a monster puzzle, a heavy choking, a neglected Tuesday." The loosest of the sections is "ROOMS," which meanders, as the section announces itself, as if "there is no use in a centre" (498). Still, the piece's organization and seemingly purposeful confusion, along with lines like "Lecture, lecture and repeat instruction" (483), indicate that there is a method at work and a will to impart it—or *something*: an orientation, a kind of susceptibility—to the reader.

The precise nature of Stein's stance toward the reader is difficult to discern. On a superficial level, *Tender Buttons* resembles a narrated slide show ("slide one, A CARAFE, THAT IS A BLIND GLASS; slide two: GLAZED GLITTER"), except that the narrator's relationship to the object displayed is cryptic and the overarching visual image is withheld. Or rather, the narrator's relationship to the object is all that matters, but it is utterly idiosyncratic as the reader is given a seemingly concrete noun that is then loosened from its familiar anchoring points. Enigmatic address reinforces this sense of obscure purpose in *Tender Buttons*. Most notably, the entreaty "please" is repeated throughout, implying an interlocutor, but the addressee is not specified: "Please spice, please no name, place a whole weight, sink into a standard rising, raise a circle" (481); "Every way oakly, please prune it near. It is so found" (489); "Please pale hot, please cover rose, please acre in the red stranger, please butter all the beef-steak with regular feel faces" (496); "a little piece a little piece please" (488).

"Please" may be an imperative, a verb, or a plea ("Please Please Me," as the Beatles put it). "Please" is a particularly erotic word for Stein; it is woven throughout "Lifting Belly" as a solicitation and an active verb: "Please be the man. / I am the man" (51); "Lifting belly can please me because it is an occupation I enjoy" (35). Pleasure, pleasing, and pleas to please nudge one another throughout, as Stein's language appears to appeal to someone or something. "Please" is a tease: a quick, exciting point of possible contact, an ambiguously promising speech act. "Please" is a particularly riveting word in Stein's lexicon because of this fungibility, and because of the possible passionate implied address of another.

"Please" is also, of course, one of the primary signifiers of diplomacy, of politeness.[27] Children are told that it is "the magic word" to produce desired results. However, it is not sufficient to simply say "please"; the rules of civility require an interrogative inflection ("Pretty please?"). Please without a question mark effectively strips the statement of solicitousness, consideration, and attentiveness to the addressee. Stein was notoriously contemptuous of question marks throughout her work. As she notes in "Poetry and Grammar" (1934):

> The question mark is alright when it is all alone when it is used as a brand on cattle or when it could be used in decoration but connected with writing it is completely entirely completely uninteresting. It is evident that if you ask a question you ask a question but anybody who can read at all knows when a question is a question as it is written in writing. . . . A question is a question, anybody can know that a question is a question and so why add to it the question mark when it is already there when the question is already there in the writing. Therefore I never could bring myself to use a question mark, I always found it positively revolting, and now very few do use it.[28]

Although Stein explains her refusal to employ question marks as a democratic transparency—"anybody can know" what she is saying—it is also indicative of an imperiousness on her part.[29] Her freewheeling sentence structure by no means always signals when a question is a question. The question mark, like the entreaty "please," would suggest a direct address to another, but Stein prefers to keep this ambiguous.

Many critics read Stein's whole oeuvre from the time she met Alice B. Toklas as one long address to her lover.[30] Others characterize Stein as writing for "everybody," while an alternative interpretation sees her as writing for an audience of one: herself.[31] Whatever the case may be, we can—and must—still read Stein in relation to other implied readers, at least linguistically implied. The sense that Stein's work may be some sort of conversation or a dialogue gives the reader a tantalizing but fleeting point of orientation. Harriet Chessman argues that Stein's primary mode is the "dialogic form, in which difference may enter without being relegated to a secondary position or subsumed under an authoritarian identity." Emphasizing the "intimacy" of Stein's writing, Chessman traces a variety of "forms of relatedness," including a mother-child dyad and a lesbian relationship.[32] While Stein does create moments of intimacy with her reader, they are not consistent or stable. Even when her writing has the overt structure of a dialogue, through what seems like direct address or questions, this is typically a fleeting impression, although the reader may sustain the illusion on her own.[33] The interrogative, solicitous mode is a teasing gesture in *Tender Buttons*, a break in the stream of associations to *possibly* focus on another person, a body, a listener, beyond. If this is intimacy, it is highly contingent and sporadic, a darting acknowledgment that there is an interlocutor who is just as quickly forgotten or ignored.

Some critics have argued that where Stein's work frustrates meaning it opens up new avenues of sensual perception. Stein writes in *Everybody's Autobiography* that "anybody can get tired of anything everybody can get tired of something and so they do not know it but they get tired of feeling they are understanding and so they take pleasure in having something that they feel they are not understanding." This argument that people enjoy disorientation is reversed in a Pathé newsreel promoting her lectures: "My lectures are to be a simple way to say that if you understand a thing you enjoy it and if you enjoy a thing you understand it. Understanding and enjoying is the same thing."[34] Both statements fold back on themselves, asserting unlikely tautologies. The ease with which Stein reverses herself suggests that her central terms—"understanding," "enjoying," and "pleasure"—may have nothing, or everything, to do with one another.

What does "understanding" mean in the context of Stein's work? And what quality of pleasure (or "excitement") does her work offer? The case is often made that Stein's sensuous approach to language is based on a "caressing" of nouns. She comments, in "Poetry and Grammar,"

When I said.
A rose is a rose is a rose is a rose.
And then later made that into a ring I made poetry and what did I
    do I caressed completely caressed and addressed a noun.[35]

But Stein dictates a range of relationships to language: "Poetry is concerned with using with abusing, with losing with wanting, with denying with avoiding with adoring with replacing the noun. . . . Poetry is doing nothing but using losing refusing and pleasing and betraying and caressing nouns" ("On Poetry and Grammar," 327). The false simplicity of the definition ("doing nothing but") is a familiar Stein tactic to mask a complex idea. Many of the gerunds here—"abusing," "losing," "denying," "avoiding," "refusing," and "betraying"—are, as Marianne DeKoven observes, "predominantly anxious and violent verbs"[36] that conflict with the last one, "caressing." Stein's work can be embracing and sensuous, but not all of her tactile effects are so affectionate. Yes, there is "rubbed purr," but Stein also rubs words—and readers— the wrong way, with her exasperating repetition or bafflingly arbitrary word choices, which can be more abrasive than tender.

Instead of caressing, which implies benevolent, gentle seduction, Stein's model of relatedness suggests the more rough action of tickling. Stein's seeming estrangement from language, her attention to its material and sensual properties, its sounds and patterns, rhythms and textures, has been likened to a kind of primal or preoedipal performance, a toying with the building blocks of linguistics. Lisa Ruddick describes Stein's work around the time of *Tender Buttons* as wordplay that operates according to its own rules, producing "childish pleasures . . . childlike jabs at the rules of grammar and diction."[37] When we enter a Stein text, language operates erratically: this is a game that does not disclose its rules, or a code that does not permit us to decipher it entirely. But tickling is not just a game, and its pleasures are not simple; it has a very particular effect and neuropsychological structure that correspond to the vicissitudes of Stein's writing.

Stein jokes about tickling. She likes the word for its onomatopoeic properties. In *A Long Gay Book*, for example, when Stein writes about the creative process, tickling is a minuet of the mouth. "All the conscience which tells that little tongue to tickle is the one that does not refer to teeth."[38] She often pairs "tickle" with "little," producing "little tickles," flickerings of the tongue. In *Saints and Singing*, Stein makes a literary pun with "tickle" and "canticle" ("[c]an tickle can tickle"; "Can tickle/He can make her purr."[39] In *The Making of Americans*, she points out the somatic and cerebral dimensions of tickling: "waiting is to me very interesting for always something is coming or else nothing is coming and there is eating, sleeping, laughing, living, talking and a little tickling in the body and the mind then that is very pleasant to any one."[40] The homology between somatic and linguistic or mental tickling is hardly new. Darwin, for example, explored the metaphor—"The imagination is sometimes said to be tickled by a ludicrous idea; and this so-called tickling of the mind is curiously analogous with that of the body."[41] However, by this account, any creative work that strikes our fancy could be said to "tickle" us. I want to suggest that Stein's writing substantially and structurally operates like tickling.

Both ancient philosophers and modern scientists consider tickling to be an enigmatic and singular form of stimulation.[42] In his *Studies in the Psychology of Sex*, Havelock Ellis proposes that ticklishness is "one form of touch sensation . . . which is of so special and peculiar a nature that it has sometimes been put aside in a class apart from all other touch sensations."[43] Earlier philosophers did indeed try to classify it as a distinctively ambiguous phenomenon. In Plato's *Philebus*, Socrates assigns tickling to the category of states that are "a combination of pains with pleasures, the balance tilting now this way now that." Although tickling is correlated with laughter, Plato specifies that "In the class in which the pains predominate over the pleasures you must count those pleasures of itching . . . and of tickling."[44] This opinion has held sway over centuries. Tickling can produce pleasurable sensation signaled by laughter, but it is laughter on the edge of discomfort, which at some point demands cessation. Anyone who has a young child will recognize this pattern: "Tickle me, tickle me . . . stop!" (There is a wonderful description of this in Carl Sandburg's review of a 1920 screening of Charlie Chaplin's *The Floorwalker*, in which he observes "a healthy rollicking kid" in the audience emitting "a steady stream of laughter—a sort of tickle-me-don't tickle-me laughter."[45])

Some scientists, looking for an evolutionary purpose for tickling to account for its aggressive dimension, have speculated that it may be a mock form of fighting.[46] Havelock Ellis addresses cases of tickling used as torture.[47] Writing for *The New York Times*, John Chamberlain likened Stein's writing to "Chinese water torture; it never stops and it is always the same."[48] Stein's own publishers described "the effect produced on the first reading" of *Tender Buttons* as "something like terror."[49] However, we do not have to go so far as torture or terror to grasp the volatile and compound nature of tickling. Adam Phillips points out in his brief essay "On Tickling" that "the tickling narrative, unlike the sexual narrative, has no climax." Tickling is "a paradigm of the perverse contract" that highlights "the irresistible attraction and the inevitable repulsion of the object, in which the final satisfaction is frustration."[50] "Frustration" is an important concept for Stein; she frustrates conventional systems of signification and linguistics, but for many Stein admirers this is explicitly a source of pleasure.

Tickling folds together affection and hostility as well as infantile and erotic impulses. It can also persist into adulthood, between adults, as erotic play. Ellis devotes a section of *The Psychology of Sex* to this. (Molly Bloom, for example, recalls of an old flame, "I tormented the life out of him first tickling him I loved rousing that dog in the motel rrrssstt awokwokawok his eyes shut and a bird flying below us he was shy all the same I liked him like that moaning" [*Ulysses*, 18:812].) Ellis suggests that ticklishness decreases "with age and sexual activity," but is related to arousal and, in extreme forms, a fetishistic fixation (11). Infantile tickling is healthy, but adult-on-adult tickling is a perverse regression. Stein criticism is notably divided between readings of her language as infantile (or preoedipal) and interpretations of it as expressing a mature female eroticism.

Aristotle pointed out that man "cannot . . . tickle himself," a phenomenon that subsequent scientists have interpreted as indicating a complex interface between the self and other. Darwin, writing about tickling in *The Expression of the Emotions in Man and Animals*, speculates that "it seems that the precise point to be touched must not be known" by oneself, and that therefore the purpose of tickling may be to establish social bonds between people, particularly children and parents.[51] In the section on "Infantile Sexuality" in *Three Essays on the Theory of Sexuality*, Freud compares tickling to thumb sucking. In both, he writes, "A rhythmic character must play a part"; "the stimuli which produce the pleasure are governed by special conditions, though we do not know what those are" (49). In fact, thumb sucking and tickling are quite different. Thumb sucking, characterized by a regular rhythm, is a form of self-soothing. By contrast, the key to ticklish pleasure is its unpredictability and discontinuity, and it has to be produced by another person.

The tickle response is epidermal, but it also has a powerful social dimension. One must be susceptible—one must be ticklish—in order for it to register as pleasurable. An unwanted tickle is an annoyance. In "What Does She See When She Closes Her Eyes" (1936) Stein explores relationships of tactile receptivity and refusal, as well as the erotic connection between caressing and tickling: "Henry Maximilian Arthur could be tickled by grasses as they grow and he could not caress but he could be caressed by Theresa as well as be tickled by grasses as they grow."[52] Tickling, like caressing, is a pleasure that requires receptivity. This, as we will see, is an important factor in readers' responses to Stein. Wyndham Lewis, who was hostile to her, makes a nevertheless relevant observation about this feature of tickling. In *Time and Western Man* (1927), he links Stein and Charlie Chaplin as "revolutionary simpleton[s]" who cultivate a repulsive "infant-cult." In his preface to *Tarr*, Lewis reflects on the related phenomenon of the *"worship of the ridiculous,"* of which Chaplin is a key idol. "The worship (or craze, we call it) of Charlie Chaplin is a mad substitution of a chaotic tickling for all the other more organically important ticklings of life."[53] To Lewis, "chaotic" tickling is annoying as well as trite. Actually, all tickling is necessarily "chaotic": jagged and intermittent. What he calls "more organically important" tickling has gravity and is supposedly mature or adult: something like arch humor or irony. Tickling is somatic and erratic, whereas irony is cerebral and calculated: traits associated with modernist stylistics. Clearly, as tickling goes, "There are some who like it" and "there are many who can never really like it."

A former student of William James, G. Stanley Hall, with whose work Stein was familiar, contributed a major publication in the modern science of tickling.[54] In 1897, Hall copublished, along with Arthur Allin, a paper on "The Psychology of Tickling, Laughing and the Comic" that identified two categories of tickling: knismesis and gargalesis. The former is a light stimulation (for example, "contact with the finest hair, wool, or cobweb," which "evokes sensations that are not only exceedingly intense, but also very widely irradiated, and also provokes reflex movements that may be convulsive in their intensity"), and the second is a "harder" touch that produces laughter but can also cross over into discomfort.[55] Hall and Allin relate this to children picking scabs, pulling off their hangnails, and so on, "often removed with great pain." Studies of gargalesis in humans and primates alike specify that there is a pronounced note of aggression in this kind of tickling. Hall and Allin make two important points: that pleasure and displeasure are closely related in tickling, and that one of the essential questions about tickling concerns whether it is an automatic response or dependent upon social context.

The jury was still out on this last question when Stein was writing, and it remains so. In 1999, two University of California scientists took up the conundrum. Christine Harris and Nicholas Christenfeld summarize the debate: "The *interpersonal* explanation suggests that tickling is fundamentally interpersonal and thus requires another person as the source of the touch. The *reflex* explanation suggests that tickle simply requires an element of unpredictability or uncontrollability and is more like a reflex or some other stereotyped motor pattern."[56] In order to test the rival hypotheses, Harris and Christenfeld built a fake "tickle machine." This contraption was "designed to look and sound like a robotic hand . . . attached by a long flexible hose to an impressive array of equipment that could plausibly control its motion. This equipment, when turned on, produced a vibrating sound that could be that of a genuine robotic apparatus" (505). Subjects were blindfolded and told that they would be tickled on their feet by, alternatingly, the machine and a human being, and were then asked to identify who or what had administered the tickling. A human experimenter did all the tickling. The subjects were not able to distinguish accurately between what they had been told was a machine and a human tickle; they had the same ticklish response to both. "The tickle-machine works," Harris and Christenfeld concluded, "because it, like another human being but unlike oneself, can produce stimulation that is unpredictable and/or not canceled by command or afferent signals. . . . The present results are generally favorable to the view that the tickle response is some form of innate stereotyped motor behavior, perhaps akin to a reflex."

Now, stereotyped motor behavior and reflex—as well as robotic hands—were of intense interest to Stein. Her earliest single-author publication was her 1898 article, "Cultivated Motor Automatism; A Study of Character in Its Relation to Attention," building on a 1896 coauthored article on "Normal Motor Automatism," in which Stein tested her own ability to become distracted or detached from conscious movement and produce "automatic writing."[57] "Habits of attention," she wrote, "are reflexes of the complete character of the individual, and again on habits of attention are dependent the different forms and degrees of automatic writing." When the famed behaviorist B. F. Skinner reviewed Stein's later writing for *Atlantic Monthly* in 1934, he claimed that the 1898 article was the key to her baffling method. He maintained that her rambling, "unintelligible" prose was simply automatic writing, a flow of unorganized words.[58] Stein resisted this interpretation; as Barbara Will points out, her claim was not that she achieved automatism but rather, even more impressively, that she could "be simultaneously engaged in the performance of automatism and outside of it," to achieve "attentive inattentiveness" and to produce unpredictable patterns, surprising herself.[59] Tim Armstrong describes this as more of a "distracted" writing than one produced by a "second self."[60]

Stein would have no doubt been amused at Harris and Christenfeld's experiment, with their fantastic fake machine. Tickling is simultaneously reflexive, a motor response, and highly context specific, involving a complex relationship between self and other. Stein's writing and tickling both depend on erratic stopping and starting. There is no predicting her next move, even when she seems to be repeating herself:

The difference between thinking clearly and confusion is the same difference that there is between repetition and insistence. A great many think that they know repetition when they see or hear it but do they. A great many think that they know confusion when they know or see it or hear it, but do they. A thing that seems very clear, seems very clear but is it. A thing that seems to be exactly the same thing may seem to be a repetition but is it. All this can be very exciting.[61]

Stein preferred the term "insistence" to repetition ("there can be no repetition because the essence of that expression is insistence, and . . . insistence . . . can never be repeating, because insistence is always alive" [288; 290]), arguing that "repetition" has a mechanical quality while "insistence" is more organic and animate, yet she explored "mechanistic" human response such as motor automatism. The ticklish parts of Stein are evident everywhere, but they necessarily appear at unpredictable intervals. Even her "insistence" or repetition is a function of intermittency. Stein locates "a little tickling in the mind and the body" as an interruption of the flow of waiting and the habitual. Likewise, when we read Stein, we wait for that little tickle amid a field of seeming random wordplay arranged, as Marjorie Perloff points out, "precisely to manifest the arbitrariness of discourse, the impossibility of arriving at 'the meaning' even as countless possible meanings present themselves to our attention."[62]

The important texture of Stein's work, then, is the contrast between tedium or disorientation and moments of intensity or excitement. In "Portraits and Repetition," Stein emphasizes the "excitement" of her word portraits: "they were exciting to me and they were exciting to others who read them" (301). She points to her writing's palpable effects: its somatic or sensual but not necessarily pleasurable properties. Along with "excitement," another word Stein employs often to describe the effect of her work is "irritating," as do many of her readers: Edith Sitwell, for example, described the writing in *Geography and Plays* as "an irritating ceaseless rattle like that of American sightseers talking in a boarding-house (this being, I imagine, a deliberate effect)."[63] In "Composition as Explanation," when Stein contrasts "classic" to new or "outlaw" art (*Selected Writings*, 514), she argues that before art becomes "a classic" it "is still a thing irritating annoying stimulating." Its "beauty" is not recognized. However, "beauty is beauty even when it is irritating and stimulating not only when it is accepted and classic" (*Selected*, 515). For Stein, repetition plays a central role in this irritating and stimulating quality. In *The Making of Americans*, she explains that she sees "All living" as "repeating" and that she loves this (*A Stein Reader*, 61). Like Freud, Stein recognizes that "Loving repeating is *always* in children" (62), but for Freud, this feeling is lost in adulthood. Like tickling, a love of repetition is thought to be normal in children, but abnormal or neurotic in adults. While Stein concedes that "repeating is very irritating," it is also a source of enjoyment, of primal pulsating pleasure. "Always more and more I love repeating" (56).[64]

The most obvious sense of irritation here is emotional annoyance or aggravation, but the term also has a somatic connotation, as in a local inflammation of a body part, particularly the skin. Excitement too is an affect that suggests sensual as well as mental agitation. Both connote a strongly embodied connection with and response from the reader. While many writers evoke sensual registers (oral, sonic) in their work, Stein draws particular attention to them in her shift away from language as a conventional system of signification. Catharine Stimpson proposes that "in Stein's more abstract writing, the body disappears into language utterly, or becomes an example of a linguistic category."[65] If the body disappears in a thematic sense, it returns through the somatically evocative nature of Stein's language. Along with sound, Stein highlights the tactility, volume, grain, and materiality of language in a way that necessarily involves the audience. As Rebecca Scherr puts it, Stein's readers' bodies are "implicated in this textual exchange."[66] Stein's tactile effects are often playful—"All the tickling is tender," she remarks in *Matisse Picasso and Gertrude Stein*[67]—but not entirely. The visceral qualities of her texts can also be frustrating, belligerent, and antagonistic to the reader. These effects are not beyond Stein's control. No matter how improvisatory her writing was, she made continuous choices. She cultivated and inscribed effects of irritation and annoyance, as well as excitement, into her work. In Stein's rhetorical (non)question, "What is the use of a violent kind of delightfulness if there is no pleasure in not getting tired of it," the double double negatives ("no pleasure," "not getting tired") and contorted syntax reinforce the oscillation between seemingly contradictory violence and delightfulness. "Not getting tired of it" indicates the sheer stamina that is required to read Stein's work: stamina that can just as easily collapse into exhaustion or boredom. Adam Phillips defines tickling as a "delightful game" that highlights "the irresistible attraction and the inevitable repulsion of the object, in which the final satisfaction is frustration" (11). Stein creates the effect of ticklish intermittency that can so easily—indeed, must—tip over into irritation and annoyance. Tickling, as Stein knew, is exciting because it is also annoying and irritating, and because it involves the subject in a simultaneously affable and antagonistic dynamic.

This suggests that Stein is the tickler and her reader is ticklish. But the picture is more complicated. Chessman's conception of Stein's work as a "dialogue" implies mutual, reciprocal pleasure, as does the interpretation of the reader and Stein collaborating. Likewise, Scherr argues that Stein's tactile aesthetic erodes the boundary between self and other: "In the bodily experience of touch, we can never locate the exact place where we end" and the other "begins. . . . Stein's tactile eroticism allows us to hover in uncertainty, in the threshold space between subject and object. . . . By prioritizing tactility and sound, meaning is created in close contact and dialogue with the reader" (204). Clearly, not all readers have a sensation of participation and collaboration with Stein; at the very least, dialogue is only one way of understanding her work.

Stein's lectures are particularly illustrative of her relational dynamic with her audience and her ticklish effects. Much of Stein's interwar writing was ostensibly given to elucidating herself in works such as "Composition as Explanation" (1926), *How to Write* (1931), *Lectures in America* (1934), and *Narration* (1935). Although Joyce, for example, talked privately about keys to his work, he did not publish them or perform them on the stage as Stein did. The modernist impulse to teach readers, to inculcate, comes across strongly in these expository pieces. (Stein's early work too was preoccupied with education—*Q.E.D.*, *Fernhurst*, "The Value of College Education for Women"—and after World War Two, she wrote several books for children that also assumed a pedagogical stance.) Her line in "Sacred Emily," "Tickle tickle tickle you for education," brings to mind Darwin's and other scientists' speculations that tickling has a pedagogical purpose in mimicking self-defense or attacks, or that an "edifying tickle" is a means of imparting information through humor, just as humorous banter and "word play teach about relationships of words, language and concepts."[68] In Stein's creative prose/poetry and her expository writing such as her lectures there is a constant friction between her management of and her seeming disregard for or implicit aggression toward her reader. We see the same tension between free play and restriction, between address to an implied audience and disregard or disrespect. Both kinds of writing display the same strategies of intermittency and repetition, obfuscation and justification, solicitation and irritation, that characterize Stein's ticklish pleasure.

A lecture is in many ways the opposite of a dialogue or collaboration. In contrast to Socratic teaching, which does take the form of a dialogue, a lecture—from the Latin root for "reading"— traditionally presents an authoritative speaker holding forth to a passive, silent audience that is perhaps allowed to ask questions at the conclusion. Stein's lectures conform to this unidirectional rhetorical model, even as she continually addresses her audience. While some critics have described her lectures as so accessible that they resemble cozy fireside chats, their structure and formal elements illustrate the push and pull of indeterminacy and the withholding of meaning that happens throughout all of her work. "Composition as Explanation," Stein's 1926 lecture written for Cambridge and Oxford audiences that was subsequently published by the Hogarth Press, opens with a promising declarative—"There is singularly nothing"—followed by a phrase that raises more questions than it answers: "that make a difference a difference in beginning and in the middle and in ending except that each generation has something different at which they are all looking." Stein seems to clarify the statement with "By this I mean so simply," but what she means is hardly simple, any more than "singularly" is singular: "that anybody knows it that composition in the difference which makes each and all of them then different from other generations and this is what makes everything different otherwise they are all alike and everybody knows it because everybody says it" (*Selected Works*, 513). What exactly does Stein mean by "explanation," here or in her title? Who or what is "all of them"? And what is it that everybody knows and says? The lecture has the structure of the titular "explanation," but both terms of the title remain puzzling throughout. Stein includes many gestures appearing to simplify matters—"Now that is all" (523)—when the opposite seems true.

The legend of Stein's American lectures in the mid-1930s has reinforced the narrative of her as populist and accessible: "Stein for everybody." The lectures are not exact transcripts; apparently, Stein improvised a great deal and sometimes ignored her notes. However, the final edited versions reveal a dramatic, performative mode of communication that is consistent in many ways with her poetry and creative prose work. There are moments of great clarity: for example, Stein's discussion of her developing method in "Portraits and Repetition" and her comments on crime novels and the Old Testament ("permanently good reading," *Narration*, 19). There are also notes of surrealism. For example, following a discussion of newspapers versus fiction, Stein suddenly blurts out, "I love my love with a b because she is peculiar" (39). Bridgman refers to this "abrupt, bizarre interruption" as an extension of a child's game in which letters are substituted for names (259). There is an example of the game in chapter 22 of *David Copperfield*: "I love my love with an E, because she's enticing; I hate her with an E, because she's engaged."[69] In typical fashion, Stein departs from the rules of the game and invents her own: the letter ("b") does not match the adjective ("peculiar") except only approximately in sound. It's a game Stein plays often, including in *How to Write* ("I love my love with a b because she is precious," 105), *Before the Flowers of Friendship Faded Friendship Faded* (poem 29)[70] and *Reread Another* ("I love my love with a z because she is exact," *Stein Reader*, 354). In the lecture, this phrase is in part a tease—a flirtatious gesture to pique her audience's interest, a coy suggestion of exposure—but it is mostly Stein's self-amusement, her game with herself. It is, above all, self-referential. While Stein's delivery and performance were by all accounts winning, her words on the page suggest that the strength of her connection with the audience was probably more by force of her charismatic delivery and physical presence than by her actual words, which are intensely engaged with herself and her work and only cursorily engaged with the audience.

Thornton Wilder's preface to Stein's *Narration* lectures framed the talks as friendly collaborations with the audience. For example, he explains one idiosyncrasy as a gesture of good will on Stein's part: "Miss Stein pays her listeners the high compliment of dispensing for the most part with that apparatus of illustrative simile and anecdote that is so often employed to recommend ideas."[71] Wilder reads this feature as Stein's faith in the audience's intelligence, but it can just as easily be read as Stein's indifference to having to substantiate her theories. In both *Lectures in America* and the four talks published as *Narration*, her direct address to the audience is deceptive. The solicitation is undermined by her imperative tone: "You will see what I mean"; "You do understand if you think about it." As with "please" throughout *Tender Buttons,* what seems like an appeal to the listener is actually a command to see things the way Stein does. She does not ask, "Do you see what I mean?" but rather tells it: "Do you see what I mean. It is very interesting. And it has an awful lot to do with everything" (*Narration*, 39). Likewise, in "Portraits and Repetition":

> Do you see my point, but of course yes you do. You do see that there are two things and not one. . . . You see then what I was doing in my beginning portrait writing and you also understand what I mean when I say there was no repetition. . . . Oh yes you all do understand. You understand this. . . . And does it make any difference to you if you do understand. It makes an awful lot of difference to me. It is very exciting to have all this be. (*Writings: 1932–1946*, 293–296)

Does it really make a difference to Stein if her audience understands? Her grammar suggests otherwise. Although the lectures are full of what seem like interrogative constructions, Stein does not pose them as such. These gestures in which Stein feigns interest in her audience constitute a kind of game, for those inclined to play and to follow the erratic twists and turns of her mind, encouraged by the occasional apostrophe. (Koestenbaum provocatively proposes that "Stein's ideal audience is a dog, mute and loyal" [*Cleavage*, 327].) The conclusions of the second and final lectures in *Narration* show Stein shifting back and forth, reversing direction, just when one would expect her to be most summative: "Perhaps narrative and poetry and prose have all come where they do not have to be considered as being there. . . . Perhaps yes, perhaps no, no and yes are still nice words, yes I guess I still will believe that I will. You will perhaps say no and yes perhaps yes" (29); "That is what makes anything everything that it has been done and so perhaps history will not repeat itself and it will come to be done. Perhaps no perhaps yes anyway this is all I know just at present about how writing is written how an audience is existing how any one telling anything is telling that thing" (62). These oscillations, like Stein's beloved "b," raise expectations and reverse them just as rapidly, bringing the listener along and then casually undermining the promise of an answer or at least a statement. Is this really a dialogue? Is Stein trying to communicate to anyone but herself? Perhaps yes, perhaps no.

The last talk in *Narration* is significantly concerned with "what is it to be an audience." Stein declares that "the audience is the thing. It helps a lot to know anything about this thing if you think are always really always thinking about the narrating of anything of narrative being existing. So then what did I know about myself as an audience (49). Meditating on herself as the audience, she then concludes by crediting her listeners with the same knowledge: "This you all of you know. Then after all what is the use as you all of you know this" (50). What exactly is known is not clear, but when Stein reframes the question, her purpose comes into focus:

> Everybody always says do you write for an audience well do you and what is an audience and is it almost impossible or is it possible to make an audience of yourself and is it almost impossible or is it possible to rid yourself of yourself as an audience. (52–53)

Stein distinguishes among different kinds of authorship and says that reading one's own lecture is a special case in which "you have a half in one of any two directions, you have been recognizing what you are writing when you were writing and now in reading you disassociate recognizing what you are reading from what you did recognize as being written while you were writing. In short you are leading a double life" (57). This experience of a self-conscious "double life" resembles the willed "self-splitting" of Stein's motor automatism. However, this is not the same as addressing an audience: it is addressing oneself. Stein's lectures and her other writing do elicit collaboration insofar as they call upon the audience to see and hear and feel the words on the page (or being read), but what we are induced to experience is what it is to be Gertrude Stein. Stein's writing may seem especially porous or participatory because its patterns are so random, but her lectures, like her other works, impress her own associations and thought process.

Here we come back to the charge that Stein has a reckless disregard for her audience. Koestenbaum, a bona fide Stein fan, states, "Above all one must remember this about Stein: *she did not care*" (*Cleavage*, 326). Stein makes no attempt to disguise this. "I was not interested in what other people would think when they read this poetry," she explained of *Tender Buttons*. "They might have another conception which would be their affair."[72] She makes clear, in "Portraits and Repetition," for example, that although she is glad for others' excitement about her work, her real investment is the excitement in herself. How does this jibe with tickling, a pleasure that requires "the enacted recognition of the other" (Phillips, 9)? One has the sense, reading Stein at length, that the author, practiced in the art of automatic writing, cultivated reflex, and split subjectivity—talking and listening at the same time, she always claimed[73]—is watching herself amuse herself. Tickling for Stein is intrapersonal, and if interpersonal, that is a secondary goal. Unlike high modernists such as Joyce, Pound, or Eliot, whose referentiality is external—"contingent difficulty"—Stein's referentiality is internal. Her methods are internal to her own language; her stylistic innovations, including her repetitions and idiosyncratic construction, are inward-looking and insular. She produces textual effects that are impossible in physical terms: self-tickling. And yet, we might think of Stein as a kind of tickling machine, with her somatic, acoustic language and her erratic and rhythmic cadences collaterally involving the susceptible reader in her circuit of pleasure.

"Stein pleases herself," Kostenbaum notes, but she also, by example, "leads the willing reader to imagine a regime of self-pleasure" (324). But not all readers. This is where Stein is running a far more daring experiment than Harris and Christenfeld's. In their project with the tickle machine, all their subjects were prepared to be tickled, by man or motor. Stein's textual effects are wildly contingent. Her texts can be a pleasure machine or a torture machine or both, depending on the reader. In *Matisse, Picasso, and Gertrude Stein,* she remarks that "Many many tickle what is not ticklish and many tickle the rest when that is not the only way to say that every bad one and every good one is the kind of a one to go away."[74] Some readers are more susceptible to Stein's tickle than others. Some are pleased, some are exasperated, some decode. Most probably, the more one reads Stein, the more ticklish one becomes.

"The teasing is tender and trying and thoughtful," Stein writes in *Tender Buttons,* and so is her tickling (486). The purpose of tickling is multifold: intimate, playful, erotic, regressive, reflexive, aggressive, and pedagogical. Recent research suggests that tickling may not, in fact, actually be pleasurable in a straightforward sense. Harris and Christenfeld conducted another experiment in which people were exposed to humorous television and then tickled. The results indicated that the laughter or giggles that result from tickling are not necessarily experienced as enjoyable; rather, the "elicitation of laughter by tickle results from its association with humour through Pavlovian conditioning. . . . Tickle [may share] an internal state with other emotions such as social anxiety and that ticklish laughter might be similar to nervous rather than mirthful laughter."[75] Conditioning: perhaps the more we are told that Stein is a difficult or a sensuous writer, the more we experience her that way. But also, anxiety: the ubiquitous parodies of Stein's writing in the teens and twenties suggest the conversion of anxious bafflement into mastery: if you can copy Stein, you must understand her. One critic in the 1920s suggested that "Reading [Stein] aloud . . . to almost any gathering is to experience an electric charging of the room; none is able to sit quiet, none is able to keep silent. Everyone shouts at once. They become more and more angry, more and more exhilarated, more and more tickled . . . until they guffaw."[76] Harris and Christenfeld's interpretation of tickling returns to Plato's original formulation of a pleasure that is also—and perhaps primarily—a discomfort, and enfolds the psychoanalytic suggestion that tickling, as a narrative with no climax, demonstrates "the irresistible attraction and the inevitable repulsion of the object, in which the final satisfaction is frustration" (Phillips, 11). If Harris and Christenfeld's findings are true, Stein's is a triumph of modernist hedonic—and anhedonic—conditioning, turning frustration and anger into laughter and, sometimes, pleasure. In her own time, Stein taught many readers to experience her style of textual difficulty as enjoyable. Her work continues to be, at least for some, a singularly difficult delight, and a testament to modernism's radical redefinition of pleasure.

3

ORGASMIC DISCIPLINE
D. H. Lawrence, E. M. Hull,
and Interwar Erotic Fiction

Is Lawrence difficult? Certainly not in the same ways that Joyce and Stein are. Although Lawrence thought of his writing as radical, as cultural "surgery" or a "bomb,"[1] his formal experimentation has often been underestimated, F. R. Leavis notwithstanding. (Leavis described Lawrence as "so much more truly creative as a technical inventor, an innovator, a master of language, than James Joyce," an assessment jarringly out of step with the current critical consensus.[2]) Since the 1960s, most critics who struggle with Lawrence do so on the basis of his politics. However, his idiosyncratic style and iterative, polemical prose have always been puzzling. Scholars have become increasingly interested in the techniques through which Lawrence guides his audience's response. Anne E. Fernald draws attention to Lawrence's "coercive language" and "abrasive method."[3] Charles Burack suggests that Lawrence "mortifies" and "assaults" his readers' sense of language, and that his "textual effects invite and channel potential reader responses."[4] A. S. Byatt, upon rereading Lawrence, admits that she found herself "irritated again by his insistent sawing noise, his making a point over and over" and his "preacherly pulpit-thumping," but concludes that Lawrence's near disappearance from U.S. college syllabi is the result of a refusal to engage with difficulty: "What has disappeared is the sense that literature is exacting, diverse, and difficult to read or to describe."[5] As a modernist pedagogue (or preacher), Lawrence is particularly overt, but his lessons have not yet been understood completely, largely because of readers' resistance to the way he delivers them. As John Worthen observes, "in some ways we are still learning to read" Lawrence.[6]

One part of Lawrence's work we are still learning to read is his representation of pleasure. He has a reputation as an innovator of sex writing who at the same time produced increasingly conservative, stereotypical images of masculinity and femininity. The Lawrence of "Tickets Please," seemingly alarmed about women's potential power, and *Lady Chatterley's Lover*, for whom "the bridge to the future is the phallus,"[7] is difficult to reconcile with the Lawrence of *Women in Love* and other work in which he explored the possibility of men and women being equal partners.[8] Lawrence's representations of eroticism are shaped by innovative and derivative impulses, and by originality and repetition; he alternately encourages and prohibits—or, more precisely, dictates—particular kinds of pleasure in his characters and in his readers. These contradictions are exemplified by the way Lawrence handles one best-selling text of pleasure: E. M. Hull's *The Sheik*.

In the first part of this chapter, I will examine the remarkable attention Lawrence and critics such as Q. D. Leavis pay to Hull's novel and the subgenre to which it belongs, desert romance, whose predictable formulas and sensational prose were viewed as epitomizing popular pleasure. *The Sheik* has a surprisingly prominent place in significant formulations of British modernism precisely because of the efficiency with which Hull manages readerly pleasure. In his effort to revive sexual experience, Lawrence turned to the tropes that he criticized in Hull's work but used them toward fundamentally different ends. Lawrence's response to Hull's writing exposes an important conflict between the modernist ambition for innovation and its reluctant recognition of popular culture's attractions. It also demonstrates an intrinsic paradox of pleasure: its dependence on both novelty and familiarity. In the second part of this chapter, I will examine how several of the features Lawrence borrows from Hull return in *Lady Chatterley's Lover*, his most explicit and radical treatment of eroticism. Here Lawrence writes about sex, not to promote pleasure but rather to discipline and even curtail it.

Figure 3.1
My Story Weekly
P.P.6004.scb, Oct. 1927, cover © The British Library Board

"ARE YOU NOT WOMAN ENOUGH TO KNOW?"

On October 15, 1927, the debut issue of *My Story Weekly* appeared in London with a cover image calculated to draw an audience: a sleek flapper, glamorous and dreamy, against a background oasis complete with camel, palm tree, and a male figure in a turban and robes. Inside, in a tone that simulates an intimate chat at the local teashop, with frequent addresses to the reader, Irene Speller's "How I Was Loved By a Sheik!" recounts the author's trip to Damascus with a British dance troupe. There, "in the East," Speller confides, she "met with adventure and romance, which make all the sheik stories ever written pale into insignificance."[9] She and her dancer friend Winnie compare their first glimpse of the Saharan sky to images they have seen on "glowing posters . . . outside the picture palace at Shepherd's Bush. Haven't you seen them too," Speller asks her reader, "outside the picture palace in your neighborhood?" (2). But the East is "not much like Shepherd's Bush," Speller and Winnie conclude, especially when a dashing sheik appears one night in the theater in which they are performing and fixes his "amazing dark eyes" on Speller ("dark, flashing eyes that you never see in the men here in England" [3]). The sheik makes his move and invites her to his elegant desert tent. Amid clichés such as "Love knows no boundaries" and "There was something in the air that night," he woos Speller while other characters repeatedly warn her that he "has got different ideas to the sort of men we know" (3). As Speller obsesses about how the sheik might kidnap her and make her his "desert queen," it becomes clear that alterity and danger are a central part of the story's thrill. And yet, as the tale's hackneyed language and multiple references to "sheik stories" indicate, the appeal of Speller's adventure is not its novelty, but its reiteration of an excitingly predictable formula with which the author assumes her readers are familiar. The narrative concludes with Speller tearfully leaving the sheik, quoting Rudyard Kipling's already clichéd "We were East and West, and, of course, it is true now that 'never the twain shall meet.'"[10]

My Story Weekly became one of the most popular British women's magazines, and its editors' choice of Speller's story for the inaugural issue is indicative of interwar reading tastes. "How I Was Loved by a Sheik!" is a less violent and sexually explicit imitation of one of the most successful fictions in early twentieth-century British publishing history, E. M. Hull's 1919 novel *The Sheik*. In this orientalist fantasy, Diana Mayo, an arrogant English aristocrat who rejects marriage and other trappings of womanliness, dares to take a trip into the Algerian Sahara with only Arab guides. She is captured by a handsome sheik and taken to his luxurious caravan in the desert, where he forces himself— along with lavish jewelry and dresses—upon her. After much bosom heaving and bodice ripping, Diana becomes conscious of her love for the "lawless savage," and she decides to stay with him in their love oasis.[11] British readers thrilled to this sadomasochistic fantasy, sending the novel through 108 reprintings in the UK by 1923.[12] Two years later, audiences clamored to see Rudolph Valentino, in the title role that made his reputation, kidnap and ravish his way through George Melford's film adaptation of *The Sheik* as well as its sequel, also based on a novel written by Hull.

Hull followed *The Sheik* with *The Shadow of the East*, *The Desert Healer*, and *The Sons of the Sheik*, which joined a plethora of fictions with similarly suggestive titles by other authors: *Desert Love*, *The Hawk of Egypt*, *The Lure of the Desert*, *Burning Sands*, *Harem Love*, and so on. *The Sheik* inspired so many imitators that we can accurately speak of an interwar desert romance genre. The elements were intensely formulaic: a beautiful woman, usually British, leaves the home country for the "Arab East" (including a diversity of locales such as Algeria, Egypt, and Morocco), which is routinely signified by the same images: endless deserts and skies, jasmine-scented nights, ill-tempered camels, and lustful, gorgeous sheiks.[13] Above all, the heroine is "swept away" and made more exquisitely feminine (that is, pleasurably passive) by her encounter with a relentlessly masculine sheik. The dominant imagery in desert romance is the cliché of "burning desire" or "consuming passion": there is no body part of the sheik that does not sear the heroine, and no emotion that is not experienced as a conflagration. While the stories were of varying degrees of sexual frankness, Hull's novel was the supreme model for "sheik stories" in the interwar period.[14]

In *The Long Week End*, Robert Graves and Alan Hodge note that "Tarzan of the Apes was the most popular fictional character among the low-brow [British] public of the Twenties; though the passionate Sheikh of Araby, as portrayed by E. M. Hull and her many imitators, ran him pretty close." The terms "Sheikh" and "Sheikhy" entered the popular lexicon as synonyms "for the passionately conquering male."[15]

Sheet music and gramophone records and a number of "sheik films" capitalized on the appetite for desert romance between the wars; at least two perfumes called "Sheik" were launched in the early 1920s.[16] And then in the 1930s the mania for desert romance waned (although the theme lives on in women's mass market romances, such as Susan Mallery's Harlequin titles, *The Sheik and the Bought Bride, The Sheik and the Christmas Bride, The Sheik and the Pregnant Bride*, etc.).[17] This was a relatively short shelf life, given the fervor with which British readers consumed "sheik stories."[18] Intriguingly, this genre—a celebration of male power and female submission—reached the pinnacle of its popularity in Britain at a time of vigorous debate about new possibilities for gender roles in the wake of World War I. Moreover, the desert romance, among the most deliberately derivative of popular fiction genres, peaked at the same moment that modernist fiction was pursuing originality and "making it new."

The broad narrative strokes as well as the linguistic details of *The Sheik* would become important to Lawrence. As Hull's novel opens, its heroine, Diana Mayo, seems an unlikely model of sexual adventurism. She appears to have no libido at all, but by the end of the story, this ice-cold androgyne is begging for the love of a "fierce desert man." The commonplace reading of *The Sheik* as a taming of the New Woman is not strictly accurate.[19] Diana has none of the political concerns of the typical New Woman (although she does have fashionably bobbed hair). Her declaration that "Marriage for a woman means the end of independence" is quickly undercut by her modification, "that is, marriage with a man who is a man, in spite of all that the most modern woman may say" (9). Diana is an orphan who was raised by her brother, Aubrey. "You have brought me up to ignore the restrictions attached to my sex" (24), she reminds him when he tries to curb her freedom. This privilege is more a matter of spoiled will than political consciousness, and Hull clearly intends Diana to seem unnatural.

Hull performs a balancing act as she encourages her reader to identify narcissistically with Diana while colluding against her. As with all romances, physiognomy is destiny. Diana is beautiful, of course, but also haughty, and she must give up her willfulness so that the romance plot can unfold. When she tells Aubrey, "I will *never* obey any will but my own," his response—"Then I hope to Heaven that one day you will fall into the hands of a man who will make you obey" (24)—is a desire that Hull develops in the reader too, and it proves to be prognostic. The story of Diana's abduction, captivity, and rape (of which more later) are told in a breathless manner culminating in victorious debasement: "The girl who had started out so triumphantly from Biskra had become a woman through bitter knowledge and humiliating experience" (102).

Against all warnings, Diana rides out into the desert with an entourage of "natives." On the second day, the party is ambushed; a turbaned figure on horseback chases Diana across the dunes and lifts her off her horse onto his with one sweep of his powerful arm. He takes her into a tent of magnificent luxury and throws her on a well-appointed divan (sartorial and interior design details feature prominently in *The Sheik*). Flinging aside his cloak, the sheik stands before her, "tall and broad-shouldered," with "the handsomest and the cruellest face that she had ever seen." Nature triumphs over culture as Diana finds herself "dragging the lapels of her riding jacket together over her breast with clutching hands, obeying an impulse that she hardly understood." In an instant, the sheik undoes Aubrey's years of cultivating boyishness in Diana, and she reverts to a performance of melodramatic womanhood.

> "Who are you?" she gasped hoarsely.
> "I am the Sheik Ahmed Ben Hassan. . . ."
> "Why have you brought me here? . . ."
> He repeated her words with a slow smile. "Why have I brought you here? *Bon Dieu!* Are you not woman enough to know?" (48)

But Hull's reader *is* woman enough to know, and this superior knowledge aligns the "womanly" reader with Ahmed and his desires.

Critics routinely describe the first encounters between Diana and Ahmed as extended rape scenarios, which they are, technically, but they are crucially qualified by Hull's language. Throughout Diana's struggles with Ahmed, Hull dwells on "the consuming fire" of his "ardent gaze" and his "pulsating body." Hull's repetition of and endless variation on "burning desire" has a cumulative effect, indicating desire and physical excitement where there is also violence and moral outrage:

> The flaming light of desire burning in his eyes turned her sick and faint. Her body throbbed with the consciousness of a knowledge

that appalled her. She understood his purpose with a horror that made each separate nerve in her system shrink against the understanding that had come to her under the consuming fire of his ardent gaze, and in the fierce embrace that was drawing her shaking limbs closer and closer against the man's own pulsating body. (49)

Without explicitly describing what is happening in this scenario, Hull's language, focusing on the sensations of pulsating and flaming, indicates somatic pleasure amid Diana's fear and horror. The body "throbs" independently of her mind, asserting itself over and against her moral response. (Ahmed even carries a smoldering prop around with him: his Turkish cigarettes. Diana comes to associate the "perfume" of his tobacco, confusingly mingled with the "faint, clean smell of shaving-soap," with his "pulsating body." The Sheik and Joyce's Blazes Boylan have these pungent Turkish cigarettes in common: it was, apparently, the choice of lotharios everywhere.) Hull generates an erotic dynamic from the oscillation between knowledge and denial, physical sensation and ethical indignation. Diana struggles to understand the meaning of her corporeal sensations, but the reader, for whom the tension between the body and the mind is spelled out, knows better.

Hull encourages her reader to identify with Diana while hoping, like the sheik himself, for her forced fall into passion.[20] In Hull's forerunners among romance, sensational, gothic, and seduction novels, a direct identification with the heroine is invariably central to the formula. No matter what the heroine's shortcomings may be, the reader is rarely encouraged to desire, with the male villain or rake, her demise. When Diana is "shaken to the very foundation of her being with the upheaval of her convictions and the ruthless violence done to her cold, sexless temperament" (78), Hull's construction suggests that her heroine's sexlessness is preposterous. Through these unorthodox arrangements of sympathy, identification, and sensation in *The Sheik*, Hull represents pleasure as simultaneously outrage and thrill, and a final surrender to everything Diana initially resisted.

At one point, Diana manages to escape the encampment right after Ahmed has asked her to "choose" whether she will submit to him or not. She says that she will and, disappointed in herself, channels the outraged spirit of a horse she has seen Ahmed tame brutally. However, once she finds herself at liberty in the desert dunes, she relaxes and begins smoking a cigarette, which she gradually realizes is one of the Sheik's:

> She had always been powerfully affected by the influence of smell, which induced recollection with her to an extraordinary degree, and now the uncommon penetrating odour of the Arab's cigarettes brought back all that she had been trying to put out of her mind. With a groan she flung it away and buried her face in her arms. The past rose up, and rushed, uncontrolled, through her brain. Incidents crowded into her recollection, memories of headlong gallops across the desert riding beside the man who, while she hated him, compelled her admiration, memories of him schooling the horses that he loved, sitting them like a centaur, memories of him amongst his men, memories more intimately connected with herself. . . . There had even been times when he had interested her despite herself. (105)

The Proustian cigarette elicits memories of Ahmed's caresses and his "handsome brown face"; Diana, "writhing on the soft sand . . . struggled with the obsession that held her" (105). As with Joyce, the at-first foul odor of the Sheik's cigarette induces the tender and "intimate" memories that Diana has not to this point admitted. When Ahmed comes after her and sweeps her up again onto his horse, she is putty in his "long, lean fingers. . . . Quite suddenly she knew—knew that she loved him, that she had loved him a long time, even when she thought she hated him" (111–112). The metaphoric flames now become a bonfire of passion into which Diana flings herself.

> Now she was alive at last, and the heart whose existence she had doubted was burning and throbbing with a passion that was consuming her. Her eyes swept lingeringly around the camp with a very tender light in them. Everything she saw was connected with and bound up in the man who was lord of it all. She was very proud of him, proud of his magnificent physical abilities, proud of his hold over his wild, turbulent followers, proud with the pride of primeval woman in the dominant man ruling his fellow-men by force and fear. (152)

At last the burning and throbbing make sense to Diana: they are the somatic symptoms of the "primeval woman" meeting her match in the "dominant man."

Throughout *The Sheik*, Hull handles racial stereotype with the same double movement of attraction and repulsion, predictability and exception that she does desire in general. Desert romance inverts the gender positions in conventional orientalism by imagining an eroticized masculine "foreigner" and casting the fantasy from a woman's perspective, but the terms of that eroticization are just as stereotypical.[21] Hull pedantically insists that "the position of a woman in the desert was a very precarious one" because of Arab men's "pitiless . . . disregard of the woman subjugated" (78). But this is all in bad faith, as Diana comes to love a version of that subjugation. The moment she realizes her feelings for Ahmed also involves such contradictions and polarizations:

> Her heart was given for all time to the fierce desert man who was so different from all other men whom she had met, a lawless savage who had taken her to satisfy a passing fancy and who had treated her with merciless cruelty. He was a brute, but she loved him, loved him for his very brutality and superb animal strength. And he was an Arab! A man of different race and colour, a native; Aubrey would indiscriminately class him as a 'damned nigger.' She did not care. It made no difference. . . . She was deliriously, insanely happy. (112–13)

That Hull emphasizes stereotypes at this turning point suggests that the frisson of alterity *and* polarity is a central part of the erotics of *The Sheik*, and it remains so long after Diana "discovers" her feelings for Ahmed and the "embraces she panted for" (123). She continues to imagine Ahmed as a "lawless savage" even after evidence to the contrary appears.

At the end of the novel, Hull springs a surprise on the reader. Ahmed is actually the son of an English earl and a Spanish mother. Hence, it would appear that the sexual compromises of the previous two hundred pages and the scandal of loving an Arab are recuperated with an aristocratic marriage to a white man. This is surely the most clichéd part of Hull's novel: the ubiquitous marriage denouement.

And yet, while the subject of marriage bookends the narrative (Diana rejects marriage at the beginning of the story but marries at the end), in between, there is no attention to marriage whatsoever. As Billie Melman observes, "both the marriage and the discovery, by Diana, of Ahmed's 'real' identity are gratuitous. At no point in the whole story is matrimony presented as a necessary alternative to an unlawful but happy concubinage" (102–103). Despite the conventional frame, *The Sheik* presents an erotic fantasy almost completely unmediated by proprietary concerns, which may well account not only for the tremendous popularity of Hull's novel but also for the unusual attention that an unlikely modernist audience gave to *The Sheik*.

"THE TYPIST'S DAY-DREAM"

The London *Times Literary Supplement* review of *The Sheik* focused exclusively on the novel's plot, without making any judgment about the quality of the writing. It was the last time that Hull would be described so neutrally. "It is a bold novelist who takes his [*sic*] heroine into the Garden of Allah by the gates of Biskra, as heroes are so hard to find there who comply alike with the requirements of the proper local culture and the conventions of romance as written for Western people."[22] Despite misattributing male authorship, the *Times* reviewer shows a canny understanding of the dilemma of genre and geography in which Hull finds him/herself. But the *Times* conclusion is amiss: "If there be a moral here in this simple tale it is one of warning to young European ladies not to ride alone into the Sahara." The translation of Hull's fantasy novel into a cautionary tale is the first of many misreadings of *The Sheik*. Hull not only inaugurated an orientalist psychogeography for women but also initiated a kind of female sexual tourism. In the early twentieth century, solo British female travelers were increasingly common, but, writes Osman Bencherif, it was "E. M. Hull who, with *The Sheik*, first put the desert on the map as an exotic place of sexual indulgence" (180). In 1924 the *Daily Express* journalist H. V. Morton wrote a multi-installment column from Biskra, "In the Garden of Allah." Although his title borrows from Robert Hichens's 1904 novel, the scene Morton describes is much more Hullian: a city full of British and American women seeking erotic adventure, "English girls, advertising the fact that they are wearing non-stop silk stockings . . . riding past on camels," in search of passionate sheiks. Morton himself admits, "I want sheiks. I want the real Edith M. Hull stuff. I want to see how perfectly ordinary people from London, Paris, and New York behave under the influence of the Sahara" (5). Zelda and F. Scott Fitzgerald wrote of Biskra that since the publication of *The Garden of Allah* and *The Sheik*, "the town has been filled with frustrated women."[23] These trends suggest that Hull's novel had a powerful effect on her readers.

In 1919 Hull's novel may have looked like a "simple tale," but critics were soon writing about *The Sheik* as a symptom of cultural decline. Q. D. Leavis's *Fiction and the Reading Public* is a key summary of this critical development. Leavis is most concerned with the fact that "what is considered by the critical minority to be the significant works in fiction"—the novels of D. H. Lawrence, Joyce, Woolf, and Forster—are not read by the public or stocked by libraries or booksellers. Leavis argues that *The Rainbow*, for example, is not read because it moves "in a slow, laboured cycle" (226), and the reading public is not willing to make this kind of commitment. Comparing contemporary best-sellers to the glory days of the eighteenth-century novel, Leavis's main critique of current fiction—"as distinct from literature"—is that it uses stale language that elicits an equally stale response from its audience.[24]

> The idiom that the general public of the twentieth century possesses is not merely crude and puerile; it is made up of phrases and clichés that imply fixed, or rather stereotyped, habits of thinking and feeling at second-hand taken over from the journalist. . . . To be understood by the majority [a serious novelist] would have to employ the clichés in which [the general public] are accustomed to think and feel, or rather, to having their thinking and feeling done for them. . . . The ordinary reader is now unable to brace himself to bear the impact of a serious novel. (255–257)

Authors like Hull, Leavis asserts, descend to the readers' idioms of banality. Leavis pinpoints as the primary problem with popular fiction "the consistent use of clichés (stock phrases to evoke stock responses)" (243). A "stock response" is inauthentic or ersatz, "interfering with the reader's spontaneities" (244). A spontaneous response, however, does not mean doing what comes naturally, but rather registering an experience of "shock." Leavis contrasts "the popular novels of the age" that "actually get in the way of genuine feeling and responsible thinking by creating cheap mechanical responses" (74) to "the exhilarating shock that a novel coming from a first-class fully-aware mind gives" (74). The metaphors Leavis uses to describe stock responses are notably somatic—"Novel-reading now is largely a drug habit" (19), she asserts, a "masturbatory" (165) form of self-indulgence—while the experience of "shock" is more cerebral, with the emphasis more on self-conscious thinking than feeling.

Leavis's example of the deluded reader is Gerty MacDowell in *Ulysses*, whose consciousness has been colonized by popular women's fiction. "For Gerty MacDowell every situation has a prescribed attitude provided by memories of slightly similar situations in cheap fiction; she thinks in terms of clichés drawn from the same source, and is completely out of touch with reality. Such a life is not only crude, impoverished, and narrow, it is dangerous" (245). Such a life is also fiction, but never mind. The example is instructive because Leavis locates in it two kinds of readers and two kinds of author-reader relationships. Gerty's relationship to popular fiction is one of uncritical identification; the space between the page and the reader has collapsed. However, as discussed in chapter 1, Joyce inscribes an ironic distance between Gerty and the reader of his "serious" novel. This effect of estrangement, for Leavis, allows for the "impact" of modernist fiction's "shock."

If Joyce had depicted Gerty as living twenty years later, she would likely be imagining Leopold Bloom through the lens of desert romances, the contemporary equivalents of *The Lamplighter* and *The Princess's Novelettes*. Leavis notes that "ten of the fourteen novelists advertised by the 3d. circulating libraries [in a catalog] specialize in fantasy-spinning" (54). A striking number of the titles are desert romances: *The Desert Dreamers, The Lure of the Desert, Sands of Gold, The City of Palms, The Mirage of the Dawn,* and *East o' the Sun* (54). Leavis argues that reading "novels like *The Way of an Eagle, The Sheik,* [and] *The Blue Lagoon*" constitutes "a more detrimental diet than the detective story in so far as a habit of fantasying will lead to maladjustment in actual life" (54–55). Presumably, one could put the methods of detection to use in real life, while "fantasying" lacks such applications and will cause the dreamer to misread real life. Leavis never substantiates this genre- and gender-biased claim. Her argument about the connection

between cliché and fantasy-driven readerly pleasure leans most heavily on women's romance, and *The Sheik* is one of the central pillars. In
a questionnaire about popular fiction that Leavis distributed to sixty
authors, *The Sheik* is one of four titles specified as examples of "great
bestseller[s]" (44). One respondent singles out *The Sheik* as his primary example of "rotten primitive stuff" (46). In demonstrating how
low the popular novel has sunk, Leavis suggests that we "Compare
Pamela with *The Sheik*, which in the year of its publication was to be
seen in the hands of every typist and may be taken as embodying the
typist's day-dream, and it is obvious that *Pamela* is only incidentally
serving the purpose for which *The Sheik* exists and even then serving
it very indifferently" (138). Rather than providing a "scaffolding for
castle-building" (138) and escapism, the eighteenth-century novel, for
Leavis, promoted the destruction of illusions and fantasy.

Leavis's throwaway line about "the typist's day-dream" reveals how
closely associated female audiences and formulaic language are in the
modernist critical paradigm of pleasure. In "The Little Shopgirls Go to
the Movies," for example, Siegfried Kracauer argues that "Sensational
film hits and life usually correspond to each other because the Little
Miss Typists model themselves after the examples they see on the
screen."[25] Again, the iconographic typist (for Eliot in *The Waste Land*,
among other modernist fictions; we will meet her again in chapter 6)
stands in for a whole demographic of female consumers whose fantasies are transparent and mindlessly imitative. The typist is a figure of
repetition rather than originality who absorbs what is put before her
rather than producing her own work. Likewise, Leavis imagines fantasy, as both an activity and a literary genre, as a passive and mindless
repetition of bromides. (The women who are supposedly trying to find
their own sheiks in Biskra represent an intriguingly active response
to fantasy texts.) For Leavis, fantasy is divorced from the processes
of creativity, distinction, and activity, all of which she associates with
modernist fiction. "A habit of reading poor novels," Leavis argues, "not
only destroys the ability to distinguish between literature and trash, it
creates a positive taste for a certain kind of writing, if only because it
does not demand the effort of a fresh response, as the uneducated ear
listens with pleasure only to a tune it is familiar with" (136–137). Here
again is the adjuration of the leisure theorists, who urge consumers to
develop tastes for more bracing and challenging activities.

Novelty and repetition are important structural issues for pleasure and aesthetic response. In *Beyond the Pleasure Principle*, repetition has a pathological, infantile character. Freud asserts that for adults, "Novelty is always the condition of enjoyment," whereas "children never tire" of repeating the same game or story (42). The repetition compulsion, of course, challenges this principle, but the way Freud chooses to characterize it (as a compulsion) suggests that it is an aberrant or undisciplined inclination. Stein's repetition was characterized as infantile on these grounds. By contrast, innovation—the cult of novelty, the shock of the new—signals intelligence, thoughtfulness, and sophistication: "Novelty is better than repetition," Eliot writes in "Tradition and the Individual Talent."[26] A similar assumption underlies the dismissal of formulaic genres as appealing to uneducated or undiscerning readers. Repetition may occur on the level of plot, as serial or genre fiction conforms to established patterns that have proven successful, or on the level of phrases, as clichés or word combinations are so familiar as to be drained of meaning. Bliss, says Barthes, summing up the view of aesthetic modernism, "may come only with the *absolutely new*, for only the new disturbs (weakens) consciousness (easy? Not at all: nine times out of ten, the new is only the stereotype of novelty)" (40). The truly new, then, is a special category of innovation that disrupts or "shocks" the reader. "The stereotype is the word repeated without any magic," and Barthes pronounces it "nauseating" (42–43). "The bastard form of mass culture is humiliated repetition" (41–42).

But how much innovation can an audience absorb? At what point does innovation become disorienting and off-putting? Some degree of linguistic or structural familiarity is a necessary condition of intelligibility. Umberto Eco points out that modernism's characterization of popular or mass culture as works of "repetition, iteration, obedience to a preestablished schema, and redundancy" that are "pleasurable but non-artistic"[27] is unsustainable, for even experimental works necessarily play on schema and formula. By the same token, serial works demonstrate variation as well as repetition, and "even the most banal narrative product allows the reader to become, by an autonomous decision, a critical reader, able to recognize the innovative strategies" (200). One reviewer of the films *The Sheik* and *The Son of the Sheik* noted that they appealed as a counterpoint to "the drabness" and "ordinariness of . . . everyday life," but complains, "what a pity that the story of both these films is so similar. A little inventiveness would not have come amiss and the later film would have been better for it."[28] Contemporary psychological studies suggest that people are most receptive to experiences that strike a balance of the novel and the familiar.[29] Radical invention can be alienating, and rote predictability can be boring, but the right combination is captivating.

Women in great numbers responded to the desert romance, it seems, out of an attraction to a kind of novelty (alterity) combined with an antinovelty (formula). The former includes an exotic locale, a certain explicitness about women's desire, and the appearance of a kind of man one ordinarily didn't meet, apparently, if one was a typist; the latter includes formulaic repetitions, clichés of genre, stereotypes, and conventional plots. This has implications for both gender politics and language. The success of Hull's novel suggests that fantasies of stereotypical gender roles continued to have a hold on the imagination at the same time that women were struggling for political equality. Even as erotic representation is often construed as the realm of transgression and novelty, fantasy and pleasure may also actively resist innovation, favoring stereotypes and cliché scenarios, which makes them antithetical to prevailing modernist tenets of originality.

For Leavis, the antidote to books such as *The Sheik* is modernist fiction, "in which words are used with fresh meanings and for ends with which [the reader] is unfamiliar": it delivers "shocks" to its readers. If popular reading is a narcotic, modernism is bracingly therapeutic (257). If only Gerty MacDowell read *Ulysses* instead of *The Lamplighter*, and typists read *The Rainbow* instead of *The Sheik*, the reading public would be uplifted. This corrective or rehabilitative approach is predicated on an understanding of pleasure as a kind of false consciousness. But modernist shock is a reading experience that runs counter to the reading public's evident tastes. Fantasy and its most solicitous literary forms, including romance and pornography, imagine pleasures that are, strikingly often, regressive or banal. Although a primary goal of modernism is to train readers to enjoy what is challenging and unfamiliar, there are concessions to less exalted tastes throughout modernist works. Lawrence's own fiction calls into question the very terms of his criticism of *The Sheik* in ways that indicate he recognized that repetition, cliché, and stereotype have attractions that can be just as powerful as novelty and innovation.

"THE THROB OF *THE SHEIK*"

In "Surgery for the Novel—or a Bomb" (1923) Lawrence begins by making the same generic distinction that Leavis does between "serious" and popular fiction. He sees "On the one hand the pale-faced, high-browed, earnest novel, which you have to take seriously"— "*Ulysses* and . . . Miss Dorothy Richardson and M. Marcel Proust"— and "on the other, that smirking, rather plausible hussy, the popular novel"— "the throb of *The Sheik* and Mr. Zane Grey."[30] However, Lawrence faults Joyce, Proust, Richardson, and Stein for self-absorption, "self-consciousness," and abstraction that fail to deliver the "new, really new feelings, a whole line of new emotion, which will get us out of the emotional rut" (520). He extends Leavis's criticism of fantasy fiction—that it is "completely out of touch with reality" and interferes with "spontaneities"—to the serious novel. In a 1928 letter, Lawrence opines that "James Joyce bores me stiff—too terribly would-be and done-on-purpose, utterly without spontaneity or real life."[31]

The flip side, the popular novel, is pedestrian and unoriginal: "Always the same sort of baking-powder gas to make you rise" (*Phoenix*, 519). However, sameness, repetition, does not have the negative connotations for Lawrence that it does for Leavis, and novelty is not a supreme virtue. Lawrence's own work, as he knew, was highly repetitive. On this count, he responded to critics in his 1919 foreword to *Women in Love*: "In point of style, fault is often found with the continual, slightly modified repetition. The only answer is that it is natural to the author: and that every natural crisis in emotion or passion or understanding comes from this pulsing, frictional to-and-fro, which works up to culmination."[32] Repetition, then, is "natural" for Lawrence; it is what comes naturally, spontaneously.

Just as Lawrence defended and practiced a certain kind of repetition, he was skeptical of novelty as an aesthetic goal. In "Introduction to These Paintings," he writes,

A cliché is just a worn-out memory that has no more emotional or intuitional root, and has become a habit. Whereas a novelty is just a new grouping of clichés, a new arrangement of accustomed memories. That is why a novelty is so easily accepted: it gives

the little shock or thrill of surprise, but it does not *disturb* the
emotional and intuitive self. It forces you to see nothing new. It
is only a novel compound of clichés.[33]

Blatant novelty is no more desirable than "shock," as evidenced by
the fact that Lawrence yokes the word that Leavis favors with "thrill,"
which Lawrence uses to distinguish empty modern sex from more profound erotic experience. For Lawrence, the pursuit of novelty in and
of itself produces overly self-conscious, too-deliberate art. The true
artist, then, struggles between novelty and cliché. Lawrence perceived
this challenge in Cézanne's attempt to transcend cliché and shallow
novelty at the same time: "Cézanne's early history as a painter is a
history of his fight with his own cliché. . . . His rage with the cliché
made him distort the cliché sometimes into parody" (576). This is a
fair description of Lawrence's own writing, which often verges on
self-parody.

As formulaic as the popular novel is, Lawrence concedes that it
invariably elicits a strong somatic response: a "throb," a "rise," whereas
the "serious" novel drives people further into their own minds. *The
Sheik* is the paradigmatic popular novel for Lawrence in "Surgery for
the Novel." He writes that "The mass of the populace 'find themselves'
in the popular novels. But nowadays it's a funny sort of self they find. A
Sheik with a whip up his sleeve, and a heroine with weals on her back,
but adored in the end, adored, the whip out of sight, but the weals
still faintly visible. . . . Sheik heroines, duly whipped, wildly adored"
(519). Lawrence's rhythmic, breathless language here betrays the stylistic resemblance between his writing and Hull's; his exaggerated
paraphrase of *The Sheik* also indicates how his imagination ran in the
same direction as hers. Ahmed strikes an insubordinate servant in one
brief scene of *The Sheik* and a horse in another, but he does not whip
Diana. Lawrence's remarks suggest that he may have conflated the
novelistic Sheik with the cinematic one, Valentino, whose sadomasochistic scenes on the screen were legendary.[34] Valentino was, as Linda
Ruth Williams points out, "the first major male star to be specifically
marketed for a female audience"; this is reflected in Lawrence's portrayal of the star as a confection designed for ravenous women's appetites.[35] In his 1928 essay "Sex Versus Loveliness," Lawrence writes that
"the so-called beauty of Rudolph Valentino . . . only pleases because it

satisfies some ready-made notion of handsomeness," arguing that such stereotypical sex appeal is inferior to the "greater essential beauty" of "Charlie Chaplin's odd face."[36] In fact, Valentino's looks and screen presence represented a challenge to dominant Hollywood conceptions of masculinity as well as ethnicity. At the same time that Lawrence wanted to dismiss Valentino as a cliché, he also recognized the star's appeal and perhaps even brought it to bear on his own charismatically exotic, brooding leading men. After Valentino's early death in 1926, Lawrence was more sympathetic; his poem "Film Passion" claims that the female cinema mob killed the star.[37]

Although Lawrence distances both the popular novel and film from significant fiction like his own, there are episodes of sadomasochistic eroticism in Hull's novel that seem right out of Lawrence's own pages. For example, in a highly charged scene, Diana sees Ahmed brutally break a colt, an encounter that is reminiscent of Gudrun and Ursula watching Gerald terrorize a mare in *Women in Love*.[38] Hull pays as much attention to the rhetoric of "will" as Lawrence does, making it a central trope of Ahmed's dynamic with Diana. Moreover, Ahmed is a man who commands other men, a posture that Lawrence found fascinating. In many ways, then, it is not just the general populace but also Lawrence who "finds himself" in Hull's novel. Lawrence complains in a 1926 letter to publisher Thomas Seltzer that he has been asked "to come back with a bestseller under my arm. When I have written 'Sheik II' or 'Blondes Prefer Gentlemen,' I'll come. Why does anybody look to me for a best seller? I'm the wrong bird."[39] The parodic titles reflect the serial quality of popular novels (yet another dose of baking powder), but the pleasures of popular fiction were not as foreign to Lawrence as he claimed. Indeed, as David Trotter points out, Lawrence "worried about the resemblance between his own radical revaluation of sexuality and the purple passages of the romancers" (*English*, 188). I will argue that, in a sense, Lawrence did write "The Sheik II" insofar as he adapted many of Hull's tropes for his own work.

After "Surgery for the Novel—or a Bomb," Lawrence returned to Hull in "Pornography and Obscenity" (1929), an essay prompted by the censorship of *Lady Chatterley's Lover*. He maintains that genuine pornography can be recognized "by the insult it offers, invariably, to sex, and to the human spirit. Pornography is the attempt to insult sex, to do dirt on it":

The pornography of today, whether it be the pornography of the rubber-goods shop or the pornography of the popular novel, film, and play, is an invariable stimulant to the vice of self-abuse, onanism, masturbation, call it what you will. . . . And the mass of our popular literature, the bulk of our popular amusements just exists to provoke masturbation. (*Phoenix*, 178)

Unlike Leavis, Lawrence does not limit this theory of pernicious masturbation to popular literature: "most of our modern literature," he asserts, shows symptoms of "self-abuse" (180). Building on this premise, Lawrence goes on to draw some unexpected distinctions among a group of diverse texts. Weighing Boccaccio, Rabelais, Richardson, Brontë, Fielding, and Keats against one another, Lawrence now includes Hull: "I'm sure poor Charlotte Brontë, or the authoress of *The Sheik*, did not have any deliberate intention to stimulate sex feelings in the reader." This is an odd interpretation, as one only has to read a couple of pages of *The Sheik* to realize that it is meant precisely to "stimulate sex feelings." Lawrence continues, "Yet I find *Jane Eyre* verging towards pornography and Boccaccio seems to me always fresh and wholesome" (174). The distinction is grounded on how the author handles his or her material. Pornographic texts treat sex as furtive and dirty instead of clean and healthy. *Jane Eyre*'s gothic thrills are more sneaky and manipulative, to Lawrence, than the overt bawdiness of *Boccaccio*. Lawrence also casts this as a question of audience, of the group versus the individual: "The mass is for ever vulgar, because it can't distinguish between its own original feeling and feelings which are diddled into existence by the exploiter. . . . The mob is always obscene, because it is second-hand. . . . It is up to the individual to ask himself: Is my reaction individual, or am I merely reacting from my mob self?" (172). What accounts for Lawrence's new reading of *The Sheik*, rescuing it from the realm of the "rubber-goods shop" and promoting it several notches up the literary genre ladder?

The Sheik is less closely related to *Jane Eyre* than it is to the anonymous mid-nineteenth-century pornographic classic *The Lustful Turk*. Emily Barlow, the supposed narrator of this epistolary novel, is a British ingénue traveling in "the East." She is swept off her horse and captured by Ali, the Dey of Algiers. ("Dey" was the title for governor used before the French conquest in 1830.) The Dey carries Emily to his "sumptuous chambers," complete with beautiful clothes, attentive maids, and contemporary novels. This gorgeous but barbarous swain immediately assaults Emily's virginity. Although she puts up a fight, the protest quickly gives way to, as Emily reports, "a sensation it is quite impossible to describe . . . [a] sudden, new and wild sensation blended with . . . shame and rage."[40] Emily's archetypically porno-graphic awakening—the rape that turns to arousal—is strikingly like Diana Mayo's, although it takes about a tenth of the time to achieve. Within just a few pages, Emily is utterly in thrall to the Dey and his wicked ways, and in no time she proves to be a gifted libertine. It is only with great reluctance that at the end of the novel she is shipped home to England, her erotic education complete. "I will never marry," Emily writes, "until I am assured that the chosen [man] possesses suf-ficient charm and weight not only to erase the Dey's impression from my heart, but also from a more sensitive part." The flimsy way mar-riage is invoked at the end of *The Lustful Turk*—more as a setup for a coy joke than anything else—is typical of pornography, in the world of which marriage is not just insignificant, but a downright turn-off. Just so, the marriage at the end of *The Sheik* is gratuitous, and Hull's main concession to traditional novel conventions is perfectly in keep-ing with its pornographic progenitor.

As Allison Pease has shown, many modern writers, including Law-rence, "strove to incorporate mass-cultural pornographic represen-tations of the body, sex, and sexuality into their works even as they affirmed the aesthetic value of their appropriations" (xii). Pease con-tends that the only representations of sexualized bodies available to the modernists were in conventional pornography, but Lawrence knew—and he says as much in "Pornography and Obscenity"—that popular fiction was already representing sex, if not in the explicit fashion of pornography, then in a language that we might call "porno-romance," the idiom of the desert romance. Indeed, Billie Melman argues that "the desert-passion industry" (104) is "one of the earliest examples of mass, commercialised erotic literature" (104).

Isolated, remote, striving to minimize historical referents and prob-lems except those that are part of the erotic frisson, the setting of desert romance resembles nothing so much as what Steven Marcus has called "pornotopia."[41] The complex double identification that Hull cultivates— the reader's alignment with Ahmed's desires against Diana's prudish arrogance—is uncharacteristic of romance. But in pornography—most notoriously, in a text such as Sade's *Justine*—the reader is commonly primed to will the heroine's chastisement or comeuppance. Just as pornography endlessly recycles a limited vocabulary without, apparently, any inhibition of its pleasurable affect, so Hull (and her readers) never seems to tire of the metaphors of smoldering passion. The episodic pacing of *The Sheik* is also reminiscent of pornography; the way Diana comes to each encounter with Ahmed as if for the first time, her feelings and his body described with only subtle variations from the last time, resembles the phenomenon of "renewable virginity" in pornography, where each episode presupposes astonishments equal to the last.

The *Sheik* gives insight into many of Lawrence's preoccupations: female consciousness, sexuality, and pleasure. Hull achieves a strong readerly response that Lawrence valued highly; she connects with the reader in a way Lawrence knew was important, even though he disagreed with the direction Hull takes this alliance. The relationship between the desert romance author and her readers is as intimate as the pornographer's with his audience, reflecting a confidence that the same scenario, told again and again from a slightly different angle or with a slightly different set of props, is sure to incite arousal. Although in *Women in Love*, Birkin tells Hermione that she is incapable of being "a spontaneous, passionate woman . . . with real sensuality," and that she wants only "pornography—looking at yourself in mirrors" (42), nowhere are clichés so effective, and readerly affect so unmediated, as in pornography. In the realm of pornography, the stock response is the ideal response, as the reader feels pleasure in tandem with the characters. As Pease describes it, pornography "invites readers to indulge their own sensations through a mimetic imaginative practice" (8). Although Hull never explicitly mentions body parts or acts, she expertly marshals euphemism so that the reader has no doubt when the sheik is aroused and when he and Diana are "intimately connected."

There is a suggestive correlation between pornography's arousing function and Lawrence's desire to wrest the reader out of passivity and into spontaneity, reviving the libidinalized body from the stranglehold of consciousness. Lawrence's reclassification of *The Sheik* in "Pornography and Obscenity" indicates that he understood the attractions of these pleasurable genres even as he tried to turn them toward another ideological and affectual purpose. Most tellingly, in the period between "Surgery for the Novel" and "Pornography and Obscenity," Lawrence's own fiction took a decidedly Hullian turn.

BECOMING WOMAN

As several critics have noted, Lawrence's story "The Woman Who Rode Away" (1924) and, even more explicitly, his novel *The Plumed Serpent* (1926), reference and rewrite *The Sheik*.[42] In both, an aloof modern heroine (American in one case, British in the other) goes to Mexico and falls in thrall to swarthy "Indian" men whose ideology is founded on Aztec cosmology, human sacrifice, and male dominance. But while critics concur that Lawrence was "adapting the clichés of the desert romance" (Horsley, 114) and "at once invoking and denigrating" popular romance (Trotter, *English Novel*, 188) in these works, the broader motivation for his turn to *The Sheik*—as a means of directing reading and erotic pleasure together in a way that lays the groundwork for his most well-known novel on contemporary sexuality, *Lady Chatterley's Lover*—has not yet been recognized.

"The Woman Who Rode Away" and *The Plumed Serpent* are variations on the common interwar theme of leaving a troubled Britain for another, less apparently complicated country. Lawrence had an unusually literal understanding of this theme, as he enacted this flight himself, to Australia, Italy, New Mexico, and other locales that seemed to offer alternatives to a moribund interwar Britain. Unlike Hull, who once praised "the really fine work that the French Government has done" in Algeria,[43] Lawrence was critical of imperialism, and his fictions support the autonomy of native cultures. Mexico, like Algeria, offered racial, religious, and linguistic otherness, a foreign landscape, and a "primitive" culture that seemed free of the gender upheavals of Britain. Finally, neither Algeria nor Mexico has a history of British imperialism (but rather French and Spanish), so the exoticism is less fettered by political complications.

"The Woman Who Rode Away" presents many of the themes that are explored in *The Plumed Serpent*, but in a different tone. The unnamed American female protagonist lives in Mexico with her children and her husband, who "admired his wife to extinction. . . . Like any sheikh, he kept her guarded." Her husband is only a sheikh in his possessiveness; he has been unable to master her in the ways that matter to Lawrence.

At thirty-three she really was still the girl from Berkeley, in all but physique. Her conscious development had stopped mysteriously with her marriage, completely arrested. Her husband had never become real to her, neither mentally nor physically. In spite of his late sort of passion for her, he never meant anything to her, physically. Only morally he swayed her, downed her, kept her in an invincible slavery.[44]

Like Diana Mayo, she is not yet a "real" woman; the ritual that was supposed to launch her into womanhood, marriage, has been ineffective except as a spiritual suppressant. She hears about a local tribe of Indians who are the "descendants of Montezuma and the old Aztec or Totonac kings" (550), and the next time her husband is traveling, she ventures out by horseback into the hills alone, where a group of "dark-faced," "strongly-built" Indian men surround her. In a less dramatic version of Hull's kidnapping scene, one of the men seizes the reins of the woman's horse and they lead her to their village, where they drug her and keep her captive. This is no sexual utopia; there is "nothing sensual or sexual" (560) in the way the men regard the woman. One man is assigned as her guard. They are alone together constantly, but to the woman,

> He seemed to have no sex, as he sat there so still and gentle and apparently submissive with his head bent a little forward, and the river of glistening black hair streaming maidenly over his shoulders.
>
> Yet when she looked again, she saw his shoulders broad and powerful, his eyebrows black and level, the short, curved, obstinate black lashes over his lowered eyes, the small, fur-like line of moustache above his blackish, heavy lips, and the strong chin, and she knew that in some other mysterious way he was darkly and powerfully male. (567)

The fault, Lawrence implies, is hers: she is so sexless that she is unable to recognize the allure of her "darkly and powerfully male" captor. Even Diana Mayo at her most resistant is aware of "the Sheik's vivid masculinity." In Lawrence's story, instead of treating the woman like a sexual being, the men subject her to earnest lectures about how the white man has stolen the Aztec sun and moon, and how only the sacrifice of a white woman will return the cosmos to its proper order. As a result of her immersion into the rhythms and cycles of nature, the woman

> seemed at last to feel her own death; her own obliteration. As if she were to be obliterated from the field of life again. . . . Her kind of womanhood, intensely personal and individual, was to be obliterated again, and the great primeval symbols were to tower once more over the fallen individual independence of woman. The sharpness and the quivering nervous consciousness of the highly-bred white woman was to be destroyed again, womanhood was to be cast once more into the great stream of impersonal sex and impersonal passion. (569)

To be cast into "impersonal sex" and "impersonal passion" is not to be made sexually passionate, but rather to find one's symbolic place in the cosmos. Diana Mayo's being "made to feel acutely that she was a woman, forced to submit to everything to which her womanhood exposed her" is the prelude to ardor. Lawrence's modern woman, by contrast, is obliterated and acquiesces to the ancient order. In the final scene of the story, the woman is taken into an ice cave, fumigated, stripped naked, and laid on a table, and the story ends with the men gathered around her, watching the sun's rays creeping into the cave and waiting for a priest to plunge a knife into her. The scene could have been a ceremonial orgy, as the woman is surrounded by naked men "in the prime of life"; instead, it becomes a deathly punctuation, a numbness. It is the anti-*Sheik*, in which the woman is not metaphorically destroyed, as Diana is by Ahmed in order to be reborn, but is poised to be literally killed. Unlike *The Sheik*, which highlights Diana's every physical sensation, Lawrence's woman, drugged and disoriented, feels almost nothing. There is a tension throughout the story between its erotic potential and the frigid effect (matching the chill in the ice cave) of the men's and the narrator's solemn, stilted sermons. This is no *Story of O* or *Philosophy in the Bedroom*, where lectures give the characters and readers time to rest up for the next sexual escapade, but rather a droning soundtrack that attempts to diminish the story's titillating elements and a prurient response from the reader. Lawrence takes up Hull's thrilling fantasy of escape and submission but tries to prevent his reader from having the same kind of erotic pleasure by literally lowering the temperature and shifting to a story of negation in the service of a lesson on "great primeval" culture.

Lawrence gives more attention to the erotic content of Hull's novel in *The Plumed Serpent*, the third of his so-called leadership novels, where antidemocratic politics are combined with male domination. The first two leadership novels (*Aaron's Rod* and *Kangaroo*) feature a British male protagonist who is disillusioned with postwar democracy and searches for a political "master" abroad, but can never bring himself to fully submit.[45] In *The Plumed Serpent*, the submission of Kate Leslie, a middle-aged woman, is achieved through a heavy narrative reliance on *The Sheik*. In Mexico City, Kate hears about a growing underground movement calling for the return of the gods of antiquity, the Aztecs' plumed serpent Quetzalcoatl, the god of culture, and Tlaloc, the god of fertility. When she meets the powerfully charismatic general Cipriano, who, with Don Ramon, is leading the Quetzalcoatl movement, Kate has a strongly imaginative response: "There was something undeveloped and intense in him, the intensity and the crudity of the semi-savage. . . . Something smooth, undeveloped, yet vital in this man suggested the heavy-ebbing blood of reptiles in his veins" (67). This is the first of many reptilian metaphors that prove aphrodisiac to Kate. When she contemplates returning to America, the thought of Cipriano's body slithering around hers makes her hesitate: "She felt like a bird round whose body a snake has coiled itself. Mexico was the snake" (72). The discourse of colonialism and imperial conquest are reversed in this embrace: the "conquering" race finds itself squeezed by the potent "semi-savages" of Mexico—and is aroused. Throughout the novel, Lawrence's idioms of eroticism—the virile and animalistic Quetzalcoatl men, the conflict between Kate's "modern" ideas and the allure of gender regression—strongly resemble Hull's. At one point, for example, Diana imagines the sheik's arms around her as "the coils of a great serpent closing round its victim" (96). Even in the transposition of the setting to Mexico, Hull's desert romance tropes creep in. Kate thinks of the Quetzalcoatl women as "harem type[s]" with "harem tricks" (397). Western influences have not diminished Cipriano's primitive virility: his Oxford education "lay like a film of white oil on the black lake of his barbarian consciousness" (82). Similarly, Hull's

Ahmed manages to keep his nails pared and his robes spotless, but these Western conventions do not ruin his primitive appeal. As Hull's Diana is able to dominate British and American men but meets her match with Ahmed, so the Quetzalcoatl men display a kind of masculinity Kate has never seen before. Lawrence's attention to the men's bodies, like Hull's to Ahmed's firm limbs and his revolver "thrust" in his waistband, leaves no doubt about where the source of their power is: "He had a secret, important to himself, on which he was sitting tight"; "on his thighs the thin linen seemed to reveal him almost more than his own dark nakedness revealed him. She understood why the cotton pantaloons were forbidden on the plaza. The living flesh seemed to emanate through them" (81; 183–184).

As with Hull's tale, Kate must undergo a stripping away of her values, an unknowing, in order to discover what is important.

> "Ah!" she said to herself. "Let me close my eyes to him, and open only my soul. Let me close my prying, seeing eyes, and sit in dark stillness along with these two men. They have got more than I, they have a richness that I haven't got. They have got rid of that itching of the eye, and the desire that works through the eye. The itching, prurient, knowing, imagining eye, I am cursed with it, I am hampered up in it. It is my curse of curses, the curse of Eve. The curse of Eve is upon me, my eyes are like hooks, my knowledge is like a fish-hook through my gills, pulling me in spasmodic desire. Oh, who will free me from the grappling of my eyes, from the impurity of sharp sight! Daughter of Eve, of greedy vision, why don't these men save me from the sharpness of my own eyes!" (184)

Kate's "itching, prurient, knowing" eye and her "spasmodic desire" evoke original sin, for which she blames Eve's lustful, restless vision. In an odd adaptation of Genesis, Kate asserts that the Quetzalcoatl men have managed to shed the curse of questing for knowledge as well as the tyranny of the sense of sight. Released from "spasmodic desire" and shame, content to be in a pre-edenic darkness, they have attained a more primal kind of knowledge that leads into political primitivism. Antidemocratic and anti-Marxist, the Quetzalcoatl movement wants to reinstate the Aztec religion and racial and gender hierarchy.

Ramón declares himself "the First Man of Quetzalcoatl," and Cipriano is named the "First Man of Huizilopochtli" (261), the god of war and sacrifice. When Cipriano asks Kate to marry him and become "First Woman of Itzpapoltl," she initially resists, wondering "how could she marry Cipriano, and give her body to this death?" (248). But

> she felt herself submitting, succumbing. He was once more the old dominant male [and] she was swooned prone beneath, perfect in her proneness.
> It was the ancient phallic mystery. . . . Ah! and what a mystery of prone submission, on her part, this huge erection would imply! . . . Ah! what a marriage! How terrible! and how complete! . . . She could conceive now her marriage with Cipriano; the supreme passivity, like the earth below the twilight, consummate in living lifelessness, the sheer solid mystery of passivity. (311)

Lawrence echoes Hull's panting, swooning language glorifying erotic surrender. As with Hull, acquiescence comes with an acceptance of unknowing; however, there is an important difference between Kate's "prone submission" and Diana's. At the beginning of *The Plumed Serpent*, Kate's libidinal drive is a crucial part of her attraction to the Quetzalcoatl men, and this is where the desert romance formula is most powerful for Lawrence. However, by the end of the novel, with Kate's marriage to Cipriano, this changes. One of many conditions Cipriano imposes upon her is that they must maintain emotional and sexual distance, and this includes control of her orgasm.

> He made her aware of her own desire for frictional, irritant sensation . . . and the spasms of frictional voluptuousness.
> Cipriano . . . refus[ed] to share any of this with her. . . . When, in their love, it came back on her, the seething electric female ecstasy, which knows such spasms of delirium, he recoiled from her. . . . And succeeding the first moment of disappointment, when this sort of "satisfaction" was denied her, came the knowledge that she did not really want it, that it was really nauseous to her. (421)

Critics have generally understood this passage as Cipriano demanding that Kate give up clitoral "spasms of frictional voluptuousness" for more "potent" (and presumably, less labor-intensive for Cipriano) vaginal orgasms. This request that she adjust her orgasm to suit him— to renounce her "seething electric female ecstasy"—is a stark example of Lawrence's disciplinary approach to pleasure. Banning "frictional, irritant sensation" and "voluptuousness," he demands distance and self-conscious unconsciousness (no easy feat) in its place. Lawrence never loses sight of the somatic, but he expands the physical description to include more abstract spiritual and moral rhetoric. More than that, though, the language here signals a quashing of conventional pleasure not just in Kate but also in the reader. Words like "disappointment" and "nauseous" are incongruous in what could be erotic scenes, particularly in a narrative that echoes the arousing tropes of desert romance and pornography. While such counterintuitive language might, in the hands of Joyce, serve a perversely libidinous function, Lawrence qualifies "ecstasy" and "spasms" as frantic and unsatisfying ("seething," "delirium"), and the passage seeks to diminish rather than cultivate aphrodisiac effects.

A central difference between Hull and Lawrence is illustrated by a comparison of the "knowledge" Kate gains (that certain forms of sexual "satisfaction" are "really nauseous to her") and Diana Mayo's erotic enlightenment. As euphemistic as Hull's narrative is, there is no question that Diana's captivity is an erotic experience, whereas, as Marianna Torgovnick argues of *The Plumed Serpent*, "Kate's attraction to Mexican men is clearly sexual, but—she insists and Lawrence insists—sex is not the point, is not more than a metaphor, a means to an end, an expression of larger, cosmic unities."[46] Sex is not exactly *not* the point; rather, what is at stake in this scene is the modification of sexual pleasure. Kate's conclusion emphasizes this "sex suppression": "Without Cipriano to touch me and limit me and submerge my will, I shall become a horrible, elderly female. I ought to *want* to be limited" (439). Falling into line with the primal order of Queztalcoatl means relinquishing her instinctual pleasures, which Lawrence codes as modern and false, and adopting prescribed ecstasies that are ostensibly more rewarding. In these scenes and others where his didacticism comes to the fore, Lawrence exerts the same attempted modification of pleasure over his reader that he does over his heroine.

Hull strives to isolate the fantasy of *The Sheik* from the "here and now" (as the hasty race change and marriage indicate), while Lawrence seeks to deploy fantasy toward an antierotic end. He adapts Hull's narrative of female eroticism to achieve an embrace of Queztalcoatl authoritarianism and a concomitant "limiting" of women's—and his reader's—pleasure. Several central features of *The Plumed Serpent*—female submission, gender primitivism, orgasmic discipline, and readerly discipline—return in *Lady Chatterley's Lover*, Lawrence's most explicit treatment of sexuality, in which pleasure is even more tightly controlled.

LADY CHATTERLEY: THE WOMAN WHO RODE BACK HOME

After several novels in which he searched for spiritual rejuvenation abroad, Lawrence turned back to England. In *Lady Chatterley's Lover*, he relocates the struggle to the heartland. In this novel, more than any other, Lawrence challenges his modern characters and, by extension, his readers to adopt the right kind of pleasure and, specifically, the right kind of orgasm. Mellors's hut, deep in the primeval forest, is the nerve center of this operation. Pornotopia is recast as a locale of spiritual resurrection effected through belabored pleasure and orgasmic discipline.

Although Lawrence cautioned against tendentious fiction, memorably remarking that "If you try to nail anything down, in the novel, either it kills the novel, or the novel gets up and walks away with the nail,"[47] his own work, particularly near the end of his life, could be jarringly didactic. Lawrence's interest in education and pedagogy, expressed both in his nonfiction and in pivotal scenes in his fiction, is also reflected in his rhetoric of sexuality. For many readers, it is this element of didacticism that is *Lady Chatterley's Lover*'s flaw, rather than its language or subject matter. F. R. Leavis, for example, pronounced that Lawrence was "too possessed by his passionate didactic purposes" in his final major novel to achieve artistic greatness.[48] The three separate versions of the novel that Lawrence produced indicate that this was a deliberate effect. Michael Squires, Ian Gregor, John Worthen, and other critics concur that *Lady Chatterley's Lover* became more didactic and polemical as Lawrence revised it. "The final version," Worthen notes, "is crisper, utterly unsympathetic, more economical, more useful to the novel's polemic. For the final *Chatterley* is a crusading novel."[49]

Lawrence set himself a number of narrative challenges in *Lady Chatterley's Lover*. He wanted to unite the body and the mind, but only in a very particular, "unconscious" way. He wanted to bring men and women together in a balancing act of union and separateness. He wanted to depict sexuality as it had never been done before, but he did not want his writing to have a pornographic effect on his audience. His high-minded purpose must always be evident, even though he claimed to be trying to wrest people out of their too conscious approach to sex. Lawrence left himself almost no margin for error. He wanted to use words like "fuck" and "cunt" in a way that was "clean" rather than obscene. He wanted his readers to understand and feel the quality of Connie's pleasure, but their sexual investment could not be dirty, secretive, or masturbatory. Lawrence wanted a strong, invested engagement from his audience, but not the close readerly alliance between Hull and her audience. The sex scenes in *Lady Chatterley's Lover*, then, steer a narrow pathway between arousal and restriction, intimacy and distance, pleasure and its extinction. Significantly, just when Lawrence was, in his own estimation, most ambitious and daring in reinventing the lexicon of sexual representation, he produced writing that feels both most like Hull's and most determinedly opposed to it.

In "A Propos of Lady Chatterley's Lover," Lawrence again blames modern technologies of pleasure for the "counterfeit" and "false" feelings people have about love and sex. "The radio and the film are mere counterfeit emotion all the time, the current press and literature the same. People wallow in emotion: counterfeit emotion. They lap it up" (312). As much as Lawrence wanted to set *Lady Chatterley's Lover* against the tropes of popular pleasure, Connie's sexual awakening and key scenes of eroticism in the novel strongly echo Hull's. Connie and Mellors both evoke, without exactly conforming to, the character types of desert romances. She is an unfulfilled, unrealized postwar woman married to a man who has been wrecked by the war. Mellors is a sort of sheik figure, a self-defined outsider whose identity is mysterious and contradictory. His first appearance in *Lady Chatterley's Lover* unsettles Connie in a way that is similar to Ahmed's debut in *The Sheik*. "A man with a gun strode swiftly, softly out after the dog, facing their way, as if about to attack them. . . . He seemed to emerge with such a swift menace. That is how she had seen him, like a sudden rush of a threat out of nowhere" (46). Lawrence qualifies this image: Mellors hardly sweeps Connie off her feet; he has softness and is "rather frail, really" (47). However, Connie consistently perceives him as "aloof, apart" and different from the modern men who surround her (except for Tommy Dukes, Lawrence's surrogate in the novel, with whom Mellors shares a tendency to preach), and he never loses this liminal quality. Like Ahmed's combination of "Western" and "Eastern" traits, Mellors's aristocratic dignity and working-class earthiness allow him to be both familiar and foreign. "He had a natural distinction, but he had not the cut-to-pattern look of her class. . . . He had a native breeding" (274). His oscillation in and out of dialect is one sign of Mellors's protean social identity; his brash pronouncements ("What is cunt but machine-fucking!" [217]) and often charmless approach ("'Lie down!' he said. 'Lie down! Let me come!' He was in a hurry now" [210]) keep the reader from seeing him as a conventional romantic figure. Most importantly, he holds himself apart from Connie. When they meet, Mellors "stared into Connie's eyes with a perfectly fearless, impersonal look, as if he wanted to see what she was like. He made her feel shy" (46). Lawrence describes Mellors's gaze as "impersonal" several times: he appraises Connie with "a curious, cool wonder: impersonally wanting to see what she looked like. And she saw in his blue, impersonal eyes a look of suffering and detachment, yet a certain warmth" (47). This is an indication of Mellors's style of lovemaking and the language Lawrence will use to describe it: attenuated, rhythmic, and insistent, but also withholding and distant, putting space between itself and the reader.

Sex, for Lawrence, needs to be handled in a similarly defamiliarizing way. Throughout *Lady Chatterley's Lover*, Lawrence treats sexual pleasure as analogous to textuality. When they are young, Connie and her sister glibly regard "the sex thing" as an experience that "marked the end of a chapter. It had a thrill of its own too: a queer vibrating thrill inside the body, a final spasm of self-assertion, like the last word, exciting, and very like the row of asterisks that can be put to show the end of a paragraph, and a break in the theme" (8). This is the way readers consume pornography, according to Lawrence: they obtain a quick fix instead of having an expansive, profound experience. They are one with the text, in a masturbatory sense, and then they move on. Unlike a text such as Hull's, in which the prose is a transparent medium for exciting content, Lawrence's novel continually draws the reader's attention to its language through conspicuous repetition, authorial intrusions, and other techniques that impose distance between the acts on the page and the reader's body. Lawrence wants his reader to pay attention to textuality itself rather than indulge in mimetic pleasure.

In "Apropos of Lady Chatterley's Lover," Lawrence casts postwar sexuality as a predicament of repetition. "The act tends to be mechanical, dull," he asserts, a "wearying repetition over and over, without a corresponding thought, a corresponding realisation. Now our business is to realise sex" (308). This enervating iteration structurally resembles Lawrence's own writing, with its "continual, slightly modified repetition." Although Lawrence uses the language of orgasm to describe his own style—"this pulsing, frictional, to-and-fro, which works up to culmination"[50]—he specifies that this rhythm, like bodies moving against each other, is desirable only because its "culmination" or "crisis" is characterized by illumination or "understanding." To be meaningful, it must be accompanied by "realization." Lawrence tries to effect this through didactic explanation, an imposed rhetorical disparity between the acts described and the narrator's exposition of their significance.

The sexual interludes in *Lady Chatterley's Lover* model different kinds of erotic and readerly response. Early on in the novel, sex is regarded by the characters as "a cocktail—they both lasted about as long, had the same effect, and amounted to about the same thing" (64). Clifford is mechanical in his attitude, hoping that he and Connie can "arrange this sex thing as we arrange going to the dentist" (44). Lawrence describes Connie's sex with the writer Michaelis in an explicit but perfunctory way, as a "thrill" that is over the moment the scene ends. (The case of Michaelis demonstrates it is not just women's orgasm that concerns Lawrence.) Disappointed because Michaelis comes too quickly, Connie figures out how to keep him inside her afterward, "while she was active, wildly, passionately active, coming to her own crisis" (29). Lawrence signals to the reader that this too is false pleasure: selfish, deliberate, and isolated. "She still wanted the physical, sexual thrill she could get with him, by her own activity, his little orgasm being over. . . . It was an almost mechanical confidence in her own prowess" (29–30). Notably, Lawrence does not describe the orgasm, but only reports that it is achieved, like a task checked off a list. There is no "realization" or insight.

Connie's orgasm with Michaelis approaches, but is not nearly as dreadful as, Bertha Coutts's diabolical desire and her beakish, castrating anatomy that Mellors describes later in the novel. His lengthy, angry tirade emphasizes that it was Bertha's orgasmic etiquette that tore them apart: "She'd try to lie still and let *me* work the business. She'd try. But it was no good. She got no feeling off it, from my working. She had to work the thing herself, grind her own coffee" (202). Such mechanical pleasure, for Lawrence, is one of the great ills of modernity. Strikingly and repeatedly in *Lady Chatterley's Lover*, Lawrence focuses on orgasm itself as the locus of spiritual and sexual dysfunction. Just as Cipriano demands that Kate alter her means of attaining ecstasy, the sex scenes in *Lady Chatterley's Lover* present Connie and the reader with a sequence of orgasmic instruction.

The first two times Mellors and Connie have sex, it is unremarkable. Like the woman who rode away, Connie is passive, "in a sort of sleep, in a sort of dream"; Mellors enters her and "She lay still, in a kind of sleep, always in a kind of sleep. The activity, the orgasm was his, all his" (116). Connie does not struggle to achieve her own orgasm, but she is not open to Mellors either, so she is unsatisfied. After he comes, she lies beside the "panting" man debating her predicament: "Her tormented modern woman's brain still had no rest. Was it real?—And she knew, if she gave herself to the man, it was real. But if she kept herself for herself, it was nothing" (117). The next time she is with Mellors, she is drawn out of this "sex in the head." "Her will had left her. A strange weight was on her limbs. She was giving way. She was giving up" (133). This surrender results in their simultaneous orgasms ("Then as he began to move in the sudden helpless orgasm, there awoke in her new strange thrills rippling inside her, rippling, rippling, like a flapping overlapping of soft flames" [133]) and Connie's palpitating release:

All her womb was open and soft and softly clamouring like a sea-anemone under the tides, clamouring for him to come in again and make a fulfilment for her. She clung to him unconscious in passion, and he never quite slipped from her. And she felt the soft bud of him within her stirring and in strange rhythms flushing up into her, with a strange, rhythmic growing motion, swelling and swelling till it filled all her cleaving consciousness. And then began again the unspeakable motion that was not really motion, but pure deepening whirlpools of sensation, swirling deeper and deeper through all her tissue and consciousness, till she was one perfect concentric fluid of feeling. And she lay there crying in unconscious, inarticulate cries. (133–134)

The repetition of "rippling," "clamouring," and "rhythm" evokes erotic movement, but Lawrence uses deliberately nebulous terms: "unspeakable" and "strange" sensations, and a "motion that was not really motion." Unlike the directly mimetic language of pornography that specifies particular body parts and actions, here pleasure is not localized or characterized as a "crisis" but is rather a slower, organic "swelling and swelling" that gradually envelops the whole body and works its way into the "tissues." This extended, lyrical scene of the rippling, swirling whirlpool could be the pinnacle of Connie's pleasure; afterward, Mellors remarks, "We came-off together that time. . . . It's good when it's like that. Most folks live their lives through and they never know it" (134). However, this kind of mutual pleasure cannot be the final word. Like the love relationships in Lawrence's other novels, this must not be too harmonious. There must be tension and apartness in a dynamic relationship, a splendid separateness between characters and also between the author and the reader. A fall into utopian pleasure or a masturbating reader is what Lawrence must preclude in his prescription for spiritual resurrection.

The next time Connie and Mellors are together, they begin with a domestic scene in his house, with Mellors taking tea and speaking mostly in the King's English, rather than in the dialect of passion. Things change when they move to the hut, where Mellors bellows at Connie, "Lie down then!" Despite their recent intimacies, she is inexplicably "afraid, afraid of his thin, smooth naked body, that seemed so powerful, afraid of the violent muscles. She shrank, afraid" (171). The menace and strangeness that Mellors first posed return, preventing the relationship from becoming too tame, tranquil, or pleasurable. Connie herself has a sort of out-of-body experience: "Cold and derisive her queer female mind stood apart," observing Mellors's "farcical" buttocks and "the wilting of the poor, insignificant, moist little penis" (172). Like the passages of "sex in the head," this jeering also sets the reader apart from the act, seeing it from a critical distance. This undoes the swirling perfection of the previous sex scene, as does the next turn of events. Lawrence takes the reader by surprise when Mellors suddenly approaches Connie from the rear. This act introduces "wonder that was also awe, terror" (175), a new kind of opposition, defamiliarization, strain, and tension that brings about the metaphorical dissolution and rebirth of Connie: "She was gone, she was not, and she was born: a woman" (174). Like Hull, Lawrence constructs a sense of transformation through negation and release: Diana "had become a woman through bitter knowledge and humiliating experience" (102). However, while Hull's scene of womanliness is followed by an expansion of sexual possibility, Lawrence's moves toward limitation.

In the first of two anal sex scenes, Lawrence describes Mellors's "potent inexorable entry inside her, so strange and terrible" (173) through another oceanic metaphor: "Oh, and far down inside her the deeps parted and rolled asunder, in long, far-travelling billows, and ever, at the quick of her, the depths parted and rolled asunder, from the centre of soft plunging, as the plunger went deeper and deeper, touching lower, and she was deeper and deeper and deeper disclosed" (174). Unlike Connie's vaginal orgasm, which spreads like diffuse ripples, this sensation drives in one direction, like a depth sounder. In the second scene, the "night of sensual passion," which is arguably the climax of the novel's sexual narrative, this rhetorical thrust is even more pronounced. Following the awkward confrontation between Mellors and Connie's sister, Mellors's anger leaves Connie "a little startled, and almost unwilling . . . a little frightened." The ensuing sex, "different, sharper, more terrible than the thrills of tenderness" (246), is described as one of obstacles and a power struggle on a different level than the couple's previous encounters. Connie's orgasmic pleasure is only very briefly described, as "piercing thrills of sensuality" (246), at the beginning rather than the conclusion of the scene. This placement indicates Lawrence's focus on the process of penetration and on instructing the reader how to interpret the act rather than depicting its pleasures. He describes the physical encounter as a feat of colonial exploration, with Mellors's penis pressing toward Connie's heart of darkness:

> And what a reckless devil the man was! really like a devil! One had to be strong to bear him. But it took some getting at, the core of the physical jungle, the last and deepest recess of organic shame. The phallos alone could explore it. And how he had pressed in on her! And how, in fear, she had hated it! But how she had really wanted it! (247)

The body's resistance is matched by a psychological resistance: "It cost her an effort to let him have his way and his will of her" (247). The language of eroticized resistance and conquest here is highly evocative of Hull's: "she was made to feel acutely that she was a woman, forced to submit to everything to which her womanhood exposed her, forced to endure everything that he might put upon her—a chattel, a slave to do his bidding, to bear his pleasure and his displeasure" (*The Sheik*, 77–78). In the anal sex scenes, far more than in the earlier scenes of vaginal penetration, Lawrence's language resembles Hull's. Here is a climactic scene from *The Sheik*, along with phrases from the second anal penetration scene in *Chatterley* in italics:

> For the first time she had pitted her will against a will that was stronger than her own, for the first time she had met an arrogance that was greater and a determination that was firmer than hers. For the first time she had met a man who had failed to bow to her wishes [*Lawrence: To find a man who dared to do it, without shame or sin or final misgiving! . . . What a pity that fine, sensual men are so rare! . . . Ah God, how rare a thing a man is!*], whom a look had been powerless to transform into a willing slave. [*Lawrence: She had to be a passive, consenting thing, like a slave, a physical slave.*] In the few hours that had elapsed she had learned fear, a terrible fear that left her sick with apprehension, and she was learning obedience. [*Lawrence: In this short summer night she learnt so much.*] Obedient now, she forced herself to lift her eyes to his, and the shamed blood surged slowly into her cheeks. [*Lawrence: It took some getting at . . . the last and deepest recess of organic shame.*] (*The Sheik*, 67; *Lady Chatterley*, 247–248)

Lawrence turns to Hull to describe a woman "forced" into sexual knowledge and to inscribe tension and struggle within eroticism. However, as with *The Plumed Serpent* and "The Woman Who Rode Away," Lawrence is striving to produce a different effect than *The Sheik*. Hull's text is arranged to make her reader swoon with arousal. Diana's shame is caused by her realization that she is sexually responsive to Ahmed and that she is helpless to fight against him. Shame, hot and burning, is an indicator of sexual stimulation for Hull; her reader knows this, even when Diana does not. As Diana blushes, the sheik's "dark, passionate eyes burnt into her like a hot flame. His encircling arms were like bands of fire, scorching her. . . . Fascinated she could not turn [her eyes] away." The language of conflagration and passion, fascination, and pure somatic voluptuousness is aimed at stoking the fires of Hull's reader. It is otherwise with Lawrence.

In *Lady Chatterley's Lover*, the first episode of anal sex, with its extended metaphor of plumbing the depths of Connie's ocean, is described as a "primordial tenderness" that culminates in her "soft, shuddering convulsion" (174). In the second episode, there is very little affect; instead, the purpose of the scene is given in a pronouncedly didactic tone. The "phallic hunt" serves to "burn out false shames and smelt out the heaviest ore of the body into purity. . . . Instead of shame, shame died." Here, Lawrence's explanation of the function of shame rhetorically overshadows the sensation of pleasure. Lawrence does not want readers to lose themselves in sensation but rather to contemplate the symbolic purpose and psychological implications of the act.

Critics have debated what Lawrence meant to achieve with his representation of anal intercourse. Pease points out that "In pornography, anal penetration is typically troped as a final frontier, the ultimate achievement in carnal sensation" (160), so it would make sense that Lawrence, who draws on pornographic imagery even as he tries to prevent a pornographic effect, follows the scene of mutual orgasm with the "phallic hunt." Jeffrey Meyers has addressed these scenes of anal eroticism, along with the one in *Women in Love*, in terms of Lawrence's ambivalence about homoeroticism and his intimation that love between men is a privileged relation beyond heterosexuality.[51] Other critics have looked at these scenes as metaphorical strategies of dissolution and initiation (Clarke) or as Lawrence's exploration of developmental, psychological impulses (Spilka). Kermode downplays what he calls "the use of buggery for high symbolic purposes," arguing that the really significant sex in *Lady Chatterley's Lover* happens in the vaginal sex scenes. As for anal exploration, Kermode asserts, there is "No need ever to do it again; [Connie and Mellors] can perhaps go back to 'tenderness.'"[52] To the contrary, the second anal penetration scene is the novel's sexual finale. After it, a pregnant Connie and Mellors are together one more time in a London hotel and the sex is unremarkable.

From the "night of sensual passion" forward, Lawrence has nothing more to prove about sexual pleasure.

Why, when the swirling mutual orgasm scene seems to fulfill Lawrence's requirement for balance, does Connie's anal impalement serve as the novel's sexual punctuation? What does the penultimate scene establish that allows Lawrence to put sex to rest, as it were? For pleasure to be meaningful, to Lawrence, it must be momentous, the opposite of a cocktail or a Hullian cliché. In *Lady Chatterley's Lover*, he argues that the postwar task, to "build up new little habitats, to have new little hopes," "is rather hard work: there is now no smooth road into the future: but we go round, or scramble over the obstacles" (5). The "hard work" of anal sex, for Lawrence, offers spiritual insight that the "smooth road" of vaginal sex does not. For Lawrence and his characters, arduous sexuality is a limit experience that offers a "really new feeling." It carries transgressive connotations that vaginal sex, in or outside of marriage, does not. Hull thoroughly covers the convergence of sex and shame; Lawrence needs to move beyond it. Anality brings with it taboo and liberation, connotations of death and disgrace, that press Connie to the limits of her mind and her body. It also presses the limits of the alliance between the author and his reader.

More than the other sex scenes, the last episode of anal penetration reflects the didactic, prophetic general tone of *Lady Chatterley's Lover*, from its opening sentence—"Ours is essentially a tragic age, so we refuse to take it tragically"—to Mellors's pessimistic letter that concludes the novel. Lawrence's authorial intrusions are particularly jarring and foreground the mediated nature of reading. (This is also the case in Mellors's letter, which is ostensibly directed at Connie but includes disconcerting directives and observations: "I'm sure you're sick of all this," he acknowledges at one point [300].) In the discussion of shame, passion, men, and women, the penultimate sex scene emphatically sidelines pleasure to focus on moral, social, and spiritual lessons. "In this short summer night [Connie] learnt so much." Connie proves an adept pupil. Directly after the second anal sex scene, she lectures her sister about "real sensuality" (253), and she goes to Europe with Hilda and exclaims, in a voice that sounds very much like Lawrence's, about shallow pleasure-seekers on the Lido ("Enjoyment! Another form of sickness"). Emerging from the night of "phallic hunting out," she is able to make the finer distinctions about pleasure (sexual and otherwise) that Lawrence wants his reader to learn.

We can only understand the nature of pleasure, Lawrence suggests, through a deliberate, arduous encounter. Sexual pleasure and readerly pleasure entail a similar kind of attention, focus, and commitment. Lawrence wants his readers to have this complex textual experience, but he does not trust them to extract the lessons without his explicit authorial guidance. While Hull assumes an alliance of sensation and knowledge with her readers, Lawrence assumes resistance and opposition. This is true of most of his later works, which are full of direct addresses to a reluctant reader, and particularly so in *Lady Chatterley*'s sexual finale. Charles Barack argues that "readers may feel either Connie or the narrator is trying to force a favorable interpretation on her experience. The language repels rather than attracts the reader."[53] Lawrence wants to both repel and attract. He anticipates opposition and resistance from the reader and, if it doesn't occur naturally, he produces it. He wants his audience to be active and to react spontaneously and strongly. So even though Lawrence enlists many of the familiar formulas of popular romance, he throws obstacles in his reader's way, whether the "friction" of repetition or disconcerting narrative details. Mellors cannot be too seductive as a leading man, and his sex with Connie cannot be so compelling that the reader merges with the scenes in masturbatory bliss. Above all, Lawrence's language cannot be transparent or too easy. In Leavis's words, the reader must "brace himself to bear the impact of a serious novel" (257). Anal sex, for Lawrence, is a paradigm for his work as a novelist: to get to the bedrock of sex and language, to give the reader a new feeling, and to revitalize sexual and literary experience together through difficult pleasure.

Although Lawrence's approach to sexuality is, in some ways, highly expansive and imaginative, his representation of pleasure is markedly dogmatic. The penultimate sodomy scene in *Lady Chatterley's Lover* is a textual rite of passage as constrained and narrow for the reader as it is for Connie. In some ways, Lawrence departs from the usual modernist treatment of pleasure in that his scenes of orgasmic discipline locate the problem of pleasure in the body, rather than externalizing it in popular pleasure, and he refuses the dichotomies of somatic versus cerebral pleasure that so many high modernists insist upon. However, he plays out the familiar drama of pleasure hierarchies within orgasm itself, deriding "cocktail" ecstasy and exalting arduous, difficult sexuality and textuality.

Lawrence's scenes of orgasmic discipline are a dramatic example of modernism's attempt to redefine pleasure. By borrowing from Hull and the kind of fiction she represents as a means of managing pleasure, even while disowning her method, Lawrence demonstrates how pleasure resides at the crossroads of novelty and familiarity, the shock of the new and the gratifications of the sure thing. Eroticism may necessarily converge with cliché, triteness, and banality in ways that are at odds with traditional definitions of modernism. Hull aims to arouse her readers, and what happens next is up to them. Despite his rhetoric about representational freedom and spontaneity, Lawrence carefully and conspicuously regulates readerly pleasure. That said, individual readers can and do react however they wish: *Lady Chatterley's Lover* was, of course, censored as obscene; since then, it has been regarded by many as a "sexy" book or even pornography, against Lawrence's explicit wishes. This irony makes manifest the ways readerly pleasure is subject to both calculation and contingency. Lawrence's representation of eroticism is one of the most striking examples of modernism's faith in its ability to mold and manipulate pleasure. However, as with the competing appeal of cliché and innovation, Lawrence's writing also demonstrates how textual pleasure can—and must—have a life of its own, of unforeseen energies, between the reader and the page.

◙ ◙ ◙

From the page, we now move to the screen—or rather, the screen rendered on the page. Just as Lawrence was concerned with forging a kind of writing that could compete with "the throb of *The Sheik*," Aldous Huxley was preoccupied with the insidious effects of popular novels and "new pleasures" such as the cinema. Both authors sought to engage the problem of pleasure through exposing the shortcomings of easy, somatic amusement and agitating for more thoughtful, exacting activities. Like Lawrence, Huxley incorporated threatening pleasures into his own writing, and in both cases, these excitements are never quite contained in the ways the authors seem to have wanted.

4

HUXLEY'S FEELIES
Engineered Pleasure in *Brave New World*

"Who will recount the pleasures of dystopia?"
—Fredric Jameson[1]

"I have just been, for the first time, to see and hear a talking picture," Aldous Huxley writes in a 1929 essay called "Silence Is Golden." "A little late in the day," he imagines his "up-to-date" readers remarking, "with a patronizing and contemptuous smile."[2] After all, the film that introduced Huxley to the world of sound cinema, *The Jazz Singer*, had been released two years earlier. The "gigantically enlarged" (21) images on the screen spouting noise send Huxley into paroxysms of scorn and fury. He is especially horrified by the scene in which Al Jolson sings "Mammy" in blackface: "My flesh crept as the loud speaker poured out those sodden words, the greasy, sagging melody. I felt ashamed of myself for listening to such things, for even being a member of the species to which such things are addressed" (23). While only half feigning his reactionary pose, Huxley condemns the talkies as "the latest and most frightful creation-saving device for the production of standardized amusement" (20), presenting one of the most popular vehicles of pleasure as a nightmare of emotional degradation and appalling physical effects.

Huxley's cranky response to *The Jazz Singer*, a film that stood as both a technological landmark and a massive box-office success, is a window onto a key moment in the history of cinema when articles such as "Silence Is Golden," "Why 'Talkies' Are Unsound," "Ordeal by 'Talkie,'" and "The Movies Commit Suicide" contended with equally impassioned defenses of sound film.[3] The crisis occasioned by the coming of sound now appears as an overblown objection to a transition that in hindsight seems inevitable.[4] But just as the cinema itself was often perceived as revolutionary—George Bernard Shaw remarked in 1914, "The cinema is going to form the mind of England. . . . The cinema is a much more momentous invention than the printing press"[5]— the coming of sound was greeted by many as a watershed moment. Beyond the changes in the industry (technological developments and the retirement of actors who had disagreeable voices, for example), the talkies raised more philosophical questions about the social, moral, and even physical implications of moving and talking images, and how those images were influencing the general public's appetite and capacity for pleasure. In particular, Huxley was interested in the didactic potential of film. Always fascinated by educational systems, whether examining the training of infants, mass pedagogy, the Dalton Plan, or liberal education, Huxley extended this concern to cinema in his essays and fiction.

Cinema history would not be accurately represented by a chronicle of technological evolution from, say, Muybridge to the present. Such a history would miss a crucial component of the story: spectatorship. Accounts from the period such as Huxley's and Iris Barry's *Let's Go to the Pictures* emphasize not just what happens on the screen but also how the audience responds.[6] Those responses are strikingly different from how we now think of cinema spectatorship, and this is particularly true of the reception of the talkies. Contemporary critics such as Tom Gunning, Miriam Hansen, Jonathan Crary, Ben Singer, Linda Williams, and Laura Marcus, following the early lead of Walter Benjamin[7] and Siegfried Kracauer, have moved away from the psychoanalytic approach that dominated film criticism of the 1980s toward a more historical and sociological model that addresses how visual modernity in general and cinema spectatorship in particular are bodily, visceral experiences.[8] Cinema is not merely a screen for psychic identifications but is experienced by an embodied, physically affected spectator. While the myth of Lumière's train sending confused audiences screaming from the screen in 1895 has been debunked,[9] writing from the time of "Silence Is Golden" illustrates Kracauer's assertion that film was thought of as a particularly somatic medium, influencing "the spectator's senses, engaging him physiologically before he is in a position to respond intellectually."[10] Gunning's description of the earliest filmmaking as a "cinema of attractions" (121) and Singer's examination of early "blood and thunder" melodrama, among other work, suggest that modern technologies of vision were experienced as mobilizing the body and actively produced new modes of spectatorship and perception. (Recent critics, such as Susan Buck-Morss, have extended this to propose that the cinema screen is a kind of prosthetic organ that "does not merely duplicate human cognitive perception, but changes its nature."[11]) This was especially true of the transition to sound.

The cinema, particularly in its avant-garde forms, offered fresh approaches to representation; techniques such as montage and close-ups inspired many modernist writers to find literary equivalents.[12] At the same time, the reception of early film (the "youngest" art, as Virginia Woolf put it in her 1926 essay "The Cinema"[13]) is very much in keeping with that of mass culture in general: intoxication, addiction, deluded reverie, and gluttony. In a 1925 *Vanity Fair* essay called "Where Are the Movies Moving?" Huxley writes that "the darkness of the theater, the monotonous music—inducing, as they do, a kind of hypnotic state—enhance in the minds of the spectators the dream-like quality of what they see on the screen" (*Essays* 1:176).[14] Kracauer's section on "the spectator" in *Theory of Film* characterizes film spectatorship as "lowered consciousness" (189). In an article for *Close Up*, Bryher describes a stupefied film audience: "To watch hypnotically something which has become a habit and which is not recorded as it happens by the brain, differs little from the drug taker's point of view."[15] Both hypnosis and intoxication influence mind and body, suggesting that the cinema spectator is vulnerable on two fronts, but Bryher's metaphor points to the common feeling that moviegoing was a particularly embodied experience, bypassing the rational mind entirely.

The reception of film had its roots in responses to elements of mass culture such as amusement parks, radio, and other leisure technologies that appealed to the body in new ways. Film was already conceived of as a bodily experience when it was silent, but the addition of sound made the association more pronounced.[16] In 1930 Charlie Chaplin maintained: "I shall never speak in a film. I hate the talkies and will not produce talking films. The American industry is transformed. So much the better or worse, it leaves me indifferent. I cannot conceive of my films as other than silent. My shadow appears on the screen as in a dream, and dreams do not speak."[17] For Chaplin, the cinematic experience of ephemeral, mute dreaming was shattered by the talkies, which forced a new kind of embodiment on the medium. Many remarked on the physical and cognitive difficulties that the sound film presented to the audience. Virginia Woolf wrote: "The eye licks it all up instantaneously and the brain, agreeably titillated, settles down to watch things happening without beseeching itself to think. . . . Eye and brain are torn asunder ruthlessly as they try vainly to work in couples" (269). The image of the brain being roused without having to function analytically—a distinction between sensual stimulation and cerebral reasoning—is an apt figure for the modernist conception of the trouble with mass culture pleasure. This sense of dislocation between the brain and the body is supported by Barry's contemporaneous observation that "Every habitual cinema-goer must have been struck at some time or another by the comparative slowness of perception and understanding of a person not accustomed to the pictures: the newcomer always misses half of what occurs" (13). The idea of a population divided between those who had been initiated into the new physical practice of cinema spectatorship and those who had not marked a unique and brief moment in film history: a narrow bridge of time between the wars in which audiences' capacity for sensual pleasure seemed to be undergoing an expansion that was not, to many critics, for the better.[18]

Despite Huxley's pose of being defiantly out of date in "Silence Is Golden," he wrote a music and theater column in the *Weekly Westminster Gazette* that kept him current, and he published essays on a wide range of cultural topics for mass-market journals including *Vanity Fair* and *Esquire*. Even so, Huxley joined other interwar critics who conflated all forms of mass or popular culture. In a 1927 article for *Harper's*, "The Outlook for American Culture: Some Reflections in a Machine Age," he writes:

The rotary press, the process block, the cinema, the radio, the phonograph are used not, as they might so easily be used, to propagate culture, but its opposite. All the resources of science are applied in order that imbecility may flourish and vulgarity cover the whole earth.[19]

The cinema is one in a series of horrors here, but elsewhere, as in his 1923 essay, "Pleasures," Huxley singles it out as an especially pernicious "ready made," collective pleasure (*Essays*, 1:356). The scene of cinema audiences who "soak passively in the tepid bath of nonsense," challenged only to the extent that they must "sit and keep their eyes open" (356), recurs throughout Huxley's writing, such as the people "sitting at the picture palace passively accepting ready-made day-dreams from Hollywood" in *Eyeless in Gaza* (1936). Even when traveling in Malaysia, Huxley manages to find a film audience to ridicule:

> The violent imbecilities of the story flickered in silence against the background of the equatorial night. In silence the Javanese looked on. What were they thinking? What were their private comments on this exhibition of Western civilization? . . . The world into which the cinema introduces the subject peoples is a world of silliness and criminality.[20]

For Huxley, cinema is largely symptomatic of cultural degeneration that goes by the name of progress, and the introduction of sound was a particularly alarming development because of its implications for pleasure. In expanding its scope to include not just the eyes but also the ears, sound cinema exerted control over even more of the sensual body.

All of Huxley's writings on cinema from the period are arranged around the dichotomy presented in "Pleasures": new and old, physical and mental, trite and meaningful.[21] It is integral to his vision of futurity in *Brave New World*, a dystopia, or, as Huxley called it, a "negative utopia," that is paradoxically organized around pleasure.[22] London in the Year A.F. (After Ford) 632 is a culture of genetic and psychological control; individuals are decanted into a state whose motto is "Community, Identity, Stability."[23] Huxley's novel is famous for its bottled babies, color-coded classes, hypnopaedic conditioning, and the pharmacological marvel *soma*. A nightmare of a totalitarian, genetically engineered future, *Brave New World* is also a cautionary tale about a world where artifacts of high culture are held under lock and key while the populace is supplied with "imbecile" entertainment. Everyone is happy, but it is the happiness of a mechanical utilitarianism aimed to produce uniform and banal satisfaction. The denizens of Brave New World follow a prescribed routine of "standardized amusement" summarized by the Resident World Controller for Western Europe, Mustapha Mond, as "Seven and a half hours of mild, unexhausting labour, and then the *soma* ration and games and unrestricted copulation and the feelies" (224).

With the feelies, Huxley extends the innovation of synchronized sound to include all the senses. The feelies have a special status among other means of mass pleasure insofar as they are aesthetic creations: Mond describes them as "works of art out of practically nothing but pure sensation" (221). In a central scene, John the Savage, newly exported from the Malpais Reservation (a parody of Lawrence's representation of primitivism in texts such as *The Plumed Serpent*), attends a feely called *Three Weeks in a Helicopter.* Billed as "AN ALL-SUPER-SINGING, SYNTHETIC-TALKING, COLOURED, STEREOSCOPIC FEELY. WITH SYNCHRONIZED SCENT-ORGAN ACCOMPANIMENT" (167), a parody of the 1920s cinema slogan, "All-Talking, All-Singing, All-Dancing,"[24] *Three Weeks in a Helicopter* is three-dimensional and scented, with tactile sensations produced by metal knobs embedded in the viewers' chairs. The pleasure that the feely transmits provokes in the Savage a rage at its sensual indulgence that is similar to Huxley's at the cheap emotion and audio excess of *The Jazz Singer.*

Mond explains to John that in the Brave New World there is "no leisure from pleasure, not a moment to sit down and think" (55). Pleasure has become a full-time job. Here Huxley would seem to fit the old stereotype of the modernist elitist who shores up the "great divide." Accordingly, *Brave New World* has typically been read as "the classic denunciation of mass culture in the interwar years."[25] Huxley's novel belongs to what is traditionally a markedly didactic genre. Pleasure is not characteristically associated with dystopic texts, in which negation and repression are common notes. The generic ambitions of the dystopia, the attempt to depict a culture gone awry, mean that images of degradation and inequity are the norm. One of Huxley's challenges, then, is to render dystopic pleasure unattractive. His own term "negative utopia" captures this contradiction.

In his essay "Aldous Huxley and Utopia," Adorno examines the status of pleasure in this imagined totalitarian state. He argues that

Huxley is "inwardly an enemy of intoxication," who is "less concerned with the dehumanization of the industrial age than the decline of its morals."

> The regularly occurring communal orgies of the novel and the prescribed short-term change of partners are logical consequences of the jaded official sexual routine that turns pleasure to fun and denies it by granting it. But precisely in the impossibility of looking pleasure in the eye, of making use of reflection in abandoning one's whole self to pleasure, the ancient prohibition for which Huxley prematurely mourns continues in force. Were its power to be broken, were pleasure to be freed of the institutional reins which bind it even in the "orgy-porgy," Brave New World and its fatal rigidity would dissolve.[26]

"Turning pleasure to fun" and denying it "by granting it" but exposing its follies is a canny description of modernism's approach to pleasure. Reversing modernism's demand that readers learn to appreciate difficult pleasures and reject easy ones, in *Brave New World* Huxley depicts a culture in which pleasure is compulsory and engineered to eliminate intellectual challenge and to produce docile citizens. However, the culture that is meant to be repulsive is secured by a wide variety of "fun" that is often, from a readerly perspective, pointedly engaging. That is, there are moments in the novel in which the reader is brought face to face with "fun" that escapes Huxley's withering critique. This ambiguity in the representation of ostensibly debased pleasure is especially evident in the feelies. For all his griping about silent cinema's transition to sound, in *Brave New World* Huxley provides unexpected insight into a time when cinema's technological innovations were not just observed but also truly felt, producing one of the most far-ranging meditations on the uses of pleasure from the period.

"EVERY HAIR OF THE BEAR REPRODUCED"

Although the feelies are pap for the public, their institutional structure indicates their importance in *Brave New World*. (While the movies were increasingly thought of as an American product, Huxley portrays the feelies as a distinctly local industry.) The "Feeling Picture" headquarters comprise twenty-two floors of the Bureaux of Propaganda in London (66), the "buildings of the Hounslow Feely Studio" sprawl over "seven and a half hectares" (62), and at the College of Emotional Engineering "Professor of Feelies" is a title of considerable status (156). John is escorted to the feelies by Lenina Crowne, to whose attractive physique, good-natured promiscuity, and provocative clothes (hot pants, boots, and zippered lingerie) Huxley calls excited attention. Word has it that *Three Weeks in a Helicopter* is an especially good feely. In the opening pages of the novel, the Assistant Predestinator tells Henry Ford, "I hear the new [feely] at the Alhambra is first-rate. There's a love scene on a bearskin rug; they say it's marvellous. Every hair of the bear reproduced. The most amazing tactual effects" (35).

Huxley's choice of venue for *Three Weeks in a Helicopter*, the Alhambra, evokes a rich history of British popular entertainment. Built on Leicester Square in 1854 and known initially as The Royal Panopticon of Science and Art, the Alhambra's first of many subsequent incarnations was as a Victorian shrine to scientific exhibitions, a combination of intellectual curiosity and industry that would fall into Huxley's category of "real" pleasure. In 1858 it became The Alhambra Circus and then, in 1864, the Alhambra Music Hall.[27] The building was demolished in 1936 to clear room for a cinema, the Odeon, as if fulfilling Eliot's apocalyptic prophecy about the passing of music hall culture and the rise of "the cheap and rapid-breeding cinema."[28] The Alhambra, with its transformations that reflected the evolution of popular culture, is a fitting forum for the feelies.

Like *Brave New World* itself—and like most dystopias, which simultaneously reference the past, present, and future, Huxley's feelies reach both back to cinema's music hall origins and forward to the imagination of technologies such as virtual reality. *Three Weeks in a Helicopter* is preceded by a performance inspired by music hall "turns" that were a feature of early cinema presentations and had more in common with vaudeville than with today's "coming attractions." The performances preceding films in the twenties were a varied roster of short acts that included humorous skits, newsreels, cartoons, travel and nature films, and musical performances. *Three Weeks in a Helicopter* begins with an overture by the Huysmans-inspired scent organ that plays a symphony of synaesthetic effects. Max Nordau's notorious critique of Huysmans's decadent hero—"a parasite of the lowest grade of atavism"—is specifically connected to the synaesthesic effect of symbolist art, which Nordau calls

> a retrogression to the very beginning of organic development. It is a descent from the height of human perfection to the low level of the mollusc. To raise the combination, transposition and confusion of the perceptions of sound and sight to the rank of a principle of art, to see futurity in this principle, is to designate as progress the return from the consciousness of man to that of the oyster.[29]

Nordau's contention that such aesthetic developments are harbingers of cultural degeneration (following Plato in asserting that the lowest form of mindless, pleasure-driven life is that of an oyster) sounds very much like Huxley, whose most "civilized" character in *Brave New World* is "the Savage." The "confusion" of sound and sight that characterized the talkies was a sign of cultural regression for many critics. "The soul of the film—its eloquence and vital silence—is destroyed," Ernest Betts opined. "The film now returns to the circus from whence it came, among the freaks and the fat ladies."[30]

Beyond the complaints about poorly executed sound films, there was a more far-reaching philosophical and aesthetic argument against the talkies: the contention that each art should stay within and develop according to its own limits, and that images rather than sound "must be/are the primary carriers of the film's meaning and structure."[31] Rudolf Arnheim's 1938 essay "A New Laocoön: Artistic Composites and the Talking Film" is a classic statement of this point, opening with the premise that there is an "uneasiness" in film audiences due to "the spectator's attention being torn in two directions," between vision and hearing.[32] Chaplin and many others reiterated the point:

> people blather of "talking films" and coloured films and stereoscopic films. I can't abide coloured etchings, and on the stage we already have a perfect three dimensions. Why, we lose half our quality if we lose our limitations! Motion, two planes, and a suggestion of depth: that is our chaos from which we will fashion our universe.[33]

Huxley makes a similar argument for retaining the limitations of each artistic medium in "Where Are the Movies Moving?" He delightedly describes a silent sequence in which his "favorite dramatic hero, Felix the Cat," is shown singing, as indicated by "little black notes" issuing from his mouth. The cartoon cat "reaches up, catches a few handfuls" of notes and makes a scooter out of them on which he rides away. "Seen on the screen," Huxley marvels, "this conversion of song into scooters seems the most natural, simple, and logical thing in the world." This example

> indicates very clearly what are the most pregnant potentialities of the cinema; it shows how cinematography differs from literature and the spoken drama and how it may be developed into something entirely new. What the cinema can do better than literature is to be fantastic.[34]

Here Huxley credits cinema with a serious advantage over literature and supports a modernist aesthetic (the abstraction and surrealism of music concretized into notes and then transformed into scooters). However, he also conservatively insists that each art should stay within its own boundaries.

By contrast, the avant-garde cinema was pushing for more porous boundaries between the arts, and exploring how cinema could be developed into something more sensually and formally innovative. Sergei Eisenstein, W. I. Pudovkin, and G. V. Alexandrov's 1928 "Statement on Sound" advocates montage and "the creation of a new *orchestral counterpoint* of sight-images and sound-images."[35] Eisenstein goes further in "Synchronization of Senses," which describes how a "single, unifying sound-picture image" might be developed as a "polyphonic structure" that "achieves its total effect through the *composite sensation of all the pieces as a whole*."[36] Pointing to examples of synaesthesic art including Rimbaud's "famous 'color' sonnet" (90) and Whistler's "color symphonies" (108), Eisenstein proposes that such effects could be achieved in cinema. "To remove the barriers between sight and sound, between the seen world and the heard world," he rhapsodizes, "To bring about a unity and a harmonious relationship between these two opposite spheres. What an absorbing task! The Greeks and Diderot, Wagner and Scriabin—who has not dreamt of this ideal?" (87). It is the ideal of the *Gesamtkunstwerk*, the "total work of art" that synthesizes multiple media: the reverse of the Laocoön argument, which Huxley advocates. Huxley believed in a certain degree of playful surrealism, but not a free fall into promiscuous sensual hyperreality, which he saw as aesthetic and generic monstrosity. The feelies are a parody of *Gesamtkunstwerk* inspired by the talkies' addition of sound to image. Kracauer made a similar connection, describing Berlin's "picture palaces" as "A glittering, revue-like creature" that "has crawled out of the movies—*the total art work* [Gesamtkunstwerk] *of effects*" that "assaults all the senses using every possible means."[37] For Huxley, film alone among other forms of mass culture has the fearsome potential to expand so promiscuously, both formally and socially. (In 1936 Huxley reported on his recent visit to "a gigantic new movie palace" in Margate: "Its name implied a whole social program, a complete theory of art; it was called 'Dreamland.'"[38] The cinematic *Gesamtkunstwerk* strives to bring about the "lowered consciousness" that Huxley saw early cinema inducing: people are not just hypnotized but put to sleep by the fantasies on the screen.)

Huxley's feelies link cultural degeneration and aesthetic decadence. The posture of the audience, "sunk in their pneumatic stalls" (evocative of both the music hall and the barnyard, as well as Eliot's Grishkin, whose "friendly bust / Gives promises of pneumatic bliss"[39]) suggests a submissive absorption of stimuli. However, the audience at the feelies is anything but drowsy. The scent organ transports its audience through a gamut of sensations that are but an *amuse-bouche* to the main attraction, *Three Weeks in a Helicopter*:

> suddenly, dazzling and incomparably more solid-looking than they would have seemed in actual flesh and blood, far more real than reality, there stood the stereoscopic images, locked in one another's arms, of a gigantic negro and a golden-haired young brachycephalic Beta-Plus female. . . . Expiringly, a sound-track superdove cooed "Oo-ooh"; and vibrating only thirty-two times a second, a deeper than African bass made answer: "Aa-aah." "Ooh-ah! Ooh-ah!" the stereoscopic lips came together again, and once more the facial erogenous zones of the six thousand spectators in the Alhambra tingled with almost intolerable galvanic pleasure. (168)

The goal of the feelies is not mere mimesis, but rather a straining at the boundaries of artificiality to create an enveloping and lurid experience of pleasurable hyperreality. The sensation produced by the feely is created by a "galvanic" or electric current, like a low-level shock treatment. It takes the audience to the edge of unpleasure: it is "almost intolerable." Notably, the one sense that is not stimulated by the feelies is taste; indeed, taste, in the sense of aesthetic judgment, is exactly what is lacking here.

Huxley's representation of mass culture in *Brave New World* explains the seeming contradiction between the two dominant accounts of early cinema—as a Benjaminian shock, on the one hand, and as a narcotic, on the other—which Buck-Morss characterizes as producing "the simultaneously hypersensitized and anaesthetized mass body that is the subject of the cinematic experience" (55). Huxley's feelies both shock and arouse but ultimately contain and subdue their audience by directing their responses in a way that renders them socially, if not sensually, passive.

The plot of *Three Weeks in a Helicopter* is "extremely simple" (168). In this respect, the feelies resemble the early "cinema of attractions," which, Gunning argues, appealed to an audience more interested in the display of spectacle and the "act of looking" than the development of a particular narrative (121). The characters sing a duet and make "a little love . . . on that famous bearskin, every hair of which . . . could be separately and distinctly felt." The "negro" develops "an exclusive and maniacal passion" for "the Beta blonde" and she is "ravished away into the sky and kept there, hovering, for three weeks in a wildly anti-social *tête-à-tête* with the black madman" (168–169). She is rescued by

> three handsome young Alphas . . . and the film ended happily and decorously, with the Beta blonde becoming the mistress of all her three rescuers. . . . Then the bearskin made a final appearance and, amid a blare of sexophones, the last stereoscopic kiss faded into darkness, the last electric titillation died on the lips like a dying moth that quivers, quivers, ever more feebly, ever more faintly, and at last is quiet, quite still. (169)

Representing the feelies is a challenge of ekphrasis that Huxley meets through language that strives for tactility as well as visuality. The moth fluttering on the lips in stuttering words reflecting the weakened beating of its wings, along with the hairs on the rug, produce sensations equal to visual spectacle. Huxley uses language that asks the reader not just to visualize the images but also to imagine their "tactual effects."

While Lenina emerges from the feely "flushed" and aroused, John is "pale, pained, desiring, and ashamed of his desire." He tells Lenina, "I don't think you ought to see things like that. . . . It was base . . . ignoble" (169–170). Although Huxley asks his reader to sympathize with John's high-minded rejection of the feelies after the fact, the language he uses to describe *Three Weeks in a Helicopter* is titillating: everyone in the audience, even John, experiences the galvanic erogenous effects. At climactic moments—specifically, when John rejects pleasure—the reader is more aligned with Lenina than with the sensitive but repressed Savage. His overreaction to the shallow and silly, but also sleazily engaging culture the feelies represent necessarily calls into question his capacity to cope with very human kinds of somatic experience. John is so appalled by it all that he retreats to the countryside, where he mortifies his body, flagellating himself. Darwin Bonaparte, "the Feely Corporation's most expert big game photographer" (252), stalks and films John's acts:

> He kept his telescopic cameras carefully aimed—glued to their moving objective; clapped on a higher power to get a close-up of the frantic and distorted face (admirable!); switched over, for half a minute, to slow motion (an exquisitely comical effect, he promised himself); listened in, meanwhile, to the blows, the groans, the wild and raving words that were being recorded on the soundtrack at the edge of his film, tried the effect of a little amplification (yes, that was decidedly better). . . . When they had put in the feely effects at the studio, it would be a wonderful film. (253)

Bonaparte's efforts culminate in a hit feely feature called *The Savage of Surrey* that "could be seen, heard and felt in every first-class feely-palace in Western Europe" (254). With its alliterative play on Robert Flaherty's popular 1922 film *Nanook of the North*, *The Savage of Surrey* assimilates John to the form of mass culture most foul to him. His flight from hedonism will be absorbed into the economy of mandatory pleasure. The feely's ensuing publicity contributes to John's suicide, and the novel's concluding scene presents his dangling feet as if shot cinematically in close-up:

> Slowly, very slowly, like two unhurried compass needles, the feet turned towards the right; north, north-east, east, south-east, south, south-south-west; then paused, and, after a few seconds, turned as unhurriedly back towards the left. South-south-west, south, south-east, east. (259)

With John's death, civilization's last chance for culture perishes. Horrified by the hedonism of the Brave New World and hunted and framed as an animal himself in *The Savage of Surrey*, John is a casualty of popular culture: death by pleasure.

GOATS AND MONKEYS

The particular feely Huxley describes in *Brave New World* is a composite of parody and allusion that draws together specific debates about the implications of sound cinema and its potential to become something more culturally significant than mere "fun." *Three Weeks in a Helicopter* seems to be an assemblage of random stupidity subordinated to its more spectacular effects, but is in fact a strategic amalgamation of the two kinds of pleasure Huxley delineates in his essay "Pleasures" as "old" and "modern." The feely's title and its memorable "tactual effects" allude to a 1907 best-selling romance novel, *Three Weeks*, by one of the most prolific genre writers of the era, Elinor Glyn. Glyn is best known now for her novel *It* and the silent film adaptation that launched Clara Bow's career as the "It Girl." After Glyn's debut as an extra in a Cecil B. de Mille film, she wrote over a dozen screenplays for major studios. Glyn was a vigorous proselytizer of high-handed ideas about romance in her numerous novels as well as her articles and her treatise *The Philosophy of Love* (1923), and a tireless promoter of her own writing, as exemplified by her four-volume series *The Elinor Glyn System of Writing* (1922), the third of which is devoted to writing "photoplays."[40] Glyn also worked extensively with Rudolph Valentino after he appeared in *The Sheik*, helping transform his screen persona from a dominating and seemingly racially exotic lover to a more aristocratic leading man.[41] To skeptics such as Huxley, Glyn represented the nadir of both contemporary fiction and popular cinema. Robert Graves and Alan Hodge observe that in the teens and twenties, "Glyn was the reigning queen of popular love literature and considered 'very hot stuff' among the 'low-brow public.'"[42] Graves and Hodge assert that she was "not read by the more discriminating," yet many modernists reference her work, including Rebecca West, F. Scott Fitzgerald, William Faulkner, and Virginia Woolf.[43] Woolf wrote about Glyn in a 1917 diary entry: "Expecting life & smartness at least I spent 8d upon a Magazine with Mrs Asquith's love letters, & they're as flat & feeble & vulgar & illiterate as a provincial Mrs Glyn might be."[44] In *Fiction and the Reading Public*, Q. D. Leavis caustically remarks that "famous authors of bestsellers are run as limited companies with a factory called 'Edgar Rice Burroughs, Inc.' or 'Elinor Glyn Ltd.'" (50). Indeed, Glyn's industriousness was remarkable, because she saw her writing as a commercial enterprise—Anne Morey dubs her "the sexual Martha Stewart of the 1920s, with all the power and vulnerability that that strategy confers upon a woman who operates as a brand"—as well as a means of promoting herself and her conceptions about men, women, sex, and love.[45] Just as Lawrence saw Hull as symptomatic of lamentable tendencies in popular writing and cinema, Huxley chose Glyn, Hollywood doyenne, to exemplify debased modern amusement. Glyn was also, even more self-consciously than Hull, an educator of mass audiences in the ways of pleasure.

Three Weeks is in many respects an inversion of *The Sheik*. It tells the story of an affair between Paul Verdayne, a listless upper-class British man, and the queen of an unnamed Eastern European nation who seems modeled on the dominant women of Sacher-Masoch. Just as Hull's Diana "learns" to be a woman through conforming to gender stereotypes, Glyn's Tiger Queen takes Paul in hand and teaches him to be a man through a combination of erotic edification and lectures. She tells him, "You must not just drift, my Paul, like so many of your countrymen do. You must help to stem the tide of your nation's decadence, and be a strong man."[46] But decadence of an order that would have enraged Max Nordau is exactly what follows. In the climactic scene of the novel, Paul finds the queen reclining on a magnificent tiger-skin rug, gripping a *fleur du mal* between her teeth. She writhes around ("like a snake," Glyn writes, no fewer than four times [86, 87, 88, 134]), and the tactile stimuli—slithery snakeskin and soft fur—are as confused as Glyn's mixed metaphors: "She purred as a tiger might have done while she undulated like a snake" (134). Paul impregnates her, becoming the pillar of strength she meant for him to be. *Three Weeks* has a strongly racialized discourse running through it (the queen's behavior is attributed to her "Slav" blood) charged with orientalist themes. Its emphasis on improving a nation's or race's "stock" through reproduction reflects the contemporary discourse of eugenics, a theme that overlapped with Huxley's interests in *Brave New World*.[47] *Three Weeks'* moral and sexual lessons are staged through, as Laura Horak puts it, Paul's "sensual education," which was extended into Glyn's cinematic contributions that "modeled and invited spectators to participate in a form of erotic, embodied spectatorship."[48] Glyn's novel was an instant success in Britain and was filmed several times. In particular, the scene with the tiger-skin rug in the 1924 version, Horak demonstrates, simulates Paul's point of view and his thralldom to the dominant Tiger Queen, thus putting the spectator in the position of experiencing the "visual arousal and physical restraint" that are at the center of Glyn's erotics in her novel (94).

Glyn played up the centrality of this scene, with its pedagogical and erotic content, by posing with such rugs in publicity photographs. This prop is rendered absurd in Huxley's novel, with the characters exclaiming about the feely's simulation of the bearskin rug. Rebecca West commented that Glyn represented an "appalling . . . school of fiction . . . that imagines that by cataloging stimuli one can produce a feeling of stimulation."[49] Indeed, like *The Sheik*, this is exactly what *Three Weeks* does, and very effectively too, judging by its popularity. In a 1915 letter in which Huxley discusses Lawrence's censorship problems with *The Rainbow*, he writes, "It is always the serious books that get sat on—how much better to suppress Mrs. Glyn," suggesting that there was something about Glyn's romances that needed to be contained.[50] However, as in Lawrence's reading of Hull, this feature of romance fiction—its arousal of the reader through sensual description and its deliberate shaping of the reader's response—could be appropriated at the same time that it was criticized, and Huxley does just this in his adaptation of *Three Weeks* in *Brave New World*.

In Huxley's oppositional equation, Glyn and the feelies represent collective, accessible, somatic pleasures that "mean a lot of agreeable sensations to the audience"; "the serious books" are represented by modernism (Lawrence) and, in *Brave New World*, by Shakespeare. Throughout *Brave New World*, beginning with its title, Huxley juxtaposes the feelies with Shakespeare. After a confused John returns from his trip to the Alhambra, he opens *The Complete Works of Shakespeare*, which he has smuggled in from the Reservation. He "turned with religious care its stained and crumbled pages, and began to read *Othello*. Othello, he remembered, was like the hero of *Three Weeks in a Helicopter*—a black man" (171).[51] Visiting Eton, John asks, "Do they read Shakespeare?" He is told that the library "contains only books of reference. If our young people need distraction, they can get it at the feelies. We don't encourage them to indulge in any solitary amusements" (163). In *Brave New World*, Shakespeare's work has been seemingly severed from its theatricality--Huxley figures it not in its enacted form, which might resemble the collective amusement he critiques, but in the more private experience of reading—and yet it is surreptitiously cited through the feelies.[52]

Most obviously, Shakespeare represents the lost values of refined and literary culture. When Mond and John discuss Shakespeare, John laments the passing of "old things" such as books because

> the new ones are so stupid and horrible. Those plays, where there's nothing but helicopters flying about and you *feel* the people kissing." He made a grimace. "Goats and monkeys!" Only in Othello's words could he find an adequate vehicle for his contempt and hatred. (219)

The words refer to Iago's speech about trying to get visual proof of Desdemona's infidelity: "It is impossible you should see this, / Were they as prime as goats, as hot as monkeys" (3.3.402–403). For John, the feelies promote voyeurism, showing publicly and en masse what should be intimate, individual experience. He insists to Mond that

> "*Othello*'s good. . . . *Othello*'s better than those feelies."
> "Of course it is," the Controller agreed. "But that's the price we have to pay for stability. You've got to choose between happiness and what people used to call high art. We've sacrificed the high art. We have the feelies and the scent organ instead."

"But they don't mean anything."

"They mean themselves; they mean a lot of agreeable sensations to the audience."

"But they're . . . they're told by an idiot." (220–221)

This discussion reiterates Huxley's formulations in "Pleasures" and goes even further in articulating the cultural divide between new, popular amusements and those of past eras. When John mistakenly calls the feelies "plays," expecting them to have meaning, and Mond corrects him that their importance is their "agreeable sensations," Huxley opposes significance to sensation. Culture can have meaning or it can deliver "agreeable sensations to the audience," but not both. Hence Mond describes the pleasure of the feelies as an empty tautology: "they mean themselves." Again, Gunning's concept of the "cinema of attractions" is apt here as Huxley suggests that the tawdry desire for stimulation remains cinema's (and the popular novel's) main appeal, while Shakespearean drama offers the dignified and valuable rewards of narrative significance and complexity. But of course, John's sense that Shakespeare solicits only noble emotions is wrong; as his own quotations show, Shakespeare was not above lust and sensationalism.[53]

Neither Huxley's nor John's use of Shakespeare is as high-minded as they might want. Shakespeare's story of a jealous "Moor" and a white woman provides the taboo pretext of *Three Weeks in a Helicopter*. The feely focuses on free love, against which the maniacal monogamy of the "blackamoor" is cast, and miscegenation. Although there is disagreement about whether Shakespeare's Moor is black or sub-Saharan, Huxley definitely casts a black man to couple with the Beta blonde. The "blackamoor" in the feely and Al Jolson's blackface in *The Jazz Singer* both link the talkies with racial exoticism, physicality, and simultaneous modernity and primitivism. While some writers, such as Una Marson, lamented the overwhelming whiteness of the cinema ("Cinema Eyes," 1937), Huxley was not alone in associating cinema with racial otherness. (*The Sheik* too, in both the novel and the film version, plays on the sexualization of racial difference that turns out to be a masquerade.) In 1929, the British film journal *Close Up* devoted a special issue to "The Negro in Film" from which, Jane Gaines observes, "One receives the impression from the special issue that the Negro was in vogue in London as never before."[54] The editor of *Close Up*, Kenneth Macpherson, "lament[ed] the passing of the silent film: he concurred with others that the only consolation was that the talkies now made it possible to *hear* the Negro for the first time" (Gaines, 1). On one level, blackness functions fetishistically for Huxley; on another level, it is a way for him to emphasize further the bodily aspects of cinematic effects. "Again and again," Miriam Hansen observes, "writings on the American cinema of the interwar period stress the new physicality, the exterior surface or 'outer skin' of things."[55] This is certainly true of *Three Weeks in a Helicopter,* with its attention to the skin color of its actors and the texture their bodies feel on the bearskin rug.

There is a curious congruence of racial mixing and the talkies throughout Huxley's work. Both "Silence Is Golden" and *Three Weeks in a Helicopter* showcase racial masquerade and miscegenation. Al Jolson's famous "Mammy" scene, to which Huxley calls such attention, has another "racial" layer beyond the image of the white man in blackface. Jolson's character is from an orthodox Jewish family; as he puts on his makeup and prepares for an opening-night performance on Broadway that will keep him from honoring his father's dying wish that he sing Kol Nidre in the synagogue, he describes his hesitations to his love interest, Mary (a "shiksa" who troubles Jolson's character's mother): "There's something, after all, in my heart—maybe it is the call of the ages—the cry of my race." "Race," or ethnicity, is both an essential trait and a "special effect" in *The Jazz Singer*, an identity that can be painted on.[56] The black-and-white film stock of the early teens and twenties was animated by contrast: the less subtle the better. Huxley does not comment overtly on the racial dimensions of *The Jazz Singer* in "Silence Is Golden," but his concentration on Al Jolson's blackface performance suggests that it drew his attention, and the film's preoccupation with racial and ethnic contrast does appear in Huxley's description of how the members of the band in *The Jazz Singer* "belong to two contrasted races. There were the dark and polished young Hebrews. . . . And there were the chubby young Nordics, with faces transformed by the strange plastic powers of the American environment into the likeness of very large uncooked muffins, or the unveiled posteriors of babes" (21). "Race" is read precisely as the "outer skin of things," as color and the consistency of flesh on the screen. But race and ethnicity went deeper for Huxley. Throughout his writings on cinema, he expresses anti-Semitic paranoia about Hollywood, which he feared was run by "Jews with money."[57] His association of cinema both with blackness and with Jewishness, and more generally with racial promiscuity, resembles nothing so much as the rhetoric of "degeneration," with its anxiety about unrestrained pleasure.

At the same time, as with the synthetic but seductive Lenina, Huxley plays on the excitement of taboo representation in the feelies. On this count, *Three Weeks in a Helicopter* has another intertext: white slavery films. This genre of "vice films," especially popular in the teens, told melodramatic stories of young girls being kidnapped and forced into "slavery," a code name for prostitution. Shelley Stamp argues that films such as *White Slave Traffic* and *Traffic in Souls* responded to anxiety about young women's new urban recreation culture, and particularly cinema. "Cinemas were described by many observers as arenas of particular carnal license, where women were alternately preyed upon by salacious men who gathered around entranceways, and themselves tempted to engage in untoward conduct."[58] The Beta blonde's sexualized "enslavement" to the blackamoor plays on the sensationalism underpinning the white slavery scare at the turn of the century as well as the fantasy of miscegenation. Huxley reaffirms racial stereotypes even as he mocks contemporary films that exploited these stereotypes.

The representation of black sexuality in films of the twenties was vexed, whether in *Birth of a Nation* (a film Huxley knew and wrote about), with its scene of a black man chasing a white woman, or "race films" like those of Oscar Micheaux. In *Three Weeks in a Helicopter* Huxley makes use of the fantasy of black male sexuality threatening white womanhood in a scene that would have been banned under the Motion Picture Production Code of 1930, better known as the Hays Code: "Miscegenation (sex relationships between the white and black races) is forbidden."[59] Indeed, everything about the feely, from the kisses to the interracial romp on the bearskin, would have been unrepresentable in mainstream cinema in 1932. Huxley uses the cover of dystopia—and the overt condemnation of the fictional culture—to depict what would otherwise have been deemed obscene or even pornographic.

Notably, at the same time that Huxley plays *Othello* for its erotic implications in the feely, John uses Shakespeare as a defense against sensual pleasure throughout *Brave New World*. When Lenina tries to seduce him, for example, "inevitably he found himself thinking of the embraces in *Three Weeks in a Helicopter*. Ooh! ooh! the stereoscopic blonde and ahh! the more than real blackamoor" (192), and he spits Shakespearean insults to keep her at bay ("Down from the waist they are Centaurs, though women all above. . . . Impudent strumpet!" [195–196]). John's quotations reflect his intelligence, but they are also a stilted means of critique. Their anachronistic and artificial quality, part of an attempt to stifle somatic pleasure through authority, are no competition for the overwhelming immediacy of the pleasure vehicles in *Brave New World*. Huxley's manner of describing dystopic pleasure necessarily produces its giddy attractions.

Despite the broad satire of the feelies' idiocy, Huxley does not choose to portray them as lacking in magnetism—like the mechanistic Tiller Girls, for example, whom Kracauer oddly characterizes as "sexless bodies in bathing suits" (*Mass*, 76)—and his opposition to intoxication, as Adorno describes it, is not uniform. The effects of *soma*, for example, are presented as a comalike daze into which characters fall, so readers do not generally experience its compelling properties as they do the feelies. *Soma* is, therefore, easier to dismiss. But Huxley dwells on the feelies' allure and efficient mobilization of the body. He does the same with the "uncommonly pretty" and "wonderfully pneumatic" Lenina Crowne, who is closely related to the feelies. Her characteristics—sensual, female, modern, available to everyone—code her as an embodiment of mass culture. She is discussed by the men who have "had" her, just as they discuss the sensual merits of *Three Weeks in a Helicopter*. The novel includes several scenes of Lenina taking off and putting on her outfits, which Huxley details as carefully as the feely scenes (e.g., "the softer rolling of those well-fitted corduroy shorts" [60]). The scene in the "GIRLS' DRESSING-ROOM," in which "eighty vibro-vacuum massage machines were simultaneously kneading and sucking the firm and sunburnt flesh of eighty superb female specimens" (36) and Lenina emerges from her bath like some futurist Aphrodite, straddles the line between critique (of conveyor-belt hygiene) and soft-core fantasy. Even more charged is the scene in which John steals into Lenina's hotel room and rapturously fondles her clothes, which unfolds in strikingly parallel terms to the feely *Three Weeks in a Helicopter*:

He opened the green suit-case; and all at once he was breathing Lenina's perfume, filling his lungs with her essential being. His heart beat wildly; for a moment he was almost faint. Then, bending over the precious box, he touched, he lifted into the light, he examined. The zippers on Lenina's spare pair of viscose velveteen shorts were at first a puzzle, then solved, a delight. Zip, and then zip; zip, and then zip; he was enchanted. Her green slippers were the most beautiful things he had ever seen. He unfolded a pair of zippicamiknicks, blushed, put them hastily away again; but kissed a perfumed acetate handkerchief and wound a scarf round his neck. Opening a box, he spilt a cloud of scented powder. His hands were floury with the stuff. He wiped them on his chest, on his shoulders, on his bare arms. Delicious perfume! He shut his eyes; he rubbed his cheek against his own powdered arm. Touch of smooth skin against his face, scent in his nostrils of musky dust— her real presence. "Lenina," he whispered. "Lenina!" (142–143)

Like the feelies, this scene commences with the stimulation of smell (of Lenina's perfume), moves on to touch and sight and sound ("Zip, and then zip") and has a vicarious quality, as Lenina's "real presence" is withheld. The sense of taste is, as in *Three Weeks in a Helicopter,* missing from John's experience. As with the feely, this is a scene of guilty pleasure that Huxley invites the reader to feel with his character. John's handling of Lenina's garments echoes Huxley's linguistic descriptions of her. Even as the author emphasizes Lenina's artificiality, he effectively simulates John's arousal through funny but also charged scenes of fetishistic desire. When John discovers Lenina sleeping in bed, "dressed in a pair of pink one-piece zippyjamas" (143), his romantic *Romeo and Juliet* sentiment quickly gives way to the desire to "take hold of the zipper at her neck and give one long, strong pull . . ." (144). Huxley's ellipsis tempts the reader to conjure the body beneath those zippyjamas.

After such erotic scenes of longing, John's rejection of Lenina, the feelies, and other sensual pleasures is represented as a puritanical hysteria, which Huxley criticizes as much as thoughtless consumption of the feelies, *soma,* and orgy porgy. When they are finally together, Lenina does a zippered striptease for John: her "white sailor's blouse" comes off with the "long vertical pull" that is denied earlier. She drops her "pale shell pink" zippicamiknicks with a "Zip, zip!" and approaches John in a kinky ensemble of shoes, kneesocks, and a "rakishly tilted round white cap" (193). John attacks her while quoting *Othello*: "O thou weed, who are so lovely fair and smell'st so sweet that the sense aches at thee" (195). Huxley depicts John's response as absurdly repressed. His hypervigilant rage against mutual attraction is excessive and goes against his own—and perhaps the reader's—desires. "Lenina's artificial charm and cellophane shamelessness," Adorno observes, "produce by no means the unerotic effect Huxley intended, but rather a highly seductive one, to which even the infuriated cultural savage succumbs at the end of the novel" (105).

The tiger skin and bearskin, the goats and monkeys, the odor of pig's dung, and the way the "big game photographer" Darwin Bonaparte tracks John all contribute to a strong sense of bestiality and mindlessness surrounding the feelies, of physical transgression and cultural regression—but also excitement and sensation—that Huxley associates with film. He presents cinematic progress as at a crossroads between new and old pleasures, between the serious, thoughtful world of *Othello* and the decadent, sybaritic, but nevertheless seductive world of Glyn. In keeping with his characteristic interest in cultural conditioning, Huxley adds a further cinematic allusion to *Three Weeks in a Helicopter* that indicates how the dangerous pleasures evoked in his "negative utopia" might be managed.

THE SAVAGE OF SURREY

The idea that people's pleasures can be upgraded through aesthetic training is a major modernist gamble. Huxley "reverse engineers" this premise in one of the founding principles of *Brave New World*: that people can be influenced, through techniques such as hypnosis and sleep conditioning to reject "old" pleasures (e.g., Shakespeare) and instead embrace more straightforward, sensational amusements. Just as Huxley was interested in how the conception of the family or individuality, for example, could be influenced by education, he was intrigued by how cinema could shape people's minds. He positions the management of pleasure in *Brave New World* as a means of bolstering the other techniques of social conditioning, such as eugenics.

John's feely epitaph, *The Savage of Surrey*, along with the other feelies mentioned in *Brave New World*—"the famous all-howling stereoscopic feely of the gorillas' wedding" (253) and *The Sperm Whale's Love-Life*, which Darwin Bonaparte considers the gold standard in feelatography—indicate that Huxley had a particular kind of film in mind when he invented this form of amusement. Although the coyly titled feelies seem ludicrously farfetched, they are not far off from real ethnographic and nature documentaries that were hugely popular in Britain in the twenties. The foremost among these was a series called *Secrets of Nature*, sponsored by British Instructional from 1922 to 1933. In her history of British cinema, Rachel Low notes that "The excellence and popular success of the *Secrets of Nature* films was one of the few bright features of the British film industry during the twenties. . . . They were liked by both ordinary audiences and highbrows."[60] Screened before feature-length films, the *Secrets of Nature* shorts focused on topics such as the habits of the cuckoo or plant growth. Their titles were often coyly suggestive: *Romance in a Pond*, for example, investigates the life cycle of newts. According to David King Dunaway, these documentaries were Huxley's favorite kind of film, and "in particular his favorite [was] *The Sex Life of Lobsters*."[61] Huxley's brother Julian, who was active in the popularization of biology, narrated and directed an Oscar-winning film called *The Private Life of the Gannets* (1935). Although both titles sound like feelies, appealing to audience prurience, Huxley often praised documentary film. In "Silence Is Golden," he lauds the "fascinating Events of The Week" newsreels. In *Heaven and Hell*, he applauds colored documentaries as "a notable new form of popular visionary art" and singles out Disney's *The Living Desert*, with "the immensely magnified cactus blossoms, into which . . . the spectator finds himself sinking."[62] In 1929 he wrote that he was "personally . . . very fond" of "the documentary film which shows me places I have never visited, strange animals, odd people, queer trades. . . . *Nanook* and *Chang* and *Moana* are delightful, imaginative liberations for those who have undergone long slavery in the world of adult interests" ("The Critic in the Crib," *Essays* 3:13–14).

In their 1934 book *Secrets of Nature*, the collaborators Mary Field ("the only Englishwoman at present directing talking pictures"[63]) and Percy Smith ("an expert on micro-cinematography") remark that when the *Secrets of Nature* series "went talky," it faced the same obstacles that other kinds of films did: "Experiments have shown that the majority of cinema-goers cannot both look and listen. When they go to the pictures they have the tendency to look, for had they wished to listen, they would have stayed at home and turned on the wireless" (214). An illustration in the book titled "Synchronizing a 'Secret of Nature'" shows a group of musicians recording a film sound track. The image indicates the seriousness with which the *Secrets of Nature* films were produced and also hints at the surrealism of the venture, as a full orchestra accompanies an arachnid rendered twice as large as a grand piano. (*The Matrimony of Mites*, one imagines the title of the finished product might go.)

From cinema's early days, there was interest in its didactic potential. In 1914, Shaw wrote,

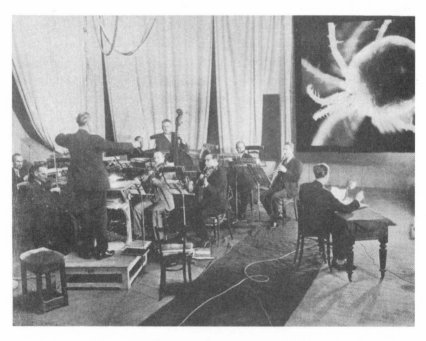

Figure 4.1
"Synchronizing a Secrets of Nature Film"
Courtesy of Studiocanal Films Limited

The cinematograph begins educating people when the projection lantern begins clicking, and does not stop until it leaves off. Whether it is shewing you what the South Polar ice barrier is like through the films of Mr Ponting [*90 Degrees South* (1911–1912)], or making you silly and sentimental by pictorial novelets, it is educating you all the time. (7)

Shaw adds that the cinema "is educating you far more effectively when you think it is only amusing you than when it is avowedly instructing you in the habits of lobsters."[64] This idea of education sneaking in under the cover of pleasure is a significant twist on statements such as Eliot's "alarming conclusion that it is just the literature that we read for 'amusement,' or 'purely for pleasure' that may have the greatest, and least suspected influence upon us." Shaw had an optimistic vision of cinema as an edifying pleasure. In "The Critic in the Crib," Huxley cites a Columbia Teachers College study that found that "class-room films can raise pupils' marks by an average of twenty-four per cent," and that most teachers thought such films were useful "in arousing and sustaining the children's interest, in improving the quantity and quality of their reading, and in aiding them to correlate features of their lessons with personal experiences and community conditions" (*Essays*, 3:13). Huxley notes, however, the findings of another team of researchers that "at no age did students like such semi-educational productions as *Nanook*, *Grass*, *Moana*, and *Chang*" (13). These seemingly contradictory conclusions are played out in *Brave New World* when John visits the Eton "Beta-Minus geography room." The students are watching an ethnographic film about the Penitentes of the Savage Reservation beating themselves. The students roar with laughter while Bernard takes advantage of "the cinematographical twilight" to make a pass at the Head Mistress. John, meanwhile, is "pained" and bewildered at the spectacle (162). The students are hardly interested in the film, but it is nevertheless working its subliminal power to imprint the cultural values of the Brave New World upon them. Huxley's vision of how educational cinema might develop is much more cynical than Shaw's; it functions, like the other forms of mass pleasure, to shore up the citizens' social conditioning. As a mass medium that appealed to people because it seemed so accessible, cinema could "form the mind of England," as Shaw predicted, but it could also *de*form the mind, as in *Brave New World*, and produce docile rather than alert citizens.

Throughout his representations of cinema, Huxley draws attention to films' sociopolitical potential, and the ways they can be used to manipulate audiences. In one of his earliest comments on film, Huxley wrote in 1916 that *Birth of a Nation*

> is said to mark quite a new epoch in cinematographic art. In time, no doubt, we shall have cinemas being bought up by the political parties for propagandist work, in which they will soon excel even the newspapers. The effect of them in China is said to be prodigious, while Rumania is described as a Cinematocracy. (*Letters*, 94–95)

Huxley only briefly remarks upon the art of De Mille's racially inflammatory epic; he is more interested in the propagandistic implications of cinema than its aesthetic possibilities. Similarly, shortly after the publication of *Brave New World*, in a 1935 *Daily Express* article, Huxley imagines "the retrospective gaze" of a future journalist to make a series of predictions about how life would look in 1960. He devotes considerable space to prophecies about the cinema. "As for the talkies . . . they took to color in the early forties and became stereoscopic about nine years later" (*Essays*, 3:423). He recalls that actors began "having themselves fitted with synthetic voices" and that politicians followed suit:

> Ministries of Propaganda found that it was possible to supply dictators, monarchs, and even democratic Prime Ministers with a brand of synthetic eloquence incomparably more moving than that of the greatest orators of previous epochs. (3:424)

Huxley was not far off with his aesthetic predictions, but his political predictions are fanciful. As in *Brave New World*, there is a gap between his sense of what is pleasurable—and his own ability to simulate that sensation, textually—and his understanding of the extent to which such entertainment could be harnessed for a political or pedagogical purpose. The way Huxley depicts pleasure and the way he wants the reader to judge it are not exactly congruent in *Brave New World*, suggesting that it is not as easy to program as Huxley imagined. This is underscored by the irony that despite Huxley's critique of the repressive, censorious, and totalitarian culture of *Brave New World*, schools still regularly ban the novel, in part because of its salacious content.[65] As with Lawrence's work, the pleasure of the text takes on a life of its own once real readers step into the picture. No matter how directly an author attempts to steer them, readers will always have the freedom to react however they want—within the limits of their social conditioning, Huxley might add. The fact that there is room for characters in *Brave New World* to reject compulsory amusement indicates that pleasure, like the cinema, can be repressive or potentially revolutionary.

Here the distinction between a dystopia and a negative utopia is significant. George Orwell's *1984*, for example, imagines a culture in which pleasure is withheld; in *Brave New World*, pleasure is imposed. Since Orwell writes about mass culture from an external perspective, the reader views it as invasive, exploitative, and dispiriting. Orwell does not generally show the reader pleasurable effects of the mass culture he denounces. Huxley's "negative utopia" takes more representational risks by beckoning its reader to imagine the allure of what is also ultimately a repressive mechanism of social control.

Huxley himself characterized John's assimilation into the Brave New World as an "insane life in a Utopia" (viii), indicating its inherent contradictions. Jameson's suggestion that dystopic literature necessarily anticipates utopianism ("the post-catastrophe situation in reality constitutes the preparation for the emergence of Utopia itself"[66]) is one way of understanding the tensions in Huxley's representation of mass pleasures. They must be appealing enough to register with the reader as such, but they must also justify John's despair and suicide. Embedded in Huxley's simultaneously attractive and repellent stimulants like the feelies, *soma*, and free and easy sex is the hope for a more perfect pleasure.

HUXLEY AND HOLLYWOOD

The problem of representing negated pleasure is one that Huxley did not completely solve, and as time went by, he moved in a new direction. In a development not anticipated by his early writings on film, in 1938—less than ten years after his screed about *The Jazz Singer*—Huxley moved to Hollywood, the home of "standardized amusement" and "Elinor Glyn Ltd.," and spent the rest of his life there. Perhaps this was no more ironic than the fact that Huxley, who was nearly blind, had such strong opinions about films he could hardly see. His friendships with figures such as Chaplin and Anita Loos allowed him access to the inner circles of Hollywood. Along with other expatriates such as Evelyn Waugh, Huxley worked as a scriptwriter for the major studios. Most of the projects with which he was involved were adaptations of literary classics—*Pride and Prejudice* (1940) and *Jane Eyre* (1944)—or similarly "highbrow" projects such as *Madame Curie* (1943). These were commercially successful examples of entertainment combining "old and "new" pleasures, a mode that had seemed elusive to Huxley in the twenties. While he continued to write about cinema satirically in *After Many a Summer Dies the Swan* (1939) and *Ape and Essence* (1948; it is presented in the form of a failed film script and includes a scene of baboons watching the cinema, bringing back the feelies' themes of cultural regression and bestiality),[67] Huxley's participation in a developing industry that produced films such as *Citizen Kane* may have changed his perception of film's possibilities.[68]

Huxley made two attempts to adapt *Brave New World* to visual forms. In a 1945 letter to Loos, he proposed a film that would "revolve around the person of a very clever but physically unattractive scientist, desperately trying to make a gorgeous blonde, who is repelled by his pimples but fascinated by the intelligence of his conversation" (*Letters*, 535). This figure, who seems to be a stand-in for Lenina (or perhaps the Beta blonde of *Three Weeks in a Helicopter*), sounds suspiciously like Loos's most famous heroine, Lorelei Lee of *Gentlemen Prefer Blondes*. "In the end," Huxley continues, the scientist "makes violent passes at the blonde, gets his face slapped and is left disconsolate among the white mice and the rabbit ova—an emblem of personal frustration who is yet the most revolutionary and subversive force in the modern world" (*Letters*, 535). The drama no longer centers on one noble man's resistance to pleasure but rather his inability to attain it.[69]

More surprising is Huxley's subsequent attempt, in 1956, to adapt *Brave New World* to perhaps the least likely genre. He writes in several letters that he is at work on

a musical comedy version of *Brave New World*—for everyone
tells me that science fiction can never succeed on the stage as a
straight play, but that it will be accepted when the medium ceases
to be realistic and makes use of music and lyrics. (*Letters*, 808)

As in his comment that "what the cinema can do better than literature
is to be fantastic," here Huxley suggests that science fiction has to be
less realistic—and more fantastic, as well as more genre-crossing—
in order to be commercially viable. The idea of *Brave New World* as a
musical is a comedic prospect, which was surely part of the point. The
exchange between film and literature had become more fluid in the
forties and fifties, and the same period was the golden age of Broadway
musicals such as *Oklahoma!* (1943), *South Pacific* (1949), *Guys and Dolls*
(1950), *West Side Story* (1957), and Loos's own *Gentlemen Prefer Blondes*
(1949). Jerome Meckier speculates that "Perhaps Huxley conceived of
musical comedy—the musical comedy of ideas—as the ideal form for
bridging the ever-widening gap between high seriousness and popular
entertainment."[70] The gap, in fact, was diminishing. Postwar culture
did not insist on the schism between "fun" and pleasure in the way
that the modernist period had, as I will show in chapter 6.

Huxley's proposed musical adaptation of *Brave New World* came
shortly after MGM's musical comedy *Singin' in the Rain* (1952), with its
humorous treatment of the talkies revolution. Cinematic musical productions, shaped around song and dance numbers, turned back, in some
senses, toward the music hall, with its combination of different kinds of
entertainment. This comes across strongly in Huxley's three-act musical
of *Brave New World*, which includes nine whimsical songs and several
equally odd dances, which include a kinetic "Death Conditioning" ballet
and a soft-shoe shuffle involving workers in the hatchery singing "Everybody's Happy Now." At another point, Huxley revisits precisely the scene
that so horrified him in *The Jazz Singer*—a scene straight from the music
hall—and replays it as pure absurdity. A character "falls on one knee, in
the attitude of Al Jolson," and sings, not "Mammy" but "Bottle of Mine,"
an ode to the bottle from which he was "decanted."[71] The sequence is
designed to elicit laughs, in contrast to the disgust and shame that Huxley claimed to have felt watching Al Jolson sing "Mammy" in *The Jazz
Singer*. The scene recasts melodrama as satire, aiming to elicit a knowing
chuckle from the audience rather than cloying sentiment.

As theater became more like film, film became, once again, more like the stage, suggesting that the strict boundaries for artistic forms that Huxley advocated earlier as a means of keeping the talkies at bay had crumbled by the mid-fifties. Huxley gave his script to several readers, including Chaplin and Leonard Bernstein, but he never managed to find someone to write the score, and the musical was never produced. While it is a weak derivative of the original, the musical *Brave New World* does show Huxley reconfiguring some of the problems that preoccupied him in the novel. Throughout, pleasure is played as comic "fun" and, at points, Huxley seems to be parodying his own work. In act 1, Joe, a Beta minus, steals and gobbles up some of Lenina's *soma* and makes a pass at her: "Listen, Baby. Let's you and I go to the feelies tonight. I hear there's a wonderful show at the Piccadilly Palace." She turns him down "with dignity": "Nothing doing. I think your behaviour is lousy and unethical." Joe persists: "Boy meets pneumatic girl on a foam rubber mattress with a chinchilla slip cover. You can feel that fur all over you—every single hair of it. They say it's terrific" (41). Riffing again on Glyn's tiger skin, Huxley makes the feelies tawdrier, but they remain more of a dirty joke than the sign of cultural decline that they are in the novel. Significantly, Huxley chose not to stage the feelies, but he does represent the newer visual technology, television, and it plays a role similar to that in Orwell's *1984*, as mass media have encroached even further into the lives of citizens, out of the feely palace and into the private home.

Another striking change is the character of Lenina, who is less sexually aggressive and more thoughtful than in the novel: she joins John in reading *The Complete Works of Shakespeare*, and she is not the free lover she was in 1932. In the conclusion of the musical, Huxley takes a "third alternative" (ix) that he mentions in his 1946 foreword to *Brave New World*, as Lenina and John depart to join a community of like-minded exiles in Tahiti. In Lenina's transformation, Huxley has traded in *Othello* for *The Tempest* and *My Fair Lady*. The conflict of sympathy with the puritanical "Savage" is resolved in the musical; John does not martyr himself but rather wins the girl. At the end of the musical, as the couple embraces, a huge television screen is superimposed on the stage and the audience watches two rival factions in Tahiti attack each other. This news broadcast is then interrupted by a commercial selling "Voluptua Hand Cream" ("Laboratory tests by famous scientists have proved that the effect of ethyl acetic aldehyde on anthropoid apes is little short of miraculous" ([103]). The final image in the musical is a Jumbo Economy Jar of synthetic pleasure ("Voluptua") poised to distract citizens from political strife. Despite abandoning the nihilistic ending of the novel (John's suicidal rage against hedonism) and despite Huxley's attempt to sell or "sell out" his novel as a musical, this conclusion reiterates the warning of Huxley's other work about the dangers of pleasure, but in a decidedly less alarming tone.

Huxley conceptualizes pleasure as a function of manipulation, whether by the state, by Hollywood studios, or by an author's machinations. In doing so, he offers a reflection on the modernist proposition that people's pleasures could be upgraded through hard work. Alongside his strong statements against contemporary, accessible, and somatic pleasure—which takes people away from political awareness—Huxley's fictions also demonstrate that the choice between "old" or "new" pleasure, between the false consciousness of the feelies or the noble struggle of Shakespeare, is itself false. *Brave New World* proves that the alert and politically aware reader can appreciate—even have *fun* with—prurient pursuits such as the feelies at the same time that she appreciates a satiric attack on them. Our capacity for pleasure can and does sustain these contradictions, suggesting that even in the completely engineered state of *Brave New World*, pleasure may elude the system. This hope would become the basis of many utopian dreams later in the century, when Norman O. Brown, Wilhelm Reich, and others would look to pleasure to break the grip of capitalism.

5

THE IMPASSE
OF PLEASURE
Patrick Hamilton and Jean Rhys

"Don't forget what happens to the audience at tragedies, will you?
Even while they're weeping, they're enjoying themselves."
—Plato, *Philebus*[1]

"Well, even in toothache there is enjoyment."
—Dostoyevsky, *Notes from Underground*[2]

The interwar fictions of Patrick Hamilton and Jean Rhys describe strikingly similar realms from different points of view, both from the margins of late modernism. Their lower middle-class, working-class, and bohemian characters totter through urban landscapes of menacing streets, dingy rented rooms, bars, pubs, cinemas, A.B.C. teashops, and Lyons Corner Houses. Hamilton is best known for his drama *Rope* (1929), which Hitchcock adapted for the screen in 1948. His interwar novels, including *The Midnight Bell* (1929), *The Siege of Pleasure* (1932), and *The Plains of Cement* (1934)—published as a trilogy called *Twenty Thousand Streets Under the Sky* (1935)—as well as *Hangover Square: A Story of Darkest Earl's Court* (1941) and *Slaves of Solitude* (1947), are tales in which women take financial advantage of men, men drink away their wages, and all narcotize themselves at the "local" and the cinema. Hamilton views the tug of war between the sexes primarily from a victimized man's perspective, while Rhys focuses on women who are perpetually displaced and impoverished. Hamilton's stories cluster tightly around a fifty-mile radius of London,[3] while Rhys ranges around England, France, the Netherlands, and the West Indies, but all of their protagonists inhabit a

claustrophobic psychic terrain, "another place which was perpetually the same."[4] These "drunken, deracinate"[5] figures view themselves
as casualties of fate, buffeted about by a cruel world and more powerful others who act upon them. It is challenging to come to terms
with such apparently unrelenting bleakness and often unsympathetic characters who sabotage themselves. Contrary to the common understanding of Hamilton's and Rhys's novels as narratives
of disempowerment and depression, this chapter will make the case
that pleasure—of an idiosyncratic texture—is a dominant concern of
their texts. Both authors convey a strong sense of civilian interwar
culture as shadowed by the past war and threatened by the gathering
storm of fascism. Their characters' affects—including boredom, frustration, disorientation, and paralysis—reflect a time of uncertainty,
dread, and helplessness. Writing in the wake of the depression and
alongside Hitler's rise to power, Mussolini's breach of the Abyssinian
border in 1935, the outbreak of the Spanish Civil War in 1936, and the
local appearance of Oswald Mosley's British Union of Fascists rallying
in Hyde Park, Rhys and Hamilton register the deepening fear of the
years leading up to World War Two, but in a different way than more
explicitly political writers such as Auden, Spender, Huxley, Orwell,
and Isherwood. Hamilton and Rhys capture the dysphoria of their
moment by registering a protest against pleasure.

Like Huxley, Lawrence, Joyce, and others from the period, Rhys and
Hamilton rework the concept of pleasure, but from a different angle
than the writers I have considered so far. Both authors are consumed
by efforts at cultural distinction and individuation; their refusal of
bourgeois values and facile amusement is characteristically modernist. But while other writers favor cerebral, complex pleasure at the
expense of easy embodiment, Rhys and Hamilton present an overwhelmingly somatic world in which distinction is won through the
ability to resist pleasure entirely. Unpleasure here is a response to the
construction of accessible mass culture as a source of corrupt consensus, but without a concomitant advocacy of high culture or intellectual
pleasure. On the one hand, Rhys's and Hamilton's characters' pride
in living a superior kind of misery is continuous with modernism's
demand that its readers embrace difficulty and discernment; on the
other, the vehemence of their outsider position entails a rejection of
both "elite" and mass sensory pleasure. For Hamilton and Rhys, there

is no realm of Kantian or Eliotic disinterest into which to withdraw—
or rather, when it is offered, the characters refuse it.

While Joyce's masochism and Lawrence's female submission, for
example, are impulses toward unpleasure, those authors both maintain
the horizon of conventional (easy, simplistic, somatic) as well as valorized (analytical, aesthetic, transformative) pleasure. For Hamilton and
Rhys, by contrast, unpleasure is a spectrum ranging from ennui to *jouissance* that is shadowed by anhedonia, an extinction of pleasure entirely.
In some respects, these affects resemble what Sianne Ngai calls "ugly
feelings" (including envy, irritation, and disgust), which are "dysphoric
or experientially negative, in the sense that they evoke pain or displeasure" (*Ugly Feelings*, 11). Like other ugly feelings, Hamilton's and
Rhys's states of unpleasure are signaled textually by "a general state
of obstructed agency," "situations of passivity," and inaction charged
by attraction. These two authors, along with contemporaries such as
Samuel Beckett and Djuna Barnes, express "at the same time pleasure
and a sense of terrible anxiety"[6] in the apprehensive interwar period.

When Hamilton's and Rhys's protagonists do experience what
could be called pleasure, it is almost always slightly inept: excessive,
off kilter, or something fleeting that has happened in the past and is
gone forever. Pleasure is a zero-sum game, usually belonging to the
other: the greedy prostitute or the sociopathic man (in Hamilton) or
the wealthy male patron (in Rhys), while the hapless main characters
wallow in their misfortune. Most contemporary critics view Rhys
and Hamilton as exposing the dystopic realms they depict, in which
characters are traumatized or disenfranchised by their class, gender,
racial, or national marginality. Interpretations of Hamilton and Rhys
as empathetic and melancholic necessarily underplay what is determinedly intransigent in their work. As Ngai remarks, unlike "potentially ennobling or morally beatific states like sympathy, melancholia,
and shame (the emotions given the most attention in literary criticism's recent turn to ethics)," ugly feelings "are explicitly *a*moral and
*non*cathartic, offering no satisfactions of virtue, however oblique, nor
any therapeutic or purifying release" (*Ugly Feelings*, 6). There is a per-
sistent complicity with and tropism toward misery and pain in Hamilton's and Rhys's characters. As Trilling sees in *Notes from Underground*
a character who "has arranged his own misery," Hamilton's and Rhys's
characters are drawn to obliteration, repetition, debasement, and self-

destruction.[7] Unpleasure here is not so much a by-product of political disenfranchisement or personal trauma as it is a chosen attraction. If pleasure, from the classical Greeks through Freud and beyond, has been defined as a lowering of tension, Rhys and Hamilton's characters seek to amplify conflict and diminish satisfaction and tranquility. They do not, however, perform a simple inversion: that is, they do not simply substitute pain for pleasure, but rather alter the value of each.

From Plato onward, pleasure has been anatomized according to class, and this is a strong element of most modernist discussions of pleasure. Rhys and Hamilton illuminate the ideological underpinnings of pleasure and how they are class- and gender-inflected. They both position their down-and-out protagonists as more sympathetic than their upper-class characters, but this sympathy is earned by individuals through their inability or refusal to take part in collective pleasure. While Hamilton perpetuates the long-standing gendering of repudiated sensational pleasure as female, Rhys calls attention to the way the female body is aligned with frivolous, dangerous, and devalued delight.

Like other writers of the period, Hamilton and Rhys are attuned to vernacular culture as the main vehicle of collective, somatic pleasure. Both authors depict a repertoire of distractions, including the cinema, romance novels, and popular songs, as well as immediate and physical experiences that are not mass-produced, such as drunkenness and prostitution, but show them as having unpleasant effects on the characters. For example, in their alcohol-sodden tales, Rhys and Hamilton literalize one of the master metaphors of modernist scorn for mass culture: intoxication. In Rhys's *After Leaving Mr. Mackenzie*, Julia remarks that "no place is a place to be sober in" (261); nearly all of Hamilton's characters frequent "Hangover Square." (Both authors were themselves alcoholics. Hamilton titled his unfinished autobiography *Memoirs of a Heavy-Drinking Man*; David Plante's portrait of the aged Rhys, in *Difficult Women*, might well be called *Memoirs of a Heavy-Drinking Woman*.[8]) In their fictions, Rhys and Hamilton realize the modernist fear of narcotized contemporary life through scenes of embodied immediacy that cannot be classified as pleasure in any simple sense.

Formally, Hamilton's and Rhys's narratives enact the intersection of pain and pleasure that their stories thematize. Their recursive, uneventful plots consist of monotonous, aggravating, frustrating repetitions and stalemate, a condition that I will call the impasse of pleasure.[9] These texts are negative, anticathartic, and politically ineffectual, defying the idea that pleasure—or literature—must have a particular use-value. In presenting the case of outsiders and marginal, self-destructive underdogs, they produce unsettling reading effects, including black humor, that push readers to their limits of tolerance. In their paeans to misery and debasement and their moments of unexpected whimsy and absurdity, Rhys and Hamilton generate a readerly affect of mixed despair and delight even as they renounce the pursuit of pleasure.

"PLEASURE ITSELF HAS BEEN FOUND WANTING": PATRICK HAMILTON

Although Hamilton is cursorily included in some literary histories of the late modernist period, his work had not received much in-depth critical attention until quite recently. He has often been dismissed as a forerunner of Bukowski, a depressive bard of alcoholism and urban squalor. Terry Eagleton pronounced Hamilton "sub-Dickensian,"[10] picking up on an argument Orwell made in his 1935 review of *Twenty Thousand Streets Under the Sky,* which faulted Hamilton for his "Priestleyan assumption that 'real life' means lower-middle class life in a large town and that if you can pack into your novel, say, fifty-three descriptions of tea in a Lyons Corner House, you have done the trick."[11] The comment, which others have noted is a fair description of Orwell's own novels of the period, points to the insistently materialist nature of Hamilton's prose, detailing the tightly circumscribed and repetitive nature of his characters' lives. Recent critical interest in Hamilton largely hinges on claims that his work offers a dialectical materialist critique of England. (Eagleton argues that Hamilton's "satiric anatomy . . . was thoroughly political in intent.") This view renders Hamilton more ideologically coherent and constructive than the fiction itself bears out. The Marxist argument that Hamilton's characters are alienated cogs in an exploitative system also fails to recognize the contorted kinds of bliss that his characters gain from that position.

For all his interest in depicting his characters' manners and the details of their environment that evokes a kind of kitchen-sink realism or naturalism, Hamilton reflects many modernist concerns and effects what Gerard Barrett calls a "low-key modernism" characteristic of the "second wave of modernist writers" such as Henry Green and James Hanley.[12] Hamilton carries out a variety of formal experiments, ranging from stream of consciousness and collage in *Hangover Square*, to the "ballooning" of his 1939 dystopic fantasy novel *Impromptu in Moribundia*. Here the narrator time- and space-travels, via a vaguely described contraption, the "Asteradio," to a world modeled on the worst of the English middle class. When characters spout clichés and advertising jingles, or when they think something that is particularly determined by mass culture or bourgeois idiocy, their words are presented in drawn dialogue balloons, as if issuing from their mouths. The culture industry has run rampant in Moribundia: "Nearly every other building . . . was either a cinema or a place of entertainment, and I have never seen so many cars, so many greyhounds, so many fur coats, so many silk stockings and so many idle people bent on pleasure in my life." Alongside these broad attacks on familiar modernist targets, Moribundian writers are themselves parodies of contemporary luminaries. "Toile S.T.," "Ecyoj," "Yelxuh," and "Ecnerwal" are said to be narcissistic, inward-looking, and sterile, and their work is "meaningless masturbation."[13] Hamilton sets himself apart from both the middle class and what he presents as the cultural elite, but the working class culture of Moribundia has no more to recommend it.

Figure 5.1
Patrick Hamilton, *Impromptu in Moribundia*
Copyright © 1939 Patrick Hamilton. Reprinted by permission of
A. M. Heath & Co Ltd.

For all this, Hamilton has an ease and fluency with vernacular culture. For example, in *Hangover Square*, the main character's sudden sociopathic moods are likened to "watching a talking film, and all at once the soundtrack had failed" (15). The return to outmoded silent film is as disorienting as the original transition to the talkies had been in the late 1920s; Hamilton extends the metaphor of this jarring shift to reflect his character's schizophrenia. Later, the physical attraction of a toxic aspiring film starlet, Netta, is described through the technology of radio:

> She was something of which he was physically sensible by some means other than that of sight or sound: she was sending out a ray, a wave, from herself, which seemed to affect his whole being, to go all through him like a faint vibration. It was as though she were a small amateur wireless station, and he alone was tuned in to her and listening.[14]

The inverse of the silent film analogy, which is a retrogressive stripping away of one sense (hearing), radio introduces an entirely new somatic dimension. In both cases, Hamilton's interest is not the message of the medium so much as the somatic effect on its audience. Here and elsewhere, Hamilton supersaturates vernacular culture with significance that is ultimately grounded in the body. Noticeably, however, he does not characterize vernacular culture as uniform or straightforwardly pleasurable.

The first novel in the *Twenty Thousand Streets Under the Sky* trilogy opens with Bob, a waiter at the pub that gives the novel its title, The Midnight Bell, near Euston and Warren Streets, dreaming that he is on a ship at sea, departing for a "momentous voyage."[15] He wakes up disoriented in "his little hovel of a room" and finds himself fully dressed and sickened as a result of getting "drunk at lunch again." It's an event, the regretful hangover, that appears *ad nauseam* in Hamilton's novels and signals the long tail of dysphoria that inevitably follows pleasurable excess. "The burden of cold and ever-recurring existence weighed down his spirit. Here he was again" (4). The scene underscores the irony of the title's play on Jules Verne's adventure-packed *Twenty Thousand Leagues Under the Sea*. Bob had once been a sailor, but the drama of the London streets he treads is hardly so daring. Rather, "the small fish in the weird teeming aquarium of the metropolis" are "uncanny, grotesquely adjusted, and obscurely motivated."[16] This urban fishbowl's equivalents of the great squid that grips the *Nautilus* are alcoholism, economic parasitism, and frustrated desire.

Bob's routine for his day off from work is a roll call of formulaic urban amusements: he walks across town to have tea at a Lyons, smoking "three cigarettes, and strangely enjoying the electric-lit, spoon-clinking liveliness of the place" (41), he browses bookshops, drinks at a bar, has a meal at the Corner House, and goes to the cinema. The real story begins when he falls in love with a prostitute, Jenny Maple, who is perpetually low on rent money. Bob, proud of the fact that he has saved eighty pounds, offers her money, which "gives him a strange thrill . . . almost as though he were making love" (76), although that is exactly what he is *not* doing. Jenny remains beyond his reach. Hamilton's pairing of "strange" with "enjoying" and "thrill" indicates the equivocal texture of Bob's pleasure. Repeatedly, with the regularity of a metronome, Bob declares that he will stop squandering his money on Jenny, but then he draws out more from his dwindling bank account to woo her. It comes as a surprise to him every time. "Would this ever end?" he wonders. "It seemed as though she were some alluring and irresistible pilot, leading him on and downwards (for his sins and weakness) through every circle of hell" (191). Not just the pilot but also the route is irresistible to Bob. At the end of the novel, after promising to take a trip to Brighton with him on Boxing Day, Jenny stands Bob up at Victoria Station. He goes on a wild drinking binge and ends up, having been robbed, in a doss house in Soho surrounded by vagrants. Devastated and financially wrecked, he thinks, "It could never have been otherwise. He had merely essayed the impossible and failed" (220). Yet he is also elated, as if this bottoming out has vindicated him.

The novel ends on an inexplicably upbeat note as Bob decides to become a sailor again; the narrator hopefully observes that "after all he had suffered, and after all he had lost, Bob was yet able to glow in this manner and resolve to go to sea" (221). But Bob is no Captain Nemo. Formally, the conclusion circles back to the novel's opening scene, the urban sailor washed up on the shore, but there is no reason to expect a heroic transformation or forward movement. (Rhys draws comparably claustrophobic narrative circles in her novels.) Indeed, the next two novels in the trilogy backtrack chronologically to tell similarly dejecting tales about other characters, and the final installment recapitulates many of the events from Bob's narrative involving other characters whose stories intersect with his, reinforcing the impression of stasis and the sense that Bob has not really departed. (These internal repetitions no doubt contributed to Orwell's pronouncement that *Twenty Thousand Streets Under the Sky* is "as shapeless and inert as a clot of frog-spawn" [390].)

The second novel in the trilogy, *The Siege of Pleasure,* describes how Jenny became a prostitute, tracing her downfall to one drunken night. *The Plains of Cement* focuses on Ella, the kindhearted barmaid at The Midnight Bell who is hopelessly love with Bob but, in lieu of his affection, becomes semiengaged to a comically pompous man she doesn't particularly like (Ernest Eccles). The trilogy is framed by two stories of unrequited love. In *The Midnight Bell*, *Siege*, and *Plains*, as well as *Hangover Square*, characters tell themselves that they want to do the sensible, bourgeois thing (save money, get married, stay sober), but they consistently do just the opposite: the thing that makes them most miserable.

For a body of work that has been characterized as "shabby, depressed" (Widdowson) and "grimy, graceless, bleak, ugly" (Doris Lessing[17]), Hamilton's novels are remarkably loquacious about pleasure. Ian Sinclair notes that "The key Hamilton terms are . . . cement, plains, pleasure. Those three words recur endlessly, as he describes the slate and limestone city."[18] John Bayley explains the apparent contradiction in the following way:

> The [London] *Times* was moved to comment in its obituary that Hamilton was "a genuine minor poet of the loneliness, purposelessness and frustration of contemporary urban life." Handsome as it seems, the tribute is misleading. Urban life is the same everywhere, and always has been, and only during the last century has it become a fashionable cliché to refer to it in these terms. Where Hamilton is concerned, it would be equally true to say he is a connoisseur of the excitements, obsessions and enjoyments of urban life, for his characters are submerged in these, as they are in the pubs, the cinemas and Lyons Corner Houses, and all the rituals and consolations of such places.[19]

In fact, it is not a matter of one or the other: frustration or enjoyment. Hamilton's fiction teeters on an edge between the two. For a more accurate description, we might shift the terms chiasmatically: Hamilton writes about the frustration of enjoyment and the enjoyment of frustration. It is no coincidence that the center of the trilogy, and the chiasmatic structure, is *The Siege of Pleasure*. Systematically and relentlessly, Hamilton's characters create impasses and obstacles to pleasure, orienting themselves toward "strange thrills" and "strange enjoyments" that undercut the notion of the pleasure principle, that people seek pleasure and avoid pain.

In a chapter on hedonism in *Principia Ethica*, G. E. Moore asserts that "The things we enjoy and the things we do not, form two unmistakable classes."[20] If only it were so clear. Hamilton's characters are in a constant state of apparent befuddlement about what they do or do not enjoy. As Freud describes it, unpleasure delays, reroutes, inverts, or distorts, but does not exclude, pleasure. Masochism and the less pathological repetition compulsion are his primary examples (although his description of erotic "fore-pleasure" versus "end-pleasure" in *Three Essays on the Theory of Sexuality* suggests a similar dynamic). Freud posits that such repetitions are aimed toward mastery or overcoming of a painful experience: an end point that produces pleasure by extinguishing tension. By this account, the goal of Hamilton's characters is reaching the lowest point—the empty bank account, the complete humiliation—that proves that the world truly is cruel after all, and that the individual really has no power, or rather, only has power to bring about misery. It is the dubious triumph of vindication that things are, indeed, as bad as one thought. However, Hamilton's characters suggest that the path to the end point itself, which maintains a steady level of frustration and tension, is more connected to pleasure than Freud allows.

"The masochist is morose," Deleuze writes, but this pose is "related to the experience of waiting and delay" that is, along with suspense and disavowal, key to masochistic pleasure. For Deleuze, the idea of a "pleasure-pain complex" or "pleasure in pain" does not describe masochistic pleasure adequately: "masochism is not pleasure in pain, nor even in punishment."[21] Rather, the masochist desires tension and waiting: "pleasure is now a form of behavior related to repetition, accompanying and following repetition, which has itself become an

awesome, independent force" (12). Deleuze proposes that the masochist's pose of powerlessness is an underhanded strategy: "What inso-
lence and humor, what irrepressible defiance and ultimate triumph lie
hidden behind an ego that claims to be so weak" (124). The masochist's
manipulations are characterized by humor and theatricality that foregrounds elaborate and apparently unwilled suffering.

The formal qualities of masochistic display that Deleuze highlights
("Fundamentally, masochism is neither material nor moral, but essentially formal," 74) certainly characterize Hamilton's and Rhys's work.
Both oeuvres have a stalled quality at the same time that they are
strikingly theatrical. Even though their main focus is the interior, psychological angst of their characters, their narratives unfold through
scenes of externalized conflict, disaster, and failure that are often
darkly funny. Hamilton sets his male protagonists against female suc-
cubi who keep men in a state of erotic suspension: a predicament that
the male characters themselves have a hand in bringing about. The
ironies and frustrations that Hamilton and Rhys set up for their readers, the behavior that strains credibility and sympathy, and the formal
repetition and stasis include masochistic dynamics but, more than
that, they are achieved through strategies that are integrally related to
the historically specific interwar discourse of pleasure. Both Hamilton
and Rhys elevate contorted, self-defeating unpleasure while casting
conventional pleasure as unethical, dispassionate, or amoral. Significantly, both authors self-consciously deploy contemporary vernacular
culture to establish dysphoria.

Hamilton's representations of intoxication and prostitution, central
experiences around which the trilogy revolves, illustrate his attitude
toward pleasure. Writing against a backdrop in which "recreational"
pleasures of the body and mass culture are commonly interpreted as
intoxicating false pleasures, Hamilton and Rhys both suggest that
drinking produces irresistible unpleasure. Inebriation here promises
initial release from woe, but the giddiness of the first drink inevitably gives way to uncontrolled consumption and the narrative careens
out of control. For example, when Bob steps out with Jenny for the
first time, things begin well: "She was phenomenally desirable, and he
was proud of her. He had never had such a delightful evening. He was
drunk" (53). But then "everything grew more and more confused. . . .
The place was beginning to reel; she was speaking with amused dispar-

agement of her other partners; he was finding himself strangely grati-
fied by the disparagement, and trying to order some more drinks" (54).
The scene becomes chaotic as Jenny dances with other men and finally,
the evening ends with Bob realizing how little is left in his wallet: "It
was hard to credit that you could spend all that on so innocent an evening. She could hardly have extracted more from him if she had been a
harpy. It occurred to him that she had never thanked him" (55). Their
successive meetings follow the same pattern. At the end of another
date, Bob has a fight with Jenny, and he rages about prostitutes: "they
got what was coming to them. There was, after all, a God. They rotted
in their own sins and diseases. . . . In the meantime, it would be best to
get drunk. . . . He did so" (127–128). After the chapter break, he wakes
up "sick and heavy . . . giddy but horribly lucid. . . . The truth was that
he was letting himself go. He was becoming debauched" (128).

For Hamilton's (and Rhys's) characters, intoxication quickly crosses
over from excitement to excess. The chapter in *Plains of Cement* that
recounts Jenny's fall into prostitution, for example, details her feelings as she imbibes port with a man she has just met: "Of course
she'd have another drink. She liked drink. She'd have as many more
as she wanted. At last she was abandoned. She was going to have some
pleasure for once. Pleasure—that was the thing—pleasure for once!"
Within a half hour, "enthroned in lucid joy" (289), she has quit her
job and is on the path to prostitution. Hamilton's representation differs from modernist condemnations of metaphorical intoxication in
that he depicts drunkenness as complex and unstable: a pleasure that
inevitably turns to unpleasure, which is actually part of its attraction.

Erotic pleasure too teeters on this edge for Hamilton's characters.
Although the three main narrative lines in *Twenty Thousand Streets*
depict vectors of desire among young, unmarried men and women,
there is almost no sex. Most sexual encounters occur in the context of
prostitution. Bob is intensely ambivalent about prostitutes, referring
to "them" and "these women." He can only account for Jenny through
clichés, noting her "utmost simplicity and tragedy. Beautiful, ill-
educated, foolish, weak, miserable, well-meaning, her beauty had been
her downfall" (136). In this disingenuous framing of Jenny's story as
a tragedy, to which I will return, Bob views her as both a "virgin" and
a "siren" (93). She is "as inaccessible, almost, as a princess" (99), but
also "A little vulgar soul with a little white body, that walked about the

West End and sold itself" (128). When she rebuffs Bob, he falls back into his original position and rages, "Fancy, at his age, imagining there was a resemblance between a harlot and a human being!" (127). Even as Bob's desire for Jenny is the motor driving this narrative, the text rarely signals any pleasure, sexual or otherwise, in their interactions. What we see instead is misery, manipulation, and frustration. The most physically intimate scene between Jenny and Bob, when he visits her Wardour Street boardinghouse, suggests depressing and pestilential sex. A "dark passage which chilled Bob's soul" (169) leads to her filthy, cramped room ("In the confined, crowded, low-ceilinged space you could hardly move" [170]), which is lined with portraits of men left by previous occupants. "Disease and delinquency were in the air: no one had ever cleaned it out. . . . Only those who had fled from toil—only unemployed servant girls, and the spoiled beauties of the slums, had filled it with the lotus odour of their indolence and unhappiness" (171). A jug and basin in the corner, which should be "a source of cleanliness," is "easily the dirtiest thing in the room" (170). Except for a kiss and dancing, this Zolaesque episode is the closest Bob gets to Jenny's body, which the language of the scene casts as grimy and polluted.

Why, then, does Bob continue to pursue Jenny? His desire for her clearly parallels the structure of addiction: "How had she gained this hypnotic ascendency over him—how, from being a rather pretty and piteous little wretch, had she subtly developed into an erotic and deadly drug now utterly indispensable alike to his spiritual and nervous system?" (155–156). Jenny is the epitome of accessible, commodified, bodily pleasure, yet Bob cannot seem to get it, which begs the question of whether he really wants it. For Hamilton, prostitution is a compromised, parasitic kind of voluptuousness: falling in love with Jenny can only produce misery for Bob. The point, however, is that misery is itself a motivation for him. Jenny has insight into the structure of both of Bob's addictions. Noting how her customers need to get drunk before a sexual encounter with her, Jenny "marvelled, as she always did, at these little men, to whom an evening of delight, apart from the money they paid for it, entailed such strenuous mental suffering" (227). "Delight" and "suffering" are closely aligned for Hamilton, in both intoxication and prostitution. Suffering is the attraction: part of the "strange enjoyments" that motivate his characters.

If sexual pleasure is elusive in *Twenty Thousand Streets*, by contrast, an explosive—even orgasmic—moment of pleasure occurs around a different kind of commodity. When Jenny takes Bob's money and dismisses him yet again, he ponders "The brutality, the low-down servant-girl meanness of her. He would never forgive her. She had betrayed and humiliated him" (125). His mood plummets and then suddenly soars as he decides to withdraw more money from the bank. "He could not, of course, humiliate himself any further"—in fact, he could and he does—"but he would have a gamble. He did not know what had come over him lately—he had been getting wild. Let him have one last fling, and then succumb. If he wooed her rightly, might [she] not be his own again?" (129). Smashed by now, he plots his next move and finds, suddenly, that he is ravenous. It is "the false hunger of the drunkard. He could eat and eat." His famished mind turns to some-thing completely unexpected. "Turkish Delight. He could eat pounds and pounds of Turkish Delight. A blind soul, surrounded by the dark-ness of the infinity of the cosmos, lay throbbing with orgiastic desire for Turkish Delight! What a life!" (130). This is one of the most libidi-nally charged, yet comical, passages in Hamilton's work. The cause of the outburst is a popular mass-produced candy that capitalized on ori-entalist fascination, a comestible companion to mass-market novels and films such as *The Sheik*. Fry's introduced its Turkish bar in 1914 as "full of Eastern Promise"; Cadbury's describes its Turkish Delight bar as a "mystical, exotic treat that lets you escape from the everyday."[22] Bob sublimates his sexual desire in a fantasy of gorging himself on the sweet, sticky, exotic treat. (C. S. Lewis would exploit Turkish Delight for the same purpose in *The Lion, the Witch and the Wardrobe* [1950], as an emblem of hedonism. The White Witch presents young Edmund with several pounds of "enchanted" Turkish Delight: "anyone who had once tasted it would want more and more of it, and would even, if they were allowed, go on eating it till they killed themselves."[23]) Hav-ing had this vision of an absurdly banal sublime that he isn't even able to execute, Bob instead settles for a spartan meal of bread, butter, and cheese foraged from the bar downstairs before he passes out in his lonely bed, the prelude to yet another hangover.

The imagined orgy of Turkish Delight, like the scenes of Bob's tipsy glee before he careens into heavy inebriation, along with his desire/repulsion for Jenny, can be correlated, at least theoretically, with *jouissance*. As Lacan puts it, "It begins with a tickle and ends in a blaze of petrol."[24] *Jouissance* flouts the traditional hydraulics of pleasure, in which tension is undesirable, and instead involves an increase of tension to a point that is unbearable. It is a feeling "closer to pain than pleasure," Frank Kermode writes; "pleasure is identified with 'cultural enjoyment and identity,'" whereas "jouissance shatters that identity and is not to be identified with enjoyment."[25] That said, *jouissance* is not quite the right word for Bob's paroxysms. Hamilton's revision of the pleasure principle is not only highly comic (it reads more than a bit like a parody of "Ecnerwal," with his orientalist eroticism), but also points down a dead-end, raptureless street. Bob's Turkish Delight fantasy only emphasizes his foolishly self-created deprivation.[26]

In contrast to Bob's imagined sugar binge or drunkenness, the cinema is an unexpectedly anhedonic zone for Hamilton, despite the fact that his characters are frequent filmgoers and idolize cinema stars. Before Jenny becomes a prostitute, she rents a room above a pet shop and has a single picture of Rudolph Valentino on the wall: "The charmer's drooping lids and sensuously ominous gaze followed her around the room." Bob has a passionate crush on a leading lady, a "large-eyed, slim and shingled blonde," and Ella "dreamed submissive dreams" of the actor Richard Dix.[27] However, the overall cinematic experience is disconnected from "amusement" or "fun." For example, when Ella and Bob go to the pictures at the new Madame Tussaud's cinema, there is an opulent, "decidedly Eastern" atmosphere and doll-like attendants— "seductresses" (80)—seat them. The promise of excitement fades when the film begins.

> In a few moments they were a part of the audience. That is to say their faces had abandoned every trace of the sensibility and character they had borne outside, and had taken on instead the blank, calm, inhuman stare of the picturegoer—an expression which would observe the wrecking of ships, the burning of cities, the fall of empires, the projection of pies, the flooding of countries with an unchanging and grave equanimity. (81)

The cinema renders its viewers depersonalized, each face a banal, blank reflection of the screen in front. At another point, Bob goes out alone on a foggy day "in a wild mood and meant to go to the pictures again," and experiences the same flattened lack of feeling. "He went to Tussaud's cinema, took a one and threepenny seat, and had no pleasure. There was a fog even in the cinema" (89–90). Hamilton reiterates popular conceptions of cinema as a technology of enforced passivity, but against the widespread contemporary concern that it was stimulating people with the wrong kind of mass-produced narratives, Hamilton presents a cinema that hardly stimulates at all, and instead renders the audience indifferent and docile ("the fall of empires" is no more serious that "the projection of pies"). Unlike alcohol, prostitution, and the frenzy of Turkish Delight, all of which heighten tension, cinema dissipates tension but leaves the spectators feeling nothing.

Two notable cinema scenes in the second and third installments of the trilogy emphasize conventional vehicles of amusement that fail to produce pleasure. At the outset of *The Plains of Cement*, which describes the period before Jenny becomes a prostitute, her suitor, Tom, takes her to a Lyons restaurant and the cinema. He spends beyond his means, foreshadowing her relationship with Bob. In fact, Bob's object of "orgiastic desire," Turkish Delight, plays a starring role in the episode. Although he cannot afford it, Tom is certain that "if he did not get Turkish Delight [for Jenny] the entire evening was endangered. For it was an axiom that, amid all the varied delights that generous nature showered, to Turkish Delight Jenny was most consistently faithful" (248). Jenny's faithfulness is as dubious as the supposed cornucopia of delights. As soon as she and Tom are seated in the cinema, "all at once, a delicious, almost salacious little rattle took place in the darkness, and Tom knew she had begun" (249). Little else in *Twenty Thousand Streets Under the Sky* comes near to being "salacious." As in Bob's fantasy of cramming his mouth with Turkish Delight, the narrator notes the alacrity with which Jenny dispatches the sweets: "A pound an hour was Jenny's usual speed with Turkish Delight." Finally Tom obtains his reward: "As far as Jenny was concerned, sensuousness advanced little beyond the realms of Turkish Delight . . . although she still allowed him to hold her hand. She did not as a rule like being 'touched.' But an exception was always made at the pictures, and he was happy because, though she in no way surrendered to him, she was placid and aquiescent" (249). As with the earlier scene, the cinema and the candy produce an anesthetization of sensation, which is required here for Tom to hold Jenny's hand. The sweets and the trip to the cinema are not pleasures freely given but rather the price of attaining sensual contact: a transaction that echoes the structure of the profession into which Jenny soon falls. Her compulsive consumption of Turkish Delight illustrates her selfishness (she is "faithful" to nothing but her own desires) and her incipient whorishness: her joyless, obligatory giving of as little of herself as she can to Tom in return for spending his money. For Bob, Turkish Delight is a fantasy consolation for otherwise unattainable delights.

The most sympathetic characters in Hamilton's fictions *feel* everything—except conventional pleasure—while his despicable characters, whose hearts are toughened, are mercenary hedonists. Denying oneself pleasure, then, becomes a principle and a mark of distinction. This is demonstrated by another cinematic sugar jag near the end of the trilogy. In the final pages of *The Plains of Cement*, Ella learns that Bob has left The Midnight Bell and London. Heartbroken, she buys herself "four ounces of Italian Cream," for which she has a "passion." Italian Cream evokes fantasies of imported splendor just as Bob's Turkish Delight alludes to the exotic Orient. She goes to the Capitol cinema, which is "a tremendous extravagance, as she knew you could not get into the Capitol under one-and-six, but she was beyond caring about extravagance, and she had to have some distraction" (518). She seeks distraction: the classic modernist description of mass culture's effect. Ella also hopes to make a decision about breaking up with the horrid Earnest Eccles.

Hamilton frames this scene with an awkward departure from the free indirect discourse that characterizes most of Ella's narrative and the intimate representation of most of his characters' emotions. In removed omniscient narration—and using the same word, "grave," as he does in the earlier cinema episode with Bob and Ella to explain the audience's affect—Hamilton comments:

> It is a sad pass when a solitary young woman in London is so low in spirits and miserable in her thoughts that she decides she must buy herself some sweets and go by herself to the pictures and sit in the gloom, to hide from the roaring world, and try to divert her mind from its aching preoccupations by looking at the shadows. You will sometimes see such lonely figures, eating their

sweets and gazing gravely at the screen in the flickering darkness of picture theatres, and it may well be that they are merely other Ellas, with just such problems and sorrows in their grey lives as hers.

It is the sweets which give the tragedy to the spectacle. To have reached such an age, to have fought so strenuously all along the line of life, and yet to have come to a stage of hopelessness and isolation wherein the sole remaining consolation is to be found in sweets! Yet this was Ella's predicament the next afternoon. (518)

Throughout the trilogy, Hamilton details the minutiae of his characters' lives—and particularly their feelings of angst and frustration. They may be identifiable as types (the barman, the barmaid, the prostitute), but they are individualized. For this scene of conventional distraction, however, Hamilton shifts to melodramatic, sentimental, and clichéd language ("It is the sweets which give the tragedy to the spectacle"), oddly combined with the high-handed voice of the sociologist that deindividuates and departicularizes his heroine ("merely other Ellas with just such problems and sorrows in their grey lives as hers"). As soon as Ella breaks free of this objectifying, flattening narrative—which she does, importantly, by seeing herself as apart from "the other Ellas"—the narrative shifts back to the usual Hamiltonian voice that aligns itself with the underdog who cannot partake in vernacular pleasure. "She had no sooner entered the imposing, lavishly mirrored portals of the Capitol than she had a feeling that her impulse to entertain herself had been a mistaken one" (519). She "tried to . . . enjoy her Italian Cream," but "she had to be careful not to make herself sick" (519). Gustatory pleasure gives way to fear of nauseating gluttony: the same degeneration of pleasure as in drinking. Rather than experiencing the diversion and amusement that cinema is supposed to deliver, Ella's heart sinks "in sudden unexpected lurches, which left a slow ache behind. . . . [Bob] had struck, as it were, a blow upon her soul which had been transmitted to her physical being." This metaphysical hurt is matched by a comically external one: "Moreover she had come in in the middle of a picture, and the children behind her kept on kicking her in the back." Her heart and body battered—and seasick, like Bob, "as though the ship of her lovelorn condition had entered even rougher water" (519)—she flees the cinema into a "teeming, roaring, grinding, belching, hooting, anxious-faced world" (520).

For characters such as Bob and Ella, there is no refuge in this type of distraction or other conventional amusements. A standard modernist complaint is that cinema is all too effective in diverting people from their problems, feeding them delusions and narcotizing them. For Hamilton's sympathetic characters, cinematic pleasure fails, but in the way that they *like* to fail. Ella goes to the cinema ostensibly expecting "distraction" and instead receives "a blow upon her soul" and a shower of kicks on her back. However, this timid character who holds herself back from sensuous Italian Cream, who never acts on her real desire for Bob and instead enters into an excruciating courtship with the buffoonish Earnest Eccles, is not a pushover. She is quick-witted and firm with the raucous clientele at The Midnight Bell. She lives independently. She is not the waif Hamilton makes her out to be in his soapbox passage. Could it be, then, that this character is doing what she wants? Is she enjoying her "tragic" loss of Bob by the fact that cinema *can't* distract her?

One reason it is difficult to put one's finger on what is driving Hamilton's characters is that they constantly insist they are not to blame for anything that happens to them. Bob tells himself that "From the first moment he had met her, to the last time he had seen her, he had never made one conscious move towards either wooing or winning [Jenny]. Indeed, he had done nothing but retreat. And yet here he was stuck with her—fully committed. Agencies beyond him had been at work" (120). Ella lets Mr. Eccles court her even as "the dungeon of his shameless and enwrapping personality" (477) repulses her. Jenny blames others for her drunken night: "It wasn't fair—them making her drunk like that" (305). Hamilton's characters "find" themselves in the same situation over and over, and make the same self-defeating decisions over and over. Hamilton once wrote,

There is only one theme for the Hardy-cum-Conrad great novel—that is, that this is a bloody awful life, that we are none of us responsible for our own lives and actions, but merely in the hands of the gods, that Nature don't [sic] care a damn, but looks rather picturesque in not doing so, and that whether you're making

love, being hanged, or getting drunk, it's all a futile way of passing the time in the brief period allotted us preceding death.[28]

This might describe the surface of Hamilton's fiction, or the narrative that his characters tell themselves, but the stories themselves tell
otherwise. His characters do have and make choices, and moments of
volition are foregrounded throughout the novels. Bob could choose to
break off with Jenny and romance the good-hearted Ella. Ella could
ditch the odious Mr. Eccles much earlier than she does. Both of them
have jobs and a place to live, and their circumstances are not so desper-
ate (although Ella has the threat of spinsterdom pressing upon her)
until they make them so. Jenny's moment of choice is most glaring of
all, as Hamilton carefully details the scene in which one glass of port
leads her into prostitution.[29]

With disavowal and underhandedness, Hamilton's characters do
what they want, even as they deny that is so. They swear to do one
thing, and then, in strikingly quick succession (sometimes in the same
sentence), do the opposite. For instance, when Bob discovers that
Jenny has skipped out on her rent and is grifting her landlord as surely
as she is grifting Bob, he vows for the umpteenth time to cut his losses
and stay away from her. "Was it relief? Was this his chance of escape?"
(158). To the contrary, he immediately goes to the area of the West End
that is her turf and begins looking for her: "he discovered himself in
that quarter, as he invariably did on Thursday evenings, and was willing to submit to fate and accident" (158). Obviously, this is no function of fate or accident. He pitifully asks Jenny why she failed to keep
their last date and she flatly tells him that she didn't want to meet him
(again, it is the unsympathetic characters in Hamilton who are able to
be open about their desires). "This was hopeless—an *impasse*" (161, italics in original), he thinks. "Were there any lower circles, he wondered,
to which he might descend in hell?" (163). The question is not rhetorical: Bob goes on to find an even lower circle and to abase himself still
further. If we read these texts literally—if we look at how the characters act—the narratives suggest that the impasse is exactly where they
want to be. The impasse, a point at which a character is impeded or
blocked, represents the collision of forces (pleasure and pain), a place of
pressure or tension without release, that defines unpleasure. No exit.

The patterns of these texts—their repetition, the characters' avowed helplessness and refusal of responsibility and agency—reflect a determined desire for abasement, tension, and deadlock. For example, when Jenny stands Bob up for the final time, at Victoria Station, he retreats to a restaurant where

> he sat there quietly contemplating his own drama. . . . He ordered a double whisky. That step was obvious. He drank it rather theatrically and rather theatrically ordered another. For the moment he could regard himself theatrically. He was, perhaps, almost enjoying himself. (210)

In moments like these, Hamilton tips his hand, indicating the payoff, the delectation of suffering, and how these experiences are self-consciously staged and narrated by the "victims" with a note of what can only be called triumph or "enjoyed discomfort." If the repetition of "theatrically" suggests Bob is not exactly trapped because he is able to observe and savor his own performance, it is more precisely a moment in which he fully admits his motivations and his desire for defeat.

Here and throughout his work, Hamilton implies that conventional pleasure is dishonorable. The characters who suffer are held up as morally superior, and misery is a mark of negative distinction. Bob's self-conscious viewing of himself as wretched and victorious mirrors the reader's view of him, and also Hamilton's. The protagonist who can't or won't participate in mass culture, at least not in the usual ways, serves as a figure for the reader who is consuming a text that is frustratingly and unrelentingly oriented toward defeat, that thwarts narratives of fulfillment, redemption, and progress as well as modernist narratives of cultural competency. All parts of the reading process are drawn into this promotion of failure, refusal, and negation.

The performance of defeat and the reader's witnessing of it takes another form at the conclusion of *Midnight Bell*. Bob tells himself, "He believed it was not [Jenny's] fault. Existence had abused her and made her what she was: poverty had crushed him and made him unable to help her" (220). "Poverty had crushed him": let us not forget that at the beginning of *The Midnight Bell* Bob had a steady job and a healthy sum in the bank. His last-minute forgiveness of Jenny is as disingenuous as his dismissal of his own hand in the drama. Not just the characters but Hamilton's narrator too is given to this kind of theatricalization of suffering, in the passage describing Jenny eating sweets in the cinema, for example, and in the conclusion of the trilogy. The narrator praises Bob, for "after all he had suffered, and after all he had lost, Bob was yet able to glow in this manner and resolve to go to sea."

> For there is this about men. You can embitter and torment them from birth. . . . You can trick them and mock them with all the implements of fate—lead them on, as Bob was led on, only to betray them, obsess them with hopeless dreams, punish them with senseless accidents, and harass them with wretched fears. You can buffet them, bait them, enrage them—load upon them all evils and follies in this vale of obstruction and tears. But, even at that, there is one thing you cannot do. You can never make them, under any provocation, say die. And therein lies their acquittal. (221)

One can almost hear the violins—or the Greek chorus—in the background. But the unpersuasive coda, which shifts the blame away from the characters to cosmic forces, is at odds with the rest of the novel and the events that led to this point. Here, as in the scene with Ella eating Italian Cream in the cinema, which is also said to be a "tragedy," there is a strong authorial address to the reader ("you") and a solicitation of sentimentalism and clichés (the "vale . . . of tears," Bob's having been ostensibly "led on," and the final, triumphant "acquittal") that Hamilton's narrative otherwise rejects. Like Lawrence and Huxley surreptitiously imitating exactly what they critique in Hull and Glyn, Hamilton cannot resist the redemption of suffering, the deliverance from the bleak world he has otherwise so consistently depicted. As in the Italian Cream scene, in which Ella becomes like "other Ellas," Bob becomes just like other unfortunate men. The passage contradicts the spirit of these characters' struggles for individuation and distinction through debasement and failure.

To the reader who has been enculturated into Hamilton's narrative world in *Twenty Thousand Streets Under the Sky*, this redemptive frame, with its evocation of tragedy, rings false. Aristotle specifies that there is an *oikeia hedone* or "proper pleasure" in the audience's response to tragedy, an emotion of "enjoyed discomfort."[30] Freud points to this as one of the culturally sanctioned forms of unpleasure: "the artistic play and artistic imitation carried out by adults, which, unlike children's, are aimed at an audience, do not spare the spectators . . . the most painful experiences and yet can be felt by them as highly enjoyable."[31] The mere word "tragedy" carries the nimbus of dignity and serious- ness of purpose. However, Hamilton's characters do not fulfill the clas- sical definition of tragic actors; they themselves want their downfall too much. And the feeling produced by Hamilton's novels is nowhere near cathartic. Instead, the off-key final pages of the trilogy, with its clumsy reach toward salvation, sounds a last note of uncomfortable dissonance, a bad aftertaste that lingers like one of Bob's hangovers or the cloying powdered sugar of Turkish Delight.

Hamilton's last major works, *Hangover Square: A Story of Dark- est Earl's Court* (1941) and *The Gorse Trilogy* (published from 1952 to 1955), are even more critical of conventional pleasure and take that critique in a political direction. The simmering resentment of cruel, parasitic women in *Twenty Thousand Streets* tips over into overt misogyny and violence. In *Hangover Square,* the male protago- nist's hopeless relationship with the actress-grifter Netta is similar to Bob's crush on Jenny in *Twenty Thousand Streets,* but it is more aggressively angry, as Bone fantasizes about killing Netta and even- tually does so. Netta is drawn to a political force that is not available to Hamilton's earlier characters—fascism: "It might be said that this feeling for violence and brutality, for the pageant and panorama of fascism on the Continent, formed her principal disinterested aes- thetic pleasure. She had few others" (154). The phrase "disinterested aesthetic pleasure," associated with Kant and Eliot, links modern- ist detachment to fascism. Yet Netta's attraction is hardly disinter- ested: "She liked the uniforms, the guns, the breeches, the boots, the swastikas, the shirts. She was, probably, sexually stimulated by these things in the same way as she might have been sexually stimulated by a bull-fight" (153). Fascism, Hamilton suggests, is the point at which the worst of popular and elitist pleasures converge; it offers imme- diate, embodied, aestheticized attractions to characters who crave stimulation and excitement, as well as a philosophy of detachment and cruelty.

Hamilton's *Rope* (1929) is perhaps his most concentrated explora- tion of the rejection of pleasure cast explicitly in terms of modernist aesthetics. The play leaves behind the seedy bars of Euston Street for the Mayfair home of a wealthy Oxford undergraduate, Brandon, who along with an accomplice, Granillo, has strangled a classmate and hosts a dinner party served on the trunk containing the corpse. Telescoping the claustrophobia of Hamilton's novels, the drama unfolds in one room and tightly focuses on one act of violence and its intellectual justification: a ghoulish parody of aestheticized pleasure. The "passionless . . . bloodless and noiseless murder,"[32] as Brandon characterizes it, is an act of pure will and intellect. Brandon declares that its "beauty and piquancy" are expressed in their arrangement of the gathering that follows (5). It is a daring and difficult stunt just to see if they can get away with it. (This is echoed in Hitchcock's decision to shoot a feature film in what seems like one single, continuous take: a formal feat that did not serve any real narrative purpose, but was its own justification.) Most of the party is dominated by the interests of "unintellectual humanity" (6), in opposition to the self-declared *übermenschen*. The guests chatter about film stars, fiddle with the wireless, and dance to the gramophone; the victim, Ronald, met his death after a trip to the Coliseum Music Hall. Brandon, Granillo, and Rupert—a "damnably brilliant poet" whom Brandon and Granillo almost invite to join them in staging the murder because they feel he "might have seen this thing from our angle, that is, the artistic one" (6)—profess ignorance or distaste for the cinema. Rupert unconvincingly remarks, "I once went to the pictures and saw Mary Pickford" (23). Brandon says, "I simply abhor the things myself. . . . They simply make me go to sleep. And all those places are so infernally stuffy" (23). Vernacular pleasure, rejected by the characters who think of themselves as exceptional men and embraced by the glibly sybaritic partygoers, is the background to the stealthy, aestheticized, and intellectualized act of violence at the center of the party.

The liquor flows as heavily throughout the play as in any Hamilton novel. Rupert arrives already drunk and proceeds to get more inebriated, although it does not seem to impair his sharp perception. While the other characters dance in the next room, Rupert peruses Conrad's last novel, *The Rover*, and discovers the dead man's ticket to the music hall, which leads him to unmask the murder. After the other guests leave, Rupert plays a game of cat and mouse with the hosts and eventually discovers the body. Brandon tells him,

Listen. I have done this thing. I and Granno. We have done it together. We have done it for—for adventure. For adventure and danger. For danger. You read Nietzsche, don't you, Rupert? . . . And you know that he tells us to live dangerously . . . And you know that he's no more respect for individual life than you, and tells us—to—live dangerously. We thought we would do so—that's all. We have done so. We have only *done* the thing. Others have talked. We have done. Do you understand? . . . For God's sake tell me you're an emancipated man. (63-64)

Rupert may be intellectually on the side of modernism (Conrad, Nietzsche, modern poetry), but his "emancipation" stops short of Brandon and Granno's cerebral exhilaration. Earlier in the evening, he concedes that he has "done murder" himself in the war, but there was no thrill to it. He berates Brandon and Granillo for their "cruel and scheming pleasure" that led them to commit "a sin and a blasphemy against that very life which you now find yourselves so precious" (64).

Like other Hamilton protagonists, Rupert rejects pleasure on both sides of the great divide. When the other party guests have left, he makes a lyrical speech about the hour: 10:35, the last call for pleasure. "It's a wonderful hour," he sighs. "I am particularly susceptible to it":

Because it is, I think, the hour when London asks why—when it wants to know what it's all about—when the tedium of activity and the folly of pleasure are equally transparent. It is the hour in which unemployed servant girls, and the spoiled beauties of slums, walk the streets for hire. . . . It is the hour when jaded London theatre audiences are settling down in the darkness to the last acts of plays, of which they know the denouements all too well. . . . For others, further horrors are awaiting. The nightclubs and cabarets have not yet begun but they will do very soon. . . . Five-and-twenty to eleven. A horrible hour—a *macabre* hour, for it is not only the hour of pleasure ended, it is the hour when pleasure itself has been found wanting. There, that is what this hour means to me. (55–56)

Here Rupert acts as the omniscient narrator for Hamilton's interwar oeuvre, vacillating between tedium and folly, pain and pleasure (he even uses a phrase from Bob's visit to Jenny's squalid room:

"unemployed servant girls, and the spoiled beauties of the slums"; Bob also speaks of prostitutes as representing "the glamour and beauty of the macabre" [42]). Baffled, Brandon asks, "My dear Rupert, do you see no earthly object in living?" "I fear not," Rupert replies, demanding another drink (56). It is always 10:35 in Hamilton's textual universe, the hour when the drinkers are about to be ejected from the pubs, the hour when Jennys begin to trawl for customers, "The hour when pleasure itself has been found wanting." And it is this, the evacuation of pleasure, that Hamilton's favored characters crave.

"FOR GOD'S SAKE WATCH OUT FOR YOUR FILM-MIND": JEAN RHYS

Critics regularly refer to "the Rhys woman": a narcissistic, self-defeating, financially dependent victim who makes dubious decisions and declares the world a hostile conspirator against her. Like Hamilton's characters, Rhys's women drink often; the effect is a temporary giddiness that inevitably gives way to crying, unsteadiness, and "making a scene." They rarely get a lucky break, and when they do, they squander it.[33] In *Good Morning, Midnight*, Sasha Jensen ends up in an awful room in an awful hotel; she thinks, "Only I would have landed here, only I would stay here" (364). There is a basic disjunction between Rhys's characters' declared desires and their actions. In *Voyage in the Dark*, after Anna sleeps with Walter for the first time, he gives her cash. "I meant to say, 'What are you doing?'" she recalls. "But when I went up to him, instead of saying, 'Don't do that,' I said, 'All right, if you like—anything you like, any way you like.' And I kissed his hand" (23). Her impulse toward independence gives way to exaggerated subservience and a self-imposed loss of agency. Similarly, in *Good Morning, Midnight*, Sasha tells herself: "I'm not going to any beastly little bar tonight. No, tonight I'm going somewhere where there's music; somewhere where I can be with a lot of people; somewhere where there's dancing. But where? By myself, where can I go? I'll have one more drink first and then think it out. . . . Not the Dôme. I'll avoid the damned Dôme. And, of course, it's the Dôme I go to" (388). Rhys's work is full of such moments, when desire and will are overruled by a counterforce of self-destruction: a dynamic that has typically been read as passivity but in fact suggests determined negation.

The general critical perception is that there is little pleasure in Rhys's fiction, but rather inertia, numbness, and misery. Pleasure does exist for Rhys, but it is often cast in the past tense: for example, the sensuous opening of *After Leaving Mr. Mackenzie* and *Good Morning, Midnight*'s account of Sasha's happy period with Enno in Paris or very fleetingly in the present, in the interval between the first and the second Pernod. Pleasure has a dangerous dimension. "Don't get excited. You know what happens when you get excited and exalted, don't you?" Sasha reminds herself. "So, no excitement. . . . Not too much drinking, avoidance of certain cafés, of certain streets, of certain spots. . . . No trailing around aimlessly with cheap gramophone records starting up in your head" (351). Pleasure, for Rhys, represented by urban pastimes such as drinking in cafés, flaneuserie, and "cheap gramophone records," is always on the verge of getting out of hand.

Rhys's characters exist in a world where women are expected to provide pleasure: mistresses find money in their bags after a sexual encounter, chorus girls are assumed to be sexually available, manicurists are asked to "be a bit nice" to their clients, and "amateurs" are part of an economy of pleasure that is far more complex than conventional prostitution in terms of agency and desire ("People are much cheaper than things," a chorus girl remarks in *Voyage in the Dark* [28]). Mass-produced vernacular culture—popular songs, films, and romance novels, for example, which are coded as feminine, passive, and somatic— gives women mixed signals about pleasure. Rhys's protagonists are unable or refuse to participate in this economy of conventional pleasure that serves male desire and stays within the boundaries of acceptable behavior for women. Pleasure for them is not release (as in the Freudian model) or escape through prefabricated fantasies (the dominant understanding of vernacular culture). Like Hamilton's characters, Rhys's characters are irresistibly drawn toward the impasse: a deadlock of movement, a heightening of tension.[34]

As with Hamilton, in Rhys the impasse has political and historical implications. Her protagonists are displaced and poor, and their stories are set in the dramatic moment, as Jane Marcus describes it, of "the end of empire and the rise of fascism colliding."[35] Yet Rhys focuses on intimate experiences, interior landscapes, and uneasy affect rather than overtly political interventions. Shari Benstock has argued that Rhys, along with Djuna Barnes and Anaïs Nin, chose "privacy over public activism," but that their fictions nevertheless "render the sense of impending catastrophe in terms of a forbidding urban landscape to be negotiated by female characters."[36] Subsequent critics have excavated the ways Rhys, like Barnes in *Nightwood*, gestures toward historical crises of colonialism and empire in texts that feature self-absorbed protagonists on the margins of society. Veronica Gregg, for example, maintains that "The reiterative character of Rhys's portrayal of the outsider is underwritten by the writer's insistence on a stubborn, unassimilable otherness" that includes "othered races, sexualities, and genders."[37] Likewise, Maren Tova Linnett has suggested that Rhys's Jewish characters reflect her protagonists' own "alienation and pain" at a time that anti-Semitism was fueling the most vicious political regimes.[38] Rhys also deploys her protagonists' capacities for pleasure in such a way as to mark them as apart from, and resistant to, oppressive consensus and conformist consolidations of national, racial, and sexual identity that would reach a terrifying pinnacle with Nazism.

Rhys and her characters have been diagnosed by critics as depressed, melancholic, schizophrenic, borderline personality, and, perhaps most commonly, masochistic. Some critics are put off by her representation of masochism, while others recuperate it as a strategy of self-representation; some see it as the dominant cultural narrative for women, and others argue that it stemmed from Rhys's personal history.[39] All of these readings locate Rhys's masochism in trauma and cultural disenfranchisement. Certainly, her characters are masochistic; however, like Hamilton, Rhys does not just recycle her own traumatic experiences but self-consciously constructs unpleasure in response to dominant narratives of pleasure and desire, particularly in vernacular culture.

Although diagnostic readings of Rhys's masochism describe, some more convincingly than others, the extravagant debasement throughout her work and its general lugubriousness, they are less persuasive when it comes to the other tonal ranges that Rhys explores. Like Hamilton, Rhys reads vernacular culture as a source of negative identification, but she also employs humor and irony in ways that run counter to the interpretation of her texts as numb or depressive. For example, in one of the exuberant periods of *Good Morning, Midnight*, when Sasha is pregnant, before her baby dies and her husband abandons her, she has dinner in her apartment with her friend Lise, a cabaret singer. In high spirits, "chuckling madly," Sasha tells Lise a story about her life in

England. A man tried to pick her up in Kensington. "Can you resist it?" he asks her. "Yes, I can," she drolly recalls her reply, "I can resist it, just plain and Nordic like that, I certainly can" (427-8). Fuming, he insists on waiting with her for her bus.

> We are standing by a lamp-post, in dead silence, waiting for the bus, and what happens? My drawers fall off. I look down at them, step out of them neatly, pick them up, roll them into a little parcel and put them into my handbag. What else is there to do? He stares into vacancy, shocked beyond measure. The bus comes up. He lifts his hat with a flourish and walks away. (428)

This is a markedly theatrical vignette of absurd physical comedy. Told in the present tense, as if the scene is unfolding in front of our eyes as well as Sasha's, the woman who first refuses the man's advances—the ice maiden, the ball-breaker—is immodestly exposed, perhaps punished for her haughtiness, by her wayward lingerie. She tries to retain her dignity through nonchalance and wittily details her cool response: she steps out of her drawers "neatly" and "roll[s] them into a little parcel." Meanwhile, the man is transformed from a rake to a prude by her scandalous display: perhaps he wanted to see her drawers, but not this way. Despite the provocative actions, both figures are affectless: Sasha's behavior is deadpan and the man "stares into vacancy" although he is "shocked." The scene is awkward and cryptic as well as funny, but it is a joke without a punch line.

There is a punch line of sorts in the scene that follows. The next day Sasha, realizing "that it is I who have lost ground," and feeling "awful about everything," calls the man. He says that he is "very vexed" about what happened but will send her a box of Turkish Delight. "Well now, what is it, this Turkish Delight?" she wonders. "Is it a comment, is it irony, is it compensation, is it apology, or what? I'll throw it out of the window, whatever it is" (428). The scene ends there, leaving the reader to picture the defenestrated candy scattered about like Sasha's perplexed questions. As with Hamilton, Turkish Delight is a substitute for the pleasure that the characters are *not* having. Here it is symptomatic of English reserve, a gesture to avoid confrontation and to smooth over the awkward exchange in the street, in which it is not clear who should apologize to whom. To Sasha,

Turkish Delight is a cipher or shorthand for something unknown. It defies interpretation. "Is it comment, is it irony . . . or what?" might well be asked of Rhys's work in a more general sense. Her protagonists are often unsure whether they are reading the world correctly, and if they are capable of behaving correctly (laughing at the right spot in the cinema, not crying in cafés, keeping their drawers up, etc.). Pleasure is something Rhys's protagonists find especially bewildering and unstable, and vernacular culture is anything but the simple, easy, standardized experience presented in the usual modernist discourse. In her representations of popular literature, songs, and especially film, Rhys points out that interwar vernacular culture is preoccupied with women's bodies and the confusing social scripts that mandate their behavior; indeed, she demonstrates how women's conformism is what secures these texts' pleasure.

Rhys continually stages vignettes with a staccato rhythm, non sequiturs, tonal disjunctions, inappropriate affect, a lack of narrative explanation or continuity, and jokes that draw attention to the female body and turn on the female protagonist's humiliation, debasement, or confusion.[40] The sequence with the falling drawers and the Turkish Delight is strongly visual and suggestive rather than narratively cohesive or conclusive. Fragmented form is a classic feature of modernism, but Rhys's constructions also reference theatrical structures. Rhys herself worked as a chorus girl, actress, and film extra during her early years in England.[41] Louis James contends that the distinctive structure of music hall influenced Rhys's sense of narrative structure, pacing, and tone: "changes of mood and use of refrain" as well as "juxtaposition of fantasy and tawdry reality."[42] The same was true of early cinema. Just after World War One, when the music hall was waning and film was still a new medium, cinematic programs perpetuated the music hall structure as short films and live performances were combined in one "bill." Rhys's scene with the falling drawers strongly recalls a saucy music hall skit, where undergarments were always good for a laugh (this could be Benny Hill). The staging is pitch-perfect cliché British (underneath a Kensington lamppost) and the man's stylized exit is also theatrical. However, both characters' feigned affectlessness is unusual in the context of theater and early film, where exaggerated emotions, double takes, and over-the-top reactions were the norm. Rhys frequently incorporates pleasure-driven vernacular culture into her narratives, but she does so to display her protagonist's estrangement from popular scripts of pleasure.

One major assumption about vernacular culture is that everyone—except those cultural critics who stand apart from "the crowd"—responds to it the same way. Both Hamilton and Rhys focus on characters who read vernacular culture in a way that is out of synch with those around them. While this is structurally similar to general modernist skepticism about mass culture, Rhys's constant mixing of highbrow, lowbrow, and middlebrow texts—classic English and French literature, music hall and jazz songs, popular women's literature—suggests that her characters are similarly heterogeneous in their class identifications. They are not exactly highbrows, although they read: Sasha defines herself as a "cérébrale"; Anna reads *Madame Bovary*. Their cultural identifications are as complex as their racial and national senses of self. Just as Rhys uses race or national difference as a means of establishing her protagonists' outsider identities, she uses vernacular culture to define her protagonists through negation of its supposed pleasures.

This often happens with songs. In *Voyage in the Dark*, for example, the unremittingly sunny "Camptown Races" becomes a dark commentary on Anna's unlucky romantic life in which "nobody wins" (95). At the opening of *Good Morning, Midnight*, Sasha is at a restaurant and is listening to a woman hum "Gloomy Sunday," otherwise known as "The Hungarian Suicide Song." Sasha says, "I like that song," but it causes her to weep so much that she must retreat to the "lavabo" (347). Rhys frequently uses the metaphor of music to explain encroachments of painful memory: "I walk along, remembering this, remembering that, trying to find a cheap place to eat—not so easy round here. The gramophone record is going strong in my head: 'Here this happened, here that happened'" (352).

Rhys's representation of her protagonists' responses to film is more elaborate and significant. In keeping with contemporary views of filmgoing, Rhys's cinema is largely a female space and its narratives are preoccupied with questions of female desire. Anna Snaith writes, "Rhys's evocation of modernist London . . . features the cinema, which, like the department store, was seen as a dangerous site of mass culture, appealing to and corrupting of women. Often called 'dream palaces,' cinemas were thought to indulge passively women's fantasies in distracting and morally harmful ways."[43] Rhys's cinema scenes typically have two features: the films' narratives highlight tensions around gender and desire, and in these scenes, Rhys emphasizes conflicts between the novel's protagonist and the rest of the cinema audience. Like Hamilton's characters, Rhys's women go to the movies as a means of retreat or an escape that never turns out to be so. The cinema is a place of negation that extinguishes conventional delight.

In *Good Morning, Midnight*, filmgoing represents other people's pleasures. One way Sasha manages to keep herself in line is by drawing up a disciplined schedule, which includes going to "a cinema on the Champs Elysées, according to programme. Laughing heartily in the right places. / It's a very good show and I see it through twice" (352). She is proud of herself for responding appropriately and successfully subverting her destructive impulses. Later, when she wants a drink in a restaurant, she uses film as a ruse, asking the waiter "to tell me the way to the nearest cinema. This, of course, arises from a cringing desire to explain my presence in the place. I only came in here to inquire the way to the nearest cinema. I am a respectable woman, une femme convenable, on her way to the nearest cinema" (409). As she orders a second Pernod, the pretense of normalcy fails. As with Hamilton's characters, the inevitable inebriation sends her resolve off track. "Now the feeling of the room is different. They all know what I am. I'm a woman come in here to get drunk. That happens sometimes" (410). Her masquerade also fails when Sasha goes to the Cinéma Danton. At first she is able to fall into line with the crowd. The comic film centers on "a good young man trying to rescue his employer from a mercenary mistress" (410). Rhys's protagonists are often mistresses, but they only take what they are given and pay dearly even for that. The film's final joke turns on the young man interrupting the employer, "a gay, bad old boy who manufactures toilet articles," and the mistress who leaves, announcing with annoyance that she's on her way to fetch "suppositoires." "Everybody laughs loudly at this," Sasha notes, "and so do I. She said that well" (411). The gold-digging mistress is stripped of her sexual power and becomes a coarse comedian. Sasha chuckles with the crowd: so far so good. When the man accidentally flings an engagement ring into a pond and "makes too wild a gesture," Sasha identifies with the predicament—"Exactly the sort of thing that happens to me"—and laughs wildly until she weeps. "However, the film shows no signs of stopping, so I get up and go out" (411). Like her drinking, which starts as a feeling of pleasure but careens into drunkenness, Sasha's response to the film tips over into uncomfortable excess. She turns back to liquor. "Another Pernod in the bar next door to the cinema. I sit at a corner table and sip it respectably, with lowered eyes. Je suis une femme convenable, just come out of the nearest cinema. . . . If I have a bottle of Bordeaux at dinner I'll be almost as drunk as I'd hoped to be" (411).

Rhys's cinematic narratives are figurative projections of her characters' conflicts. In *After Leaving Mr. Mackenzie*, Julia's trip to a women-run cinema leaves her weeping at the "old fashioned" romance of the film: a plot that is unavailable to her, arguably, because she chooses circumstances that make it impossible. Another woman in the audience loudly proclaims the movie "dingo" (259). Later, in a cinema on Edgware Road, Julia is equally out of synch with the rest of the audience as she watches a "comic film" of male athletes running around a track who are then joined by women, "at which the audience rocked with laughter" (301). The image of women exhausting themselves by emulating men renders the contemporary bid for gender equality comical to the audience, but it is disappointing to Julia: it is "a strange anticlimax." Screen femininity is equally maladroit in the film *Hot Stuff from Paris*. Despite its title, Julia observes that "The girls were perky and pretty, but it was strange how many of the older women looked drab and hopeless, with timid, hunted expressions. They looked ashamed of themselves, as if they were begging the world in general not to notice that they were women or to hold it against them" (273). Although the cinema of this period was commonly understood as an escapist space of communal, collective, female experience and a primary locus of women's pleasure, Rhys emphasizes the rifts in spectatorship and the venue's coercive nature.

Voyage in the Dark features an especially telling cinema scene. The novel's protagonist, Anna, who comes to England from the Caribbean, is often ill and feels like a ghost or as if she is in a dream.[44] After she is cast off by her wealthy lover, Walter, Ethel Matthews convinces her to go to the Camden Town High Street cinema to distract her from her woes. They go to see the silent film "Three-Fingered Kate, Episode 5. Lady Chichester's Necklace." The ensuing scene draws a contrast between Anna's response and that of the other cinemagoers, and Rhys constellates the film with two other intertexts about female pleasure. The Three-Fingered Kate film begins with a series of observations about the cinematic atmosphere.

> The piano began to play, sickly-sweet. Never again, never, not ever, never. Through caverns measureless to man down to a sunless sea. . . .
> The cinema smelt of poor people, and on the screen ladies and gentlemen in evening dress walked about with strained smiles. (67)

Rhys introduces the cinema scene with the usual musical accompaniment and also with a line from classic English poetry, "Kubla Khan." It is a reflection of Anna's hopelessness: just before the cinema scene, Anna has been thinking about drowning and despair after Walter has rejected her (61, 65). Coleridge's vision of the pleasure dome intersects with many of Rhys's images. The luscious garden "Where blossomed many an incense-bearing tree" is an orientalist Eden that physically resembles Anna's descriptions of her native Caribbean island. Rhys closes the section with a soothing flashback: "my lovely life . . . a garden with a high wall round it—and every now and again thinking I only dreamt it it never happened" (84), repeating Coleridge's idea of a paradise dreamed up and lost. Pleasure is inherently unruly for Coleridge; its negative energies include a gothic "woman wailing for her demon lover," an image that resonates with Rhys's unhappy female protagonists in *Voyage, Quartet, After Leaving,* and *Good Morning, Midnight,* and strikingly anticipates Bertha in *Wide Sargasso Sea.* Rhys draws suggestive parallels between Coleridge's romantic sublime and contemporary unpleasure.

The film that "Kubla Khan" prefaces in *Voyage* is a tale of rebellious female desire chastised. The tale of Three-Fingered Kate is wildly appealing to Anna's fellow cinemagoers but dysphoric to her. She observes, "On the screen a pretty girl was pointing a revolver at a group of guests"; she robs the society people, taking a pearl necklace. "When the police appeared everybody clapped. When Three-Fingered Kate was caught everybody clapped louder still." The screen announces the next installment in the series: "Three-Fingered Kate, Episode 6. . . . Five Years Hard. Next Monday." Anna resents the audience and their reactions: "'Damned fools,' I said. 'Aren't they damned fools? Don't you hate them? They always clap in the wrong places and laugh in the wrong places'" (67). Although the audience in the cinema smells "poor," there is no class alliance here; they side with the aristocrats and their protectors, the police, against the female outlaw. As Celia Marshik points out, "Anna's eventual criminality is prefigured by her sympathy for 'Three-Fingered Kate. . . . When Anna curses the crowd that applauds Kate's capture, readers can see the novel's own sympathies in miniature" (191).

Anna's sympathy for Kate is even more significant given Rhys's departure from the actual *Three-Fingered Kate* series. Elizabeth Carolyn Miller notes that "Rhys describes two Three-Fingered Kate films that never actually existed."[45] The real films, produced between 1909 and 1912, "pit Kate against the wealthiest and most privileged members of her society: bankers, barons, colonels, and lords. The goods she steals are luxury items of the rich: jewelry, art, and priceless colonial loot" (118). Analyzing the one extant film in the series, Miller reads Kate's adversary, Baker Street detective "Sheerluck," as a "protector of bourgeois property, clients, and values," while Kate is "the female consumer gone criminal, the lady shopper gone mad" (116, 123). Thus far, Rhys's fabrication stays close to the original. However, Miller observes, "In the tradition of the populist outlaw, Kate's crimes do not alienate audiences, but attract them" (118). Rhys "presents the series as conservative and moralizing, which it wasn't. . . . The actual films were firmly on the side of Kate rather than the police" (*Framed*, 121–122). Indeed, Alex Marlow-Mann characterizes the Kate series as anomalously sympathetic to the female outlaw, "an arch-criminal and mistress of her own destiny."

> Each episode ends with a final shot, completely extraneous to the story as a whole, in which Kate defiantly raises her mutilated hand to the camera. In "The Wedding Presents," having committed her robbery she repeats the gesture with her hand turned the other way—a far more vulgar gesture directed at her victims and the forces of order. Kate, then, is a daring, ironic, proto-feminist criminal, far ahead of her time.[46]

Kate is a grinning, swaggering female Robin Hood. She aggressively pursues her desires and hoodwinks the bourgeois order, giving it the finger(s). Kate's missing digits, displayed so prominently in the last shot of each film, imply that Kate is somehow phallic and castrated at the same time. The footage from the sole existing film—*Kate Purloins the Wedding Presents*—presents her flouting that most sacred of heterosexual institutions, as well as the telos for women's popular romance narratives.

Three-Fingered Kate would seem to be a very apt figure of identification for Rhys's protagonists. Why, then, does the author fabricate a punishing conclusion for Kate and reverse the audience's sympathies? Miller speculates that "Rhys reimagines the films to accentuate her society's penchant for punishing wayward women." She does this by dramatically separating Anna's spectatorship from her peers'. Ethel's response to the French actress who played Kate—"she had this soft, dirty way that foreign girls have," while "An English girl would have respected herself more" (68)—and the ensuing conversation about sex suggest that there is something lascivious about Kate. She is perceived not just as a legal outlaw but as a lewd sexual presence on the screen. Anna identifies with Kate as a "foreign" woman; other characters insinuate that her Caribbean background sets her apart, racially and sexually, from the English—e.g., "The girls call her the Hottentot" (7). Like Kate, who is missing two digits, the Hottentot Venus (an African woman who was displayed as a freakish attraction in nineteenth-century Britain) was perceived as a physiognomic oddity whose bodily features denote her lustfulness.

Cinematic narratives are alienatingly conventional to Rhys's protagonists, and as such confirm their outlier spectatorship. Despite desultory attempts to assimilate to their surroundings, they do not fully desire conformity: they seek out this alienation. As Ford Madox Ford comments in his preface to *The Left Bank*, Rhys has "a terrifying insight and a terrific—an almost lurid!—passion for stating the case of the underdog."[47] For Rhys, there is no pleasure without negation; for her characters, to share the same popular pleasures as everyone else would compromise the ways they are marked and identify as outsiders.

There is still more to the Three-Fingered Kate scene from a narrative point of view. Like the falling drawers scene, Kate's story is one episode—one "turn"—in a sequence that needs to be read together. "Three-Fingered Kate" is followed by "a long Italian film about the Empress Theodora, called 'The Dancer-Empress.'" Empress Theodora was a scandalous figure of sexually voracious power. In his posthumously published *Secret History*, Procopius tells a scurrilous story of "Theodora-from-the-Brothel" who rose from working as an actress/dancer/prostitute to the Empress of Byzantium as the wife of Justinian I. Procopius insists on Theodora's nymphomania and tells stories of her enormous sexual appetite and numerous abortions, along with her outrageous stage acts.[48] Less sensational accounts confirm the basic trajectory of her life but point out the conflation of female entertainers (actresses and dancers) with prostitutes at Theodora's time—not so different from Rhys's time. Though she was an historical novelty, Theodora was no doubt, like Kate, an analogue of the New Woman, a figure of exaggerated sexual appetites and newfangled freedoms who seemed "modern" in her independence, sensuousness, and mobility. Rhys does not describe the film in any detail, other than noting that Anna watches all of "The Dancer-Empress." Theodora's combination of professions echoes Anna's own drift through the female pleasure industry, from a chorus girl/actress/dancer, to a manicurist who is told to "be a bit nice" to the men, to a prostitute (an "amateur"): a bitter inversion of Theodora's ascent to the throne.

Many critics have commented on how Rhys elides actual sex in her narratives, even as her female characters are caught up in an economy that turns on their status as sexual commodities.[49] I suggest that the cinema is one important place where Rhys explores the dangers and pleasures of female sexuality. In her work on cinema history, Linda Williams observes that "for women, one constant of the history of sexuality has been a failure to imagine their pleasures outside a dominant male economy."[50] This makes itself felt in the cinema, and particularly in pornography, as a preoccupation with the mystery of women's sexual pleasure driven by, Williams argues, a lack of visual "proof" signifying women's orgasm—unlike the visible male "money shot." Women's pleasure—both sexually and more broadly—is a conundrum for cinema. Of course, neither "Three-Fingered Kate" nor "The Dancer-Empress" is pornography, but both films feature women of aggressive libidinal appetites (kleptomania and nymphomania) who are coded as criminal or pathological. The double-feature in *Voyage in the Dark* projects the conflict between female rebellion and the demand for conformity with which Rhys's protagonists struggle. Together the films create a complicated picture of female pleasure that is (at least in the first film) defined by negation and punishment—punishment that is, importantly, invented by Rhys in her rewriting of the Three-Fingered Kate serial. Here and elsewhere, punishment becomes constitutive of female pleasure for Rhys. The end of *Good Morning, Midnight* foregrounds questions of female sexual pleasure through the vehicle of cinema. Sasha tells Réne, a gigolo who tries to hustle her, "'Don't tell me that I'm like other women— I'm not. . . . I'm a cérébrale, can't you see that?'" René goes on to define a cérébrale as "a woman who doesn't like men or need them . . . a woman who likes nothing and nobody except herself and her own damned brain or what she thinks is her brain." In her interior monologue, Sasha comments, "So pleased with herself, like a little black boy in a top-hat. . . . In fact, a monster" (443). For René, a cérébrale is a woman without other-oriented pleasure, who "likes nothing and nobody except herself." Such a woman (thinking, independent, refusing all but narcissistic pleasure) is compared with a black boy in fancy dress; both are regarded as equally anomalous and bizarre. Like many of Rhys's protagonists, Sasha identifies with blackness, which she associates with oppression and cultural liminality. Both monsters, then, including the cérébrale who doesn't like men—and especially who doesn't *need* men—appeal to her.

When René tells Sasha, "I want absolutely to make love to you," she dismisses him, suggesting that she is uninterested in sex: "I told you from the start you were wasting your time." He insists that he can overcome what she has described as frigidity. "'What I know is that I could do this with you'—he makes a movement with his hands like a baker kneading a loaf of bread—'and afterwards you'd be different'" (452). In her mind, Sasha transforms René's sexual proposition, which she calls "an unimportant thing," into a lurid vision that takes up the earlier one of a black boy wearing a top hat: "I watch the little grimacing devil in my head. He wears a top-hat and a cache-sexe and he sings a sentimental song—'The roses all are faded and the lilies in the dust.'" Sentimentality, the trade of romantic love, is rendered irreverent, derisive, and obscene; a g-string calls attention to what it is supposed to hide ("cache-sexe"). As they travel to her hotel in a taxi, René whistles the song of the Foreign Legion, an organization that invites national border-crossing; it triggers a fantasy in Sasha's mind of herself in a "whitewashed room," warmed by the sun, wearing a short black dress. She waits—the suspenseful posture of masochism—for a man who

> ill-treats me, now he betrays me. He often brings home other women and I have to wait on them, and I don't like that. But as long as he is alive and near me I am not unhappy. If he were to die I should kill myself.
> My film-mind. . . . ("for God's sake watch out for your film-mind. . . .")
> "What are you laughing at now?" [René] says.
> "Nothing, nothing. . . ." I do like that tune. Do you think I could get a gramophone record of it? (452–453)

The story produced by Sasha's "film-mind" unfolds in a distinct narrative mode. Most obviously, it is in the first person—like Rhys's account of films and theatrical episodes such as the falling drawers scene—and Sasha is both the narrator and the starlet.[51] While the story starts in the present tense, like Sasha's descriptions of the films she sees on the screen, she also uses the historical present to give background ("He often brings home other women and I have to wait on them"), which indicates that this is an ongoing tale or a serial, like the installments of films such as *Three-Fingered Kate* or *The Perils of Pauline*. Unlike the films onscreen, in which the motivations behind the actions are opaque to Sasha, here she explains the feelings behind the images. But—as with the real films—her response is incongruous. She laughs.

The sadomasochistic feature that Rhys's "film mind" plays is strongly related to what Rhys critics refer to as "the Mr. Howard story," a sequence that appears in a notebook, known as the Black Exercise Book (BEB), which critics have dated to when Rhys was composing *Good Morning, Midnight*.[52] Rhys prefaces the Mr. Howard episode dramatically: "I was just at this stage when it happened—the thing that formed me made me as I am" (BEB). When she was fourteen, "a handsome old English man of about seventy two or three" visited her family. She was "captivated by this elegant speech." Mr. Howard takes her out for a walk and they sit on a secluded bench:

> He says
> How old are you? I'm fourteen. Fourteen he said fourteen—

quite old enough to have a lover. . . . A lover. I hadn't much about
lovers & then very ignorantly. . . . A lover—a lover is tall and
beautiful and strong. A lover smiles at you And hurts you.

I feel ["I feel" crossed out]. My dress ["My dress" crossed out]
buttoned. . . . his hand touches my breasts.

I sit perfectly still staring at

I'd flirted with [crossed out] (BEB)

The scene, critics agree, is a sexual violation. Rhys describes it as a
repressed memory with the characteristics of a trauma: "What happened was that I forgot it ["!" on top of "?"] It went out of my memory
like a stone." While there was clearly a physical violation, Rhys calls the
experience a "mental seduction." She emphasizes that as the walks continued, they revolved around Mr. Howard spinning out what Rhys calls
an "intoxicating . . . irresistible" narrative, a "serial story." She recounts
one episode. "We were living He + I in a large house on one of the other
islands. . . . I saw the huge rooms smelt the flowers that decorated them
heard the venetian blinds flap saw the moon rise over the hills the bats
fly out at sunset. . . . My arms were covered with bracelets my hands
with rings I laughed and danced but I was not happy or unhappy I was
waiting doomed Sometimes I sat at the long table decorated with flowers My bracelets and tinkled when I moved sometimes quite naked I
waited on the guests" (qtd. in Rosenberg, 10). This story bears a clear
resemblance to the narrative produced by Sasha's "film-mind" in *Good
Morning, Midnight*. Both accounts are very sensuous, focusing on smell,
hearing, and sight. The girl's role is subservient; in both narratives, she
waits, held in suspense, for the man's attention ("I am watching for the
expression on the man's face when he turns round").

Most critics have taken this fantasy as a "painful" and "dissociated"
replaying of the Howard trauma.[53] The scenes are also full of markers
of Rhysian pleasure and unpleasure. For a start, Rhys is not just an
actor in this memory: she takes over the narration from Mr. Howard.
In the Black Exercise Book, where she might well have used reported
speech, she uses the first person, and this carries over into Sasha's narrative, where it is attributed to her "film-mind." In both, the narrator
emphasizes her complicated reactions to the experience.[54] Rhys writes
in the Black Exercise Book that the installments of Mr. Howard's story
have an narcotizing effect on her: "After two or three doses of this

drug because thats what it was I no longer struggled." Pleasure and punishment are inextricably linked in Sasha's fantasy and the Howard narrative:

> I only rebel enough enough to make it fun to force me to submit
>
> Cruelty submission utter submission that was the story—I see now that he might have made it alot worse this rare & curious story.—After all Id been whipped alot. I was used to the idea—
>
> He could be nice too Mr Howard. Probably with someone healthier like water off a ducks back.
>
> But the terrible thing was the way something in the depths of me said Yes that is true—pain humiliation submission that is for me.
>
> It fitted in with all I knew of life with all Id ever felt It fitted like a hook fits an eye.

However she felt in the original moment, Rhys produces a kind of satisfaction through the narrative repetition of this story. For example, her comments in the Black Exercise Book that "Sometimes too my mind would sidetrack a bit" while she was listening to Mr. Howard, and "these dresses for instance Id like to hear a bit more about them," imply a narrative detachment as well as a relish in embellishing the details of the scene. Similarly, "Sometimes listening to him . . . my lover was no longer Mr Howard no he was young and dark and splendid like—the man in Quo Vadis," suggests a distance from the scenario in which fantasy was generated. In both the Black Exercise Book and the scene of the girl in the short black dress in *Good Morning, Midnight*, Rhys casts the sadomasochistic fantasy as mediated by intertextuality. Just as Sasha attributes the fantasy in *Good Morning, Midnight* to her "film-mind," and therefore correlates it with the narratives of female repression elsewhere in the novel, Rhys connects the Howard story in the Black Exercise Book to popular sadomasochistic narratives. Henryk Sienkiewicz's popular novel *Quo Vadis: A Narrative of the Time of Nero*, which was made into film versions in 1912 and 1924, features a strong man devoted to a young girl and is replete with sadomasochistic imagery (Moran, 108). In the Black Exercise Book, Rhys also associates the Howard memory with reading *High Wind in Jamaica*: "I was reminded of myself as a child. The little Creole girl who is beaten in the thoroughgoing West Indian fashion is . . . whom the sailors use as a prostitute loathed and finally . . . I think throw overboard. It is good. The whole book is good. But he makes her idiotic. That is a mistake." Rhys often mentions how much she enjoyed narratives of female subjugation. She claimed that her favorite book was Robert Hichens's 1904 novel *The Garden of Allah*, a forerunner of Hull's *The Sheik*.[55] Like Hull's Diana Mayo, whose tale is one of learned gender polarity and erotic subjugation, Hichens's Domini begins as an all too independent woman, but in the desert, she falls in love with a mysterious dark man to whom she learns to submit.[56]

Rhys seemed proud of what she called her "kink" that set her apart from other women (BEB), just as her protagonists resist most mainstream narratives of pleasure while embracing others. There was, as we saw in the case of *The Sheik*, a widespread interwar appetite for books about women's eroticized subjugation. Rhys's comment in *Smile Please* that "the whole business of money and sex is mixed up with something very primitive and deep. . . . It is at once humiliating and exciting,"[57] reflects the sexual politics of contemporary vernacular narratives as much as it does Rhys's own psychology. This may be the key to Sasha's sly laughter at the end of the whitewashed room fantasy. As she attributes the sequence to her "film-mind," like the "cheap gramophone records starting up in [her] head" (351), Sasha's laugh suggests there is a conscious and ironic kind of narration at work. It implies that she knows she is a product of the clichés and gender stereotypes she has seen up on the screen. She may fancy herself a woman apart from others—it is crucially important to Rhys's characters that they not experience what she depicts as conventional pleasure—but her fantasy also draws on popular narratives.

Significantly, in both the Black Exercise Book and *Good Morning, Midnight*, Rhys is equivocal about the affect of the girl in the scenario: "I was not happy or unhappy I was waiting"; "I am not unhappy." This state of being in thrall and in between extreme emotions (pain, pleasure, "!/?") is replicated in the frame of *Good Morning, Midnight*. The novel's opening sequence assembles a series of oppositions, beginning with the polarities of Emily Dickinson's poem of soured romance that serves as the epigraph: "Day got tired of me—. . . Morn didn't want me" (346). Rhys's first image is a room with a big and a smaller bed for madame and monsieur, respectively, that poses another set of opposites: "'Quite like old times,' the room says, 'Yes? No?'" The answer is both yes and no—what follows will be more of the same, but also new, a pulse of unresolvable opposition. Appropriately, "the street outside is narrow, cobblestoned, going sharply uphill and ending in a flight of steps. What they call an impasse" (347). The architecture of the impasse, its relation to pleasure, and the gendered nature of this relation, are striking in Dickinson's poem, which resolves in the paradoxical "Good morning, Midnight!" and "good night, Day!" Rhys's characters actively seek that architecture. "The room welcomes me back. / 'There you are,' it says. 'You didn't go off then?' / 'No, no. I thought better of it. Here I belong and here I'll stay'" (367). Rhys's characters not only find themselves in the impasse, they gravitate toward it. It is a place where they are "very passive" (349) in terms of momentum, but active in terms of narrativizing that experience. There is a strong correlation with the Mr. Howard story. However psychologically debilitating the experience was, Rhys insists that it was central to her creative powers. The energy of her writing is derived from these moments of paradox and impossibility, when pleasure and unpleasure are bound together though narration. ("Tristesse, what a nice word!" Sasha rhapsodizes. "Tristesse, lointaine, langsam, forlorn, forlorn. . . ." [372])

The final, puzzling scene of *Good Morning, Midnight*, which has been interpreted as variously as a murder and transcendence, is Rhys's most chilling representation of the impasse.[58] When René follows her back to her hotel, she is initially excited but then put off and tells him to go. He refers to her refusal of him as an act, a "comedy" (455), and accuses her of performing a trick, a "good truc . . . women like you, who pretend and lie and play an idiotic comedy all the time" (456). He describes a gang rape while they struggle on the bed. Finally, he leaves. Sasha weeps and imagines a voice jeering at her: "Well, well, well, just think of that now. What an amusing ten days! Positively packed with thrills. The last performance of What's-her-name And Her Boys or It Was All Due To An Old Fur Coat. Positively the last performance. . . . Go on, cry, allez-y. Encore" (458). Like Bob's performance of debasement in the bar near the end of *The Midnight Bell*, Sasha splits herself between spectator and performer. She takes up René's theatrical metaphor to belittle herself as an aging, grotesque music hall star who refuses to leave the stage. Tunes running through her head, she tells herself "I mustn't sing any more—there you are. Finie la chanson. The song is ended. Finished" (458). Although there is, as with Bob, a kind of detached irony as well as self-effacing black humor (structurally in keeping with Kantian disinterested—and modernist—pleasure), the scene immediately goes in a different direction of harrowing immediacy and embodiment.

There is another act: the voice in Sasha's head calls it "the sequel" (459). In taking the awful commis voyageur, with his "mean eyes," to her bed, Sasha withdraws completely from the economy of pleasure. This man has frightened and disgusted her throughout the novel, reminding her of death itself. With René, despite the violence and exploitation between them, she is attached to and energized by their game of cat and mouse. With the commis voyageur, Sasha becomes anesthetized. Her final words, "I put my arms round him and pull him down on to the bed, saying: 'Yes—yes—yes . . . ,'" signal an act of anhedonic calculus. Her words of affirmative punctuation and the language of lovemaking contrast with what we know to be her repulsion for and fear of this man. Unlike Hamilton, whose conclusion to *Twenty Thousand Streets Under the Sky* finally capitulates to the tyranny of pleasure, bringing his distinct characters into line with narratives of optimism and progress that are otherwise foreign to his texts, Rhys presses the distinction of negation and unpleasure to its furthest point. She concludes on an unsettling note between negation and affirmation: violence in sex, disaster in stasis, death in life.

If there is to be disaster, at least let there be tragedy. No such luck. The conclusion of *Good Morning, Midnight* is profoundly anticathartic. Barthes proposes that "of all readings, that of tragedy is the most perverse" because it entails "an effacement of pleasure and a progression of bliss" (*Pleasure of the Text*, 47, 48). This is a fair description of Hamilton's and Rhys's readerly affect. However, neither conforms to classical tragedy but rather to the modern "tragicomedy" of authors such as Beckett, which denies any kind of catharsis except textual performance and the savoring of lacerating negation.[59] While Hamilton and Rhys challenge readers to see the world through their characters' perspectives, they also actively block readerly identification and sympathy by their characters' intractability, which is compounded by belittling comedy. When Mr. Mackenzie condescendingly tells Julia, after leaving her, "Surely even she must see that she was trying to make a tragedy out of a situation that was fundamentally comical. The discarded mistress—the faithful lawyer defending the honour of the client. . . . A situation consecrated as comical by ten thousand farces and a thousand comedies" (*After Leaving*, 250–251), he denies her both the enjoyed despair of tragedy and the energizing destruction of nihilism. Instead, he diminishes her situation as a generic farce or comedy. Again and again, Rhys prevents us from running the tragic narrative of the woman who has no choices and must live a life of pain and misery. Her characters do exercise choice; however, they make choices that steer them away from pleasure and happiness. At the same time, the "comical" elements of these narratives are corrosive and further increase the protagonists' alienation. As Katharine Streip points out, Rhys's humor preserves a distance between the reader and Sasha. "It is unlikely that Sasha means for us to share her vision, or her laughter, with any enthusiasm," and "we remain spectators with an uneasy feeling that our response to Sasha contributes to her exhibition of unhappiness as well" (130). As if watching the Hottentot Venus displayed on the stage or the woman with her drawers falling down under the lamppost, readers are kept at an uncomfortable distance from Rhys's protagonists. At the same time that readers are inside Sasha's head, her interior monologue, Rhys stages scenes in which we "see" her from the outside. The foreignness these characters feel in relation to the culture around them extends to readers; their unpleasure is singular and ours is too. Even as Hamilton's and Rhys's narratives are unconstructive, noncathartic, and fiercely individualistic, their implicit critique of the consensus that they see as the basis of contemporary vernacular pleasure can be read as an argument against the political regimes whose enforced conformity gained frightening power in the mid- to late thirties.

In a discussion with Frank Kermode about pleasure and literary canonicity, John Guillory called for critics to pay "renewed attention to the formal properties of literary works as aesthetic works, which means taking account both experientially and theoretically of their aims, including the aim of giving pleasure."[60] But why do we assume that pleasure is the goal of writing or reading? In Freud's (and Plato's) terms, constant tension is experienced as unpleasure, and pleasure results from the elimination of tension. But there are works—like those of Celine, Beckett, Barnes, Hamilton, and Rhys—in which the baseline of tension and negativity challenges the notion that readers seek conventional textual pleasure, catharsis, or closure. If these worlds are depressing, they are also testaments to the creative and malleable nature of bliss. If the lives that Rhys and Hamilton depict seem stiflingly narrow and limited, the texts themselves are expansive in their ingenious contortions of pleasure.

◈ ◈ ◈

I try to decide what colour I shall have my hair dyed, and hang on to that thought as you hang on to something when you are drowning. Shall I have it red? Shall I have it black? Now, black—that would be startling. Shall I have it blond cendré? But blond cendré, madame, is the most difficult of colours. It is very, very rarely, madame, that hair can be successfully dyed blond cendré. It's even harder on the hair than dyeing it platinum blonde. First it must be bleached, that is to say, its own colour must be taken out of it—and then it must be dyed, that is to say, another colour must be imposed on it. (Educated hair. . . . And then, what?) (*Good Morning, Midnight*, 375)

To shift from the world of Rhys and Hamilton to the world of Anita Loos's *Gentlemen Prefer Blondes* is to step almost through the looking glass. Rhys's Sasha agonizes over her hair and, predictably, decides to impose "the most difficult of colours" upon herself. Once she is in the salon chair, she is surrounded by women's magazines that mock her: "No mademoiselle, no, madame, life is not easy. Do not delude yourselves. Nothing is easy" (382). By contrast, Loos's characters seem to have sprung from those magazine pages like blonde Venuses for whom everything is easy, education is a joke, and pleasure is their birthright. ("Because I'm worth it" might be their motto.) A recurring theme of the previous chapters has been a reactionary stance to pleasure, and a valorization of unpleasure as a defense against forms of culture that seemed to be threatening literature, the life of the mind, and individuality. Loos represents a conspicuous shift. Working in both literature and cinema, as well as creating a space in between, Loos developed a comedic voice that combined innovation and unabashed triviality, in which brazenly shallow entertainment exists alongside sharp, self-reflexive wordplay. It is not surprising that this voice emerged in America, and specifically in Hollywood, which was, for many modernists, the locus of low pleasure. What was perhaps surprising was that the idiom Loos devised was one that many modernists, and particularly those most invested in the exercise of distinction, found irresistible.

6

BLONDES HAVE MORE FUN
Anita Loos and the Language
of Silent Cinema

Anita Loos's best-selling 1925 novel *Gentlemen Prefer Blondes* has been all but eclipsed by the voluptuous shadow of Marilyn Monroe. Any text would have trouble competing with Monroe's spun-sugar hair, bursting bodice, and slick lipstick pout in Howard Hawks's 1953 film adaptation of the novel. In its own time, however, few other popular novels received as much attention from both general readers and cultural critics of note. Well into the 1930s and 1940s, *Gentlemen Prefer Blondes* had considerable cultural traction and was adapted to nearly every medium imaginable—magazine, stage play, silent film, musical, sound film, comic strip, dress fabric, and wallpaper.[1] While the novel's superficial signifiers (champagne, diamonds, and dancing vamps) could be captured on film or paper a room, its most important characteristic, its voice, was paradoxically silenced with the coming of the sound film. This is particularly striking given that Loos's novel is fashioned from a convergence of literature and film.

The narrator of *Blondes* is Lorelei Lee, a gold-digging ditz who spends most of her time wheedling jewelry out of her paramours, shopping, dining at fashionable clubs, or lounging in her "negligay." Lorelei is a sybarite who, when traveling in France with her sugar daddy, "Gus

Eisman the Button King," and her sardonic best friend, Dorothy, frets that she cannot "tell how much francs is in money," but decides that "Paris is devine" when she sees "famous historical names, like Coty and Cartier" along with the "Eyefull Tower."[2] She begins keeping a diary when one of her admirers urges her to put her thoughts down on paper. "It would be strange if I turn out to be an authoress," she muses. "I mean I simply could not sit for hours and hours at a time practising for the sake of a career. . . . But writing is different because you do not have to learn or practise" (*B*, 4–5). Although writing appeals to Lorelei, she confides, "the only career I would like to be besides an authoress is a cinema star" (*B*, 6).

Critics of *Blondes*, from its initial appearance to now, have taken their cue from Lorelei's two aspirations (cinema and literature) and have tried to place the novel in the cultural spectrum from mass culture to modernism. Lawrence yoked "Blondes Prefer Gentlemen" and *The Sheik* together as the kind of best-seller that was beneath him.[3] For Q. D. Leavis, Cyril Connolly, and Wyndham Lewis, *Blondes* epitomized popular culture's frivolity and idioms of idiocy. However, James Joyce, H. L. Mencken, Aldous Huxley, William Empson, George Santayana, Edith Wharton, and William Faulkner were positively giddy in their embrace of the novel. Mencken, Loos's friend, whose predilection for dim-witted platinum beauties was said to have inspired *Blondes*, wrote in a review, "This gay book has filled me with uproarious and salubrious mirth. It is farce—but farce full of shrewd observation and devastating irony" (*B*, xi). Others who had no personal connection to Loos at the time were similarly enthralled. Huxley wrote that he was "enraptured by the book."[4] In 1926, Joyce wrote to Harriet Shaw Weaver that he had been "reclining on a sofa and reading *Gentlemen Prefer Blondes* for three whole days," an image that figuratively reverses Eve Arnold's 1955 photograph of Monroe in a bathing suit reading *Ulysses*.[5] Recently, some critics have attempted to locate *Blondes* within paradigms of modernism.[6] In fact, it makes more sense to view it as anticipatory of the aesthetic developments later in the century.

Loos's "Blonde book," as Faulkner called it, has proven tricky to categorize. As Faye Hammill points out, "The primary difference between the admiring and the critical readers of *Gentlemen Prefer Blondes* is that the former consider Loos as an ironic and perceptive commentator on mass culture and the latter see her as an emanation from that culture and a producer of its commodities."[7] Hammill proposes that "middlebrow" is a useful term to describe Loos's writing, which responds parodically to both modernist and mass culture. Rather than perpetuating the battle of the brows, I suggest that the significance of Loos's work lies not in its adherence to existing literary paradigms, but rather in its creation of a distinct style that incorporates the kinds of linguistic projects modernism cast as unpleasure into a more buoyant form of vernacular textuality.

Lorelei's blonde "ambishion" of intertwining literature and cinema unwittingly reflects Loos's development of a literary style that had affinities to some of the most radical aesthetic projects of early twentieth-century art from within popular culture. Loos herself was a star "authoress" of cinema, having written over a hundred one- and two-reelers, along with features for Douglas Fairbanks and D. W. Griffith, two pillars of American filmmaking, and screenplays such as *Red-Headed Woman* (1932) and the adaptation of Clare Booth Luce's *The Women* (1939). There has been a recent resurgence of interest in Loos, signaled by a series of trenchant articles on *Blondes* and by *Anita Loos Rediscovered*, which presents a selection of her extensive cinema writing.[8] During the silent era, Loos was widely known as one of the most innovative writers of titles (variously called intertitles, subtitles, or leaders). Her contributions to cinema and literary history have only recently begun to be formally connected.

Film historians have presented the main story of early cinema as the controversy about the coming of sound, but there was also a passionate debate about titling, and Loos was an important part of this. Challenging the separation of literature and cinema as high and low culture, Loos develops a mode of writing in which literature and cinema together unmoor the conventional relationship of the image to the word. In both media, words exceed their contexts and signify not only through their meaning but also through their literal status as objects: letters printed on the page or projected on the screen. As Brooks E. Hefner points out, Loos inaugurated a "new way of thinking about how film relates to modernist modes of fictional representation and structure" (108). Taken together, Loos's titles and *Blondes* show a cross-genre relationship of exchange that brings modernist ideas about language into the vernacular culture that had been thought antipathetic to them. Like modernist writers such as Joyce and Stein, Loos

changed reading practices, but she did so without resorting to strategies of unpleasure. Her narrative innovation in both film and literature
pivots around the profusion, rather than the curtailment, of pleasure.

REVOLUTIONARY SIMPLETONS

Blondes appeared at the height of the modernist parsing of pleasure
based on the exercise of cultural distinction. The novel—like all of
Loos's writing—draws much of its comedy from this discourse in
which certain (feminine, bodily, visual, sensual, collective: "blonde")
pleasures are constructed as culturally corrosive and others (cerebral,
individualized, written) are favored as edifying and worthwhile. Loos,
for whom both modes are compelling, slyly demonstrates how acts of
cultural classification (and their undoing) are themselves pleasurable.

Leavis's *Fiction and the Reading Public* designates *Blondes* as representative of popular fiction published in 1925, asserting that the novel's
"slick technique is the product of centuries of journalistic experience
and whose effect depends entirely on the existence of a set of stock
responses provided by newspaper and film." The correlation of *Blondes*
and cinema, intended as a slight, is an acute observation. However,
Leavis's conception of mass culture—"crude and puerile," "made up of
phrases and clichés that imply fixed, or rather stereotyped, habits of
thinking and feeling"—is willfully reductive: she could only wish that
the attractions of mass culture were so nugatory. Leavis's contrast
between the pleasures of popular culture—bodily, auditory (music,
voice), or visual (cinema)—and those of high culture—cerebral and
textual ("the free play of ironical intelligence in *Passage to India* and
To the Lighthouse")—is the very paradigm around which Loos shapes
Blondes.[9] Leavis seems amazingly (conveniently?) unaware of the fact
that Loos both indulges in and satirizes idioms of mass culture.

Like Leavis, Wyndham Lewis describes Loos's language as distinctively colloquial and verbal (spoken and heard rather than written) in
his surprising comparison of Loos and Gertrude Stein, in which he
calls *Blondes* "the breathless babble of the wide-eyed child."[10] (In *The
Long Week End*, Graves and Hodge also highlight the "artless pseudo-
baby language" of *Blondes*.[11]) Lewis joins Leavis in emphasizing Loos's
affiliation with cinema, dubbing her, together with Charlie Chaplin,
"revolutionary simpletons."[12] Continuing this taxonomy of body and

cinema versus mind and text, Cyril Connolly's *Enemies of Promise* (1938) places *Blondes* in the category of "Vernacular," as opposed to "Mandarin" literature (for example, Eliot's *Poems* and Woolf's *Mrs. Dalloway*). Hemingway is "the outstanding writer of the new vernacular"; he writes in "a style in which the body talks rather than the mind, one admirable for rendering emotions; love, fear, joy of battle, despair, sexual appetite, but impoverished for intellectual purposes."[13]

For all these critics, the distinctions between low and high, popular and elite, image and word, cinema and literature, are functions of the quality of pleasure produced. As we have seen, these polarized classifications of pleasure, in which cinema is inevitably the placeholder for cultural degeneration, are often so strict as to be farcical, and seem almost to beg to have their terms tousled. For Loos, such ideological inconsistency, whereby those who claim to be most invested in cultural distinction are receptive to the voluptuous allure of denigrated pleasures, is a springboard to satire. Loos cannily named Lorelei after a mythological Rhine Maiden, a Siren, that figure around whom Horkheimer and Adorno shape their Enlightenment dichotomies (modernism versus mass culture, mind versus body, bourgeois intellectual versus proletarian laborer, and "'masculine' rationalization" versus "'feminine' pleasure," as Rita Felski puts it.[14]) Many intellectuals, lashed to the mast of cultural distinction, savored the giddy pleasures of *Blondes*. (It is a happy coincidence that, at least according to Heine, the Teutonic Lorelei was, like Loos's siren, a blonde.)

In a context in which approved pleasures are deliberate, complex, and cerebral, Loos's novel is strategically lightweight. When Lorelei is traveling through "the central of Europe" (*B*, 75), she goes to Vienna and sees the great doctor himself for psychoanalysis. "Dr. Froyd" marvels at the fact that Lorelei has no inhibitions and does not seem to dream at night. She explains, "I mean I use my brains so much in the day time that at night they do not seem to do anything else but rest." She appears to have no capacity for psychological conflict, sublimation, interiority, self-consciousness, or depth: in short, none of the interests of literary modernism. Lorelei recalls that Freud "seemed very very intreeged at a girl who always seemed to do everything she wanted to do" (*B*, 90). Loos gives Lorelei virtually all of the characteristics of mass culture: female, seductive, ravenously materialistic, American, and cinematic.

Blondes looks quite different if, instead of reading it as symptomatic of the degraded idiom of journalism or cinema, we see it as based on historically specific cinematic effects. The novel is framed by Lorelei's film career: when it opens, she has retired, and her triumphant return to the movies closes the book. In between, she flits among some of Hollywood's major names, meeting "Mr. Chaplin once when we were both working on the same lot in Hollywood" and lunching with "Eddie Goldmark of the Goldmark Films," who is based on the film mogul producer Samuel Goldwyn (*B*, 6, 16). More fundamentally, the language of the novel and its visual qualities are drawn from the distinctive voice Loos developed ten years earlier within silent film.

GOING TO THE MOVIES TO READ

The story of literary modernity includes mass-produced texts such as newspapers and magazines, billboards, and other forms of advertising that inspired, for example, the skywriting in *Mrs. Dalloway* and the skittering Hely's sandwich-board men in *Ulysses*. However, the huge words that silent cinema routinely cast in front of audiences are rarely a part of this historical narrative. Titles were introduced into silent film as the functional heirs of the nickelodeon projectionist who read out information to the audience. In early Edison films, titles were explanatory devices that patched over gaps in the narrative; in the early 1910s, they started to include direct dialogue.[15] For the most part, titles were perfunctory, establishing only basic narrative facts; most filmmakers and critics regarded them as a crude but necessary tool indicating the technological limitations of silent film. In his influential *Photoplay: A Psychological Study* (1916), Hugo Münsterberg opines that intertitles should be regarded as "extraneous to the original character of the photoplay"; they are "accessory, while the primary power must lie in the content of the pictures themselves."[16] Manuals for aspiring photoplay writers published in the 1910s insisted that "the use of a leader [title] is a frank confession that you are incapable of 'putting over' a point in the development of your plot solely by the action in the scenes— you must call in outside assistance, as it were."[17] (Elinor Glyn repeats the same point almost verbatim in *The Elinor Glyn System of Writing*: "If possible, make your plot clear without using any sub-titles; for the use of one is the frank confession that you are not able to bring out certain phases of your plot without resorting to the written word."[18]) The vigorous discussion about titling in film magazines and newspapers in the 1910s and early 1920s, Laura Marcus observes, raised "fundamental questions about the nature of film language and, indeed, the extent to which cinematic images could be understood as elements of a language." Captions and intertitles were an "intrusion of the literary into what should be an essentially pictorial realm."[19] They were not, in the early 1910s, considered an artistic form for individual authorship, only anonymous and banal placeholders. Loos changed this.

Loos's debut in cinema was precocious and auspicious. D. W. Griffith bought one of her first scenarios, which became a 1912 one-reeler, *The New York Hat,* starring Mary Pickford and Lionel Barrymore. Her early scenarios were fairly conventional, but she was already experimenting with words not just as representations of ideas but also as objects with their own material status. Loos's 1914 one-reeler *The School of Acting* features Professor Bunk's drama school, in which thespians are taught to emote according to "large cards, about two feet square, [on which Bunk] has printed in big type the names of the different emotions; such as 'Anger,' 'Jealousy,' 'Love,' 'Hope,' etc."[20] Comedy ensues when actors are shown the cards in inappropriate circumstances and cannot help but act them out. The cards suggest titles, which cinema audiences read in tandem with the actors in the film, causing a metatextual collapse of viewer/actor and word/image. In "By Way of France," a young Frenchwoman is kidnapped upon her arrival in New York; she manages to drop a note pleading "au secours! au secours!" but efforts to save her are thwarted because the man who finds the note cannot read French. Finally he locates a French dictionary and rescues her; they exchange a note: "Je t'aime" (*AL Rediscovered,* 28–29). Both films revolve around texts as concrete images—material combinations of letters—and the complications caused by faulty readings of words. The titles do not just elucidate the plot but are themselves the plot. Both films express anxiety about literacy and cinema audiences' ability or willingness to extend their attention to reading.

In the mid 1910s, Loos's future husband, John Emerson, pitched some of her screenplays to Griffith, who pointed out that they did not follow the usual protocol: "most of the laughs are in the dialogue which can't be photographed," he said, and "people don't go to the movies to read."[21] Nevertheless, in 1916, Loos displayed her idiosyncratic style of titling in her first of many screenplays for Douglas Fairbanks, *His Picture in the Papers*. Loos led with a lengthy text: "Publicity at any price has become the predominant passion of the American people. May we beg leave to introduce you to a shining disciple of this modern art of 'three-sheeting,' Proteus Prindle, producer of Prindle's 27 Vegetarian Varieties." Parodying the Heinz Corporation with its "57 varieties" and the current fad for vegetarianism, Loos addresses her readers sarcastically ("a shining disciple of this modern art") and peppers her sentences with alliteration, mixing precious locutions ("May we beg leave to introduce you") with slang ("three-sheeting"). A saucy title announces a scene in which Pete Prindle, the carnivorous son of Proteus Prindle (and brother of "PEARL AND PANSY . . . KNOWN AS '28' AND '29'"), kisses his girlfriend, who has previously received a "hygienic kiss" from a vegetarian: "Wherein it is shown that beefsteak produces a different style of love-making from prunes." Late in the story, a title comments about Pete: "Ain't he the REEL hero?" This punning voice establishes an autonomous level of commentary that self-consciously gestures at the film's REEL medium and the title's REAL textuality.

The film was considered a milestone in titling, and Loos received widespread attention in industry and general interest publications. Louella Parsons declared in the *New York Telegraph* that Loos had "revolutionized" titling.[22] Fairbanks signed an exclusive contract with Loos in 1916 to write the titles for all his films. In an article for *Everybody's Magazine* called "The Handwriting on the Screen," Fairbanks told Karl Schmidt that "Time and again . . . I have sat through plays with Miss Loos and have heard the audience applaud her subtitles as heartily as the liveliest scenes."[23] Even an antititling critic such as Vachel Lindsay, who bemoaned that "'Title writing' remains a commercial necessity," conceded that "in this field there is but one person who has won distinction—Anita Loos," who was as "brainy" as anyone could be "and still remain in the department store film business."[24] Loos saw titling as a locus of linguistic creativity and authorial power in film. "Titling pictures had all the fascination of doing crossword puzzles but was a lot more fun," she remarked (*GI*, 103), using a metaphor that is not far off from the serious whimsy of modernists such as Joyce. Loos's titles, which film historian Kristin Thompson calls "the Loos-style title," or the "'literary' inter-title," instigated the recognizable shift to witty and prolix titles in some films of the late 1910s.[25] Fundamentally changing the concept of cinematic pleasure as passive vision ("they need only sit and keep their eyes open," Huxley writes in "Pleasures"), Loos's titles presumed and even created an active audience to whom they offered a new kind of pleasure: *literary* visual pleasure. Loos did not just coax people to read; she taught them to view words as images. *American Aristocracy* (1916), another Fairbanks film, is an exemplary "Loos-style" script. The opening title asks, "Has America an aristocracy? We say yes! And to prove it we take you to Newport-by-the-Sea, where we find some of our finest families whose patents of nobility are founded on such deeds of daring as the canning of soup, the floating of soap and the borating of talcum."

Satirizing the insular Newport colony, where capitalism produces its own aristocracy ("patents of nobility"), the film's titles include puns, euphemisms, mock Latin, and other fairly intricate jokes, along with written documents—letters, newspapers, ads—that were commonly used in films at the time. But while the interpolated documents are incorporated into the plot in the conventional way (that is, the audience reads them as the characters read them), the intertitles are often detached from the plot, either commenting upon it or embarking on an entirely new conversation. Thompson refers to this aspect of Loos's titles as "double functioning," in which "almost every expository title that begins a scene also makes a verbal joke of its own"—a style quickly taken up by other comic writers, including Buster Keaton and Harold Lloyd.[26]

The hero of *American Aristocracy*, played by Fairbanks, is introduced by a title:

Now, Narraport Aristocracy possesses no interest for Cassius Lee of Virginia, amateur entomologist,* who has arrived in these parts on the trail of the migratory caterpillar.

*Entomologist—High-brow term for bug hunter

The footnote creates a level of diegesis two times removed from the cinematic plot (film diegesis: intertitle: footnote to intertitle). Moreover, the footnote splits the author's voice between one that uses a "high-brow" term (and a pseudo-scholarly flourish like a footnote)

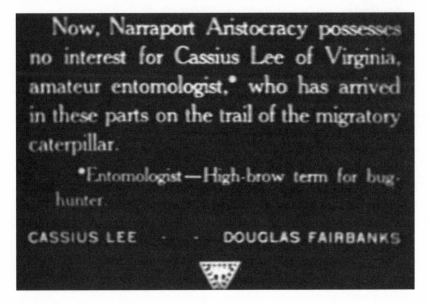

Figure 6.1
American Aristocracy, Lloyd Ingraham, 1916.

and another that undermines this pretension. Loos never missed an opportunity to set high and low against each other.

In "The Handwriting on the Wall," Loos told *Everybody's Magazine* that her "most popular subtitle introduced the name of a new character. . . . The name was something like this: 'Count Xxerkzsxxv.' Then there was a note, 'To those of you who read titles aloud, you can't pronounce the Count's name. You can only think it.'"[27] The title, as described by Loos, establishes a direct relationship between the audience and the writer that entirely excludes the film. It insists that this jumble of letters cannot be treated as an oral artifact. Language here is neither visual nor audible, but rather located in an abstract realm of thought. Words don't just represent ideas: they are ideas in themselves. The fact that Loos considered this title—explicitly allusive and self-reflexive—her "most popular" suggests how differently she imagined her audience from most critics of the time. Loos's cinema offered the pleasures of interpretation and irony—those "mandarin," "subtle," and "intelligent" pleasures that Leavis, Connolly, Huxley, and others claimed were the purview of serious literature. Loos invited audiences to enjoy the collision of different levels of cultural pleasure.

This was an exceptional historical moment when film could be exploited for literary purposes, and Loos did just that, by flouting current theories that film should strive to be a purely visual form and the idea of cinema as a seamless illusion with invisible techniques. Ignoring the injunction of critics such as the *New York Dramatic Mirror*'s Frank Woods that, "the spectators are not part of the picture, nor is there supposed to be a camera there making a moving photograph of the scene,"[28] Loos's titles directly addressed the spectator, the cinematic equivalent of breaking the fourth wall. Against the idea of film functioning like hieroglyphics (promulgated by Vachel Lindsay) or as a universal language healing the linguistic fragmentation of the Tower of Babel (associated with Griffith),[29] Loos crafted a highly idiomatic cinema that cultivated tension, rather than harmony, between text and image. In her cinema writing and subsequently in *Blondes*, she employs a number of techniques to promote this pleasurable conflict between word and image: visual and graphic subordination (subtitles, captions, footnotes), punning, homophones, phonetic spelling, a split voice, and a kind of artistic synesthesia (asking audiences to read images and see words).

Loos's 1919 short story "The Moving Pictures of Blinkville" dramatizes the process by which the pleasures of the text compete with the pleasures of the image. A trickster pretends to be a filmmaker. After the town's denizens pose for his camera, he takes an old parade film and transforms it "by long and labored work at scratching and clouding the film," like a form of writing. The resulting movie "projected on the curtain was not a picture—it was a series of blurs and blotches, with here and there a human form indicated amid the surging storm of scratches."[30] He shows it to great acclaim as "Scenes of Blinkville." The word, which is supposed to be subordinate to the visual spectacle, is rendered concrete and assumes a starring role. Audiences, without realizing it, are induced to "read" a film. Zelda and F. Scott Fitzgerald's "Our Own Movie Queen" (1925) demonstrates the effects of this new style of intertitling. When a small-town girl is all but cut out of a film in which she thinks she is going to be the lead, she and her boyfriend exact revenge by inserting new images and intertitles (set off from the regular text in the story to simulate the shape of the screen) to make her the star.[31] Thanks to Loos, titles had their own kind of textual autonomy.

At no other time in cinema history did the word exert so much power. Loos continued to capitalize on the battle between the image and the word and the related disputes about hierarchies of cultural pleasure in *Blondes*. One film project was unexpectedly influential for Loos and for *Blondes*: *Intolerance*.

"A BATHTUB FULL OF DIAMONDS": *INTOLERANCE*

While Fairbanks's films represent classic Hollywood cinema, Griffith was a figure caught between convention and innovation, pulling back toward the theater and forward toward cinema's future with innovative techniques that inspired experimental filmmakers such as Sergei Eisenstein and have led more recent critics to view Griffith as an early modernist.[32] Loos was invited to collaborate with Griffith and Frank Woods on the titles of *Intolerance* (1916). The film, approximately three hours long, presents a sweeping metanarrative, the "history of how hatred and intolerance, through all the ages, have battled against love and charity." *Intolerance* has a fuguelike structure that uses parallel montage to intercut among four narratives set in different eras (Babylonian, biblical, seventeenth-century France, and modern day). Each narrative features characters (many of whom are given generic titles such as "The Dear One," "The Boy," and "The Friendless One") who act out analogous scenarios of oppression or "intolerance." In the Babylonian narrative, one priest violently represses a more hedonistic sect; in the biblical narrative, Jesus is martyred; in the French narrative, Huguenots are slaughtered on St. Bartholomew's Day; and in the modern-day story, a workers' strike is violently suppressed and a self-righteous group of female reformers destroy a family.[33]

Loos claims that she was "the first viewer ever to see *Intolerance* [in the editing room]. I must be honest and say I thought D. W. had lost his mind. . . . In that era of the simple, straightforward technique for telling picture plots, Griffith had crashed slam-bang into a method for which neither I nor, as was subsequently proved, his audiences had been prepared" (*GI*, 102). The dominant models of spectatorship—intoxication or passive escape—fail to account for *Intolerance*, which requires its audiences to synthesize four widely disparate historical narratives and to relate allegorical images (the Book of Intolerance, the woman—Lillian Gish—rocking the cradle) to the stories around them. *Intolerance* calls upon its audience to construct its meaning, but it gives assistance through didactic titles, beginning with a sequence that addresses the viewer and explains how to watch the film—"you will find our play turning from one of the four stories to another, as the common theme unfolds in each"—and marking many of the bridges between the film's different time frames. The titles are remarkably variable in style and tone, reflecting, no doubt, the three different authors who worked on them. Many titles are bombastic and heavy-handed (for example, "My Lord, like white pearls I shall keep my tears in an ark of silver for your return. I bite my thumb! I strike my girdle! If you return not, I go to the death halls of Allat").

In most cases, we can only speculate which writer was responsible for which title, but the stylistic differences are suggestive. Loos was clear about her role. In her memoir, she recalls, "D. W. bade me put in titles even when unnecessary and add laughs wherever I found an opening. I found several" (*GI*, 103). Interspersed among the instructive and weighty inscriptions are lighter and more ironic captions that seem more reflective of the "Loos style." For example, in the scene in which The Dear One, who has jealously watched a woman's undulating walk draw men's attention on the street and decides to imitate it by tying her skirt into a hobble, a title dryly comments, "The new walk seems to bring results," as men flock to her ridiculous gait. In the marriage market in Babylon, when no one bids on the feisty Mountain Girl, she shouts at them, "You lice! You rats! You refuse me? There is no gentler dove in all Babylon than I."

Some titles are more subtle, as when the repressive High Priest of Bel-Marduk is threatened by the rival cult of Ishtar. The title remarks, "He angrily resolves to reestablish his own god—incidentally himself." The final modifier sarcastically comments from outside the action in a distinctly contemporary idiom. The tone does not match the image, and the title elicits a snicker whereas the image is aiming for sober drama. Later in the film, in the modern narrative, when The Boy is framed and put in jail, the title remarks, "Stolen goods, planted on the Boy, and his bad reputation, intolerate him away for a term." The verb form "intolerate" can be read as a teasing poke at Griffith's tendentious insistence upon the word and the concept of intolerance, which often seems like an elaborate defense against criticism of his race politics in *Birth of a Nation*.

Griffith shared with Loos an interest in making films more porous to high culture, as reflected by his use of Whitman and other literary and artistic intertexts. However, while Griffith used this material in a fairly traditional style, as epigraph or thematic support, Loos's literary intertexts are usually cheeky. The one title for which Loos routinely claimed credit—the most controversial title in *Intolerance*—is such a text. She recalls, "At one point I paraphrased Voltaire in a manner which particularly pleased D. W.: 'When women cease to attract men, they often turn to reform as second choice'" (*GI*, 103). It may seem odd that Loos would claim authorship of a quotation that is arguably misogynist, but she never hesitated to distance herself from feminism. Loos's idea of female empowerment is more *Sex and the Single Girl* than suffragette, and she was always at pains to emphasize her girlishness and insignificance even as she, like her titles, stole the spotlight. (Writing about how *Blondes* had been inspired by Mencken's barbs aimed at his fellow Americans, she remarks, "My book was certainly an offshoot of Mencken's point of view, just as a gadget can be produced by the important theory of a scientist" [*GI*, 217]). Loos flaunted superficial signifiers of cultural capital in her intertitles, not so much to make films "smarter" but to disrupt the expected relationship between the image and the word, vacuous mass culture and clever high culture. The epic complexity of *Intolerance*—its heterogeneity, didacticism and suggestion, melodrama and innovation—challenged Loos to produce a subtle, insinuating voice for a film that defied current cinematic conventions and concepts of cinematic pleasure.

Vachel Lindsay writes, "Anita Loos once said to me that *Intolerance* was 'a bathtub full of diamonds'. . . . It was a humorous way of proclaiming that there were enough suggestions in *Intolerance*, to producers of imagination, to last the motion picture world for fifty years."[34] This is certainly the case, but here Loos speaks, significantly, in the idiom of Lorelei: "kissing your hand may make you feel very very good but a diamond and safire bracelet lasts forever" (*B*, 55). Loos explicitly connects *Intolerance* to the world of *Gentlemen Prefer Blondes* by giving Lorelei a cameo in the film. "I was doing quite well in the cinema when Mr. Eisman made me give it all up," Lorelei remarks at the beginning of

Blondes (*B*, 6). Her "last cinema," was *Intolerance*, in which she played "one of the girls that fainted at the battle when all of the gentlemen fell off the tower" (*B*, 8). The battle in question is the fall of Babylon, which indicates Lorelei's definition of "gentlemen." Lorelei's appearance in the film is preposterous but also has a particular logic to it.[35]

As Miriam Hansen notices, one of *Intolerance*'s dominant themes is the "fate—and fatal power—of unmarried female characters throughout the ages" and how their environment thwarts or supports them; Michael Rogin adds that many of the narrative threads in the film promote female sexuality and public pleasure.[36] The Babylonian narrative in which Lorelei acts features open eroticism, feasting, and elaborate dance sequences (according to accounts from the set of *Intolerance*, some of the extras hired to appear seminude in the scenes were, as Lorelei would say, "not nice"[37]). Griffith's film is sympathetic to women of pleasure who are the victims of intolerance: the temple prostitutes/"Virgins" in Mesopotamia, Mary Magdalen, and the women who are herded out of the bordello under the gleeful eyes of the modern-day reformists (the subjects of Loos's "female reformers" title). Both Griffith and Loos were fascinated by hypocritical reformers. Henry Spoffard, who becomes Lorelei's husband, is a wealthy cinema "senshur" who likes to assemble the "riskay" scenes he has excised into a sort of reformist stag film that he watches recreationally with other men (*B*, 102). At one point in *Blondes*, Spoffard tells Lorelei that she "seemed to remind him quite a lot of a girl who got quite a write-up in the bible who was called Magdellen. So then he said that he used to be a member of the choir himself, so who was he to cast the first rock at a girl like I" (*B*, 93).

Loos leads her reader to infer a somewhat seamy quid pro quo underpinning the economics of Lorelei's glamorous life, but critics are divided about exactly what goes on. Barbara Everett describes Lorelei as "a cherubic-faced nail-hard amateur whore" (254); Regina Barecca remarks that Lorelei and Dorothy are "closer to con artists than to whores . . . far from professional courtesans" (xvii); Katharina von Ankum states that Lorelei "preserves her virginity" until she marries Spoffard.[38] All these readings are technically plausible. "Memoirs of a Woman of Pleasure" is as euphemistically apt a subtitle for *Blondes* as "The Illuminating Diary of a Professional Lady," which Loos, always taking advantage of structural subordination, subtitled her novel.

Figure 6.2
Intolerance, D. W. Griffith, 1916.

What is certain is that Lorelei, like the profession to which she gravitates, the cinema, is in the business of selling pleasure. Loos went on to
exploit *Intolerance*'s linguistic subtleties and thematics of pleasure in
Blondes, where she plays Griffith's vast historical epic as local comedy.

GENTLEMEN PREFER TYPISTS

According to Lorelei, she has "been" three careers. Back when she was
still going by her given name, Mabel Minnow, her father sent her to
"the business colledge" in Little Rock, but after just a week, a lawyer
named Mr. Jennings hired her to be his new stenographer. She reports

that she "stayed in his office about a year"—doing exactly what, she does not say (B, 24). Lorelei's first job links her to one of modernity's favorite female icons, the secretary or typewriter girl,[39] who embodies the paradoxes of female pleasure and technologies of writing in ways that anticipate the cinema spectatrix and the cinema writer. On the one hand, the stenographer/typist/secretary earns money and works in the public sphere. On the other hand, hers is a labor of automatism, Marx's "dead labor," regurgitating the words of others. She is connected to writing, but only in the passive sense of recording or transposing someone else's (usually her male boss's) thoughts. Her job is copying, transposing, correcting errors, and rendering her work transparent; she has no distinctive authorial signature. She bears a remarkable resemblance to the cinema titler before Loos transformed that role.

The typist's primary identity is as a worker, but there is, as Christopher Keep notes, an "excessive, almost obsessional fascination . . . with the assumed promiscuity of the female typist."[40] As Lawrence Rainey remarks, "The typist, after all, is repetition personified," but she is also imagined as "represen[ting] the promise of modern freedom: an allegedly new, autonomous subject whose appetites for pleasure and sensuous fulfillment were legitimated by modernity itself."[41] But the nature of the typist's pleasures tends to be imagined as analogous to her production of language: anonymous, automatic (like Eliot's robotic typist in The Waste Land, for whom sex is anhedonic). Loos wrote several screenplays exploring the misreadings accruing around this amanuensis of alienated words. Erik von Stroheim's The Social Secretary (1916) follows a stenographer who loses several jobs because she is harassed by her male employers, including a boss at the office of the New York Purity League who looks at "riskay" pictures—a forerunner of Henry Spoffard. Virtuous Vamp (1919) also features a talented stenographer who is fired because she distracts the men around her from their work. In Red-Headed Woman, Jean Harlow plays the stenographer as a "sex pirate."[42] By giving Lorelei a brief past as a stenographer, Loos invokes all the narrative clichés associating debased writing and pleasure that surround this handmaiden of modern literature. Even more significantly, it is through this so-called career that Lorelei is "discovered."

Lorelei's stenography stint comes to an end when she catches Mr. Jennings with "a girl there who really was famous all over Little Rock for not being nice" (B, 24–25). Lorelei recalls that when she "found out that girls like that paid calls on Mr. Jennings I had quite a bad case of histerics and my mind was really a blank and when I came out of it, it seems that I had a revolver in my hand and it seems that the revolver had shot Mr Jennings" (B, 25). Lorelei's revolver is part Hedda Gabler, part Mae West, but it is recast as an instrument that conveniently— like the typewriter—erases her agency. During her murder trial, Mabel Minnow seduces the jury with her damsel-in-distress routine and is acquitted. The judge, who appreciates her act, bestows upon her a ticket to Hollywood and the stage name Lorelei Lee. "I mean it was when Mr. Jennings became shot," she remarks, "that I got the idea to go into the cinema" (B, 25). Never has the passive tense been deployed so tactically.

In making stenography the gateway to stardom, Loos cannily invokes the popular discourse of the 1920s that associates the type-writer girl with cinema.[43] As Kracauer remarks, "Sensational film hits and life usually correspond to each other because the Little Miss Typ-ists model themselves after the examples they see on the screen."[44] Iris Barry argues that one of cinema's key consumers is "The typist in search of a thrill."[45] The typist career and the spectatrix pastime seem to support each other; as Freidrich A. Kittler puts it, "at night [women] are at the movies and during the day they sit at their typewriters."[46]

The typewriter and the cinema are connected materially (both are American, individuality-flattening technologies that traffic in copies) as well as imaginatively. Both are understood as feminized and offer-ing paradoxical pleasures. Early film critics describe cinemagoing as an experience of fantasy and escape, but they also imagine cinematic pleasure as banal and standardized. ("That which determines the rhythm of production on a conveyer belt is the basis of the rhythm of reception in the film," Walter Benjamin remarks in "On Some Motifs in Baudelaire."[47]) Even Barry, one of early cinema's greatest advocates, describes "The second-hand experience derived from the pictures, the imitation excitement," as "almost as standardized as a church service or a daily newspaper." She laments, "I wish that the public could, in the midst of its pleasures, see how blatantly it is being spoon-fed, and ask for slightly better dreams."[48] This is modernism's familiar double bind: it must account for the fact that mass culture is enormously compel-ling but also a kind of false consciousness.

Loos turns to the typewriter girl to constellate—and also recast—the connection among mechanized writing, debased pleasure, and cinema writing. Lorelei, we can safely assume, is not much of a typist: she writes her diary in longhand, and not very well at that. And Lorelei is not a spectatrix but a would-be actress. The cinema turns out to be the closest thing to a true profession for her. In making cinema a place of production rather than consumption, Loos alters the standard trope of passive celluloid just as her trademark cinematic style diverges from the paradigm of hypnotic spectatorship. The titler herself is historically positioned like the typist, alienated from her labor; Loos alters that by reinventing the form.

Loos fashioned not just Lorelei but also herself through the typist–cinema correlation. In her memoir *A Girl Like I*, a phrase taken from Lorelei (Loos often slips into such Loreleisms, in her essays as well), Loos chose to reproduce a Ralph Barton sketch of herself, a well-known cinema writer, as a cutely infantile typewriter girl. Antonia Lant suggests that the proliferation of publicity shots of female cinema writers at their typewriters in the 1920s was a way of solving the "awkwardness in efforts to signify women's acts of film writing, given the cultural desire to make her an object of visual study."[49] Loos uses the standard shot to render writing visual in a much more complicated way, adding a caption to the image in which she adopts the voice of Lorelei: "The only thing wrong with this picture is that an authoress like I never learned how to type" (*GI*, unnumbered insert between 150 and 151). Like her cinema titles, this text that is supposed to be subordinate to and explain the image instead upstages it. Ostensibly revealing Loos's shortcomings, it in fact makes her superior to the typist. The sentence reflects the anxiety that cinema titling is regarded like typewriting: debased, anonymous and subordinate, an inartistic stream of banal formulas rather than the individualized, scripted work of a legitimate writer.

On the same page of *A Girl Like I*, below Barton's drawing, is a photograph of Loos sitting at a desk with a pen in her hand, a seemingly straightforward portrait of the artist at work. Yet Loos adds this caption: "My sole preparation for a career was to buy a fountain pen and a large yellow pad: no dictionary or grammar required. Some day I'll give a course on how to succeed in literature without any learning." This idea of producing literature without learning is as ironic the usage of

Figure 6.3
Ralph Barton cartoon of Anita Loos
Courtesy of Beinecke Rare Book and Manuscript Library, Yale University

the words "education" and "literary" in *Blondes*. While Lorelei inflates these words and her own "literary" labor, Loos deflates them and the self-important disingenuousness with which they are deployed by the many would-be seducers who "educate" Lorelei through showing her art and bestowing upon her highbrow books. Loos implicates the typist and the caption writer (analogous to the subtitler as a producer of text linked to an image) to position herself between low and high cultural pursuits.

In her film writing, Loos routinely disrupts visual pleasure and puts in its place the pleasure of the text. In *Blondes* she follows the same principles, but because of her medium, the effect is slightly different. Her cinematic language creates literary visual enjoyment and her novelistic language creates visual literary pleasure. Lorelei, acting as authoress in *Blondes*, writes in language that induces the reader to see words as images.

"TRANSPARENT NEGLIGAYS AND ORNAMENTAL BATH TUBS"

Blondes is a visual novel in several senses. Most obviously, it is illustrated by Ralph Barton, who was under contract with *Harper's Bazar: A Repository of Fashion, Pleasure and Instruction* (it became *Harper's Bazaar* in 1929), where *Blondes* first appeared in serialized form. Loos was not responsible for the images, but they are routinely included in editions of the novel, so they have become part of its textual apparatus. As it happens, they reflect Loos's preoccupation with technologies of writing. The first illustration shows Lorelei at her desk with a pen, writing in her diary: exactly the same pose as Loos's publicity photo. The humorous caption Loos appended to her own portrait is perfectly appropriate for this occasion: Lorelei has "succeeded in literature without any learning." Barton's second illustration shows Lorelei on a couch with a stack of books scattered around her, looking perplexed. When a "literary" admirer (a novelist) gives Lorelei "a whole complete set of books for my birthday by a gentleman called Mr. Conrad" in an effort to "educate" her, she asks her maid to read and summarize them; she comes to the conclusion that "They all seem to be about ocean travel" (*B*, 8). Lorelei is only marginally literate, but her mistakes have the effect of calling attention to the concrete qualities of her writing.

Lorelei's voice is reminiscent of other unreliable or idiosyncratic narrators—John Dowell, Nick Carraway, Molly Bloom—and Loos adds a linguistic layer of textual play through Lorelei's misspellings and malapropisms. Even as Loos constantly signals toward the textual production of *Blondes* through these mistakes, critics such as Leavis, Lewis, and Connolly take her narrator literally ("But writing is different because you do not have to learn or practice") and understand her voice as purely physical—oral, idiomatic, and "artless pseudo-baby language." They focus on the verbal qualities of Lorelei's narrative and perceive it as "uncrafted" bodily speech rather than scripted language.

Lorelei's phonetic spelling and punctuation errors, along with Loos's innuendos, euphemisms, and double entendres, do lend themselves to this reading—for example, Lorelei's explanation that "of course when a gentleman is interested in educating a girl, he likes to stay and talk about the topics of the day until quite late," or Dorothy's suspicions about a girl in Paris who claims to be eighteen: "how could a girl get such dirty knees in only 18 years?" (B, 4, 66). However, most of the humor of *Blondes* depends upon visual wordplay.

Lorelei's trip to Europe affords Loos an opportunity to make multilingual puns (for example, Lorelei's adventure with the French con artists "Louie and Robber," and her visit to "Fountainblo" and "Momart" [B, 63]). Lorelei remarks that "French is really very easy, for instance the French use the word 'sheik' for everything, while we only seem to use it for gentlemen when they seem to resemble Rudolf Valentino" (B, 69). Loos frequently crafts homophone puns such as "Sheik"/"chic" or "Hofbraü"/"half brow" (B, 86), which, although based on words sounding alike, have to be seen to be perceived (like the "real"/"reel" pun in *His Picture in the Papers*). As with the cinema title about the unpronounceable Count Xxerkzsxxv—which looks like a vengeful secretary has pounded on random typewriter keys—Loos's language in *Blondes* highlights the details of its construction.

Faulkner's 1925 letter to Loos illustrates the many levels of voice and awareness in *Blondes*:

> Please accept my envious congratulations on Dorothy—the way you did her through the intelligence of that elegant moron of a cornflower. Only you have played a rotten trick on your admiring public. How many of them, do you think, will ever know that Dorothy really has something . . . My God, it's charming . . . most of them will be completely unmoved—even your rather clumsy gags won't get them—and the others will only find it slight and humorous. The Andersons [Sherwood and Elizabeth] even mentioned Ring Lardner in talking to me about it. But perhaps that was what you were after, and you have builded better than you knew. . . .[50]

It is no wonder that Faulkner prefers Dorothy, Lorelei's brunette sidekick, who is the voice of overt irony, modernism's signature rhetoric, in *Blondes*. Faulkner divides the readers of Loos's novel into those aligned with Lorelei (the "admiring public") and those aligned with Dorothy (educated readers). Faulkner is not so sure where Loos herself falls. Mentioning Lardner, the acknowledged master of modern American vernacular, Faulkner then revokes the compliment by suggesting that the effect was not deliberate, but also jokes back at Loos by imitating Lorelei: "you have builded better than you knew." Faulkner assumes two separate and hierarchical audiences who experience two different reading effects (irony versus mere humor), two different levels of comprehension, and hence two different kinds of pleasure. He does not acknowledge the ways Lorelei (who is hardly "elegant"), as scripted by Loos, is an only half-proficient writer but a master of strategy. Lorelei's voice is, in fact, more complex than Dorothy's sophisticated but straightforward irony. Her grasp of language is comical, but she is nevertheless skilled in dissimulation. She is a surreptitious editor of her own diary, expurgating all evidence that would contradict her carefully constructed image of herself and successfully manipulating everyone around her. Lorelei is not as dumb as she seems or as smart as she thinks she is. Making her a barely literate writer has the effect of estranging the reader from language. Loos makes sure we do not mistake these strategies for modernism—Lorelei is quick to dispatch the Conrad novels to her maid—but rather sustains the juxtaposition of mass and high culture.

At least Molly Bloom reads her own novels, even if they are "smutty." But while Molly's undulating run-on sentences are most intelligible when read aloud, Lorelei's language, if read verbally (the way Leavis, Connolly, and Lewis seem to have approached it) would produce only a few laughs at the "rather clumsy gags" (e.g., "A girl like I"; "champagne always makes me feel philosophical"). If we are fooled into thinking that we are hearing Lorelei's voice rather than seeing her script (transcribed by an unknown typist into the book before us), we are failing to see what is in front of us on the page. There is almost no descriptive imagery in *Blondes*, which is odd, given the "lookist" visual economy that rules the novel. Instead, Loos directs the reader to look at the words on the page, much in the same way that she scolds the cinema viewer who tries to pronounce 'Count Xxerkzsxxv.' One has to read and analyze the words on the page to *see* Loos's more intricate jokes. *Blondes* follows the principles of her cinema writing and asks its audience to view language materially, as visual images.

One reader who paid close attention to the words on the page, despite his declining vision, was James Joyce. In the same 1926 letter in which Joyce tells Harriet Shaw Weaver that he has read *Blondes*, he describes his "Work In Progress," which he put aside to read the novel. The next week (November 15), in a letter signed "Jeems Joker," he sends Weaver the opening paragraph of *Finnegans Wake*.[51] It is not hard to imagine why *Blondes* would have appealed to Joyce. Lorelei's voice resonates with those of Joyce's own Sirens (who appear, like Dorothy and Lorelei, "bronze by gold"), his Nausicaa, and his Penelope. In Joyce's own exploration of a contemporary, uneducated woman's voice in the final chapter of *Ulysses*, he merely jettisons punctuation, while Loos toys with all levels of language except syntax. Lorelei's mangling of several languages—French and German as well as "the english landguage" (*B*, 88)—corresponds to the riot of languages in *Finnegans Wake*. Lorelei's felicitous phrases (e.g., her "Eyefull Tower") may have stayed with Joyce ("a waalworth of a skyerscape of most eyful hoyth entowerly.")[52] More than specific puns, however, it is Loos's comic choreography of concretized language that seems relevant for Joyce. As Beckett remarked of *Finnegans Wake*, "Here form *is* content, content *is* form. You complain that this stuff is not written in English. It is not written at all. It is not to be read—or rather it is not only to be read. It is to be looked at and listened to. His writing is not *about* something; *it is that something itself*."[53] We are familiar with this argument made about modernist art, but not about vernacular culture.

Loos was keenly aware of modernist and avant-garde writing and art, joking about the contrivances of cubism and the daffyness of Dada.[54] She visited Stein at the rue de Fleurus, but claimed to be less interested in her writing—which she described through Sherwood Anderson's summary: "one should look on it as one looks at the palette of a painter, appreciate the words merely as words, and pay no attention to the context in which she placed them"—than she was in finding Stein, among Hemingway and Fitzgerald, "the most manly of the lot" (*GI*, 228). Loos routinely calls attention to the surface of words, like Stein's word portraits, or Picasso's *Still Life with Chair Caning* (1912), in which newsprint letters "JOU" are incorporated into the image as literary artifact and also as a pun. What is remarkable about Loos is that she deploys the "mandarin" mode of heightened textuality as the guiding principle of vernacular forms of culture without being gnomic, obscure, or inaccessible. For her, there was no inherent contradiction between these ostensibly different orders of pleasure, only systems of cultural classification—including elitism masquerading as "education"—that made this seem so.

When Lewis compared Loos to Stein, he argued that the former "intended to reassure the reader of the mass-democracy that all is well, and that the writer is one of the crowd . . . not a detested 'highbrow.'"[55] But Loos had a much wider audience in mind, and she aims to disarm rather than reassure, always sustaining the tension of cultural hierarchy as she views distinction from the middle of the great divide. Lorelei eagerly asserts the ways she is "literary"; simultaneously, Loos targets the self-styled "intelectuals" (modeled on Mencken) who fall for Lorelei but attempt to maintain their vaunted values of distinction. At the end of the novel, Lorelei convinces Spoffard to become a producer of titillating "pure films" (B, 120); their first production, "a great historical subject which is founded on the sex life of Dolly Madison," stars Lorelei (B, 114). Simultaneously, she collaborates on scripts with her man on the side, Mr. Montrose, a frustrated screenwriter who "had quite a hard time getting along in the motion picture profession, because all of his senarios are all over their head. Because when Mr. Montrose writes about sex, it is full of sychology, when everybody else writes about it, it is full of nothing but transparent negligays and ornamental bath tubs" (B, 115). Loos's work found a wide audience precisely because it allowed viewers and readers the pleasure of participating in cultural distinction and its undoing: a testimony to general audiences' capacity to embrace the wit of linguistic play, and to "highbrow" audiences' susceptibility to the pleasures of "transparent negligays and ornamental bath tubs." Loos's success suggests that she produced her ideal audience: a consumer who could read images and see words.

Other popular writers and artists began to reflect modernism back to itself. Several of Loos's female contemporaries—including Mae West, Dorothy Parker, and Gypsy Rose Lee—similarly manipulated modernist sensibilities and stereotypical, conventional pleasures to forge new kinds of vernacular culture. Gypsy, for example, was dubbed the "Striptease Intellectual" for her idiosyncratic burlesque act in the late 1920s and 1930s, in which she delivered a sly lecture on art, literature, or classical music, or deconstructed the practice of striptease itself, with lines quoted from the likes of Algonquin Round Table wit Dwight Fiske, all while peeling off her clothes. Like Loos, Gypsy poked fun at the pretentions of pedagogy that sought to shore up the great divide. Gypsy also wrote pulp noir fiction, including the detective novel *The G-String Murders* (1941), plays, occasional essays for *The New Yorker*, and a sparkling memoir. Loos wrote about Gypsy in a section of *A Cast of Thousands* called "Women to Remember": "Gypsy Rose Lee and I had some curious traits in common. . . . In early youth we had each appeared in rather basic vaudeville skits, during which period we whiled away some of our childhood hours reading *The Critique of Pure Reason* by Immanuel Kant. Why? Possibily [*sic*] as a counter-irritant to the gag lines we were forced to learn" (184). Gypsy and Loos both cultivated a distinctive voice (one wised-up, one dumbed-down) within their respective genres, using humor and cultural name-dropping to assert female pleasure. Throughout her career, Gypsy, like Loos, teasingly unsettled ideas about class, gender, and the perceived divide between high and low culture.[56]

The sound film put an end to the linguistic play of *Gentlemen Prefer Blondes*. Hawks's 1953 film drastically revises the plot of the novel (Lorelei and Dorothy, now showgirls, sail to Europe for Lorelei's wedding to Gus Esmond, and all but a few minutes of the film are set on the ship) and, most crucially, jettisons Loos's first-person narration. What we gain in iconic sex appeal, we lose in textual complexity. Significantly, Dorothy's jokes—broad irony—translated well to the sound film, while Lorelei's did not. The only witticisms retained in Hawks's film are obvious grammatical mistakes and malapropisms—for example, the phrase "A girl like I," and Lorelei asking for directions to "Europe, France." The pleasure of the text has dissipated. The disappearance of the text in cinema was strikingly marked within the film industry by the first Academy Awards in 1929, which gave the first and only Best Title Writing award to Joseph Farnham. (Gerald C. Duffy was posthumously nominated for his work on *The Private Life of Helen of Troy*, a film that sounds like a Spoffard production, or one of Huxley's feelies.) The same year, a special award was given to Warner Brothers for *The Jazz Singer*, signaling what was to come. Ironically, some viewers, such as Q. D. Leavis, complained that the sound cinema further distanced people from the written word: "the 'talkie' . . . does not even offer captions."[57]

Although Loos's literary-visual voice disappeared from most film, her playful approach to cultural signification would become the stock in trade of the next generation. For writers such as William Burroughs, Jeanette Winterson, Kathy Acker, and Thomas Pynchon and artists such as Jeff Koons, Andy Warhol, and Cindy Sherman (whose respective images of Marilyn Monroe signal the paradoxical emptiness and thrill of replication[58]), consciousness about the divisions that marked modernism became sources of humor, critique, or self-reflection. The giddy juxtapositions of the sort that Loos performed exist in postmodernism in tandem with the lingering critique of pleasure.

CODA
Modernism's Afterlife in the
Age of Prosthetic Pleasure

"[I] never knew as much pleasure and as little contentment."
—Anaïs Nin, *Diaries*, October 5, 1935[1]

"I finally had an orgasm, and my doctor told me that it was the wrong kind."
"Did you have the wrong kind, really? I've never had the wrong kind, ever. My worst one was right on the money."
— *Manhattan* (Woody Allen, 1979)

We began with Jean Rhys's Sasha trudging the streets of Paris, set ironically against her peers in the "after-war generation" who were "mad for pleasure." For modernist writers, pleasure was a problem. It was a force that seemed to have run amok in contemporary culture: in the cinema, in popular literature, and in the public's enthusiasm for fun. While general audiences, living through a time of political and social upheaval, dazed from one war and about to enter another, embraced mass culture amusement, modernist writers took up the mantle of arduous, deliberate pleasure as a defense of language, contemplation, and the autonomy of art. As their work confirms, even as they expounded the charms of unpleasure, they were constantly aware of the attractions of "the tepid bath of nonsense," as Huxley put it.

Cut, now, from Paris in the 1930s to the Upper West Side of Manhattan in our time, to Symphony Space, a venue known for its annual live reading of selections from *Ulysses* on June 16. The Bloomsday celebration, like others around the country and the globe, indicates how modernism—even high modernism—has been embraced and absorbed not just into the academy but into contemporary culture. And yet on the 100th anniversary of Bloomsday in 2004, British and American

newspapers noting the event found a way to emphasize *Ulysses*'s reputation as the most famous unread novel of the twentieth century. *The
New York Times* observed that *Ulysses* "has come to stand as the apogee
of 'elitist' literature" because of its "byzantine difficulty." NPR pointed
out that "the difficulty of reading *Ulysses* is as legendary as the novel
itself." And the BBC commented that "for all its renown and notoriety,
it is a book that few have read and even fewer comprehend."[2]

In April 2012, Symphony Space sponsored another modernist event:
a month-long festival called "Gertrude's Paris":

> The Paris of Gertrude Stein was wild and exhilarating with the
> creative spirits of the time collaborating, canoodling, and conspir-
> ing, and at the center of it all—Stein's salon. Join in our month-
> long celebration of this magical time of music, film, literature, and
> art. Come to Symphony Space, and make her world yours.[3]

"Gertrude's Paris" included wine tasting, jazz performances, a fashion show, a photography exhibit, films, and a discussion of Fitzgerald's
Tender Is the Night. However, amid all the "collaborating and canoodling," the main works of Stein herself that were presented were accompanied by music and dancing. In the same way that Stein's libretto for
Four Saints in Three Acts was set to a distinctly nonmodernist score
by Virgil Thomson and staged with Florine Stettheimer's decorative
sets, the raw, linguistically complex Stein was not center stage at "Gertrude's Paris." Similarly, the 2011 traveling exhibition "Seeing Gertrude
Stein: Five Stories" focused on her clothes, art collecting, and circle of
famous friends: that is, more on the "pop," visual, sybaritic Stein in
keeping with the lovable, lumpy Stein of *Midnight in Paris*, rather than
the obscure, challenging Stein on the page. Writing for *The New York
Review of Books*, Michael Kimmelman noted the conflux of Steiniana—
including "The Steins Collect," an exhibition of Leo and Gertrude's art
collection at the Metropolitan Museum of Art; Barbara Will's *Unlikely
Collaborators: Gertrude Stein, Bernard Faÿ, and the Vichy Dilemma*; and
a new edition of Stein's novel *Ida*—and concluded that while "Stein
endures," her novels and poems remain "unread as always."[4]

Clearly, modernism is alive in and outside the academy. However,
it is worth noting which parts of modernism are foregrounded and
which are sidelined or minimized. While the generation that canonized

modernism and New Criticism promoted it as a thorny, complicated body of work, those features are not emphasized as much in recent modernist studies, which has notably sought to integrate the vernacular modernisms of "Gertrude's Paris" into the field. Perhaps it is inevitable that once we have mastered modernism's maneuvers, its knots are unraveled and its edgy energy is diminished. Modernist unpleasure, a defining feature of this literature, may register most forcefully with the first-time reader who struggles with linguistic and narrative innovation. To sense this textual unpleasure is to recover what made modernism surprising, shocking, and challenging in its own time.

One important reason for the shift in the meaning of modernism in the second half of the twentieth and the early twenty-first century is that postmodern culture has reframed some of the central tensions that motivated modernism's ambivalence about pleasure. The perceived opposition of high and low culture driven by different kinds of pleasure is not so much of a dilemma for postmodern art—or contemporary scholarship—as it is a generative condition. Postmodernism has inherited the discourse of differential pleasures, but usually references it in a spirit of self-conscious play rather than embattled defense. Nor does the opposition between somatic and cerebral pleasure hold sway as it once did. One major event in the genealogy of pleasure after modernism was when the so-called sexual revolution of the 1960s and early 1970s fueled an explosion of explicit art, literature, and utopian hedonism, and theorists such as Wilhelm Reich, Nancy Friday, and Shere Hite suggested that pleasure could be a revolutionary force.[5] Friday and Hite, in particular, point to the crucial development of twentieth-century feminism. Women, who had long been cast as the ground of somatic, nonintellectual pleasure, were speaking for themselves.

Still, unpleasure remained a darkly magnetic force. The legacy of modernism's anxiety about and hierarchization of pleasure is felt strongly in David Foster Wallace's Infinite Jest (1996).[6] Since his death in 2008, critics and peers have affirmed Wallace's central place in postmodern literature and Infinite Jest, a massive novel with innumerable intersecting nonlinear narratives, has been canonized as a classic of postmodern metafiction. With its stories within stories, self-referentiality, and Nabokovian endnote apparatus that includes graphs and sub-footnotes, the novel is a virtual encyclopedia of postmodern strategies. Throughout, Wallace's sly critique of late capitalism and commercialism (for example, each year is sponsored by a product, and much of the action occurs during The Year of the Depend Adult Undergarment) is combined with a zeal for and humor about the popular culture that it interrogates. Wallace's fascination with technology and technophobia, his invocation and spoofing of strict ideological hierarchies, along with his criticism of capitalist commodification while also gleefully mocking its idioms, are typical of what Linda Hutcheon has called postmodernism's "deliberate refusal to resolve contradictions."[7]

One of the major themes of *Infinite Jest* is addiction and pleasure disorders. A prominent narrative strand that cuts across the novel's many plots, and whose importance is indicated by its titular role, is a mysterious film by one James Orin Incandeza, Jr. called *Infinite Jest*. Known as "the Entertainment" or "the samizdat," the film is "a recorded pleasure so entertaining and diverting it is lethal" (321). Once people start viewing it, it is so mesmerizing that they obsessively watch until they die. A group of radical Quebeçois separatists want to use *Infinite Jest* as a terrorist weapon against Americans, who, one character remarks, "would die for this chance to be fed this death of pleasure with spoons, in their warm homes, alone, unmoving" (318).

What makes "the lethal cartridge" so compelling? The brief and possibly fallacious descriptions of the film—for no one who sees it is supposed to survive that viewing—sketch a scenario in which an extraordinarily beautiful woman appears as "some kind of maternal instantiation of the archetypal figure of Death, sitting naked, corporeally gorgeous, ravishing, hugely pregnant . . . explaining in very simple childlike language to whomever the film's camera represents that Death is always female, and that the female is always maternal" (788). Shot from the perspective of a child in a crib, the film shows the woman bending over the infant and uttering apologies: "I'm so sorry. I'm so very sorry. I am so, so sorry" (939). The "ultimate pleasure" here is intimately connected to the maternal body and to infantile regression, drawing not only from psychoanalytic discourse but also from the centuries-old association of the female body with pleasurable passivity and also anxiety. The samizdat calls to mind T. S. Eliot's assertion that mass culture appeals to a "desire to return to the womb."[8]

Infinite Jest alludes to other pleasure technologies, such as Reich's orgone accumulator, the Excessive Machine in Roger Vadim's *Barbarella* (1968), and David Cronenberg's *Videodrome* (1983).

Wallace explicitly connects the Entertainment to the historical discourse and science of pleasure. At one point, some of the characters in *Infinite Jest* discuss the discovery in the 1970s, by a neuroscientist named Olders, that "firing certain electrodes in certain parts of the lobes gave the brain intense feelings of pleasure" (470). These areas are called "*p*-terminals" (pleasure-terminals). Building on the data, Canadian scientists implanted electrodes in a rat's brain and "found that if they rigged an auto-stimulation lever, the rat would press the lever to stimulate his *p*-terminal over and over, thousands of times an hour, over and over, ignoring food and female rats in heat, completely fixated on the lever's stimulation, day and night, stopping only when the rat finally died of dehydration or simple fatigue" (471). The artificial stimulation of the *p*-terminal overrides opportunities for real carnal pleasure ("food and female rats in heat"). Wallace adds a twist to this fictionalized version of James Olds and Peter Milner's famous rat experiments in the 1950s: when word gets out about the studies, people start lining up to volunteer for pleasure implants. "We would choose dying for this, the total pleasure of a passive goat" (474).

Wallace's depiction of a society of individuals drowning in but not enjoying pleasure offers a culmination to Rhys's Sasha and other early twentieth-century pleasure seekers. Rhys, Huxley, Eliot, Lawrence, and other authors merely imagine cinema audiences rendered passive and narcotized. Wallace goes further in creating a vehicle of entertainment that literally kills its viewers with pleasure as they neglect everything else and give themselves over to hedonism. The modernist metaphors of intoxication and hypnosis are now a deadly addiction. This is a Freudian version of Plato's oyster, "merely a body endowed with life," without the exercise of reason or intellect, and a pure receptor of pleasure. It is also the ultimate regressive fantasy, akin to the sort Huxley found so revolting in Al Jolson's "Mammy" song, and an abandonment of the intellect.

While *Infinite Jest* is in many ways a dystopic text and the samizdat a nightmarish invention, it is only a limit case for the kinds of questions about the philosophical and ethical implications of pleasure that Wallace often raised in his fiction and nonfiction. For example, in the first-person "A Supposedly Fun Thing I'll Never Do Again," he reports with near-Huxleyian contempt on a "mass-market Luxury Cruise" that he took for a *Harper's* magazine assignment: "they'll microman-age every iota of every pleasure-option so that not even the dreadful corrosive action of your adult consciousness and agency and dread can fuck up your fun. Your troublesome capacities for choice, error, regret, dissatisfaction, and despair will be removed from the equation."[9] The cruise line's slogan is "Your Pleasure is Our Business": a motto that would be equally apt for Huxley's *Brave New World*, where there is "no leisure from pleasure." The modernist dystopia, Wallace suggests, has been visited upon contemporary culture. Wallace's father, James D. Wallace, was a philosopher whose publications include "Pleasure as an End of Action" (1966), a consideration of classical hedonism and the relationship between freedom and pleasure.[10] The younger Wal-lace also meditates on philosophies of pleasure throughout his work. In an essay on "Joseph Frank's Dostoevsky," Wallace asks, "Is the real point of my life simply to undergo as little pain and as much pleasure as possible? My behavior sure seems to indicate that this is what I believe, at least a lot of the time. But isn't this kind of a selfish way to live?"[11] In interviews too, Wallace often voiced concern about how in contemporary Western culture "pleasure becomes a value, a teleologi-cal end in itself." He argued that "it's impossible to spend that many slack-jawed, spittle-chinned, formative hours in front of commercial art without internalizing the idea that one of the main goals of art is simply to 'entertain,' give people sheer pleasure. Except to what end, this pleasure-giving?"[12]

Consistent with modernist views of pleasure, Wallace proposed that "mass-market" and "commercial" amusement, with their atten-dant "fun," could be countered by "serious" art. When asked about television, he observed that

audiences prefer 100 percent pleasure to the reality that tends to be 49 percent pleasure and 51 percent pain. Whereas "serious" art, which is not primarily about getting money out of you, is more apt to make you uncomfortable, or to force you to work hard to access its pleasures, the same way that in real life true pleasure is usually a by-product of hard work and discomfort. So it's hard for an art audience, especially a young one that's been raised to expect art to be 100 percent pleasurable and to make that pleasure effortless, to read and appreciate serious fiction.[13]

Infinite Jest is anything but a passive descent into narrative pleasure. It bombards its readers with proliferating plots, detours, obscure
lexicon, and tricky constructions. Wallace does not experiment much
at the level of the word, like Joyce, or break up the sentence to the
same degree that Stein, for example, does. However, *Infinite Jest*'s
intricate narrative structures, including its rabbit hole digressions,
have a highly self-conscious and self-mocking tone that demand an
alert patience, discipline, and a sense of the text as both work and play.
Wallace conceded that his writing expresses "a kind of hostility to the
reader . . . sometimes in the form of sentences that are syntactically
not incorrect but still a real bitch to read. Or bludgeoning the reader
with data. Or devoting a lot of energy to creating expectations and
then taking pleasure in disappointing them."[13] The solution to a culture of compromised pleasure, for Wallace, is aesthetic difficulty and
even alienation: refusing readers the bliss of the samizdat and offering
them instead a demanding cognitive experience. Language, and specifically an antagonistic writerly stance toward readers—bombarding,
discomforting, bludgeoning, disappointing—is the antidote to "fun."
Wallace looks to modernist-inaugurated reading effects as a source of
cultural resistance and rigor.

From one angle, *Infinite Jest* looks like a parody of modernist views
of pleasure, but from another, it is an elaborate extension of those
ideas. For Wallace, as for many modernists, the difference between
serious and commercial art turned on the distinction between an
experience that is learned and earned, and a kind of "fun" that comes
all too easily. And yet, his work everywhere signals a hyperconscious-
ness about the biases that inform that position and a recognition of
the inevitability and intricacy of the audience's relationship to mass
culture. In postmodernism, mass culture is not so much a guilty pleasure as it is the white noise of our time. But for some writers, like
Wallace, pleasure itself as a broader category of experience remains
suspect, and the role of "serious" art is still thought to be the presentation of aesthetic tension as a bulwark against trite amusement. So
even though postmodernism can be irreverent about the kinds of cultural classification modernism espoused, those hierarchies still shape
the way some writers understand art.

That said, we are in the midst of a major paradigm shift in pleasure.
Wallace's samizdat is about sixteen years old, and its technology—the

"cartridge" that is passed from hand to hand—is already obsolete. Its materiality marks it as antiquated. Instead, we are surrounded by digital technologies that stimulate our "p-terminals" by artificial means. Pharmaceuticals such as SSRIs and Viagra, and recreational drugs such as ecstasy, have perfected chemical hedonism, and the Internet gratifies with unprecedented speed and accuracy. We live in an age of prosthetic pleasure. The modernist nightmare of bliss on demand has been realized, at least for those who can afford it. Modernism's suspicions about pleasure were always accompanied by an anxiety about new pleasure-producing technologies: indeed, the rhetoric of machine-age sensation runs throughout these chapters. However, in postmodernism, the anxiety about technologized pleasure overtakes the anxiety about somatic pleasure.

In particular, the modernist fear that easy, accessible pleasure (of the cinema, magazines, etc.) would threaten literature and deep thought has taken a new technological form. We are reading more, but our reading practices have changed. We are reading on computer screens, where text and words, choice and manipulation, firsthand and vicarious or virtual experience are colliding in unprecedented ways. The lament for the lost art of reading and the imperiled book is stronger than ever—its rhetoric of distraction, excessive accessibility, and inauthenticity comes right out of the interwar period— but the message feels strained, for much of the time those laments appear online.[14]

Where does this leave us? We might think about Barthes's "doubly perverse" reader, who "keeps the two texts in his field and in his hands the reins of pleasure and bliss," and "enjoys the consistency of his selfhood (that is his pleasure) and seeks its loss (that is his bliss)" (14). However, we do not have to view these as parallel but never-meeting experiences. Bliss and pleasure are not the distinct entities that Barthes postulates, nor do they so reliably produce the respective capitulation and destruction he imagines. As we have seen, modernism, even at its most aesthetically radical, participated in the kinds of pleasure it derided. The problem with pleasure arises when we conceptualize these different kinds of pleasure as mutually exclusive and their mixture as "perverse." The fascination with what's difficult and the satisfaction derived from doing complex tasks do not have to be jeopardized by amusement that appeals to the senses, the body, or the lax mind. There is a place for "Gertrude's Paris" and a place for close readings of recondite texts. The challenge is to hold on to modernism's aesthetic ambition and critical consciousness but relinquish the idea that they can only be achieved by dismissing or opting out of other experiences.

It is an exhilarating and an alarming moment. As we try to strike a balance somewhere between naïve enthusiasm and reactionary anxiety, the modernist response to pleasure—its insistence on mental vigor, critical thinking, and artistic innovation—seems more relevant than ever. Modernism's counterintuitive negation, difficulty, and appeal to the power of unpleasure could provide a productive tension at a time when many new pleasures have unsettling implications. The modernist legacy, its essential ambivalence, continues, and let us hope that it does, for it signals not only the continuing problem with pleasure but also pleasure's continuing potency.

Notes

INTRODUCTION: THE REPUDIATION OF PLEASURE

1. Lauren Berlant, "Love, a Queer Feeling," in *Homosexuality and Psychoanalysis*, ed. Tim Dean and Christopher Lane (Chicago: University of Chicago Press, 2001), 436.

2. Jean Rhys, *The Complete Novels* (New York: Norton, 1985), 397–399.

3. T. S. Eliot, *T. S. Eliot: The Collected Poems, 1909–1962* (New York: Harcourt Brace Jovanovich, 1991), 62.

4. See Stephen Halliwell's discussion of Aristotle's and Plato's discriminations among different kinds of pleasure. *Aristotle's Poetics* (Chicago: University of Chicago Press, 1998), 62–81.

5. Horace, "Ars Poetica," *The Norton Anthology of Theory and Criticism*, ed. Vincent B. Leitch (New York: Norton, 2001), 124–135.

6. Jonathan Culler, *Literary Theory: A Very Short Introduction* (New York: Oxford, 1997), 92. Harold Bloom, *How to Read and Why* (New York: Scribner, 2000), 22, 19.

7. Andreas Huyssen, *After the Great Divide: Modernism, Mass Culture, Postmodernism* (Bloomington: Indiana University Press, 1986).

8. Lionel Trilling, "The Fate of Pleasure," in *The Moral Obligation to Be Intelligent: Selected Essays* (New York: Farrar, Straus & Giroux, 2000), 434.

9. Virginia Woolf, "Modern Fiction," in *The Common Reader*, ed. Andrew McNeillie (New York: Harcourt, 1984), 152.

10. Trilling, "The Fate of Pleasure," 448. Theodor Adorno makes a similar point about "the dark works of modernism" such as Kafka's and Beckett's. *Aesthetic Theory*,

ed. Gretel Adorno and Rolf Tiedemann, tr. Robert Hullot-Kentor (New York: Continuum, 2004), 402.

11. Virginia Woolf, *Mrs. Dalloway* (New York: Mariner Books, 1990), 31.

12. Virginia Woolf, *A Room of One's Own*, ed. Mark Hussey (New York: Mariner Books, 2005), 18. Similarly, when a writer such as Hemingway takes refuge in simple pleasures—"We ate well and cheaply and drank well and cheaply and slept well and warm together and loved each other"—his characters cling to these physical and emotional needs in the face of cultural crisis, particularly after the war. *A Moveable Feast: The Restored Edition*, ed. Seán Hemingway (New York: Simon and Schuster, 2009), 43.

13. For an unreservedly hedonic meal, by contrast, see Audre Lorde's description of the buffet in *Zami*, with its sculpturally vulval roast beef. *Zami: A New Spelling of My Name* (Freedom, CA: The Crossing Press, 1982), 242.

14. James Joyce, *Ulysses*, ed. Hans Walter Gabler (New York: Vintage, 1986), 4:3–5. All subsequent references are to this edition.

15. Richard Poirier, "The Difficulties of Modernism and the Modernism of Difficulty," in *Critical Essays on American Modernism*, ed. Michael J. Hoffman and Patrick D. Murphy (New York: Hall, 1992), 105.

16. Terry Eagleton, *Literary Theory: An Introduction* (Minneapolis: University of Minnesota Press, 1996), 25. See also Gerald Graff's *Professing Literature: An Institutional History* (Chicago: University of Chicago Press, 1989).

17. Jeremy Bentham, *An Introduction to the Principles of Morals and Legislation*, in *Utilitarianism and Other Essays*, ed. Alan Ryder (New York and London: Penguin, 1987), 65.

18. For overviews of the psychology and neurobiology of pleasure, see Paul Bloom's *How Pleasure Works: The New Science of Why We Like What We Like* (New Haven: Yale University Press, 2010) and Morten Kringlebach's *The Pleasure Center: Trust Your Animal Instincts* (New York: Oxford University Press, 2008).

19. Frank Kermode, *Pleasure and Change: The Aesthetics of Canon*, ed. Robert Alter (New York and Oxford: Oxford University Press, 2004), 58.

20. James Olds and Peter Milner, "Positive Reinforcement Produced by Electrical Stimulation of the Septal Area and Other Regions of Rat Brain," *Journal of Comparative and Physiological Psychology* 47 (1954): 419–427.

21. Diogenes Laertius, *Lives and Opinions of Eminent Philosophers*, tr. R. D. Hicks (Cambridge: Loeb Classical Library, 1925).

22. Plato, *Philebus*, tr. Robin H. Waterfield (New York and London: Penguin Classics, 1983), 5.

23. Aristotle was more willing to acknowledge physical pleasure than Plato was, but he introduces a more complex classification scheme that includes features such as "softness" and "incontinence." For example, in *The Nicomachean Ethics*: "The lover of amusement . . . is thought to be self-indulgent, but is really soft. For amusement is a relaxation, since it is a rest from work; and the lover of amusement is one of the people who go to excess in this": self-indulgence is worse than incontinence. Aristotle, *The Nicomachean Ethics*, tr. David Ross and Lesley Brown (New York and Oxford: Oxford University Press, 2009), 131.

24. Thomas Carlyle, *Latter-Day Pamphlets* (London: Chapman and Hall, 1870), 379–381.

25. Jeremy Bentham, *The Rationale of Reward*, in *The Classical Utilitarians: Bentham and Mill*, ed. John Troyer (Indianapolis: Hackett, 2003), 94.

26. John Stuart Mill, *Utilitarianism and Other Essays*, ed. Alan Ryder (New York and London: Penguin, 1987), 281.

27. Immanuel Kant, *Critique of Judgment*, tr. James Creed Meredith (Oxford: Clarendon Press, 1991).

28. Adorno, *Aesthetic Theory*, 14.

29. Pierre Bourdieu, *Distinction: A Social Critique of the Judgement of Taste*, tr. Richard Nice (Cambridge, MA: Harvard University Press, 1987), 491.

30. G. E. Moore, *Principia Ethica* (New York: Barnes and Noble, 2005), 89. In chapter III, Moore mulls over the different theories of Hedonism offered by Aristippus, Epicurus, Bentham, Mill, Herbert Spencer, and Henry Sidgwick. Moore concludes that "the hedonistic principle, 'Pleasure alone is good as an end,'" is not consistent with views such as Mill's that "one pleasure may be of a better quality than another. We must choose between them: and if we choose the latter, then we must give up the principle of Hedonism" (83). See also Michael Levenson, *A Genealogy of Modernism: A Study of English Doctrine 1908-1922* (Cambridge: Cambridge University Press, 1984), 92.

31. Roger Fry quoted in Ann Banfield, *The Phantom Table: Woolf, Fry, Russell and the Epistemology of Modernism* (Cambridge: Cambridge University Press, 2000), 364.

32. Quoted in Banfield, *The Phantom Table*, 262.

33. "Epilogue," tr. Arthur Symons, *Baudelaire, His Prose and Poetry*, ed. T. R. Smith (New York: Boni and Liveright, 1919), 58.

34. Oscar Wilde, *The Picture of Dorian Gray*, ed. Joseph Bristow (New York and Oxford: Oxford University Press, 2008), 67.

35. Roland Barthes, *The Pleasure of the Text*, tr. Richard Howard (New York: Hill and Wang, 1975), 34.

36. Frederic Jameson, "Pleasure: A Political Issue," in *Formations of Pleasure*, ed. Frederic Jameson, Tony Bennett, et al. (London and Boston: Routledge & Kegan Paul, 1983), 1.

37. Barthes, *The Pleasure of the Text*, 57.

38. Peter Brooks's narratological theory of "textual erotics," for example, is largely focused on readerly desire rather than pleasure. *Reading for the Plot: Design and Intention in Narrative* (New York: Vintage, 1984), 37. Jonathan Culler too describes "the pleasure of narrative" as the function of desire. *Literary Theory* (New York: Sterling, 1997), 92. Tonya Krouse defines pleasure as "the *opposite* of desire" (3) and proposes that modernist novels "use representations of sex and sexuality as focal points of tension in narrative, and as such, the scene of sex operates as a locus for modernist aesthetics" (*The Opposite of Desire: Sex and Pleasure in the Modernist Novel* [Lanham, MD: Lexington Books, 2009], 3). This seems right, although I will argue that modernists construe a wider field of sensual phenomena, including but not limited to sexuality, as the basis of their argument about pleasure.

39. See, for example, *Enjoy Your Symptom! Jacques Lacan in Hollywood and Out* (New York and London: Routledge, 2001).

40. Gilles Deleuze, "Desire and Pleasure," in *Two Regimes of Madness: Texts and Interviews 1975–1995*, tr. David Lapoujade (New York: Semiotext[e], 2006), 130–131.

41. Jacques Lacan, *Feminine Sexuality: Jacques Lacan and the école freudienne*, ed. Juliet Mitchell, tr. Jacqueline Rose (New York: Norton, 1985), 147, 146.

42. Huyssen, *After the Great Divide*, 221.

43. Robert Scholes, *The Paradoxy of Modernism* (New Haven, CT: Yale University Press, 2006), xii.

44. Hansen writes, "I am referring to this kind of modernism as 'vernacular' (and avoiding the ideologically overdetermined term 'popular') because the term vernacular combines the dimension of the quotidian, of everyday usage, with connotations of discourse, idiom, and dialect, with circulation, promiscuity, and translatability." "The Mass Production of the Senses: Classical Cinema as Vernacular Modernism," *Modernism/Modernity* 6, no. 2 (April 1999): 59–77.

45. See, for example, David Chinitz's *T. S. Eliot and the Cultural Divide* (Chicago: University of Chicago Press, 2005); James Naremore and Patrick Brantlinger's *Modernity and Mass Culture* (Bloomington: Indiana University Press, 1991); Maria Di Battista and Lucy McDiarmid's *High and Low Moderns* (Oxford: Oxford University Press, 1996); Michael North's *Around 1922: A Return to the Scene of the Modern* (Oxford: Oxford University Press, 1999); Barry J. Faulk's "Modernism and the Popular: Eliot's Music Halls," *Modernism/Modernity* 8 (2001): 603–621; Jennifer Wicke's *Advertising Fictions: Literature, Advertisement, and Social Reading* (New York: Columbia University Press, 1988) and "Joyce and Consumer Culture," in *Cambridge Companion to James Joyce*, ed. Derek Attridge (Cambridge: Cambridge University Press, 2004); Allison Pease's *Modernism, Mass Culture, and the Aesthetics of Obscenity* (Cambridge: Cambridge University Press, 2000); and Karen Leick's "Popular Modernism," *PLMA* 123, no. 1 (January 2008): 125–139.

46. Q. D. Leavis, *Fiction and the Reading Public* (London: Pimlico, 2000), 3, 134, 221, 225.

47. Max Horkheimer and Theodor W. Adorno, *Dialectic of Enlightenment*, tr. John Cumming (London: Verso, 1997), 137.

48. D. H. Lawrence, *Lady Chatterley's Lover*, ed. Michael Squires (London: Penguin, 1994), 259, 256.

49. Aldous Huxley, *Brave New World* (New York: Perennial/HarperCollins, 2006), 221.

50. *Selected Prose of T. S. Eliot*, ed. Frank Kermode (New York: Harvest Books, 1975), 103.

51. Friedrich Nietzsche, *Thus Spoke Zarathustra* in *The Portable Nietzsche*, tr. Walter Kaufman (New York: Penguin, 1982), 208.

52. C. E. M. Joad, *Diogenes or the Future of Leisure* (London: K. Paul, Trench, Trubne; New York: E. P. Dutton, 1928), 9, 25, 98–99. See also Henry Durant's *The Problem of Leisure* (London: George Routledge & Sons, 1938).

53. Henry Thomas Moore, *Pain and Pleasure* (New York: Moffat, Yard and Company, 1917), 63.

54. Aldous Huxley, *Complete Essays*, vol. 1, ed. Robert S. Baker and James Sexton (Chicago: Ivan R. Dee, 2000), 355–356.

55. "Wanted, a New Pleasure," *Aldous Huxley: Complete Essays*, Vol. 3, 1930–1935, ed. Robert S. Baker and James Sexton (Chicago: Ivan R. Dee, 2001), 264. Enda Duffy takes up this claim as the premise of *The Speed Handbook: Velocity, Pleasure, Modernism* (Durham: Duke University Press, 2009).

56. Q. D. Leavis, *Fiction and the Reading Public*, 165, 19.

57. Horkheimer and Adorno, *Dialectic of Enlightenment*, 140.

58. George Orwell, *The Collected Essays, Journalism, and Letters of George Orwell*, vol. 4, *In Front of Your Nose, 1945–1950* (New York: Harcourt, Brace & World, 2000), 81.

59. George Steiner's taxonomy includes contingent, modal, tactical, and ontological difficulty. *On Difficulty and Other Essays* (New York: Oxford University Press, 1978). See also John Guillory, *Cultural Capital and the Problem of Literary Canon Formation* (Chicago: University of Chicago Press, 1993).

60. See also Cleanth Brooks's comment that "The modern poet has, for better or worse, thrown the weight of the responsibility upon the reader. The reader must be on the alert for shifts of tone, for ironic statement, for suggestion rather than direct statement. He must be prepared to accept a mode of indirection." *The Well Wrought Urn: Studies in the Structure of Poetry* (New York: Harcourt, 1970), 76.

61. T. S. Eliot, "The Metaphysical Poets," *Selected Prose of T. S. Eliot*, 65.

62. Dorothy Richardson, *Journey to Paradise: Short Stories and Autobiographical Sketches of Dorothy Richardson*, ed. Trudi Tate (London: Virago, 1989), 139.

63. Quoted in Richard Ellmann, *James Joyce* (New York and Oxford: Oxford University Press, 1959), 703; James Joyce, *Finnegans Wake* (New York and London: Penguin, 1999), 120.

64. Leonard Diepeveen, *The Difficulties of Modernism* (New York: Routledge, 2002), 150.

65. George Orwell, *Keep the Aspidistra Flying* (New York: Harvest, 1956), 239, 34. Gordon's poem strives, as Orwell wrote in "Inside the Whale" of poems such as *Sweeney Agonistes*, to "achieve the difficult feat of making modern life out to be worse than it is." *Collected Essays*, vol. 1, 493–526: 507.

66. Graham Greene, *Brighton Rock* (New York: Vintage, 2004), 184.

67. George Orwell, "Good Bad Books," in *The Collected Essays, Journalism and Letters of George Orwell*, vol. 4, ed. Sonia Orwell and Ian Angus (London: Penguin, 1968), 37–41.

68. Huyssen notes that, "The autonomy of the modernist art work, after all, is always the result of a resistance, an abstention, and a suppression—resistance to the seductive lure of mass culture, abstention from the pleasure of trying to please a larger audience, suppression of everything that might be threatening to the rigorous demands of being modern and at the edge of time" (*After the Great Divide*, 55).

69. Clement Greenberg, "Avant-Garde and Kitsch, *Partisan Review* 6, no. 5 (1939): 34–49. Robert Boyers extends Trilling's argument to the realm of modern art, and how

it was thought to "affor[d] pleasure by virtue of its affirming difficulty and a permanent state of tension." "Pleasure Revisited," *Raritan* 30, no. 1 (Summer 2010): 118–132.

70. Langer qtd. in Pierre Bourdieu's *Distinction: A Social Critique of the Judgment of Taste*. Tr. Richard Nice (Cambridge, MA: Harvard University Press, 1984), 505.

71. Frank Kermode, introduction to Eliot, *The Waste Land and Other Poems* (New York and London: Penguin, 1998), xi, xiii. Kermode returned to this formulation in his 2001 Berkeley Tanner Lectures. *Pleasure and Change*, 58.

72. C. J. Hubback translates "Unlust" as "pain" (with inverted commas) and "Schmerz" as pain, with no commas. Freud, *Beyond the Pleasure Principle* (London, Vienna: International Psycho-analytical Press, 1922). Strachey translates "Unlust" as "Unpleasure" and "Schmerz" as "pain." *Beyond the Pleasure Principle*, tr. James Strachey, ed. Peter Gay (New York and London: Norton, 1989).

73. Freud, *Beyond the Pleasure Principle*, 4.

74. Leo Bersani, *The Freudian Body: Psychoanalysis and Art* (New York: Columbia University Press, 1986), 38-39.

75. Laura Mulvey, "Visual Pleasure and Narrative Cinema," *Screen* 16, no. 3 (Autumn 1975): 6–18.

76. Sianne Ngai, *Ugly Feelings* (Cambridge, MA: Harvard University Press, 2005), and Lauren Berlant, *The Female Complaint: The Unfinished Business of Sentimentality in American Culture* (Durham, NC: Duke University Press, 2008).

77. *The Collected Stories of Katherine Mansfield* (Hertfordshire, England: Wordsworth Editions, 2006), 69.

78. Wolfgang Iser, *The Act of Reading: A Theory of Aesthetic Response* (Baltimore: Johns Hopkins University Press, 1978).

79. Walter Benjamin, "On Some Motifs in Baudelaire," trans. Harry Zohn, in *Illuminations: Essays and Reflections* (New York: Schocken, 1968), 175.

80. "Surgery for the Novel—or a Bomb" (1923), in *Phoenix: The Posthumous Papers of D. H. Lawrence*, ed. Edward David McDonald (London and New York: Penguin, 1936), 517.

81. French modernism, for example, is generally different from contemporaneous British modernism in its approach to pleasure and is more connected to traditions of decadence. Many modernist American poets seem to be less conflicted about pleasure than British prose writers of the same period, for whom Americanness is itself shorthand for suspect pleasures. Wallace Stevens, for example, looks for a way to reconcile the concrete and sensual ("the greatest poverty / is not to live in a physical world, to feel that one's desire / Is too difficult to tell from despair") with abstraction and difficulty. Art, he specifies, "Must Give Pleasure," even as it is demanding. *The Collected Poems of Wallace Stevens* (New York: Vintage, 1990), 325.

82. See Deborah McDowell on how the history of slavery in America created myths about "black women's libidinousness" that some later writers countered with "caution and reticence about black female sexuality" as an effort to emphasize racial "uplift" and social purity. Introduction to Nella Larsen, *Quicksand and Passing* (New Brunswick, NJ: Rutgers University Press, 1986), xii.

83. Joyce, *Finnegans Wake*, 219.

1. JAMES JOYCE AND THE SCENT OF MODERNITY

1. T. S. Eliot, *T. S. Eliot: The Collected Poems, 1909–1962* (New York: Harcourt Brace Jovanovich, 1991), 5.

2. James Joyce, *A Portrait of the Artist as a Young Man*, ed. Chester G. Anderson (New York: Penguin, 1977), 86.

3. See, for example, Judith Brown's *Glamour in Six Dimensions: Modernism and the Radiance of Form* (Ithaca, NY: Cornell University Press, 2009) and Mary E. Davis, *Classic Chic: Music, Fashion, and Modernism* (Berkeley: University of California Press, 2008).

4. Jennifer Wicke, "Joyce and Consumer Culture," in *The Cambridge Companion to James Joyce*, ed. Derek Attridge (Cambridge: Cambridge University Press, 1990), 234–253.

5. Jacques Derrida observes that Leopold Bloom thinks so much about perfume in *Ulysses* that he (Derrida) might have written "a treatise on perfumes—that is, on the pharmakon—and I could have called it *On the Perfumative in Ulysses*." "*Ulysses* Gramophone: Here Say Yes in Joyce" in *Acts of Literature*, ed. Derek Attridge (New York: Routledge, 1991), 253–309. Bernard Benstock offers a catalog of odors in Joyce's texts in "Olfactory Factor," in *Joycean Occasions: Essays from the Milwaukee James Joyce Conference*, ed. Janet Egleson Dunleavy, Melvin J. Friedman, and Michael Patrick Gilles (Cranbury, NJ: Associated University Presses, 1991), 152.

6. *Roland Barthes by Roland Barthes*, tr. Richard Howard (Berkeley: University of California Press, 1994), 135.

7. James Joyce, *Selected Letters of James Joyce,* ed. Richard Ellmann (New York: Viking, 1975), 359.

8. Jennifer Wicke, "Joyce and Consumer Culture," in *Cambridge Companion to James Joyce*, ed. Derek Attridge (Cambridge: Cambridge University Press, 2004), 247.

9. Plato's *Timaeus* is a major source for this classification scheme. See Carolyn Korsmeyer on how "the conventional ranking of two of the five senses as superior . . . accords with the elevation of mind over body; of reason over sense; of man over beast and culture over nature. It also lines up with another ranked pair of concepts . . . the elevation of male over female and with 'masculine' traits over those designated 'feminine.'" *Making Sense of Taste: Food and Philosophy* (Ithaca, NY: Cornell University Press, 1999), 30. It should be noted, however, that Plato places smell in the middle of the sense hierarchy in *Republic* and the *Philebus*.

10. Korsmeyer, *Making Sense of Taste*, 24. For Havelock Ellis, smell "remains close to touch in the vagueness of its messages," and "the difficulty of classifying" and "controlling" such olfactory messages makes it impossible "as to found upon them any art." *Studies in the Psychology of Sex,* vol. 1, part 3 (New York: Random House, 1942), 52.

11. Condillac quoted in Constance Classen, David Howes, and Anthony Synnot, eds., *Aroma: The Cultural History of Smell* (New York and London: Routledge, 1994), 89.

12. Immanuel Kant, *Anthropology from a Pragmatic Point of View*, tr. Robert B. Louden (Cambridge: Cambridge University Press, 2006), 50–51.

13. Charles Darwin, *The Descent of Man and Selection in Relation to Sex*, ed. James Moore and Adrian Desmond (New York and London: Penguin Classics, 2004).

14. See chapter IV in Freud's *Civilization and Its Discontents*, tr. James Strachey (New York: Norton, 2005).

15. Sigmund Freud, *Three Essays on the Theory of Sexuality*, tr. James Strachey (New York: Basic Books, 1996), 51.

16. This association continued into the twentieth century, including Patrick Süskind's murderer-genius in *Perfume: The Story of a Murderer* (tr. John E. Woods [New York: Random House, 1985]) and Nabokov's Humbert Humbert, who notes that he once worked in the perfume business and has "such wonderful taste in textures and perfumes" (*The Annotated Lolita*, ed. Alfred Appel, Jr. [New York: Vintage, 1970], 50).

17. Havelock Ellis, *Studies in the Psychology of Sex*, vol. 1, part 3, 82. Ivan Bloch also argues that "Like taste, to which it is closely allied, smell is an affective sense, which means that, necessarily, it is imbued with an obscurity of ideas. For logical thought to rely exclusively upon the presentation of smell or taste would be impossible." *Odoratus Sexualis: A Scientific and Literary Study of Sexual Scents and Erotic Perfumes* (New York: American Anthropological Society, 1933), 12.

18. Ellis, *Studies in the Psychology of Sex*, vol. 1, part 3, 55.

19. Piet Vroon, *Smell: The Secret Seducer*, tr. Paul Vincent (New York: Farrar, Straus, & Giroux, 1997), 13.

20. Aristippus is said to have steeped himself in perfumes; in Xenophon's *Symposium* (chapter 2) Socrates casts doubt on the nobility of perfuming oneself. *Xenophon: Memorabilia. Oeconomicus. Symposium. Apologia*, tr. O. J. Todd (Cambridge: Loeb Classical Library, 1923).

21. See Classen, Howes, and Synnot, *Aroma*, chapter 2, "Following the Scent: From Middle Ages to Modernity."

22. Richard Stamelman. *Perfume: A Cultural History of Fragrance from 1750 to the Present* (New York: Rizzoli, 2006), 97.

23. Luca Turin quoted in Chandler Burr, *The Emperor of Scent: A True Story of Perfume and Obsession* (New York: Random House, 2004), 206. See also Mary E. Davis on how Chanel No. 5's "mix of over eighty synthetic aldehydes" produced "a smell so fresh and unusual that some contemporary critics resorted to describing it in terms customarily associated with avant-garde visual art, calling it 'abstract'" (*Classic Chic*, 164).

24. Lilian Pizzichini, *The Blue Hour: A Life of Jean Rhys* (New York: Norton, 2009), 1. http://www.guerlain.com/int/en/base.html#/en/home-parfum/catalogue-parfums/women-fragrances/parfums-femme-lheurebleue/.

25. The class implications of the invention of synthetics are complicated. On the one hand, artificial substitutes brought the price of perfume down so that it was accessible to more people. According to Mandy Aftel, synthetics were "the decisive factor in making perfume an affordable luxury for the masses" (*Essence and Alchemy: A Natural History of Perfume* [Layton, UT: Gibbs Smith, 2004], 6). On the other hand, some of the abstract and complex synthetic effects were of limited appeal. "Until World War I," Richard Stamelman asserts, "only a sophisticated elite was ready to accept synthetic scents. Only later, when perfumes began to vaunt the 'art' of their chemistry and flaunt their originality as creations 'beyond nature,' did they successfully project

a seductive allure" (97). Synthetics, like other forms of artistic modernism, were an acquired taste.

26. See Chandler Burr's "Meow Mix," *New York Times*, October 21, 2007.

27. Classen, Howes, and Synnot, *Aroma*, 82–87.

28. Alain Corbin, *The Foul and the Fragrant: Odor and the French Social Imagination*, tr. Miriam Kochan (Cambridge, MA: Harvard University Press, 1988), 185.

29. Luca Turin, *The Secret of Scent: Adventures in Perfume and the Science of Smell* (New York: Ecco, 2006), 22.

30. Mary Douglas, *Purity and Danger: An Analysis of Concepts of Pollution and Taboo* (London: Routledge, 2003).

31. See Julia Kristeva, "Baudelaire, or Infinity, Perfume, and Punk," in *Tales of Love*, tr. Leon S. Roudiez (New York: Columbia University Press, 1989).

32. *Against the Grain/À Rebours*, tr. John Howard (New York: Albert and Charles Boni, 1930), 170, 163.

33. Des Esseintes aims for perfumes that are not mimetic: "The artist who dared to borrow nature's elements would only produce a bastard work which would have neither authenticity nor style, insasmuch as the essence obtained by the distillation of flowers would bear but a distant and vulgar relation to the odor of the living flower, wafting its fragrance into the air" (*À Rebours*, 169).

34. Augustin Galopin, *Le parfum de la femme et le sens olfactif dans l'amour* (Paris: E. Dentu, 1886).

35. One of Bayley's more exotic scents was "The 'Ess. Imperial,'" described as "a novelty, being distilled from flowers culled from each of our colonies." *Pharmaceutical Society of Great Britain's Pharmaceutical Journal*, December 6, 1902, 625.

36. Aldous Huxley, *Brave New World* (New York: Perennial/HarperCollins, 2006), 166–167.

37. D. H. Lawrence, "Surgery for the Novel—or a Bomb" (1923), in *Phoenix: The Posthumous Papers of D. H. Lawrence*, ed. Edward David McDonald (London and New York: Penguin, 1936), 517.

38. T. S. Eliot, *The Waste Land* in *T. S. Eliot: The Collected Poems, 1909–1962* (New York: Harcourt Brace Jovanovich, 1991), 56.

39. Eliot, *The Collected Poems*, 17–18.

40. Eliot, *The Collected Poems*, 46.

41. Colleen Lamos, *Deviant Modernism: Sexual and Textual Errancy in T. S. Eliot, James Joyce, and Marcel Proust* (Cambridge: Cambridge University Press, 1999), 92–93.

42. Eliot, *The Waste Land: A Facsimile and Transcript of the Original Drafts,* ed. Valerie Eliot (New York: Harvest Books, 1971), 23, 27.

43. *The Diary of Virginia Woolf vol. 1, 1915–1919*, ed. Anne Olivier Bell and Quentin Bell (New York: Harvest Books, 1977), 58.

44. In Orwell's *1984*, Winston is writing in his diary and trying to recall a scene with a prostitute from three years earlier, which in turn leads to the memory of his wife. "He seemed to breathe again the warm stuffy odor of the basement kitchen, an odor compounded of bugs and dirty clothes and villainous cheap scent, but nevertheless alluring, because no woman of the Party ever used scent, or could be imagined

as doing so. Only the proles used scent. In his mind the smell of it was inextricably mixed up with fornication." *1984* (New York: Signet Classics, 1961), 64-65. The smell is "synthetic violets"—a formula invented in 1893, as part of the synthetic revolution (Stamelman, 96–97).

45. *The Letters of Virginia Woolf, vol. 4, 1929–1931,* ed. Nigel Nicolson and Joanne Trautmann (New York: Mariner, 1981), 366.

46. On Alpers's response, see Lorna Sage, *Moments of Truth: Twelve Twentieth-Century Writers* (London: Fourth Estate, 2001), 54.

47. *The Collected Stories of Katherine Mansfield* (Hertfordshire, England: Wordsworth Editions, 2006), 153, 476, 262.

48. *Portrait of the Artist as a Young Man,* 7.

49. Dante Alighieri, *Inferno,* tr. Allen Mandelbaum (New York: Bantam, 1982), 95.

50. James Joyce, *Ulysses,* ed. Hans Walter Gabler (New York:, 1986), 4:3–5. All subsequent references to this edition.

51. *New York Times,* May 22, 1922. http://www.nytimes.com/books/00/01/09/specials/joyce-ulysses.html.

52. Smell, Havelock Ellis argues, "is a primitive sense which had its flowering time before men arose; it is a comparatively unaesthetic sense; it is a somewhat obtuse sense." *Studies in the Psychology of Sex,* 84.

53. Richard Brown writes that "there are a number of coincidences of information and terminology which suggest [that Joyce had a] deeper knowledge of *Studies in the Psychology of Sex,*" which includes a lengthy discussion of olfaction and sexuality. *James Joyce and Sexuality* (Cambridge: Cambridge University Press, 1985), 83. See also Hugh Davis, "'How Do You Sniff?': Havelock Ellis and Olfactory Representation in 'Nausicaa,'" *James Joyce Quarterly* 41, no. 3 (Spring 2004): 421–440.

54. Margot Norris reads "the language of perfume" and flowers in Joyce's work, following the "redolent trail" of heliotrope as a means of avoiding overly schematic approaches to the work that come "at the price of missing the pleasure of the text." "Joyce's Heliotrope," in *Coping with Joyce: Essays from the Copenhagen Symposium,* ed. Morris Beja and Shari Benstock (Columbus: Ohio State University Press, 1989), 5.

55. John Bishop, "A Metaphysics of Coitus in 'Nausicaa,'" in *James Joyce's Ulysses: (En)gendered Perspectives,* ed. Kimberly J. Devlin and Marilyn Reizbaum (Columbia: University of South Carolina Press, 1999), 198–99.

56. The second half of the chapter supports Mary Douglas's provocative argument that "The importance of incense is not that it symbolizes the ascending smoke of sacrifice, but it is a means of making tolerable the smells of unwashed humanity" (*Purity and Danger,* 30).

57. Don Gifford and Robert J. Seidman, *Ulysses Annotated: Notes for James Joyce's Ulysses,* 2nd ed. (Berkeley: University of California Press, 1989), 396.

58. By contrast, one might consider George Orwell's notorious statement in *The Road to Wigan Pier* that he was taught, in his "lower-upper-middle class" childhood, that "the lower classes smell." His primary example of this is how "Race-hatred, religious hatred, differences of education, of temperament, of intellect, even differences of moral code, can be got over; but physical repulsion cannot. You can have an

affection for a murderer or a sodomite, but you cannot have an affection for a man whose breath stinks—habitually stinks, I mean. However well you may wish him, however much you may admire his mind and character, if his breath stinks he is horrible and in your heart of hearts you will hate him." *The Road to Wigan Pier* (New York: Harcourt, 1972), 128.

59. Bloom, Molly remarks, "thinks nothing can happen without him knowing he hadnt an idea about my mother till we were engaged otherwise hed never have got me so cheap as he did he was 10 times worse himself" (18:282–284); critics have debated if this means that Lunita Laredo was a prostitute.

60. See Celia Marshik's discussion of Gerty's combination of exhibitionism and declaredly high morality and how "Joyce's text aligns her with the fallen woman she would reject." *British Modernism and Censorship* (Cambridge: Cambridge University Press, 2006), 153.

61. See Carol Mavor's "Odor di Femina: Though You May Not See Her, You Can Certainly Smell Her," in *The Smell Culture Reader*, ed. Jim Drobnick (Oxford and New York: Berg, 2006), 277–288.

62. For example, when Blazes Boylan, fresh from "ploughing" Molly, holds his forefinger to Lenehan and proudly tells him to take a whiff of the "lobster and mayonnaise" (15:3753), this is a torturous turn-on for Bloom.

63. Gifford and Seidman note that costly musk was replaced by an artificial version in 1888. *Ulysses Annotated*, 398.

64. Arthur Power, *Conversations with James Joyce* (Dublin: Lilliput Press, 2000), 85-86.

65. Yaara Yeshurun, Hadas Lapid, Yadin Dudai, and Noam Sobel, "The Privileged Brain Representation of First Olfactory Associations," *Current Biology* 19.21, no. 9 (November 2009): 1869–1874.

66. Djuna Barnes, *Collected Poems: With Notes Toward the Memoirs*, ed. Phillip Herring and Osias Stutman (Madison: University of Wisconsin Press, 2005), 251.

67. See *Gardeners' Chronicle: A Weekly Illustrated Journal* (London, vol. xli [January 19, 1907], 45) and Dottie Booth, *Nature Calls: The History, Lore, and Charm of Outhouses* (Berkeley: The Speed Press 1998).

68. Hugh Kenner, *The Pound Era* (Berkeley: University of California Press, 1971), 42.

69. Quoted in Havelock Ellis, *Affirmations* (Boston and New York: Houghton Mifflin, 1915), 190.

70. Judith Harrington, "What Perfume Does Your Wife?" *James Joyce Literary Supplement* 16, no. 1 (Spring 2002): 1–7.

71. George William Septimus Piesse, *The Art of Perfumery and the Methods of Obtaining the Odours of Plants* (London: Longmans, Green, 1879), 169.

72. *To-Day: A Weekly Magazine-Journal*, ed. Jerome K. Jerome (London: 1893), vols 16–17, 197. See also Pauline Stevenson, who quotes a correspondence in *The Queen* from 1900 in which an inquiry about how to perfume handbags is answered that one could "obtain the necessary powder, either violet, Peau d'Espagne or any other scent she may choose from Atkinson, New Bond Street." *Edwardian Fashion* (London: Ian Allen, 1980), 18.

73. Like Bloom, Molly spends a great deal of time pondering odors, including "the smell of those painted women" (18:57), dogs, incense, rainwater in tanks, old dishcloths, and "the smell of the sea," which, she says, "excited me of course the sardines and the bream in Catalan bay" (18:973). Of Bloom, she thinks, "I wish hed even smoke a pipe like father to get the smell of a man" (18:508–509). She smells her own flatulence and recalls her fetishistic attachment to a handkerchief soiled with Mulvey's semen (18:862–864).

74. Bishop argues that "Whether they repulsively deromanticize or merely familiarize, the range of minuscule and humanizing smells that Bloom recalls here has the effect of eroding with particularity the conventional portraits of lovemaking drawn in the first part of 'Nausicaa'" ("Nausicaa," 200).

75. Woolsey quoted in Elisabeth Ladenson, *Dirt for Art's Sake: Books on Trial from Madame Bovary to Lolita* (Ithaca, NY: Cornell University Press, 2007), 97–98.

76. Richard von Krafft-Ebing, *Psychopathia Sexualis*, tr. F. J. Rebman (Chicago: W. T. Keener, 1901), 178. For a broader discussion of masochistic impulses in *Ulysses*, see my discussion in "With This Ring I Thee Own: Masochism and Social Reform in *Ulysses*," *Genders* 25: *Sex Positives?: The Cultural Politics of Dissident Sexualities* (New York: New York University Press, 1997), 225–264.

77. Wells cited in Joseph Brooker, *Joyce's Critics: Transitions in Reading and Culture* (Madison: University of Wisconsin Press, 1994), 17.

78. For Jennifer Wicke, *Sweets* is "an incredibly rich text as consumed by Bloom, who takes it up into his own psychosexual, class, and national orbit and gets extraordinary mileage from rearrangements of its fantasy components." "Joyce and Consumer Culture," *Cambridge Companion to James Joyce*, 251. Don Gifford and Robert J. Seidman suggest that Bloom's reading of *Sweets* is an example of "*sortes Biblicae* (or *Virgilianae* or *Homericae*), divination by the Bible (or Virgil or Homer), in which a passage is selected at random and treated as revelatory or prophetic." *Ulysses Annotated*, 272. William Stephenson argues that *Sweets* exemplifies "Barthesisan bliss." "Eroticism and Lightness in 'Wandering Rocks,'" *Joyce's "Wandering Rocks,"* ed. Andrew Gibson and Steven Morrison, European Joyce Studies, 12 (Amsterdam and New York: Rodopi, 2002), 121–140.

79. Thomas Scott Matthew Henry and William Jenks, *The Comprehensive Commentary on the Holy Bible* (Brattleboro, VT: Brattleboro Typographic Company, 1837), 128.

80. Alison Shell, *Catholicism, Controversy, and the English Literary Imagination, 1558–1660* (Cambridge: Cambridge University Press, 1999), 44, 46.

81. The liturgical connection is underscored when *Sweets of Sin* resurfaces in "Circe" as part of the Daughters of Erin's parody of the Litany of the Sacred Heart: "Kidney of Bloom, pray for us. Flower of the Bath, pray for us. . . . Wandering Soap, pray for us. Sweets of Sin, pray for us" (15.1941–52).

82. James Joyce, *Giacomo Joyce*, ed. Richard Ellmann (London: Faber and Faber, 1984), 12.

83. Allison Pease, *Modernism, Mass Culture, and the Aesthetics of Obscenity* (Cambridge: Cambridge University Press, 2000), 89–90.

84. *James Joyce Letters*, vol. 2 (New York: Viking, 1966), 366.

2. STEIN'S TICKLE

1. Gertrude Stein, *Tender Buttons*, in *Selected Writings of Gertrude Stein*, ed. Carl Van Vechten (New York: Vintage, 1990), 480.

2. Gertrude Stein, *Geography and Plays* (Boston: The Four Seas Company, 1922), 181.

3. William James, *The Principles of Psychology*, vol. 1. (New York: Henry Holt, 1890), v.

4. Gertrude Stein, "The Making of the Making of Americans," in Gertrude Stein, *Selected Writings*, 250.

5. William James, *The Varieties of Religious Experience* (New York: Longmans, Green, 1903), 136.

6. See also James's generally critical review of Henry R. Marshall's *Pain, Pleasure, and Aesthetics* (1894) that nevertheless credits the author with identifying "the essentially mutable and shifting character of our enjoyments and displeasures," *Essays, Comments, and Reviews*, vol. 15 (Cambridge, MA: Harvard University Press, 1987), 341, 492.

7. Ulla E. Dydo and William Rice, *Gertrude Stein: The Language That Rises: 1923–1934* (Evanston, IL: Northwestern University Press, 2003), 63.

8. Richard Bridgman, *Gertrude Stein in Pieces* (New York: Oxford University Press, 1970), xiii.

9. David Lodge, *Modes of Modern Writing: Metaphor, Metonymy, and the Typology of Literature* (London: Edward Arnold, 1977), 154.

10. George Steiner, *On Difficulty and Other Essays* (New York: Oxford University Press, 1978).

11. See Karen Leick's detailed examination of Stein's reception in *Gertrude Stein and the Making of an American Celebrity* (New York: Routledge, 2009).

12. Charles Bernstein, for example, argues that his "primary and continuing response to Stein's poetry is one of intense pleasure in the music of the language: of hearing a palpable, intense, I'm tempted to say absolute, sense-making: you can almost taste it; a great plenitude of meaning of possibility for language, in language. Reading a Stein poem I feel an enormous satisfaction in the words coming to mean in their moment of enfolding outward and a correlative falling away of my need to explain, to figure out." "Professing Stein/Stein Professing," in *A Poetics* (Cambridge, MA: Harvard University Press, 1992), 142–143.

13. Ann Douglas, *Terrible Honesty: Mongrel Manhattan in the 1920s* (New York: Farrar, Straus & Giroux, 1995), 127, 135.

14. Leisl Olson, "'An invincible force meets an immovable object': Gertrude Stein Comes to Chicago," *Modernism/modernity* 17, no. 2 (April 2010): 331–361.

15. Wayne Koestenbaum, "Stein Is Nice," in *Cleavage: Essays on Sex, Stars, and Aesthetics* (New York: Ballantine, 2000), 309–333, 71.

16. On the range of accounts of Stein's reception, see Leick as well as Dana Cairns Watson in *Gertrude Stein and the Essence of What Happens* (Nashville: Vanderbilt University Press, 2005), 89–118.

17. Edmund Wilson, *Axel's Castle: A Study of the Imaginative Literature of 1870–1930* (New York: Scribner's, 1931), 252.

18. Cyril Connolly, *Enemies of Promise* (Chicago: University of Chicago Press, 2008), 59.

19. Marianne DeKoven connects Stein's writing to antipatriarchal French feminism and presymbolic logic in *A Different Language: Gertrude Stein's Experimental Writing* (Madison: University of Wisconsin Press, 1983) and *Rich and Strange: Gender, History, Modernism* (Princeton, NJ: Princeton University Press, 1991). Lisa Cole Ruddick asks "Why . . . when Stein comes forward as an embodied, sensual 'teller,' is her pleasure much (like) that of the bowel?" and speculates that Stein "is playfully discovering something about the link between (all?) literary repetition and the primitive pleasure people take in filling up with an excreting matter." *Reading Gertrude Stein: Body, Text, Gnosis* (Ithaca, NY: Cornell University Press, 1991), 81. Ellen E. Berry addresses the different kinds of pleasure and readerly response elicited by Stein in *Curved Thought and Textual Wandering: Gertrude Stein's Postmodernism* (Ann Arbor: University of Michigan Press, 1992).

20. See, for example, Robert R. Provine, "Laughing, Tickling, and the Evolution of Speech and Self," *Current Directions in Psychological Science* 13, no. 6 (December 2004): 215–218.

21. Wyndham Lewis, "'Time' Children. Miss Gertrude Stein and Miss Anita Loos" and "The Prose-Song of Gertrude Stein" in *Time and Western Man* (Berkeley, CA: Gingko Press, 1993); Wayne Koestenbaum, *Cleavage*, 312.

22. Pamela Hadas says of *Tender Buttons,* "No certain criticism being possible in such a case, all we can do is try to translate into more common language, at least for the moment, a piece here and there (it is so all here and there)." "Spreading the Difference: One Way to Read Gertrude Stein's *Tender Buttons,*" *Twentieth Century Literature* 24 (1978): 72. Marjorie Perloff asserts that "The meaning" of any given sequence in the piece, "like that of the title *Tender Buttons*, remains latent, impossible to translate into something else." *The Poetics of Indeterminacy: Rimbaud to Cage* (Evanston, IL: Northwestern University Press, 1999), 107.

23. "Lifting Belly" (from *Bee Time Vine*), in *The Yale Gertrude Stein,* ed. Richard Kostelanetz (New Haven, CT: Yale University Press, 1980): 41. All references to "Lifting Belly" are taken from this edition.

24. Susan Holbrook points out the "oddly contradictory critical responses" to "Lifting Belly," which are divided between claims that the work is among Stein's most explicit and erotic and claims that the work is "veiled and coded." "Lifting Bellies, Filling Petunias, and Making Meanings Through the Trans-Poetic," *American Literature* 71, no. 4 (December 1999): 751–771, 751.

25. *The Virginia Woolf Reader*, ed. Mitchell A. Leaska (New York: Mariner Books, 1984), 210.

26. Sianne Ngai, *Ugly Feelings* (Cambridge, MA: Harvard University Press, 2005), 248–297.

27. One passage of *How to Write* encapsulates all these possibilities: "Yes please. Why yes please. Why please. Why to please. Yes please, why yes please, why please, why to please. An authority in sentences. / Why please why not please why yes please

why to please why as to a place to piece why it pleases." *How to Write*, ed. Patricia Meyerowitz(Mineola, NY: Dover, 1975), 124.

28. Gertrude Stein, *Writings 1932–1946* (New York: Library of America, 1998), 316–317.

29. By contrast, Dana Cairns Watson reads Stein's "questions without answers" as demonstrations that she is "willing to be open-ended, inconclusive, and less authoritative." She reminds us of Stein's supposed last words, "What is the answer . . . in that case what is the question?" (*Gertrude Stein and the Essence of What Happens*, 116).

30. See Bridgman, *Gertrude Stein in Pieces,* and Koestenbaum, *Cleavage,* for example.

31. Janet Flanner remarks that Stein "wrote for no one but herself"; Mike Gold proposes that "In Gertrude Stein, art became a personal pleasure, a private hobby, a vice." Quoted in Barbara Will, *Gertrude Stein, Modernism, and the Problem of "Genius"* (Edinburgh: Edinburgh University Press, 2000), 81, 80.

32. Harriet Scott Chessman, *The Public Is Invited to Dance: Representation, the Body, and Dialogue in Gertrude Stein* (Stanford, CA: Stanford University Press, 1989), 3, 13.

33. For Susan Holbrook, "Bridgman's assumption of a clear dialogic structure" is "a little facile; it is impossible to know who the two speakers are, or even if there are indeed two different speakers here" ("Lifting Bellies, Filling Petunias," 765). Barbara Will asserts that "For Stein, language is . . . a site of discursive exchange," but notes the "pronominal slippage" in Stein's texts, and the ways in which "the text parodies and reverses its own hierarchical strategies" (*Gertrude Stein, Modernism*, 148).

34. Quoted in Olson, "'An invincible force meets an immovable object,'" 343.

35. Stein, "Poetry and Grammar" in *Writings: 1932–1946*, 327.

36. DeKoven, *Rich and Strange,* 198.

37. Ruddick, *Reading Gertrude Stein,* 145.

38. Stein, *A Long Gay Book* in *A Stein Reader*, ed. Ulla E. Dydo (Evanston, IL: Northwestern University Press, 1993), 246.

39. Stein, *Saints and Singing*, in *A Stein Reader*, 388.

40. Gertrude Stein, *The Making of Americans: Being a History of a Family's Progress* (Normal, IL: Dalkey Archive Press, 1995), 514.

41. Charles Darwin, *The Expression of the Emotions in Man and Animals* (New York: Appleton and Company, 1873), 201.

42. For Freud, tickling illustrates the extent to which psychology is "still so much in the dark in questions of pleasure and unpleasure." *Three Essays on the Theory of Sexuality*, tr. James Strachey (New York: Basic Books, 1996), 49.

43. Havelock Ellis, *Studies in the Psychology of Sex*, vol. 1, part 3 (New York: Random House, 1942), 11.

44. *Plato's Examination of Pleasure: A Translation of the Philebus*, ed. R. Hackworth (New York: Cambridge, 2001), 91.

45. *"The Movies Are": Carl Sandburg's Film Reviews and Essays, 1920–1928*, ed. Arnie Bernstein (Chicago: Claremont Press, 2000), 40.

46. See Christine Harris's summary of various hypotheses about the purpose of tickling in "The Mystery of Ticklish Laughter," *American Scientist* 87, no. 4 (1999): 344 ff.

47. Havelock Ellis, *Studies in the Psychology of Sex,* vol, 1, part 3 (New York: Random House, 1942), 14.

48. John Chamberlain quoted in Watson, *Gertrude Stein and the Essence of What Happens,* 102.

49. Quoted by Leick, *Gertrude Stein and the Making of an American Celebrity,* 44.

50. Adam Phillips, *On Kissing, Tickling, and Being Bored: Psychoanalytic Essays on the Unexamined Life* (Cambridge, MA: Harvard University Press, 1993), 10-11.

51. Darwin, *The Expression of the Emotions in Man and Animals,* 202.

52. *The Yale Gertrude Stein,* ed. Richard Kostelanetz (New Haven: Yale University Press, 1980), 65.

53. Wyndham Lewis, *Tarr: The 1918 Version* (Santa Rosa, CA: Black Sparrow Press, 1990), 15.

54. Stein cites Hall's article, "A Study of Fears," in her "Cultivated Motor Automatism."

55. G. S. Hall and A. Allin, "The Psychology of Tickling, Laughing and the Comic," *The American Journal of Psychology* 9, no. 1 (October 1897): 1–41.

56. Christine R. Harris and Nicholas Christenfeld, "Can a Machine Tickle?" *Psychonomic Bulletin & Review* 6, no. 3 (1999): 504–510.

57. Gertrude Stein, "Cultivated Motor Automatism; A Study of Character in Its Relation to Attention," *Psychological Review* 5, no. 3 (May 1898): 295–306; Leon M. Solomons and Gertrude Stein, "Normal Motor Automatism," *Psychological Review* 3, no. 5 (September 1896): 492–512.

58. B. F. Skinner, "Has Gertrude Stein a Secret?" *The Atlantic Monthly* (January 1934): 50–57.

59. Barbara Will, *Gertrude Stein,* 27. See Tim Armstrong's detailed discussion of Skinner's view that Stein's is "a writing predicated on the body rather than mind; and in particular . . . a de-somaticized body washed clean of 'depth' and acting as a language-machine." *Modernism, Technology, and the Body: A Cultural Study* (Cambridge: Cambridge University Press, 1998), 206.

60. Armstrong, *Modernism, Technology, and the Body,* 187–219.

61. "Portraits and Repetition," in Stein, *Writings 1932–1946,* 292.

62. Perloff, *The Poetics of Indeterminacy,* 76.

63. Dana Cairns Watson, *Gertrude Stein and the Essence of What Happens,* 60.

64. Repetition was one of the many issues over which Stein parted ways with William James. Ruddick points out that "Nothing in James's scheme would correspond to the sexualized inner pulsations Stein calls loving repeating. . . . James's theory of the mind has no erotic axis" (*Reading Gertrude Stein,* 96).

65. Catharine R. Stimpson, "The Somagrams of Gertrude Stein," *Poetics Today* 6, no. 1/2 (1985): 74.

66. Rebecca Scherr, "Tactile Erotics: Gertrude Stein and the Aesthetics of Touch," *LIT: Literature, Interpretation, Theory* 18, no. 3 (July 2007): 193–212.

67. *Matisse Picasso and Gertrude Stein with Two Shorter Stories* (Charleston: Biblio-Bazaar, 2007), 274.

68. Carol Kaesuk Yun, "Anatomy of a Tickle is Serious Business at the Research Lab," *New York Times,* June 3, 1997.

69. Charles Dickens, *David Copperfield* (Mineola, NY: Dover Thrift Editions, 2004), 274.

70. Quoted in *Gertrude Stein: The Language That Rises*, 36.

71. Gertrude Stein, *Narration: Four Lectures* (Chicago: University of Chicago Press, 2010), xvii.

72. Robert Bartlett Haas, "Gertrude Stein Talking—A Translantic Interview," quoted in Leick, *Gertrude Stein and the Making of an American Celebrity,* 43.

73. Stein writes "To begin with, I seem always to be doing the talking when I am anywhere but in spite of that I do listen. . . . I always as I admit seem to be talking but talking can be a way of listening" ("The Gradual Making of the Making of Americans," *Selected Writings,* 270); and "it is necessary to be at once talking and listening, doing both things, not as if there were one thing, not as if they were two things, but doing them, well if you like, like the motor going inside and the car moving, they are part of the same thing." *Look at Me Now Here I Am: Writings and Lectures, 1911–1945,* ed. Patricia Meyerowitz (London: Owen Peter Limited, 2005), 170.

74. Stein, *Matisse Picasso and Gertrude Stein with Two Shorter Stories,* 241.

75. Christine R. Harris and Nicholas Christenfeld, "Humour, Tickle, and the Darwin-Hecker Hypothesis," *Cognition and Emotion* 11, no. 1 (1997): 103–110.

76. John Crawford, "Incitement to Riot," *New York Call* (August 19, 1923). Quoted in Leick, *Gertrude Stein and the Making of an American Celebrity*, 81.

3. ORGASMIC DISCIPLINE: D. H. LAWRENCE, E. M. HULL, AND INTERWAR EROTIC FICTION

1. "Surgery for the Novel—or a Bomb" (1923), in *Phoenix: The Posthumous Papers of D. H. Lawrence,* ed. Edward David McDonald (London and New York: Penguin, 1936), 517–520.

2. F. R. Leavis, *The Great Tradition* (Harmondsworth: Peregrine, 1962), 36. Richard Poirier, by contrast, addresses how Lawrence is often not considered a modernist because his prose is "easy" to read. "Modernism and Its Difficulties," in *The Renewal of Literature* (New York: Random House, 1987), 99.

3. Fernald remarks that "Since Lawrence values ideas as much as he values relationships, scenes of coercion and alienation emerge as signs of the struggle to change people's minds; the importance of this struggle is matched by its difficulty." "'Out of It': Alienation and Coercion in D. H. Lawrence," *Modern Fiction Studies* 49, no. 2 (Summer 2003): 183–203.

4. Charles M. Burack, "Mortifying the Reader: The Assault on Verbal and Visual Consciousness in D. H. Lawrence's *Lady Chatterley's Lover,*" *Studies in the Novel* (Winter 1997): 491–511.

5. A. S. Byatt, "The one bright book of life," *The New Statesman,* 16 December, 2002. Byatt reviews Gary Adelman's *Reclaiming D. H. Lawrence: Contemporary Writers Speak Out* (Lewisburg: Bucknell, 2002).

6. Introduction to *Women in Love,* ed. David Farmer, Lindeth Vasey, and John Worthen (London and New York: Penguin, 1995).

7. D. H. Lawrence, "A Propos of *Lady Chatterley's Lover,*" *Lady Chatterley's Lover,* ed. Michael Squires (London: Penguin, 1994), 327.

8. See Hilary Simpson's discussion of Lawrence's "abrupt espousal of male supremacy which coincides with the end of the war" in *D. H. Lawrence and Feminism* (DeKalb: Northern Illinois University Press, 1993), 66, and also Carol Siegel's *Lawrence Among the Women: Wavering Boundaries in Women's Literary Traditions* (Charlottesville: University of Virginia Press, 1991).

9. Irene Speller, "How I Was Loved by a Sheik!," *My Story Weekly*, October 15, 22, 29; November 5, 1927: 3.

10. Ibid, November 5, 1927. Rudyard Kipling, "The Ballad of East and West" (1889), in *The Collected Poems of Rudyard Kipling* (Ware, Hertfordshire: Wordsworth Editions, 2001), 245–248.

11. *The Sheik* (London: Virago, 1996), 112.

12. David Trotter, *The English Novel in History: 1895–1920* (London: Routledge, 1993), 185. Billie Melman estimates that "The first filmed version of *The Sheik* (1921) was seen by 125 million viewers, the majority of them—to judge from the contemporary press reports—women." *Women and the Popular Imagination in the Twenties: Flappers and Nymphs* (London: Palgrave MacMillan, 1988), 90.

13. A 1926 review of desert romance films describes their psychogeography the same way as the novels: "the wide spaces, the moonlit nights, horseriding across glinting sands, for men the all-conquering male seizing in his strong arms the woman he loves, for women the thrill of capture (albeit willing and docile captivity with a little well designed camouflage to keep up appearances." Winifred Horrabin, "*The Sheik* and *The Son of the Sheik*," *Lansbury's Labour Weekly* (London), October 16, 1926, reprinted in *The Red Velvet Seat: Women's Writing on the First Fifty Years of Cinema*, ed. Antonia Lant and Ingrid Periz (London: Verso, 2006), 437–438. Melman argues that "the desert romance is one of the most consciously topographical and ethnological genres in popular fiction" (95) and describes the different styles of its main geographical areas.

14. For contemporary responses to desert romance and *The Sheik*, see Evelyn Bach, "Sheik Fantasies: Orientalism and Feminine Desire in the Desert Romance," *Hecate: An Interdisciplinary Journal of Women's Liberation* 23, no. 1 (1997): 9–40; Karen Chow, "Popular Sexual Knowledges and Women's Agency in 1920s England: Marie Stopes's *Married Love* and E. M. Hull's *The Sheik*," *Feminist Review* 63 (Autumn 1999): 64–87; and Elizabeth Gargano, "'English Sheiks' and Arab Stereotypes: E. M. Hull, T. E. Lawrence, and the Imperial Masquerade," *Texas Studies in Literature and Language* 48, no. 2 (Summer 2006): 171–186. See also Tania Modleski, *Loving with a Vengeance: Mass-Produced Fantasies for Women* (Hamden, CT: Archon Books, 1982), for more general observations about fantasy and the romance genre.

15. Robert Graves and Alan Hodge, *The Long Week End: A Social History of Great Britain, 1918–1939* (New York: Macmillan, 1941), 41.

16. "Sheik," by Alys in 1921, and by Floral Products in 1925.

17. Most critics agree that the desert romance was largely an interwar genre. See, for example, Melman, *Women and the Popular Imagination*, 90; Osman Bencherif, *The Image of Algeria in Anglo-American Writings, 1785–1962* [Lanham, MD: University Press of America, 1997]; and Patricia Raub, "Issues of Passion and Power in *The Sheik*," *Women's Studies* 21 [1992]). However, its forerunners include novels by Ouida, Marie

Corelli, Kathlyn Rhodes, and especially Robert Hichens's 1904 novel, *The Garden of Allah*, which is often associated with *The Sheik* but is more complex, as it includes a strong theological narrative.

18. Although *The Sheik* and its film adaptation were immensely popular in America as well as Britain, according to Raub, "With the exception of *The Sheik* it appears these British-written [desert romances] were much more popular with British women readers than with American readers. None of these romances appeared on the American *Booklist*'s monthly lists of best-selling fiction during this period, much less upon the yearly best-seller lists" ("Issues of Passion and Power in *The Sheik*," 128).

19. See Lee Horsley, *Fictions of Power in English Literature: 1900–1950* (London: Longman, 1995). Billie Melman and Gaylyn Studlar, for example, read Diana as a "New Woman."

20. Trotter, pointing out that a reader may identify with different elements of fantasy at different points in the narrative, argues that Diana "can do nothing; but the narrative can do what it wants with her, and for her. It all depends not so much on the reader's identification with Diana Mayo as on her understanding of genre," noting how the novel switches from a captivity romance to a "conventional romance" (*English Novel*, 186). I will argue that the identification Hull cultivates is a matter not just of genre (and that *The Sheik* draws on another, racier, genre) but of readerly affect.

21. See Reina Lewis, *Gendering Orientalism: Race, Femininity and Representation* (London: Routledge, 1996), and Meyda Yegenoglu, *Colonial Fantasies: Towards a Feminist Reading of Orientalism* (Cambridge: Cambridge University Press, 1998), on gender and orientalism.

22. *Times Literary Supplement*, "*The Sheik*" (review), November 6, 1919, 633.

23. Zelda and F. Scott Fitzgerald, *The Crack-up*, ed. Edmund Wilson (New York: New Directions, 1945).

24. Q. D. Leavis, *Fiction and the Reading Public*, xxxiv.

25. Siegfried Kracauer, "The Little Shopgirls Go to the Movies," in *The Mass Ornament: Weimar Essays*, ed. and tr. Thomas Y. Levin (Cambridge, MA: Harvard University Press, 1995), 291–304: 292.

26. *Selected Prose of T. S. Eliot*, ed. Frank Kermode (New York: Harvest Books, 1975), 38.

27. Umberto Eco, "Innovation and Repetition: Between Modern and Postmodern Aesthetics," *Daedalus* (Fall 2005):192, 200. See also Eco's *The Role of the Reader: Explorations in the Semiotics of Texts* (London: Hutchinson, 1981).

28. Horrabin, "*The Sheik* and *The Son of the Sheik*," *The Red Velvet Seat*, 437–438.

29. See, for example, the review of literature on "novelty, familiarity, and liking" in David J. Hargreaves, *The Developmental Psychology of Music* (Cambridge: Cambridge University Press, 1996), 111ff; and Karl Halvor Teigen, "Intrinsic Interest and the Novelty-Familiarity Interaction," which asserts that "According to the interaction hypothesis of interest, the inherent interestingness of a communication or a situation will be maximal when novel *and* familiar elements are simultaneously present." *Scandinavian Journal of Psychology* 28, no. 3 (September 1987): 199–210.

30. "Surgery for the Novel—or a Bomb," 517-520: 517.

31. A couple of weeks earlier, Lawrence expressed the same sentiments in a letter to Aldous and Maria Huxley, complaining about Joyce's "deliberate, journalistic dirty-mindedness—what old and hard-worked staleness, masquerading as the all-new!" but noting that Gertrude Stein "is more amusing." *The Letters of D. H. Lawrence*, ed. Aldous Huxley (New York: Viking, 1932), 759, 750.

32. *Women in Love*, ed. David Farmer, Lindeth Vasey, and John Worthen (London and New York: Penguin, 1995), Appendix I, 486. David J. Gordon calls these patterns Lawrence's "sexualization of style." "Sex and Language in D. H. Lawrence," *Twentieth-Century Literature* 27, no. 4 (Winter 1981): 362–375. Michael Squires describes the patterns of linguistic repetition and variation in Lawrence's work as a series of "loops." *The Creation of* Lady Chatterley's Lover (Baltimore, MD: Johns Hopkins University Press, 1983), 22. See also John M. Swift, "Repetition, Consummation, and 'This Eternal Unrelief,'" in *The Challenge of D. L. Lawrence*, ed. Michael Squires and Keith Cushman (Madison: University of Wisconsin Press, 1990), 121–128.

33. D. H. Lawrence, "Introduction to These Paintings," in *Phoenix: The Posthumous Papers of D. H. Lawrence*, ed. Edward David McDonald (London and New York: Penguin, 1936), 576.

34. Miriam Hansen writes at length about Valentino's unusual screen presence. She notes that "There are few Valentino films that do not display a whip, in whatever marginal function, and most of them feature seemingly insignificant subplots in which the spectator is offered a position that entails enjoying the tortures inflicted on Valentino or others." *Babel and Babylon* (Cambridge: Cambridge University Press, 1991), 285, and "Pleasure, Ambivalence, Identification: Valentino and Female Spectatorship," *Cinema Journal* 25, no. 4 (Summer 1986): 6–32. See also Gaylyn Studlar's chapter on Valentino in *This Mad Masquerade: Stardom and Masculinity in the Jazz Age* (New York: Columbia University Press, 1996) and "'Out-Salomeing Salome': Dance, the New Woman, and Fan Magazine Orientalisms," in *Visions of the East: Orientalism in Film*, ed. Matthew Bernstein and Gaylyn Studlar (New Brunswick, NJ: Rutgers University Press, 1998), 99–100.

35. Linda Ruth Williams, *Sex in the Head: Visions of Femininity and Film in D. H. Lawrence* (Detroit: Wayne State University Press, 1993), 6.

36. Lawrence, "Sex Versus Loveliness" in *Phoenix II: Uncollected Writings*, ed. Warren Roberts and Harry T. Moore (New York: Viking, 1970), 529. Lawrence also alludes to or explicitly names Valentino in his stories, including "In Love" and "Mother and Daughter." Lawrence, *The Complete Stories*, vol. 3 (New York: Penguin, 1981), 647–660; 805–826.

37. D. H. Lawrence, *Complete Poems, vol. 2*, ed. Vivian de Sola Roberts and Warren Pinto (New York: Penguin, 1993), 538.

38. See Horsley and also David Trotter's reading of *Women in Love* and *The Sheik*, "A Horse Is Being Beaten: Modernism and Popular Fiction," in *Rereading the New: A Backward Glance at Modernism*, ed. Kevin Dettmar (Ann Arbor: University of Michigan Press, 1992), 191–220.

39. *The Letters of D. H. Lawrence*, vol. v: 1924–1927, ed. James T. Boulton and Lindeth Vasey (Cambridge: Cambridge University Press, 1989), 574.

40. Anon., *The Lustful Turk* (Ware, Hertfordshire: Wordsworth Editions, 1995), 16. For a reading of *The Lustful Turk* in the context of orientalist art and fiction, see Ruth Bernard Yeazell, *Harems of the Mind: Passages of Western Art and Literature* (New Haven: Yale University Press, 2000).

41. Steven Marcus, *The Other Victorians* (New York: Basic Books, 1966).

42. See, for example, Simpson, *D. H. Lawrence and Feminism*; Melman, *Women and the Popular Imagination*; Trotter, *English Novel*; and Horsley, *Fictions of Power*.

43. Hull, "Why I Wrote the Sheik,'" *Movie Weekly*, November 19, 1921, 3.

44. D. H. Lawrence, "The Woman Who Rode Away," *The Complete Short Stories* vol. 2 (New York: Penguin, 1981), 547.

45. D. H. Lawrence, *Aaron's Rod,* ed. Mara Kalnis (Cambridge: Cambridge University Press, 1988); *Kangaroo* (New York: Penguin, 1980); *The Plumed Serpent*, ed. L. D. Clark (New York: Cambridge University Press, 1987).

46. Marianna Torgovnick, *Gone Primitive: Savage Intellectuals, Modern Lives* (Chicago: University of Chicago Press, 1990), 164.

47. D. H. Lawrence, "Morality and the Novel," in *Phoenix: The Posthumous Papers of D. H. Lawrence*, ed. Edward David McDonald (London and New York: Penguin, 1936), 528.

48. F. R. Leavis, "The New Orthodoxy," *Spectator*, February 17, 1961, 229.

49. John Worthen, *D. H. Lawrence and the Idea of the Novel* (Totowa, NJ: Rowman and Littlefield, 1979), 179. See also Squires, *The Creation of* Lady Chatterley's Lover.

50. *Women in Love*, 486.

51. Jeffrey Meyers, *Homosexuality and Literature 1890–1930* (London: Athlone Press, 1977).

52. Frank Kermode, Colin Clarke, Mark Spilka, and George H. Ford, "On 'Lawrence Up-Tight': Four Tail-Pieces," *NOVEL: A Forum on Fiction* 5, no. 1 (Autumn 1971): 54–70.

53. Charles Barack, "Revitalizing the Reader: Literary Technique and the Language of Sacred Experience in D. H. Lawrence's *Lady Chatterley's Lover*," *Style* (Spring 1998): 120.

4. HUXLEY'S FEELIES: ENGINEERED PLEASURE IN *BRAVE NEW WORLD*

1. Fredric Jameson, "Then You Are Them," *London Review of Books* 31, no. 17 (September 2009): 7–8.

2. *Complete Essays,* vol. 2, ed. Robert S. Baker and James Sexton (Chicago: Ivan R. Dee, 2000), 19.

3. See the appendix on "Spectrum of Opinion, 1928–1929" in Harry M. Geduld, *The Birth of the Talkies: From Edison to Jolson* (Bloomington: Indiana University Press, 1975). For general discussions of the advent of sound cinema, see the essays in Rick Altman, *Sound Theory/Sound Practice* (London: Routledge, 1992); Donald Crafton, *The Talkies: American Cinema's Transition to Sound, 1926–1931* (Berkeley: University of California Press, 1999); and James Lastra, *Sound Technology and the American Cinema: Perception, Representation, Modernity* (New York: Columbia University Press, 2000). Lastra argues that hearing, as well as vision, was "transformed . . . dislocated, 'mobilized,' restructured, and mechanized" (3) during the modern period.

4. Huxley's article undermines the argument that films were never silent, since music was always a part of the spectacle. See also Rick Altman, *Silent Film Sound* (New York: Columbia University Press, 2004), 193.

5. *Bernard Shaw on Cinema*, ed. Bernard F. Dukore (Carbondale: Southern Illinois University Press, 1997), 9. Shaw's thoughts on the cinema were not always out of step with Huxley's. In a 1914 *New Statesman* interview, Shaw remarked that "the cinema tells its story to the illiterate as well as to the literate; and it keeps its victim (if you like to call him so) not only awake but fascinated as if by a serpent's eye. And that is why the cinema is going to produce effects that all the cheap books in the world could never produce" (9).

6. *Let's Go to the Pictures* (London: Chatto and Windus, 1926). Published later in America as *Let's Go to the Movies* (New York: Arno Press, 1972).

7. "On Some Motifs in Baudelaire" and "The Work of Art in the Art of Mechanical Reproduction" (217–252). *Illuminations: Essays and Reflections*, ed. Hannah Arendt (New York: Schocken, 1968).

8. See, for example, Tom Gunning, "An Aesthetics of Astonishment: Early Film and the (In)credulous Spectator," in *Viewing Positions: Ways of Seeing Film*, ed. Linda Williams (New Brunswick, NJ: Rutgers University Press, 1994), 114–133; Miriam Hansen, *Babel and Babylon* (Cambridge: Cambridge University Press, 1991) and "The Mass Production of the Senses: Classical Cinema as Vernacular Modernism" in *Modernism/ Modernity* 6, no. 2 (April 1999): 59–77; Jonathan Crary, *Techniques of the Observer: On Vision and Modernity in the Nineteenth Century* (Cambridge: October Books, 1992) and *Suspensions of Perception: Attention, Spectacle, and Modern Culture* (Cambridge: October Books, 2001); Ben Singer, *Melodrama and Modernity: Early Sensational Cinema and Its Contexts* (New York: Columbia University Press, 2001); and Linda Williams, "Film Bodies: Gender, Genre, and Excess," in *Film Genre Reader 2*, ed. Barry Keith Grant (Austin: University of Texas Press, 1995), 142.

9. See Martin Loiperdinger, "Lumière's Arrival of the Train: Cinema's Founding Myth," *The Moving Image* 4, no. 1 (Spring 2004): 89–118.

10. Siegfried Kracauer, *Theory of Film: The Redemption of Physical Reality* (Princeton, NJ: Princeton University Press, 1960), 158.

11. Susan Buck-Morss, "Prosthesis of Perception: A Historical Account," in *The Senses Still: Perception and Memory as Material Culture in Modernity*, ed. C. Nadia Seremetakis (Chicago: University of Chicago Press, 1996), 45–62, 48.

12. As David Trotter points out, "Experimental cinema—a cinema of 'surprise juxtapositions'—only arrived in Britain with the founding of the London Film Society in 1925." "T. S. Eliot and Cinema," *Modernism/modernity* 13, no. 2 (April 2006): 237–265.

13. Virginia Woolf, "The Cinema," in *Collected Essays*, vol. 2 (London: Hogarth, 1966), 268-272.

14. Cinema shares many of these features with theater, but critics typically maintained that there is a "striking difference between [the filmgoer] and the theatergoer" (Kracauer, *Theory of Film*, 159).

15. Qtd. in Jeffrey Richards, "Modernism and the People: The View from the Cinema Stalls," in *Rewriting the Thirties: Modernism and After*, ed. K. Williams and S. Matthews

(London: Longman, 1997), 199. In her generally enthusiastic *Let's Go to the Movies*, Barry flatly states that "The cinema is a drug" (53). As Kracauer notes, "from the 'twenties to the present day, the devotees of film and its opponents alike have compared the medium to a sort of drug and have drawn attention to its stupefying effects," suggesting that "the cinema has its habitués who frequent it out of an all but physiological urge" (*Theory of Film*, 159).

16. See Tim Armstrong's discussion of the "bodily effects" associated with the coming of sound in *Modernism, Technology, and the Body: A Cultural Study* (Cambridge: Cambridge University Press, 1998), 222–247.

17. *Theatre Arts Monthly*, November 1930. Qtd. in Donald Crafton, *The Talkies*, 374.

18. Michael North takes exception to this idea that "human perception was somehow changed in the later nineteenth and twentieth centuries." *Camera Works* (Oxford: Oxford University Press, 2007), 30. The frequent insistence that sound film was initially difficult for people to take in suggests otherwise; Buck-Morss notes that "Viewers only gradually adapted to the cinema screen" ("Prostheses of Perception," 48). The measurable alterations of attention spans and cognitive functions in response to digital technologies such as the Internet should caution us against dismissing out of hand the possibility of tangible historical shifts in perception and cognition.

19. Huxley, *Complete Essays*, vol. 3, ed. Robert S. Baker and James Sexton (Chicago: Ivan R. Dee, 2000), 188.

20. *Eyeless in Gaza* (New York and London: Harper & Brothers, 1936), 355. *Jesting Pilate: Travels Through India, Burma, Malaya, Japan, China, and America* (New York: Paragon House, 1991), 224–225.

21. That cinematic pleasures are the product of "interminable democracies" is an insight into Huxley's politics of the 1930s. For an account of his conflicted feeling about democracy and his interest in eugenics, see David Bradshaw, *The Hidden Huxley: Contempt and Compassion for the Masses, 1920–36* (London: Faber and Faber, 1994).

22. Aldous Huxley, "Utopias, Positive and Negative," *Aldous Huxley Annual* 1 (2001): 1–5.

23. *Brave New World* (New York: Perennial/HarperCollins, 2006), 3.

24. The 1929 film *Broadway Melody* first used this slogan, which was mocked by Ernest Betts in 1930 as "All Singing, All Dancing, All Nothing." *Close Up: 1927–1933*, ed. James Donald, Anne Friedberg, and Laura Marcus (Princeton, NJ: Princeton University Press, 1999), 312.

25. John Carey, *The Intellectuals and the Masses: Pride and Prejudice Among the Literary Intelligentsia 1880–1939* (London: Faber and Faber, 1992), 86.

26. Theodor Adorno, "Aldous Huxley and Utopia," in *Prisms*, tr. Samuel and Shierry Weber (Cambridge, MA: MIT Press, 1967), 103–104.

27. See Jeffrey Richards's description of the Alhambra in *The Age of the Dream Palace: Cinema and Society in Britain, 1930–1939* (London: Keegan Paul, 1984).

28. T. S. Eliot, "Marie Lloyd" (1923), in *Selected Prose of T. S. Eliot*, ed. Frank Kermode (New York: Harvest Books, 1975), 174.

29. Max Nordau, *Degeneration* (New York: Appleton, 1895), 142.

30. Ernest Betts, *Heraclitus or The Future of Film* (London: Kegan Paul, 1928), 88.

31. Rick Altman, "The Evolution of Sound Technology" in *Film Sound: Theory and Practice,* ed. Elisabeth Weis and John Belton (New York: Columbia University Press, 1985), 51.

32. Rudolf Arnheim, *Film as Art* (Berkeley: University of California Press, 1971), 199.

33. Chaplin quoted in *Charlie Chaplin: Interviews,* ed. Kevin J. Hayes (Jackson: University of Mississippi Press, 2005), 82.

34. Huxley, *Complete Essays,* vol. 1, 174–175.

35. Sergei Eisenstein, W. I. Pudovkin, and G. V. Alexandrov, "Statement on Sound," in *Close Up: 1927–1933,* ed. James Donald, Anne Friedberg, and Laura Marcus (Princeton, NJ: Princeton University Press, 1999), 84.

36. Sergei Eisenstein, *The Film Sense,* tr. Jay Leyda (New York: Harcourt, Brace, 1947), 73, 77.

37. Siegfried Kracauer, "Cult of Distraction: On Berlin's Picture Palaces," in *The Mass Ornament: Weimar Essays,* ed. and trans. Thomas Y. Levin (Cambridge, MA: Harvard University Press, 1995), 324.

38. Huxley, "Writers and Readers" in *Complete Essays,* vol. 4, 25.

39. "Whispers of Immortality" in *T. S. Eliot: The Collected Poems, 1909–1962* (New York: Harcourt Brace Jovanovich, 1991), 45.

40. Elinor Glyn, *The Philosophy of Love* (New York: Macaulay, 1923) and *The Elinor Glyn System of Writing* (Auburn: The Authors' Press, 1922).

41. See Laura Horak, "'Would you like to sin with Elinor Glyn?': Film as a Vehicle of Sensual Education," *Camera Obscura* 25 (2010): 85.

42. *The Long Week End: A Social History of Great Britain, 1918–1939* (New York: Macmillan, 1941), 42.

43. Faulkner jokes about Glyn in a letter (James G. Watson, *William Faulkner: Self-Presentation and Performance* [Austin: University of Texas Press, 2000], 151). Nigel Brooks argues that Fitzgerald reworks *Three Weeks* in *The Great Gatsby* ("Fitzgerald's *The Great Gatsby* and Glyn's *Three Weeks,*" *The Explicator* 54 [1996]: 233–236). Anita Loos compared Glyn to Lawrence: "In those days Elinor's books were considered extremely 'broad.' Her best-seller, *Three Weeks,* was based on adultery, but she handled the subject in so dainty a manner as to make D. H. Lawrence's *Lady Chatterley's Lover,* with its identical plot, a sewer of clinical realism" (*A Girl Like I* [New York: Viking, 1966], 118, 119).

44. *The Diary of Virginia Woolf,* vol. 1, ed. Anne Olivier Bell and Quentin Bell (New York: Harvest Books, 1977), 71.

45. Anne Morey, "Elinor Glyn as Hollywood Labourer," in *Film History: An International Journal* 18, no. 2 (2006): 110–118.

46. Elinor Glyn, *Three Weeks* (London: Virago, 1996), 199.

47. For sociopolitical readings of Glyn's novel, see David Trotter, *The English Novel in History, 1895–1920* (London: Routledge, 1993); George Robb, "The Way of All Flesh: Degeneration, Eugenics, and the Gospel of Free Love" in *The Journal of the History of Sexuality* 6, no. 4 (April 1996): 589–603; and Chris Waters, "New Women and Eugenic Fictions" in *History Workshop Journal* 60 (Autumn 2005): 232–238. Frank Kermode considers *Three Weeks* as an exploration of national identity and masculinity typical

of its time ("The English Novel, circa 1907" in *Essays on Fiction* [London: Routledge & Kegan Paul, 1983], 45–56).

48. According to Horak, there was "a 1914 US version, a 1915 British parody, and a 1917 Hungarian version" of *Three Weeks* as well as a 1924 adaptation, directed by Alan Crosland, that was supervised by Glyn. "'Would you like to sin with Elinor Glyn?': Film as a Vehicle of Sensual Education," *Camera Obscura* 25 (2010): 94.

49. Rebecca West, *The Young Rebecca: Selected Essays of Rebecca West, 1911–1917*, ed. Jane Marcus (London: Virago, 1983), 73.

50. *Letters of Aldous Huxley*, ed. Grover Smith (London: Chatto & Windus, 1969), 85.

51. This slip—the "blackamoor" is the hero and not the villain?—is unexplained.

52. The film industry frequently turned to Shakespeare in an effort to elevate the medium's status. The irony of "silent Shakespeare" led to vigorous debates about the relationship between cinema and theater (Altman, "Introduction," 13). The competition became much more intense once sound film began to challenge what had previously been thought to be the stage's advantage in language. In this discussion, Shakespeare is constantly invoked as the best that theater has to offer and the best that British culture offers against the onslaught of popular culture that was increasingly identified as American. Asked in a 1915 interview "What the Films May Do to the Drama," Shaw replied that "When they can see and hear Forbes-Robertson's Hamlet . . . well produced, it will be possible for our young people to grow up in healthy remoteness from the crowded masses and slums of big cities without also growing up as savages" (*Shaw on Film*, 18). This is a rare vision of cinema as harmonious rather than competitive with theater. For commentary on early adaptations of Shakespeare for the screen, see John Collick, *Shakespeare, Cinema, and Society* (Manchester: Manchester University Press, 1989); John P. McCombe, "'Suiting the Action to the Word': The Clarendon Tempest and the Evolution of a Narrative Silent Shakespeare," *Literature Film Quarterly* 33 (2005): 142–155; Roberta E. Pearson, "Shakespeare's Country: The National Poet, English Identity, and British Silent Cinema," in *Young and Innocent? The Cinema in Britain 1896–1930*, ed. Andrew Higson (Exeter: University of Exeter Press, 2002), 176–190.

53. James Sexton has pointed out that the theme of sexual jealousy in the feely is central to *Othello* and to the Savage's tormented relationship with Lenina Crowne. "*Brave New World*, the Feelies, and Elinor Glyn," *English Language Notes* 35 (1997): 35–38.

54. Jane Gaines, *Fire and Desire: Mixed-Race Movies in the Silent Era* (Chicago: University Of Chicago Press, 2001), 1.

55. Hansen, "The Mass Production of the Senses," 71.

56. For readings of ethnicity and race in *The Jazz Singer*, see Michael Rogin's *Blackface, White Noise: Jewish Immigrants in the Hollywood Melting Pot* (Berkeley: University of California Press, 1996) and Linda Williams's *Playing the Race Card: Melodramas of Black and White from Uncle Tom to O. J. Simpson* (Princeton, NJ: Princeton University Press, 2001).

57. See, for example, Huxley's 1926 letter to Smith (*Letters*, 266).

58. Shelley Stamp, *Movie-Struck Girls: Women and Motion Picture Culture After the Nickelodeon* (Princeton, NJ: Princeton University Press, 2000), 47. See also Celia Marshik's *Modernism and Censorship* (Cambridge, MA: Cambridge University Press, 2006).

59. See Susan Courtney, *Hollywood Fantasies of Miscegenation: Spectacular Narratives of Gender and Race, 1903–1967* (Princeton, NJ: Princeton University Press, 2005). See also Lucy Bland, "White Women and Men of Colour: Miscegenation Fears in Britain After the Great War," *Gender History* 17, no. 1: 29–61.

60. Rachael Low, *The History of the British Film, vol. 4* (London: George Allen & Unwin, 1971), 130–131.

61. *Huxley in Hollywood* (New York: Harper and Row, 1989), 351.

62. Huxley, *Essays*, vol. 2, 20; *The Doors of Perception and Heaven and Hell* (New York: Perennial, 1990), 168.

63. Mary Field and Percy Smith, *Secrets of Nature* (London: Faber, 1933). See also Field's "Can the Film Educate?" (1934) in *The Red Velvet Seat: Women's Writing on the First Fifty Years of Cinema*, ed. Antonia Lant and Ingrid Periz (London: Verso, 2006), 28–334.

64. Shaw, 7. Rachel Low notes that in 1934, "the first group of classroom films to be issued in Britain, were *Shakespeare*, a one-reeler . . . about Shakespeare's biographical and historical background, and three physiology one-reelers, *Breathing, The Blood* and *Circulation*" (vol. 5, 26). In *Brave New World*, Huxley constellates the feelies with both Shakespeare and educational documentary.

65. Allison Flood, "*Brave New World* Among Top 10 Books Americans Most Want Banned," *The Guardian* (London), April 12, 2011.

66. Fredric Jameson, "Then You Are Them," *London Review of Books* 31, no. 17 (September 2009): 7–8.

67. Aldous Huxley, *After Many a Summer Dies the Swan* (New York and London: Harper, 1939) and *Ape and Essence* (New York: Harper, 1948).

68. Alongside this transformation, Huxley's views of recreational pleasures, and particularly drugs, changed radically. Not only did Huxley find value in the use of drugs such as LSD, he also proposed that drugs could serve socially useful purposes, expanding consciousness and creativity.

69. The project never got off the ground because RKO owned the dramatic rights to the novel and would not allow it to be produced. Virginia M. Clark, *Aldous Huxley and Film* (Metuchen, NJ: Scarecrow Press, 1987), 62.

70. Jerome Meckier, "Afterword" to *Brave New World: A Musical Comedy* (1956), ed. Bernfried Nugle, *Aldous Huxley Annual* 3 (2003): 106. Kracauer wrote enthusiastically about how musicals could be great "cinematic entertainment," praising Fred Astaire's dance films as "veritable landmarks" (*Theory of Film*, 147).

71. Aldous Huxley, *Brave New World: A Musical Comedy* (1956), 44–45.

5. THE IMPASSE OF PLEASURE: PATRICK HAMILTON AND JEAN RHYS

1. Plato, *Philebus*, trans. Robin H. Waterfield (New York and London: Penguin Classics, 1983), 55.

2. Fyodor Dostoevsky, *Notes from Underground, The Double, and Other Stories,* trans. Constance Garnett (New York: Barnes & Noble Classics, 2003), 243.

3. See P. J. Widdowson, "The Saloon Bar Society: Patrick Hamilton's Fiction in the 1930s," in *The 1930s: A Challenge to Orthodoxy,* ed. John Lucas (Hassocks, Sussex: Harvester Press, 1978), 117.

4. Jean Rhys, *Voyage in the Dark, The Complete Novels* (New York: Norton, 1985), 3. All subsequent references to this edition unless otherwise noted.

5. Widdowson, "The Saloon Bar Society," 118.

6. Djuna Barnes, *Nightwood* (New York: New Directions, 1961), 113.

7. Lionel Trilling, "The Fate of Pleasure," in *The Moral Obligation to Be Intelligent: Selected Essays* (New York: Farrar, Straus & Giroux, 2000), 439.

8. David Plante, *Difficult Women: A Memoir of Three* (New York: Atheneum 1983).

9. Rachel Bowlby has highlighted the impasse as a rhetorical figure in Rhys's work. "The Impasse: Jean Rhys's *Good Morning, Midnight*" in *Still Crazy After All These Years: Women, Writing and Psychoanalysis* (London and New York: Routledge, 1992).

10. Terry Eagleton, "First-Class Fellow Traveller," *London Review of Books* 15, no. 23 (December 2, 1993): 12.

11. *The Complete Works of George Orwell.* Vol. 10: *A Kind of Compulsion* (London: Martin Secker & Warburg Ltd., 1998): 390–392, 390.

12. Gerard Barrett, "Hamilton and the Nets of Language," *Critical Engagements* 1, no. 1 (2007): 226, 213. Widdowson calls Hamilton's prose "'interpretative' or 'synthetic' realism" ("The Saloon Bar Society," 122); John Lucas argues that Hamilton and writers such as Sylvia Townsend Warner and Henry Green "deliberately move outside the apparently solid realism in which their fiction seems to be housed in order to discover a radicalism which is at once technical and political." "From Realism to Radicalism: Sylvia Townsend Warner, Patrick Hamilton and Henry Green in the 1920s," in *Outside Modernism: In Pursuit of the English Novel, 1900–30,* ed. Lynne Hapgood and Nancy L. Paxton (Basingstoke, England; New York: Macmillan; St. Martin's, 2000), 204.

13. Patrick Hamilton, *Impromptu in Morbundia* (London: Faber and Faber, 2011), 138, 162–163.

14. Patrick Hamilton, *Hangover Square* (New York: Europa Editions, 2006), 58.

15. Patrick Hamilton, *The Midnight Bell, Twenty Thousand Streets Under the Sky* (London: Vintage, 2004), 3. All subsequent references to the trilogy are from this edition.

16. Patrick Hamilton, *The Plains of Cement, Twenty Thousand,* 367.

17. Doris Lessing writes of "the grimy, graceless, bleak, ugly, dreadfulness of the England described by Orwell and by Patrick Hamilton" in *Under My Skin* (New York: HarperCollins, 1994), 149.

18. "Pulped Fictions" *The Guardian,* March 12, 2005.

19. John Bayley, "Falling in Love with the Traffic Warden," *London Review of Books,* October 1, 1987, 6–8.

20. G. E. Moore, *Principia Ethica* (Cambridge: Cambridge University Press, 1993), 112.

21. Gilles Deleuze, *Masochism: Coldness and Cruelty and Venus in Furs* (New York: Zone Books, 1991), 71, 89.

22. Jonathan Brown, "The Lion, the Witch, and the Turkish Delight," *The Independent* (London), December 5, 2005.

23. In C. S. Lewis's *The Lion, the Witch and the Wardrobe* (New York: HarperCollins, 2009), Edmund, enthralled by the White Witch's offering, "thought only of trying to shovel down as much Turkish Delight as he could, and the more he ate the more he wanted to eat. . . . He still wanted to taste that Turkish Delight more than he wanted anything else" (39–40). In Dorothy Sayers's *Strong Poison* (1930), a murderer is addicted to chocolate creams and Turkish Delight, described as a "nauseating mess" that "gluts the palate and glues the teeth, [and] also smothers the consumer in a floury cloud of white sugar" (New York: HarperPerennial, 1993), 241. See also Liesl Schillinger, "The Lion, the Witch, and the Really Foul Candy: In Pursuit of Turkish Delight," Slate, Dec. 9, 2005, http://www.slate.com/articles/life/food/2005/12/the_lion_the_witch_and_the_really_foul_candy.html.

24 Jacques Lacan, *The Other Side of Psychoanalysis: The Seminar of Jacques Lacan, Book XVII*, tr. Russell Grigg (New York: Norton, 2007), 72.

25. Kermode, *Pleasure and Change: The Aesthetics of Canon* (New York: Oxford University Press, 2004), 22. See Jane Gallop's account of how American feminists have handled—or declined—the translation of *jouissance*. "Beyond the Jouissance Principle," *Representations* 7 (Summer 1984): 110–115. In Barthes's *Pleasure of the Text, plaisir* is contrasted with *jouissance* and yet, as Gallop observes, the terms are often used interchangeably.

26. Lawrence himself sent up orientalist romance in his short story "Mother and Daughter," in which an aging, fat, and unattractive suitor, who has nevertheless "a strange potency" (819) and is "curiously virile" (820), and whose presence is referred to as serpentlike and "reptilian," "patriarchal and tribal," and "sheiky" (821)—all of which invokes Lawrence's Hullian turn—but is also lampooned as "Turkish Delight" (818). Lawrence, *The Complete Stories*, vol. 3 (New York: Penguin Books, 1981): 805–826.

27. *The Siege of Pleasure*, 252; *Midnight Bell*, 81, 79.

28. Nigel Jones, *Through a Glass Darkly: The Life of Patrick Hamilton* (London: Abacus, 1991), 147.

29. In *The Siege of Pleasure*, which Hamilton called "my prostitute [book]" (Jones, *Through a Glass Darkly*, 142), he is even less empathetic toward Jenny than in the previous novel: "It is doubtful whether Jenny could be said to be the owner either of a character or conscience" (252). Although she begins as a meticulous servant (a "treasure," her employers exclaim), the narrator describes her downward slide into crime as inevitable: "the pleasures and perils of drink" "unlocked her destiny" along with "her ignorance, her shallowness, her scheming self-absorption, her vanity, her callousness, her unscrupulousness" (*Twenty Thousand*, 336).

30. See A. D. Nuttall, *Why Does Tragedy Give Pleasure?* (New York and Oxford: Oxford University Press, 2001).

31. *Beyond the Pleasure Principle*, tr. James Strachey, ed. Peter Gay (New York and London: Norton, 1989), 17.

32. Patrick Hamilton, *Rope* (New York: Samuel French, 2011), 3.

33. When Sasha gets a weekly stipend from a relative in *Good Morning, Midnight*, she remarks, "Well, that was the end of me, the real end. Two-pound-ten every Tues-

day and a room off the Gray's Inn Road. Saved, rescued and with my place to hide in—what more did I want? I crept in and hid. The lid of the coffin shut down with a bang. Now I no longer wish to be loved, beautiful, happy or successful." Jean Rhys, *The Complete Novels* (New York: Norton, 1985), 369. All subsequent references to this edition unless otherwise noted.

34. Rachel Bowlby makes the case that *"Good Morning, Midnight* . . . is structured like a rhetorical impasse . . . since all its positive terms are already excluded with the force of impossibility (once there might have been hope for change, for a long time there has been none)" (57).

35. Jane Marcus, *Hearts of Darkness: White Women Write Race* (New Brunswick, NJ: Rutgers University Press, 2004), 4.

36. Shari Benstock, *Women of the Left Bank: Paris, 1900–1940* (Austin: University of Texas Press, 1986), 424.

37. Veronica Gregg, *Jean Rhys's Historical Imagination: Reading and Writing the Creole* (Chapel Hill: University of North Carolina Press, 1995), 169.

38. Maren Tova Linett, *Modernism, Feminism, and Jewishness* (Cambridge: Cambridge University Press, 2007), 172.

39. Mary Lou Emery suggests that Rhys's masochism is a default position for women: "no cultural myth other than that of female masochism is available to [Rhys] as a means by which to transform the meaning of her degradation to renew her life." *Jean Rhys at World's End: Novels of Colonial and Sexual Exile* (Austin: University of Texas Press, 1990), 119. Cathleen Maslen also contends that "masochism is inextricably linked to ideological repression: it is the 'choice' one makes when there is no choice." *Ferocious Things: Jean Rhys and the Politics of Women's Melancholia* (Cambridge: Cambridge University Press, 1998), 84. Sheila Kineke ("'Like a Hook Fits an Eye': Jean Rhys, Ford Madox Ford, and the Imperial Operations of Modernist Meaning," *Tulsa Studies in Women's Literature* 16, no. 2 [Autumn 1997]) and Leah Rosenberg ("'The Rope, Of Course, Being Covered with Flowers': Metropolitan Discourses and the Construction of Creole Identity in Jean Rhys's 'Black Exercise Book,'" *Jean Rhys Review* 11, no. 1 [1999]: 5–33) argue that masochism is a strategy of self-definition and critique. Patricia Moran proposes that Rhys develops a masochistic aesthetic of repetition, suspense, and confusion between fantasy and reality that has its origin in sexual trauma. *Virginia Woolf, Jean Rhys, and the Aesthetics of Trauma* (London: Palgrave Macmillan, 2007).

40. Katharine Streip identifies Rhys's sense of comedy as "ressentiment humor" in which "an initial sense of injury and rage become transformed into comedy through self-laceration." Streip connects Rhys to Beckett, as both implicate the audience in their humor. Citing Freud's definition of humor, in *Jokes and Their Relation to the Unconscious*, as "a means of obtaining pleasure in spite of the distressing affects that interfere with it," she argues that Rhys's characters such as Sasha "turn wounds into occasions for pleasure" as "ressentiment humor aims for discomfort without catharsis" (122, 123, 128). "'Just a Cérébrale': Jean Rhys, Women's Humour, and Ressentiment," *Representations* 45 (Winter 1994): 118. See also Laura Wainwright, "'Doesn't that make you laugh?': Modernist Comedy in Jean Rhys's *After Leaving Mr Mackenzie* and *Good Morning, Midnight,*" *Journal of International Women's Studies* 10, no. 3 (March 2009): 48–57.

41. Rhys told David Plante, "If you had an evening gown at that time, that was all you needed to get into the crowd scene of a film. I made a little money that way. But not enough, not enough for the landlord" (*Difficult Women*, 15).

42. Louis James, *Jean Rhys* (London: Longman, 1979), 27, 13.

43. Anna Snaith, "Jean Rhys and London" in *Geographies of Modernism: Literatures, Cultures, Spaces*, ed. Peter Brooker and Andrew Thacker (New York: Routledge, 2005), 81.

44. Laurie tells Anna, "you always look half-asleep and people don't like that" (80) and complains about her getting too drunk. Ethel complains that Anna has "never a joke or a pleasant word" and is sick "all the time" (102–103).

45. Elizabeth Carolyn Miller, *Framed: The New Woman Criminal in British Culture at the Fin de Siècle* (Ann Arbor: University of Michigan Press, 2008), 121.

46. Alex Marlow-Mann, "The Exploits of Three-Fingered Kate," British Film Institute, http://www.screenonline.org.uk/film/id/727128/index.html.

47. Jean Rhys, *Tigers Are Better-Looking: With a Selection from The Left Bank* (London and New York: Penguin, 1972), 138.

48. James Allan Evans, *The Empress Theodora* (Austin: University of Texas Press, 2002).

49. Elaine Savory observes that "Sex in Rhys's texts is always heterosexual, but mostly, for the female partner, a matter of absence, inertia, coldness or distraction, with the dramatic exception of Antoinette's early passion for her husband" in *Wide Sargasso Sea. Jean Rhys* (Cambridge and New York: Cambridge University Press 1998), 60.

50. Linda Williams, *Hard Core: Power, Pleasure, and the "Frenzy of the Visible"* (Berkeley: University of California Press, 1999), 4.

51. For a variety of interpretations of Sasha's "film-mind," see Emery, *Jean Rhys at World's End*; Sue Thomas, *The Worlding of Jean Rhys* (Santa Barbara, CA: Praeger, 1999); Maren Tova Linett, *Modernism, Feminism, and Jewishness* (Cambridge: Cambridge University Press, 2007); and Judith Kegan Gardiner, "Good Morning, Midnight: Good Night, Modernism," *boundary 2* 11, no. 1–2 (Autumn 1982): 233–251.

52. The Black Exercise Book is part of the Jean Rhys Archives (Collection number 1976–011, Department of Special Collections and University Archives, McFarlin Library, University of Tulsa). My thanks to the library for permission to use this material. Elaine Savory generously shared her copy of the notebook with me. On "Mr. Howard," see Thomas, *The Worlding of Jean Rhys*; Teresa O'Connor, *Jean Rhys: The West Indian Novels* (New York: New York University Press, 1986); Gardiner; Moran; Carole Angier, *Jean Rhys: Life and Work* (New York: Little, Brown, 1991); Rosenberg, "'The Rope, Of Course,'"; Coral Ann Howells, *Jean Rhys* (New York: Macmillan, 1991).

53. Thomas reads the Howard story as a traumatic paradigm of colonial and racial subjugation, arguing that Mr. Howard is a "turn-of-the-century sex tourist, exploiting differences in age of consent legislation" by imposing his "brothel fantasies" on a young girl (30). Rosenberg writes, "it is clear that Mr. Howard does not erotically arouse Rhys" ("'The Rope, Of Course,'" 24) and proposes that Rhys deliberately writes sexual desire and pleasure out of the Howard scenario in order to contest both colonial English and Freudian discourse that cast women as promiscuous. "Rhys responds . . . by erasing sexual pleasure from her account entirely" (18).

54. The Howard story is reworked in "Good-bye Marcus, Good-bye Rose." While the narrator bemoans Captain Cardew's "ceaseless talk of love," she listens "shocked and fascinated," and ultimately rejects having children and a "normal" life as "The prospect before her might be difficult and uncertain but it was far more exciting." Jean Rhys, *The Collected Short Stories* (New York: Norton, 1987), 287, 290.

55. According to Carole Angier, Rhys sat for the Oxford and Cambridge Higher Certificate in English Literature, but did unexpectedly poorly because "she'd chosen as her favourite book a 'modern' novel, *The Garden of Allah*, by Robert Hichens" (*Jean Rhys*, 43).

56. Of her youthful reading, Rhys remarks in *Smile Please*, "I liked books about prostitutes, there were a good many then, and vividly recollect a novel called *The Sands of Pleasure* written by a man named Filson Young." *Smile Please: An Unfinished Autobiography* (New York: Harper & Row, 1979), 50–51. While this title sounds like a desert romance, it is in fact a 1905 novel set in bohemian Paris that details a young man's exploration of the world of Montmartre cafés and clubs and his infatuation with a prostitute. See Betsy Draine's "Chronotope and Intertext: The Case of Jean Rhys's *Quartet*," in *Influence and Intertextuality in Literary History*, ed. Jay Clayton and Eric Rothstein (Madison: University of Wisconsin Press, 1991).

57. *Smile Please: An Unfinished Autobiography* (New York: Harper & Row, 1979), 97.

58. For example, Judith Kegan Gardiner, contrasting, the last scene in *Good Morning, Midnight* to the conclusion of *Ulysses*, writes, "When [Sasha] accepts the white-robed fellow traveler, she does not abandon herself to Molly's sensual oblivion or to Joyce's artistic detachment. Instead, she accepts the burdens of a full humanity possessed of the ironies of having been incarnated female in a patriarchal society" ("Good Morning, Midnight," 249).

59. A. D. Nuttall addresses the question of "tragic pleasure" in relation to modernist difficulty, arguing that both are tastes for "enjoyed discomfort." *Why Does Tragedy Give Pleasure?* (New York and Oxford: Oxford University Press, 2001), 2.

60. Frank Kermode, *Pleasure and Change: The Aesthetics of Canon*, ed. Robert Alter (New York and Oxford: Oxford University Press, 2004), 72.

6. BLONDES HAVE MORE FUN: ANITA LOOS AND
THE LANGUAGE OF SILENT CINEMA

1. Anita Loos, *Fate Keeps on Happening: Adventures of Lorelei Lee and Other Writings*, ed. Ray Pierre Corsini (New York: Dodd, Mead, 1984), 59.

2. Anita Loos, *Gentlemen Prefer Blondes and But Gentlemen Marry Brunettes*, intro. by Regina Barreca 1998 [1925 and 1928] (New York: Penguin,), 44, 4, 53, 51, 52, 54. Henceforth abbreviated *B*.

3. *The Letters of D. H. Lawrence*, vol. V: 1924–1927, ed. James T. Boulton and Lindeth Vasey (Cambridge: Cambridge University Press, 1989), 574.

4. Anita Loos, *A Cast of Thousands* (New York: Grosset and Dunlap, 1977), 205.

5. Stuart Gilbert, ed., *Letters of James Joyce*, vol. 1 (London: Faber and Faber: 1957), 246.

6. Susan Hegeman, "Taking *Blondes* Seriously," *American Literary History* 7, no. 3 (1995): 525–554; Barbara Everett, "The New Style of 'Sweeney Agonistes,'" *The Yearbook of English Studies* 14 (1984): 243–263; and Brooks E. Hefner, "'Any Chance to Be Unrefined': Film Narrative Modes in Anita Loos's Fiction," *PMLA* 125, no. 1 (January 2010): 107–120.

7. Faye Hammill, *Women, Celebrity, and Literary Culture Between the Wars* (Austin: University of Texas Press, 2007), 75. See also Sarah Churchwell, "'Lost Among the Ads': *Gentlemen Prefer Blondes* and the Politics of Imitation," in *Middlebrow Moderns*, ed. Lisa Botshon and Meredith Goldsmith (Boston: Northeastern University Press, 2003), 135–166.

8. Cari Beauchamp and Mary Anita Loos, eds., *Anita Loos Rediscovered* (Berkeley: University of California Press, 2003).

9. Q. D. Leavis, *Fiction and the Reading Public* (London: Pimlico, 2000), 218, 255, 76.

10. Wyndham Lewis, *Time and Western Man* (Berkeley, CA: Gingko Press, 1993), 55.

11. Robert Graves and Alan Hodge, *The Long Week End: A Social History of Great Britain, 1918–1939* (New York: Macmillan, 1941), 135.

12. Lewis, *Time and Western Man*, Book One, "The Revolutionary Simpletons," 3–125.

13. Cyril Connolly, *Enemies of Promise* (Chicago: University of Chicago Press, 2008), 62–65.

14. Rita Felski, *The Gender of Modernity* (Cambridge, MA: Harvard University Press, 1995), 6.

15. See Rick Altman, *Silent Film Sound* (New York: Columbia University Press, 2004); William K. Everson, *American Silent Film* (New York: De Capo Press, 1998); and Tom Gunning, *D. W. Griffith and the Origins of American Narrative Film: The Early Years at Biograph* (Champaign: University of Illinois Press, 1991).

16. Hugo Münsterberg, *The Photoplay: A Psychological Study* (London: D. Appleton & Co., 1916), 79.

17. Joseph Berg Esenwein and Arthur Leeds, *Writing the Photoplay* (Springfield, MA: The Home Correspondence School, 1913, rev. ed., 1919), 221.

18. Elinor Glyn, *The Elinor Glyn System of Writing*, Book III (Auburn, NY: The Authors' Press, 1922), 266–267.

19. Laura Marcus, *The Tenth Muse: Writing About Cinema in the Modernist Period* (Oxford and New York: Oxford University Press, 2007), 290. See also Kamilla Elliot, *Rethinking the Novel/Film Debate* (Cambridge and New York: Cambridge University Press, 2003).

20. Beauchamp and Loos, eds., *Anita Loos Rediscovered: Film Treatments and Fiction by Anita Loos*, 16.

21. Anita Loos, *Kiss Hollywood Good-by* (New York: Ballantine, 1975), 6 and *A Girl Like I* (New York: Viking, 1966), 98. Henceforth abbreviated *K* and *GI*.

22. Louella Parsons, "To Whom Hath Shall Be Given," *New York Telegraph*, March 16, 1919.

23. Carl Schmidt, "The Handwriting on the Screen," *Everyman's Magazine* 36 (May 1917): 622–623.

24. Rachel Lindsay, *The Art of the Moving Picture* (1922; reprint, New York: Liveright, 1970), 14, 34.

25. Kristin Thompson, "The Formulation of the Classical Narrative," in *The Classical Hollywood Cinema: Film Style and Mode of Production to 1960,* ed. David Bordwell, Janet Steiger, and Kristin Thompson (New York: Columbia University Press, 1985), 187.

26. Thompson, "The Formulation of the Classical Narrative," 186–187.

27. Schmidt, "The Handwriting on the Screen," 622.

28. Frank Woods, quoted in Miriam Hansen, *Babel and Babylon* (Cambridge: Cambridge University Press, 1991), 82.

29. See Hansen's discussion of hieroglyphics in *Babel and Babylon* and also Michael North's in *Camera Work* (Oxford: Oxford University Press, 2007).

30. Loos, *Anita Loos Rediscovered*, 110.

31. Zelda and F. Scott Fitzgerald, "Our Own Movie Queen," *The Red Velvet Seat*, ed. Antonia Lant (London and New York: Verso, 2006), 607–623.

32. Sergei Eisenstein, "Dickens, Griffith, and the Film Today," in *Film Form: Essays in Film Theory*, ed. Jay Leyda (New York: Harcourt, 1969), 195–256. See Hansen, *Babel and Babylon,* 129–140.

33. For a detailed analysis of *Intolerance*'s influences and production, see William M. Drew, *D. W. Griffith's* Intolerance: *Its Genesis and Its Vision* (Jefferson, NC: McFarland, 1986).

34. Vachel Lindsay, "The Artistic Position of Douglas Fairbanks," in *The Progress and Poetry of the Movies* (Lanham, MD: Scarecrow Press, 1995), 167.

35. Loos's comment that Constance Talmadge's role in *Intolerance* (The Mountain Girl) was that of a "Babylonian flapper" suggests that she was imagining ways to associate *Intolerance* with her own contemporary interests (*GI*, 93).

36. Hansen, *Babel and Babylon*, 122; Michael Rogin, "The Great Mother Domesticated: Sexual Difference and Sexual Indifference in D. W. Griffith's *Intolerance*," *Critical Inquiry* 15, no. 3 (Spring 1989): 518, 520.

37. See, for example, Kevin Brownlow, *The Parade's Gone By* (Berkeley: University of California Press, 1976), 64.

38. Everett, "The New Style," 254; Barreca, *B,* xviii; Katharina Von Ankum, "Material Girls: Consumer Culture and the 'New Woman' in Anita Loos's *Gentlemen Prefer Blondes* and Irmgard Keun's *Das Kunsteidene Mädchen*," *Colloquia Germanica* 27, no. 2 (1994): 159–172.

39. Iris Barry notes that the British "Typist" is equivalent to the American "Stenographer." *Let's Go to the Movies* (1926; reprint, New York: Arno Press, 1972), 277.

40. Christopher Keep, "The Cultural Work of the Type-Writer Girl," *Victorian Studies* 40, no. 3 (Spring 1997): 418.

41. Lawrence Rainey, "Eliot Among the Typists: Writing *The Waste Land*," *Modernism/Modernity* 12, no. 1 (January 2005): 55.

42. Loos, *Kiss Hollywood Good-by*, 42. This film opens with a self-referential joke by Loos. A lounging Harlow quips, "So gentlemen prefer blondes, do they?"

43. Fictional examples of this formulation include Ada Negri's 1928 story "The Movies," in which a friendless, orphaned typist whose only passion is film is run over

after watching a movie. Antonia Lant, ed., *The Red Velvet Seat* (London and New York: Verso, 2006), 111–115.

44. Siegfried Kracauer, *The Mass Ornament: Weimar Essays,* ed. and tr. Thomas Y. Levin (Cambridge, MA: Harvard University Press, 1995), 292.

45. Barry, *Let's Go to the Movies,* 8.

46. Freidrich A. Kittler, *Gramophone, Film, Typewriter,* tr. Geoffrey Winthrop-Young and Michael Wutz (Stanford, CA: Stanford University Press, 1999), 174.

47. Walter Benjamin, "On Some Motifs in Baudelaire," tr. Harry Zohn, in *Illuminations: Essays and Reflections* (New York: Schocken, 1968), 175.

48. Barry, *Let's Go to the Movies,* 8, 5, 73.

49. Lant, ed., *Red Velvet Seat,* 574.

50. William Faulkner, cited in John T. Matthews's "Gentlemen Defer Blondes: Faulkner, Anita Loos, and Mass Culture," in *Faulkner, His Contemporaries, and His Posterity,* ed. Waldemar Zacharasiewicz (Tubingen: Francke, 1993), 207–221.

51. *Letters of James Joyce,* ed. Stuart Gilbert, vol. 1, 247.

52. James Joyce, *Finnegans Wake* (New York and London: Penguin Classics, 1999), 4.

53. Samuel Beckett, "Dante . . . Bruno . . . Vico . . . Joyce," *Our Examination Round His Factification for Incamination of Work in Progress* in *I Can't Go On, I'll Go On: A Samuel Beckett Reader,* ed. Richard Seaver (New York: Grove Press, 2007), 117.

54. See Loos's *Harper's Bazaar* story, "Why Girls Go South," which includes a fictional playwright, Hans Pfeffer, "the important exponent of modern German Explosionism" (*Fate Keeps On Happening,* 289), and "the great futurist painter Art D. Stroyer" in the scenario "Where Does Annie Belong?" (*Anita Loos Rediscovered,* 97–99).

55. Wyndham Lewis, *Time and Western Man,* 113.

56. See my article, "Not So Dirty Dancing," *Bookforum* (April/May 2009), http://www.bookforum.com/inprint/016_01/3546.

57. Q. D. Leavis, *Fiction and the Reading Public,* 56.

58. See Warhol's *Marilyn Diptych* (1962) and Sherman's *Untitled (As Marilyn Monroe)* (1982).

CODA: MODERNISM'S AFTERLIFE IN THE AGE OF PROSTHETIC PLEASURE

1. Anaïs Nin, *Fire: From A Journal of Love: The Unexpurgated Diary of Anaïs Nin, 1934–1937* (New York: Harvest, 1993), 149.

2. "Bloomsday, 1904," Opinion, *New York Times,* June 16, 2004, http://www.nytimes.com/2004/06/16/opinion/bloomsday-1904.html. "The Difficulty of Navigating *Ulysses,*" NPR, June 16, 2004; http://www.npr.org/templates/story/story.php?storyId=1959559. Neil Smith, "Cheat's Guide to *Ulysses,*" BBC, June 16, 2004, http://news.bbc.co.uk/2/hi/3810193.stm.

3. http://www.symphonyspace.org/series/167.

4. Richael Kimmelman, "Missionaries," *The New York Review of Books,* April 26, 2012. It remains to be seen how Barbara Will's alternate narrative of "collaborating

and canoodling," in *Unlikely Collaboration: Gertrude Stein, Bernard Faÿ, and the Vichy Dilemma* (New York: Columbia University Press, 2012), will shape Stein studies.

5. See, for example, the section on "Pleasure and Rebellion: 1965–1980" in Dagmar Herzog, *Sexuality in Europe: A Twentieth-Century History* (Cambridge: Cambridge University Press, 2011), 133–175.

6. *Infinite Jest* (Boston: Back Bay Books, 1997).

7. Linda Hutcheon, *A Poetics of Postmodernism: History, Theory, Fiction* (New York and London: Routledge, 1988), x.

8. T. S. Eliot, *Notes Towards the Definition of Culture* (New York: Harcourt Brace, 1949).

9. David Foster Wallace, *A Supposedly Fun Thing I'll Never Do Again: Essays and Arguments* (Boston: Little, Brown, 1997), 267. Originally published as "Shipping Out: On the (Nearly Lethal) Comforts of a Luxury Cruise," *Harpers* (January 1996): 33–56.

10. James D. Wallace, "Pleasure as an End of Action," *American Philosophical Quarterly* 3, no. 4 (1966): 314. See Stephen J. Burt, "*Infinite Jest* and the Twentieth Century: David Foster Wallace's Legacy," in *Modernism/Modernity* 16, no. 1 (January 2009): 12–19.

11. *Consider the Lobster and Other Essays* (Boston: Little, Brown, 2005), 261.

12. Larry McCaffery, "An Interview with David Foster Wallace," *Review of Contemporary Fiction* 13, no. 2 (Summer 1993): 129, 130.

13. McCaffery, "An Interview with David Foster Wallace," 128.

13. McCaffery, "An Interview with David Foster Wallace," 130.

14. See, for example, Nicholas Carr, "Is Google Making Us Stupid?: What the Internet Is Doing to Our Brains," *Atlantic Magazine* (July/August 2008), and Caleb Crain, "Twilight of the Books," *The New Yorker* (December 24, 2007).

Index